BETWEEN ASSIMILATION
AND INDEPENDENCE

Between Assimilation and Independence

THE TAIWANESE ENCOUNTER NATIONALIST CHINA, 1945–1950

Steven E. Phillips

STANFORD UNIVERSITY PRESS

STANFORD, CALIFORNIA

2003

Stanford University Press
Stanford, California

Portions of Chapters 3 and 4 adapted from Murray A. Rubinstein, ed., *Taiwan:
A New History* (Armonk, N.Y.: M.E. Sharpe, Inc., 1999), pp. 275–319.
Copyright © 1999 by M.E. Sharpe, Inc. Used with permission.

Printed in the United States of America
On acid-free, archival-quality paper

Library of Congress Cataloging-in-Publication Data
Phillips, Steven E.
  Between assimilation and independence: the Taiwanese encounter Nationalist
China, 1945–1950 / Steven E. Phillips.
     p. cm.
  Includes bibliographical references and index.
  ISBN 0-8047-4457-2 (alk. paper)
   1. Taiwan — Politics and government — 1945–1975. 2. Local
government — Taiwan — History — 20th century. 3. China — Politics
and government — 1945–1949. I. Title.
DS799.816.P48 2003
951.24'905 — dc21
2002015660

Original Printing 2003

Last figure below indicates year of this printing:
12 11 10 09 08 07 06 05 04 03

Typeset by BookMatters in Sabon

For Barbara and Samantha

Contents

Preface

Chalmers Johnson, in his introduction to *The Taiwan Experience*, put it best: "The most distinctive problem of Taiwan's development has been the management of the fissure between the majority group of native Taiwanese — or descendents of earlier mainland immigrants — who comprise about 85 percent of the population, and the mainland Chinese who moved to the island in 1949." My interest in this problem spawned a dissertation, that, much revised, has become a book. To concentrate my efforts, I investigated a limited number of people, prominent Taiwanese; a single issue, local self-government; and a relatively short time, 1945 to 1950, when the Nationalist government led by Jiang Jieshi consolidated its control over the island.

Why discuss the Taiwanese provincial elite, a relatively small group of men with education beyond high-school level, most of whom were employed in medicine, education, trade, industry, or the government bureaucracy during both the Japanese and Nationalist Chinese eras? Their attempt to negotiate the difficult transition from Japanese to Nationalist rule is fascinating. Furthermore, these Taiwanese have provided a rich written record of their aspirations and attitudes through autobiographies, oral histories, essays, private papers, and official documents.

Local self-government offers a way to connect pre- and post-1945 Taiwan, and Taiwan and Republican China. The promotion of local self-government, a position rejecting both independence and complete assimilation into China's polity, became an important tool for the Taiwanese elite to "protect" themselves from the problems of a war-torn China ruled by a collapsing Nationalist government. The legacy of fifty years of Japanese rule complicated the drive to maximize autonomy within China. Some Taiwanese recalled positive aspects of the colonial experience, such as economic development, in order to justify calls for greater autonomy. The colonial legacy, however, was a double-edged sword. The Taiwanese had to legitimize themselves by proving that they were loyal citizens of China who had not been "tainted" by collaboration with their former overlords. The Nationalists viewed the promotion of expanded local self-government as defined by the Taiwanese as the rejection of reintegration into China and refusal to embrace decolonization. The clash between these perceptions mirrored the overall relationship between state and society on Taiwan.

When discussing Taiwan under Nationalist Chinese rule, American scholars have tended to concentrate on a few topics: economic development from the 1950s to present, relations with the United States during the Cold War, democratization since the 1980s, and most recently cross-Strait relations. The 1945 to 1950 period is crucial background for understanding these topics and the development of relations between the Taiwanese and the Nationalists. For example, that prominent Taiwanese had been cowed into submission during these five years facilitated the imposition of land reform, a policy widely hailed as key to the island's "economic miracle."

The question of Taiwan's ties to the mainland remains one of the most heated disputes in East Asia, a major obstacle in Sino-American relations, and a central issue in the island's domestic politics. Supporters of independence and unification each struggle to prove that the island is a nation or a province of China. I have tried to avoid reading today's political agendas back into the 1945–50 period. At the same time, within this volume I have emphasized that relations between Taiwanese and the Nationalist state immediately after World War II were built on opposing visions of local self-government, each supported by a version of the island's history or mainland struggles for centralization and national strength. There is no way to avoid the occasional conflict between history as the way some Taiwanese or Nationalists honestly understood their past, history as a consciously created tool to build legitimacy or to rally support, and history as written by an American fifty years after the events.

Professors Nancy Bernkopf Tucker and Howard Spendelow at Georgetown University and Professor William Rowe at Johns Hopkins University provided advice and encouragement in the dissertation stage and later. Whatever strengths I have as a scholar are due to their efforts. Like a growing number of young scholars, I was fortunate to receive Professor Tucker's persistent prodding to complete the dissertation, and then the manuscript. John Witek, James Reardon-Anderson, and other members of the faculty at Georgetown also gave me guidance during the early stages of this project.

I hope this book will help alert historians in the United States to the efforts of scholars on Taiwan. In particular, the graduate students and faculty at National Chengchi University's History Department, led by then-chair Chang Che-lang, helped me locate historical materials and provided opportunities to test my ideas. Hou Kunhong and He Fengjiao at the Academia

Historica; Xu Xueji, Zhang Yanxian, Lai Tse-han, and Hui-yu Caroline Ts'ai at the Academia Sinica; and the staff at the Historical Research Commission of Taiwan Province, the Taiwan Branch of the Central Library, and the Tainan City Library all offered constructive criticism of my work and pointed me toward important materials. Li Guoqi's graduate course on the history of Taiwan provided a wonderful introduction to the scholarship in the field. Our good friends Julienne Hu and Tony Zhao opened their home to my wife and me, and provided an introduction to life on Taiwan. Finally, like so many other scholars, I owe a debt of gratitude to the dedicated staff and teachers at the Inter-University Program for Chinese Language Study ("Stanford Center"), then located in Taibei. They showed enthusiasm for improving my reading skills and tolerance of my pronunciation errors.

Ramon Myers at the Hoover Institution provided an incisive critique of this project in its early stages and brought primary source materials to my attention. Douglas Fix at Reed College offered a helpful assessment of my work at a conference sponsored by Washington University in St. Louis. I am also grateful to Murray Rubinstein for his thoughtful advice and the opportunity to publish a shortened version of one chapter in *Taiwan: A New History*. I thank heartily the readers of this manuscript, including David Barrett, John Fitzgerald, and Alan Wachman. Their comments on content and style were invaluable, and saved me from countless embarrassing errors.

I was fortunate to work for employers sympathetic to the needs of preparing a manuscript: Douglas Helms at the Natural Resources Conservation Service, Michael Birkner at Gettysburg College's History Department, Ted Keefer at the Department of State's Office of the Historian, and Cindy Gissendanner at Towson University's History Department.

Generous financial support came from the History Department at Georgetown University, the Inter-University Program, the Pacific Cultural Foundation, and the Chengchi University–Georgetown University exchange program. Julie Meyerson provided the excellent maps in this volume. Muriel Bell and the staff at Stanford University Press were encouraging, and remarkably tolerant of my incessant questions. I owe a great debt to Richard Gunde, who copyedited the manuscript; to Anne Holmes and Rob Rudnick, who created the index; and to Anna Eberhard Friedlander, who oversaw the production of the final product. I, of course, am solely responsible for any errors or omissions.

My wife, Barbara Cavanaugh Phillips, read and reread the manuscript. It was only because of her support that I earned my doctorate and brought this work to fruition.

For reasons of uniformity, and in recognition of the fact that electronic databases and card catalogs increasingly utilize pinyin romanization, I have used that system throughout the volume.

BETWEEN ASSIMILATION
AND INDEPENDENCE

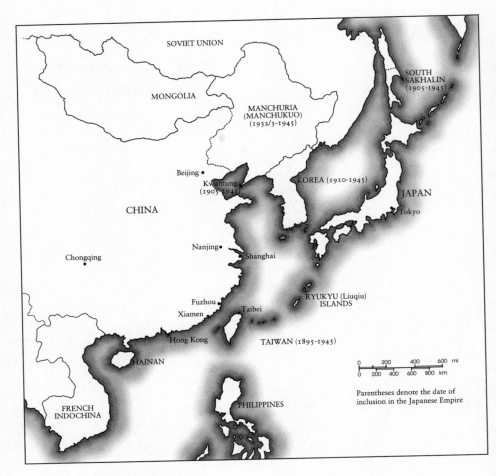

SOVIET UNION

MONGOLIA

MANCHURIA
(MANCHUKUO)
(1932/3-1945)

SOUTH
SAKHALIN
(1905-1945)

Beijing •

Kwantung
(1905-1945)

KOREA (1910-1945)

JAPAN

CHINA

Tokyo

Nanjing•

Chongqing
•

Shanghai

RYUKYU (Liuqiu)
ISLANDS

Fuzhou

Xiamen

Taibei

TAIWAN (1895-1945)

Hong Kong

HAINAN

0   200   400   600 mi
0   200   400   600   800 km

Parentheses denote the date of
inclusion in the Japanese Empire

FRENCH
INDOCHINA

PHILIPPINES

MAP 1. Japan's Colonial Empire

1 *Introduction*

A Chinese official in the 1720s complained that "the situation of Taiwan's order and disorder does not match our expectations." The island enjoyed civil rule (*wen*), consisting of circuits, prefectures, and counties, as well as a military infrastructure (*wu*), including officers, soldiers, and forts. Yet the Taiwanese, Han Chinese immigrants to the island, were less than impressed by the Qing state and one, a duck farmer named Zhu Yigui, led a revolt in 1721 that quickly overran part of the island. "How could we have predicted this?" lamented the official, Lan Dingyuan.[1] Over the next three centuries, understanding the Taiwanese has not become any easier.[2] The official's solution was a broad-based program to upgrade the quality and quantity of government bureaucrats, increase security, and improve education — in effect make the island more like what existed across the strait. Although little came of this, it was a harbinger of later attempts to "solve" the problem of Taiwan's relationship with the mainland by transforming the island into an idealized version of China.

Taiwan, more than simply a province of China, but less than a nation in the eyes of the international community, continues to defy expectations. From 1945 to 1950, the interaction between the Taiwanese and the Nationalist Chinese government led by Jiang Jieshi (Chiang Kai-shek) illustrated the complex relationship between nation and state and the difficulty of reconciling local political agendas with national loyalty.[3] Taiwanese and Nationalist Chinese struggled to define the nation and their place in it — a process little different from the efforts of scholars today. Benedict Anderson defines the nation as an "imagined community" of shared culture, values, language, and beliefs.[4] In his overview of nationalism, Ernest Gellner points out that mutual recognition or acknowledgment is key — a community is a nation because its members identify themselves as one.[5] There also exists a geographical component to the nation. Germaine A. Hoston's analysis of nationalism in China and Japan builds upon Gellner's ideas, and points out that "nation" stems from the Latin *natio*, which "referred not to a political unit but to a breed or stock of people." Nationalities "are ethnic peoples with shared histories, languages, cultures, and consciousness thereof, usually sharing a given territorial space." Hoston then goes on to define nationalism as the drive to make the nation and political unit congruent.[6] Thus, the nation is one type of community, and nationalism is the ideology that undergirds that community.

Nation, state, and province come with their own ideology and expectations. For example, killing people of another nation, or dying for one's nation, is acceptable today, although cities or provinces fighting one another appears backward, and is often denigrated as "feudal." The nation is generally recognized as the focus of political loyalty and often becomes the most important unit of history. History and the nation reinforce each other, as the development of the nation is seen as the primary "stuff" of history and as the idea of the nation is buttressed by historical research. There are other expectations for the nation, and its relationship to the state, the "institution or set of institutions concerned specifically with the enforcement of order," that few bother to question.[7] At the apex of the state stands the central government, the administrator of the nation. Those in control of the state or seeking to dominate it attempt to use nationalism to build their influence. Whoever controls the state is expected to seek uniformity among the jurisdictions under their control, limiting what they perceive as divisive regional or provincial differences. In fact, few scholars or political leaders even credit the province with an ideology—the nation has its nationalism and is guarded by the state, but there is little room for such sophistication with the province, which is portrayed as little more than an administrative subdivision of the state or a base for antinational loyalties.

Prasenjit Duara, in reflecting upon nationalism, could be describing the conflict over Taiwan's place in China when he writes, "In place of the harmonized, monologic voice of the Nation, we find a polyphony of voices, contradictory and ambiguous, opposing, affirming, and negotiating their views of the nation."[8] On Taiwan, between 1945 and 1950 these negotiations took tangible form through conflicts over local self-government (*difang zizhi*). In a chaotic and war-torn China governed by Jiang Jieshi's collapsing state, the Taiwanese attempted to revive a debate that the Nationalists felt they had settled decades before. Islanders searched for a middle ground: they accepted membership in the Chinese nation and the ultimate authority of the central government, but based on historical experience, contemporary events, and self-interest, attempted to maximize provincial autonomy and limit the impact of mainland events upon the island. This clashed directly with the Nationalists' vision of the province's relationship with the Chinese nation and the central government. To the Nationalists, support of their state and loyalty to the Chinese nation were one and the same. Furthermore, the Nationalists believed the purpose of local self-government was to fulfill the administrative needs of the state as dominated by the central government, not increase local autonomy as Taiwanese hoped. Although ultimately the centralizing efforts of the regime led by Jiang Jieshi were successful, the debate over local self-government presents a fascinating study of alternative images of nation and province in late Republican China.[9]

A History of Ambiguity

Since the 1600s, Taiwan has been defined as a small part of something else. The island was home to non-Han Chinese peoples for millennia, then became a prefecture of China's Fujian Province in 1684, a full-fledged province in 1885, a Japanese colony in 1895, a province of the Republic of China (ROC) in 1945, the *only* province of the ROC in 1949, and eventually a virtually independent nation, which it remains today. With the exception of the last transition, central governments located far from the island initiated these changes. These top-down shufflings of the jurisdictional deck are relatively easy to study and have attracted the attention of historians, but what do they have to do with the Taiwanese and their political agendas? In particular, did the transition from Japanese colony to Nationalist Chinese province change the islanders' political aspirations? If reconciling national and provincial prerogatives is difficult for historians today, between 1945 and 1950 it was agonizing for the Taiwanese, who sought to situate themselves between independence (claiming nationhood) and assimilation (becoming what they perceived as a typical province of China).

Islanders have had a contentious relationship with three different types of central governments — Qing empire, Japanese colonial regime, and Nationalist Chinese nation-state. Taiwanese dissatisfaction with specific government policies and vacillation over their place in each of these larger entities spawned a political agenda that was neither purely separatist nor assimilationist. Few islanders sought to overthrow these regimes and establish an independent nation, and even fewer felt this was possible. At the same time, Taiwanese were rarely satisfied with the treatment they received from central governments or their representatives — whether county magistrates, colonial police officers, or Nationalist bureaucrats. The goals of the Taiwanese were remarkably consistent: to minimize the central government's interference, particularly in business and trade, and to limit its demands (such as taxes), while maximizing "services," including public security and improved infrastructure. In this sense, Taiwan differed little from other provinces of China, or any other subunit of a larger political entity. Distance from the political center, however, both facilitated and strengthened these feelings.

The complex cross-strait relationship was born first of geography, as Taiwan is China's only major island other than Hainan.[10] The island lies between southeast China, Korea, Japan, the Philippines, and mainland Southeast Asia. This location brought the advantages of commerce and contact with diverse peoples, but also attracted the attention of any power wishing to play a role in the region, including the Chinese, Spanish, Dutch, Japanese, and Americans. Because of adverse ocean currents, Taiwan was one of the last-settled parts of the Middle Kingdom.[11] The earliest known inhabitants of the island were not Han Chinese but those who are now known as aborigines (*yuanzhumin*), peoples closely related to the Malayo-Polynesian inhabitants of the islands of Southeast Asia.[12] The Chinese official record, the dynastic histories, indicates that the Confucian elite had little interest in or knowledge of Taiwan until the late Ming dynasty (1368–1644).[13]

During the Ming, Taiwan was not under the control of the Chinese state, although traders, fishermen, and pirates from Fujian Province had established themselves on the west coast of the island. Political upheaval on the mainland helped link Taiwanese and Chinese history. When the Ming collapsed in 1644, Taiwan became a redoubt for a fallen regime that claimed to represent the true China and its culture against alien rule, an image the Nationalists revived after 1949. The life and career of Zheng Chenggong (1624–62), known in many Western histories as Koxinga, a regional strongman and pirate who gained increasing influence as the Ming collapsed, linked Taiwan to the mainland's political history.[14] Zheng's support of the Ming court against the non-Han Manchu invaders made him a permanent icon of Chinese patriotism. Even today he remains a particular source of local pride in Tainan, the city on the site where Zheng's forces brought about the Dutch evacuation from their small colonial outpost in 1662. A combination of effective military strategy and generous peace terms, however, in 1683 enticed Zheng's heirs to surrender to the Manchu Qing dynasty (1644–1912).

China absorbed Taiwan more as a little-wanted appendage than as part of any grand imperial design. The Manchu founders of the Qing dynasty, as horsemen from the northeast, displayed little curiosity about sea travel or Taiwan.[15] Their Han Chinese supporters, who also had almost no knowledge of this frontier island, were divided over whether to make it a part of China or simply abandon it. Official interest in the island was based primarily upon negative factors — denying the island to possible invaders or rebels against the dynasty. The Qing grudgingly made Taiwan a prefecture (*fu*) of Fujian Province in 1684, thus transforming the Han Chinese immigrants into subjects of the Qing dynasty. China's rulers sought to legitimize themselves by emphasizing their role as holders of the mandate of heaven and as protectors of Confucian culture. Those in Beijing had limited influence, however, since they had little interest in controlling local affairs and often lacked the ability to impose their will on the island's inhabitants even when they sought to do so.

The island lay on China's physical, political, and cultural periphery. The educated elite on the mainland saw it as on the edge of or outside civilization (*huawai*), which was defined largely by the philosophical, intellectual, cultural, and social tenets of Confucianism. One way to understand Taiwan's place in imperial China is through the model of the Great Tradition (*da chuantong*). Despite its name, the Great Tradition ideal was actually based upon a small part of China, the North China Plain. The plain represented the symbolic center of an idealized Middle Kingdom, a place dominated by Confucian scholars and populated by humble peasants, an "agrarian-bureaucratic heartland."[16] The main elements of the Great Tradition included small-holder agriculture as the base of society; the vital role of the scholar/gentry class; the relatively low status of merchants; the centrality of Confucian ideology in shaping the social and political order; and the ideal of a bureaucratic and meritocratic administrative apparatus.[17]

The Great Tradition can be juxtaposed to the image of Maritime China, a region that includes Taiwan and the provinces along the southeast coast of China. Although the terms Great Tradition and Maritime China are recent constructs of Western historiography, the notions they encapsulate coincide with the biases expressed in the corpus of Qing-era gazetteers.[18] Here, Maritime China is a subset of, and often inferior to, the "real" China of the North China Plain.[19] This view highlights mainland perceptions of the island's place in China, and would shape the relationship between the Taiwanese and the Nationalist state after 1945.

Taiwan was not known as an abode of peaceful peasants. On the contrary, revolts against the local administration, feuds between groups of immigrants from the mainland, and conflicts with aborigines were endemic.[20] The island gained the reputation of being a place with a history of small revolts every three years and large revolts every five years (*sannian yi xiaoluan, wunian yi daluan*). The idealized social structure of Great Tradition China, which placed scholars first and merchants last, was the opposite of reality on Taiwan, which had a history of extensive cross-strait and regional commerce. Although the phenomena seen on Taiwan also existed in the southeast coastal region, the degree of variation from the Great Tradition ideal set the island apart.[21]

During the Qing, as would be the case under the Japanese and Nationalist Chinese, Taiwanese alternated between avoiding the state and its exactions on one hand, and decrying the lack of assistance from the government on the other. Taiwan was no one's Confucian "old home" (*laojia*), but rather

INTRODUCTION

a place to make money or escape problems on the mainland. A persistent ambivalence toward central authority and high culture common among what scholars today call frontier societies (*yiken shehui*) or immigrant societies (*yimin shehui*) shaped the Taiwanese people. In the politically charged academic environment of Taiwanese history, these two terms have very different connotations: Frontier society suggests the island was assimilating into China (*neidihua*); immigrant society emphasizes the differences between the mainland and Taiwan, and is connected to the idea of indigenization (*tuzhuhua*). Immigrant society also connotes greater similarities to overseas Chinese communities in Southeast Asia than to the mainland.[22]

Of particular importance during the Qing were Taiwanese perceptions of government policies toward the island, which Taiwanese often portrayed as conservative (*baoshou*) or passive (*xiaoji*).[23] The state was blamed for retarding the island's development by limiting immigration and refusing to help Han Chinese immigrants crush the aborigines. There were many disputes and small wars as Han Chinese settlers pushed aborigines off their land, generally forcing them into more mountainous (and less fertile) areas. John Shepherd, in his examination of Qing-dynasty policy toward the island, emphasizes that the state in truth was not passive. For example, officials tried to control the settlers' pressure upon aborigines because the government wanted to avoid expensive military campaigns on the island. Han Chinese immigrants, however, interpreted this as a passive or conservative approach to rule. These same conflicts between local needs and central government policies existed on the mainland, but seem to have been more prevalent and more deeply felt on Taiwan.[24]

Despite the formal inclusion of Taiwan within the administrative boundaries of the Middle Kingdom, many Chinese-language histories claim that the central government's relative indifference to Taiwan did not change until the island was threatened by Japanese and Western imperialism in the late nineteenth century.[25] Qing reformers then recognized the importance Maritime China as a result of Western imperialism. State-sponsored reform and modernization were part of the Self-Strengthening Movement (Ziqiang yundong) of 1860 to 1890.[26] Increasing official interest in Taiwan became part of a larger debate within Qing officialdom over the need to concentrate defensive efforts on the far northwest to counter the threat posed by Russian incursions or on the coastal provinces in order to limit imperialist pressure there. In reality, the state was rarely an important help or hindrance to islanders. Taiwanese settled most of the island with little reference to the government; more often than not, they ignored the central government and its representatives on the island. Only rarely did officials stationed on Taiwan encourage immigration or call for more government assistance to develop the island.

The extent of Taiwanese participation in Qing-era government is closely connected to the issue of the island's historical relationship with the mainland which, in turn, forms part of the debate over the island's independence from China today. As one of the last parts of China settled and brought into the Middle Kingdom, Taiwan was more weakly tied to the central government and Confucian culture than other areas populated by Han peoples. For example, the Qing imperial bureaucracy had been less developed on the island than in mainland provinces. This made it easier for the Japanese to rule once they acquired the island, since there existed few leaders with strong political ties to the former central government to compete for legitimacy. As the historian Chen Ching-chih writes, "there were no more than 5,350 degree holders in Taiwan on the eve of the Japanese takeover. This figure would give Taiwan, which had a population of 2,546,000 in 1896, 21 degree holders for every 10,000 people. Taiwan thus proportionately contained a smaller group of degree holders than each of the eighteen provinces in China."[27]

The decisive defeat of the Qing dynasty in the Sino-Japanese War of 1894–95 marked a major turning point in Taiwan's history. The island became distinct from the mainland in an important way — of all China's provinces, it was the only one surrendered completely and permanently to imperialists by the Qing.[28] The island was no longer tied to a chaotic and crumbling China, but became part of an increasingly powerful and economically developed Japan. Colonial rule created the island's post-1945 elite and shaped its attitudes toward a national-level government. Under the Japanese, the Taiwanese experienced the benefits of a relatively efficient and honest administration as well as its rigid and intrusive demands. Islanders were excluded from full citizenship in the Japanese nation, even as the colonial regime held out the prospect of limited participation in the state. The Japanese era presented a tangle of contradictions: law and order with repression in a police state; economic development and exploitation; and education and employment opportunities limited by systematic discrimination. Wealthy and educated Taiwanese reacted ambivalently, organizing a series of reformist political movements that vacillated between seeking further assimilation into the empire and demanding greater autonomy from it. In particular, the elite's attitude toward the dual character of Japanese rule became clear in its attempt to expand self-government without seeking independence — setting a pattern for interaction between the islanders and Jiang Jieshi's regime after 1945.[29]

The history of peoples under colonial rule is often portrayed as a linear progression from ineffectual resistance by the ancien régime, to domination through direct or indirect rule, to attempts to reform the colonial state, to armed struggle that defeats the imperialists and establishes a modern nation-state.[30] In some places, such as the Dutch East Indies/Indonesia, the shared experience of colonial rule built a national consciousness among otherwise heterogeneous peoples who eventually overthrew their oppressor and estab-

lished a new state encompassing the same territory as the colonial administration. In other places, Korea under the Japanese for example, colonial domination of a people with a common language, culture, and government (the
Yi dynasty) spurred the development of a broad-based nationalist movement.
In short, colonialism leads to the struggle for an independent nation-state.
The experience of Taiwan represents an important variation from these patterns. Before 1895, islanders did not see themselves as a nation in their own
right and did not become one under colonial rule. Further, the island's elite
proved unable and unwilling to accept as their own the culture and history
of the Japanese nation. In this context the elite's political agenda mirrored
the contradictions of colonial rule. Taiwanese found it suited their interests
to defer the difficult question of nation in order to focus on improving their
position vis-à-vis the state. The Taiwanese struggled to reform Japanese rule,
symbolized by the Governor-General's Office (Taiwan sōtokufu; Chin.,
Taiwan zongdufu), through a variety of movements designed to expand the
island's autonomy within the empire.

Colonial rule left the Taiwanese with a dual legacy. It advanced the island
economically and industrially and insulated it from the chaos of warlords,
civil war, and invasion that plagued the mainland during the previous
decades. As the Taiwanese would emphasize after retrocession, their standard of living, level of education, and sanitary conditions all exceeded those
of the mainland, even Manchuria (which had been under Japanese control
since 1931). Acknowledging these benefits, many Taiwanese became loyal
subjects of the empire and eager participants in the Japanese-sponsored program of modernization.[31] In fact, wealthy islanders shared an interest with
the colonial regime in preventing Taiwanese farmers and workers from
organizing. Another aspect of the legacy, however, was negative. The
Taiwanese endured systematic discrimination, frustrated political aims, limited economic development geared to Japan's requirements, and wartime deprivation. The islanders' ambiguous role in the Japanese empire set the stage
for a struggle to expand self-government under the Nationalists, and led to
a difficult, and sometimes tragic, decolonization and reintegration into China.

Taiwan Province in Republican China

Retrocession did not solve the long-term problem of Taiwan's relationship with a central government, but did place it in a new political context. Between late 1945 and early 1947, the history of Japanese domination
and the immediate difficulties caused by Nationalist misrule spurred a
lively debate over Taiwan's relationship with China and the Republic of
China. The island's colonial-era economic development and political expe-

rience spawned mirror images of how the island should fit into the imagined community of the nation and the administrative structure of the state. The Nationalists sought tight control of Taiwan for two reasons. First, they harbored suspicions of the islanders' loyalty because of the latter's long association with the Japanese; and second, they wanted to exploit the island's relatively well-developed industrial base to serve the state and its goal of economic reconstruction. On the other hand, Taiwanese hoped their relatively prosperous society would be kept apart from the civil war and chaos on the mainland. Islanders also felt that their colonial-era material development, experience in political movements, and high levels of education justified reform of the state to create a relatively loose relationship between the central government and the province.

In one important way, the colonial era did not end in late 1945, as the Taiwanese elite relied heavily upon the collective memory of Japanese rule to shape their political agenda after retrocession.[32] Certain aspects of colonialism helped prominent Taiwanese establish minimum standards of effective government. During the previous fifty years, there had existed an implicit "deal" between rulers and ruled. Taiwan's colonial masters made improvements in education, sanitation, and health care, and major investments in industry and infrastructure. In exchange, the Taiwanese accepted second-class status, life in a police state, and strict limits on political activity. At the very least, Taiwanese hoped that this relationship would continue under the new regime. Nationalist misrule — the inability to meet those standards — strengthened some memories of the Japanese era, such as respect for law and order, while causing others to receive less attention, such as institutionalized discrimination. This attitude embarrassed, then antagonized the mainlander-dominated government because it highlighted the positive aspects of colonial rule. To the Nationalists, nostalgia for the Japanese era suggested that the Taiwanese were at best ignorant of, and at worst disloyal to, the Chinese nation.

A half century of bitter experience on the mainland made the Nationalists determined to build a strong central government and limit provincial autonomy. In the decade after the collapse of the Qing dynasty, Nationalist leader Sun Zhongshan (Sun Yat-sen) flirted briefly with a more decentralized system when the political party he founded, the Guomindang (Nationalist Party), was unable to control China's central government. During the last years of his life, however, Sun came firmly down in favor a highly centralized state and a Guomindang reorganized along the Leninist model. The fate of this political party was portrayed as indivisible from that of the Chinese nation. Sun's successor, Jiang Jieshi, followed the broad outlines of policies set by Sun and explicitly rejected federalism. Jiang redefined local self-government as a tool to assist administration but not as a source of a sovereign power in its own right.[33] The Nationalists defeated or co-opted war-lords, overpowered movements to promote provincial autonomy in places like Zhejiang, Guangxi, and Yunnan, and crushed armed uprisings against their rule in Sichuan. To Jiang's supporters, local self-government outside of their program was a code word for anti-Nationalist (and in their minds, anti-nationalist) loyalties.

Retrocession, however, raised Taiwanese expectations. They dreamed of obtaining greater influence over the state than they had enjoyed during the colonial era and of greater personal freedom as full citizens of the nation. From 1895 to 1945, the Taiwanese had deferred the difficult question of their participation in a nation in order to devote themselves to improving their position within the state through expanded self-government. After October 1945, islanders assumed they would reap the benefits that they believed came with full citizenship. Here, too, they were to be disappointed as the taint of "Japanization" made it easy to question their patriotism and suitability for even limited autonomy within the Republic of China.

By 1946, an increasingly restive elite openly criticized the Nationalist state as corrupt and incompetent and the Chinese nation as backward and chaotic. Returning to a pattern of political activity set under the Japanese, prominent islanders saw expanded local self-government as an answer to their concerns.[34] Many Taiwanese had hoped that looser political ties would insulate the island from economic crises and civil war on the mainland, as well as reduce the power of the central government and its representatives. The Japanese-era experiences of economic development and political activism became the justification for requests for political reform in the guise of expanded self-government. Local self-government also represented an attempt to bridge the gap between Taiwan the colony of Japan and Taiwan the province of China. To the elite, Taiwan's progress during the colonial era met the standards of development spelled out by the official ideology of the Nationalists, Sun Zhongshan's Three Principles of the People.

While the island's elite engaged in a nonviolent political struggle, ordinary Taiwanese faced a more immediate crisis of food shortages and unemployment. The concerns of both the elite and the common people, amorphous at the time of retrocession, became linked to increasingly specific criticism of Nationalist policies during 1946, and exploded in early 1947 in what became known as the February 28 Incident. This event epitomized the conflict between decolonization and reintegration, when the legacy of Japanese rule and the drive for local self-government clashed with the centralizing mission of Jiang Jieshi's Nationalist regime. Unemployed youth, workers, students, peddlers, and small merchants briefly wrested control of Taiwan from the provincial administration. The island's elite suddenly found itself caught between the mainlander-dominated state and Taiwanese society. Although prominent Taiwanese had not initiated armed resistance to the central government, they did act to manipulate the situation in their own interests. The elite moved initially to limit violence and to restore order, then used the opportunity to press for reforms under the broad rubric of local self-government. Over the course of negotiations with the provincial administration, islanders enlarged their demands to the extent that they threatened to weaken drastically Taiwan's ties to the central government. The reforms they proposed would have expanded the powers of the province beyond what was acceptable to the Nationalists. After a week of increasing tensions, reinforcements from the mainland arrived and massacred thousands — those integrally involved in the incident, those who had made enemies among the Nationalists, and others unfortunate enough to be on the streets. This brutal retribution changed the face of the island's politics for decades.

In the incident, the Taiwanese moved briefly onto the national stage, courting disaster in two ways. First, urbanites had used force to usurp state control over a province of China, an act anathema to the central government and humiliating to Nationalist officials and military leaders on the island. Second, the island's elite became embroiled in this uprising, and compounded its problems by advocating reforms that fundamentally challenged the centralizing efforts of the Nanjing government. The Nationalists' response to the incident revealed how the island had stumbled into the mainstream of the mainland's political history.

Taiwan Province as the Republic of China

Nationalist policies on Taiwan represented an extension of those implemented on the mainland. The regime combined harsh authoritarian rule with carefully managed reform, setting a pattern that would last for the next forty years. In particular, in the first three years following the chaos and violence of the February 28 Incident, the Nationalists systematized their repression on the island. This grew into a mixture of anti-Communist ideology and police state known as the White Terror. Although the Taiwanese were unlikely to challenge the state after the February 28 Incident, Nationalist rule became more oppressive as the state began to arrest anyone with even the flimsiest tie to Communists and to define almost all criticism as subversive. In fact, the Nationalists obtained a greater degree of control over Taiwan than they enjoyed in any province on the mainland. Simultaneously, they undertook limited reforms, guided firmly from the top down. A key aspect of the reforms was local self-government. Taiwan's political, economic, and social landscape was further restructured by a program of rent reduction, followed by land reform. Some of these changes, particularly those related to local self-government, appeared to meet the requests of islanders prior to and during the February 28 Incident. The actual implementation and the results that followed, however, reflected the needs of the state and its centralization efforts.

Local self-government as implemented on Taiwan highlighted the Nationalists' view of the island's relationship with the nation (China) and the state (the Republic of China). This program was based upon the experiences, goals, and biases of the mainlanders in Jiang's government — part of the "n/Nationalization" of the island's politics. The Nationalists hoped to prove the validity of their policies by implementing them in what they claimed was a microcosm of China. Just as the Taiwanese discussions of local self-government before and during the February 28 Incident reflected one understanding of the island's history and relationship with China, now the Nationalists' plans for administrative reform required a different version of the history of local self-government and its applicability to Taiwan. In particular, the justification for and content of reforms grew from mainland experiences — the ideas of Sun Zhongshan, conflicts with warlords, critiques of federalism, and state-building programs of Jiang Jieshi. The sensitive issue of Taiwan's status was avoided, as the new administrative system did not address the relationship between the province and the central government, but dealt with the county level and below. The system implemented in the late 1940s and early 1950s created a highly centralized political structure — a goal of the Nationalists on the mainland for almost half a century. Ironically, only after his greatest defeat could Jiang create a tightly controlled government under his personal command.

The island's experience with local self-government also revealed the Nationalists' complex approach to political participation. Jiang needed the Taiwanese because someone had to do the work of government at the provincial level and below. His regime, however, sought to create a citizenry that would always choose to do that which served the interests of the central government. This marked the continuation of trends that began on the mainland. In his recent book, *Awakening China*, John Fitzgerald builds upon the models of nation and nationalism developed by Benedict Anderson, and posits two sources of nationalist sentiment: a spontaneous enthusiasm from below, and a more systematic manipulation of media, education, and administration from above in order to serve the state. In this sense, Taiwan is a case study of a part of China that had little of the former and much of the latter source of nationalism.[35]

In order to create a system to serve the administrative needs of the state, not to promote autonomy, the Nationalists utilized a broad array of methods to control the discourse and policies concerning local self-government. They wrote a constitution, laws, and regulations to strengthen the central government and to limit local, particularly provincial, autonomy. These rules for political participation were backed up by the police state that developed after the February 28 Incident and grew into the White Terror. On Taiwan, the regime could concentrate its attention, as well as police and military resources, much more effectively than it had ever been able to do across the strait. If all else failed, the suspension of the constitution and the declaration of martial law would allow Jiang to override any potential opposition.

Postwar Taiwan offers another avenue to examine the regime's state-building — stripped of conflicts with warlords, Communists, and foreign invaders, and without the need to court a rural landholding elite. In the face of Nationalist defeat, many mainlanders saw the island as a laboratory where they could implement programs they had been unable to carry out on the other side of the Taiwan Strait. In this respect, the Nationalists did not change, but "China" did, that is, the island that was to represent the Republic of China. To central government leaders, the Taiwanese would have to think and act in accord with the Nationalists' priorities — which became equated with the welfare of the Chinese nation. In light of this "n/Nationalization" of Taiwanese politics, the island's elite came to realize that the safe way to discuss local self-government was in the context of building a strong China and struggling against Communism. This marked a great success for the government's program of training and propaganda, and set the tone for relations between Taiwanese and the Nationalist state for the next forty years.

Between 1945 and 1950 the Nationalists molded the kind of provincial elite on Taiwan that they had sought on the mainland. This elite changed in three ways: ideology, membership, and internal unity. It grew more compliant to Nationalist wishes, consisted of fewer leaders from the Japanese era, and split into mutually antagonistic factions. The island's leaders changed in the way they thought and acted, becoming more willing to accept the Nationalists' view of the island, its place in China and the Republic of China, and the need to make anti-Communism central to all political activity. Discussions of local self-government and Taiwan's role in a crusade to retake the mainland demonstrated these changes. The Taiwanese elite increasingly consisted of people unlikely to complain because those who were too openly opposed to government policies had died, fled, or retired. Many of the advocates of expanded islandwide autonomy were replaced in elected assemblies and official posts by younger men or by islanders who had moved to the mainland during the colonial era and had developed a close relationship with the Nationalist government and the Guomindang. Those who remained active in politics became caught up in competing against one another for benefits from the government rather than attempting to reform the system itself.

After the Nationalists' defeat on the mainland, Taiwan became head-quarters of a nation under a state that insisted the island was no more than a province, with a people who often acted as through they were living in a colony. Of course, the Nationalists did not accept that their rule of the island could be characterized as colonialism, but instead insisted on the differences between their regime and the Japanese. At the same time, the way the islanders reacted to Nationalist rule and divided themselves into groups that accommodated themselves to outside rule, resisted it, or avoided political activity suggested that Taiwanese had situated themselves toward the nation and the state in a way reminiscent of the Japanese era. Just as neither assimilation nor independence express adequately Taiwanese goals, however, the term "colonialism" does not convey fully the reality of Nationalist policies on the island.[36] Perhaps this lack of clarity is to be expected in postwar Taiwan. If nationalism is a reaction to "pure" colonialism, then the advocacy of local self-government corresponds to the island's complex situation.

Historiography's Orphan

The troubled relationship between the Taiwanese people and the Nationalist state has been the most important, and least studied, political issue on the island for the past fifty years. This historiographical blind spot can be attributed to the Cold War in Asia, an unresolved civil war in China, and the fact that Taiwan defied neat categorization as a nation or a province.[37] Until the late 1980s, the political agendas of those who have studied Taiwan most intensively—Nationalists, Communists, independence activists, and Americans—left little room for questioning, much less synthesizing, province and nation. Authoritarian rule on Taiwan and the mainland severely limited the ability of scholars to investigate the island's modern history. In particular, Nationalists and Communists rejected any discussion of Taiwan as a nation and insisted that the island was simply a province of China.[38] For decades, those on both sides of the strait often contended that conflict between the Taiwanese and the Nationalist government arose from the activities of Communists or the machinations of outsiders, specifically Americans and Japanese, seeking to control the island.[39] The Nationalists portrayed their rule of Taiwan as the fulfillment of Sun Zhongshan's dreams for China; Communists described the island as one of the remaining parts of China awaiting liberation and reunification with the fatherland (*zuguo*).[40] On the other hand, independence activists claimed the island was a nation in its own right, and suffered from colonial rule under the Nationalists.[41] Their discourse is dominated by the idea of a Taiwanese nation, ignoring the "provincial" aspects of islanders' political activity. They treated local self-government as a precursor to nationalism or a watered-down version of it. The contending justifications for various degrees of provincial autonomy illustrate the complicated intersection of politics and history. All sought to build consistency between the past and present, thus creating intellectual frameworks that dominated the island's politics for decades — concepts that frequently "bled over" to scholarship in the United States.

Beginning in the 1950s, American political and academic circles largely disregarded the Taiwanese, and instead examined the Nationalist government on the island, or studied Taiwan as a microcosm of China. The Cold War attracted the interest of American leaders and academics to Taiwan as the island related to Jiang's contribution to the anti-Communist struggle. In this context, Americans either avoided the issue of nation by stating that the island's final status had not been determined, or simply ignored Taiwanese political aspirations.[42] There was little room for ambivalence, uncertainty, or ambiguity in this highly charged atmosphere. In one key way, American scholarship, even that undertaken by liberals opposed to Jiang's regime, served the Nationalists' agenda. By taking Taiwan as a case study for the rest of China (a place impossible to visit, much less perform field research until the 1970s), scholars helped further the image of the island as simply one province in a large nation. Other than a few works promoting independence from China, there was little interest in the Taiwanese or their political agenda.[43]

Political reform in the mid-1980s on Taiwan opened the door to more nuanced examinations of the island's recent history.[44] It also made the problems of national identity and legal status more urgent by unleashing an increasingly vocal and powerful independence movement. In this atmosphere of greater interest and academic freedom, many recent Chinese-language monographs and dissertations are grounded in extensive primary source research and take advantage of newly available materials such as personal papers and oral histories. The English-language work has generally followed trends that began with scholars on Taiwan. Changes in the political and academic environments enable scholars today to examine complex and sensitive topics such as the Taiwanese elite's interaction with the Nationalist state. Although the island's relationship with the Chinese nation — whether the Nationalists' Republic of China or the Communists' People's Republic — has serious international repercussions, it is now possible to shift the focus of inquiry away from "proving" that Taiwan is a province or a nation, and toward examining the *process* by which the roles of nation, state, and province were negotiated in late Republican China.

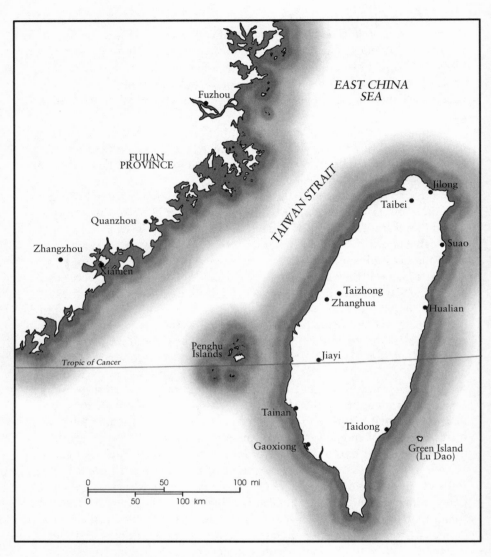

MAP 2. Taiwan and Coastal Fujian Province

2 Creating a Colonial Legacy

Understanding politics in Taiwan after retrocession must begin with the colonial experience, which shaped the island's elite and its attitudes toward government at the islandwide and national levels. The Japanese colonial regime was in many ways a progressive despotism: with one hand it promoted political stability, economic development, public health, and popular education; with the other, it crushed dissent and implemented discriminatory measures in employment and education. In the context of the limited benefits of Japanese rule and the hopelessness of an armed uprising, the Taiwanese reaction was less resistance than accommodation, as many prominent islanders danced around the "problem" of national identity while focusing on specific political issues related to improving their position vis-à-vis the colonial regime. Wealthy and educated Taiwanese organized a series of reform-oriented political movements that fluctuated between demanding local self-government within the empire and seeking further assimilation into it.

Colonial Administration, Economy, and Education

After a devastating defeat in the first Sino-Japanese War, China's beleaguered Qing dynasty ceded Taiwan to Japan in the April 1895 Treaty of Shimonoseki. The colonizers established their rule through brute force, concentrating first on eliminating armed resistance, which did not prove unduly difficult since the Taiwanese were inadequately armed and led, and divided among themselves.[1] Indeed, many wealthy islanders preferred the potential stability of Japanese rule to the lawlessness of those resisting colonization.[2] Also, the apparent willingness of Qing officialdom to abandon Taiwan gave islanders little motivation to fight.[3] For the next fifty years, China's internal difficulties and Japan's military superiority meant that the Taiwanese had no prospect of rejoining the mainland. However, when compared to the mainland—with its whirlwind of anti-Qing revolution, imperialist pressure, warlord struggles, civil war, and finally Japan's outright invasion—the island enjoyed relative peace and order. The colonial regime did not seek to restructure radically the island's society, but rather to create a situation where the Taiwanese relied upon and obeyed the government. For members of the island's elite, this stability and preservation of their status in Taiwanese society required that they accept foreign rule and strict limits on their political activities. Attempts to bring about reform were stifled; revolutionary movements or calls for the end of Japanese rule were crushed.

In the realm of material progress, there existed an implicit "deal" between rulers and ruled. Beginning in 1898 under Governor-General Kodama Gentarō and his chief administrator, Gotō Shimpei, Taiwan's colonial masters made major improvements in areas such as sanitation and health care. For example, the Japanese took great pride in the fact that the island had 180 doctors trained in Western medicine by 1904.[4] Education through primary and technical schools became widely available, and a small percentage of very able Taiwanese studied at Japanese universities. The Japanese unified measurements and currency; created postal, banking, and telegraph systems; built infrastructure including harbors, railroads, and power plants; and developed industry in areas such as sugar, aluminum, cement, iron, chemicals, textiles, and lumber. The Japanese focused islanders' energies on economic pursuits; the sphere most open to ambitious Taiwanese with ability was business. Other cooperative Taiwanese obtained low-level positions in the institutions that served the colonial empire, including the bureaucracy, Japanese-controlled companies, schools, and hospitals. Development, however, also meant domination by outside companies and an economy structured to benefit the so-called home islands (that is, Japan itself).[5] The education and employment provided by colonial rule—and the status that came with them—required working within the political and economic structures established by the state. Further, institutionalized discrimination severely limited upward mobility.

Three interrelated aspects of colonial domination shaped the Taiwanese elite and its relationship with the state: the virtual dictatorship of the governor-general, the island's economic role in the Japanese empire, and policies related to education and employment. Under a series of governors-general, Taiwan became an "empire within an empire."[6] In the late 1890s, Law 63 established the framework for Japanese rule by giving the governor-general (*Taiwan sōtoku*) broad powers over the military, administrative, regulatory, police, and judicial organs on the island, with only limited interference from Tokyo.[7] The laws passed by the Imperial Diet related to political rights did not apply to Taiwan. The first governors-general were active-duty military officers, but beginning in 1919, civilian bureaucrats held the governor-general's post, symbolizing the slight liberalization of colonial policies in Taishō-era Japan.[8]

Taiwanese political activity — primarily in the form of publications and organizations devoted to reforming the colonial system — expanded rapidly during the 1920s. The political environment shifted again in the 1930s as the military increasingly dominated Japan's domestic politics and tensions rose with China. After 1937, as the Japanese began to mobilize the island's population for the war effort, only military officers served as governor-general. In order to promote loyalty to the empire, even the most moderate independent Taiwanese organizations were banned or absorbed by government-controlled groups.

The governor-general presided over a police state. Backed by the military, the police became the most frequent point of contact between the Taiwanese and the government. In addition to enforcing criminal codes, police managed household registration, price controls, and sanitation regulations. They also monitored political activity — harassing and arresting those considered a threat to the state. The Japanese were capable of great brutality. For example, in the early years of colonial rule the regime frequently used public executions to terrorize the local population. As Taiwanese author Wu Zhuoliu (born Wu Jiantian) recounted later, the people feared the police "as though they were ghosts."[9] Demonstrating one of the many moral and political dilemmas of colonialism, some Taiwanese obtained low-level positions in the police force — where they often earned a reputation for bullying their fellow islanders.[10] Such participation in the colonial system represented one of many ways the Taiwanese planted the seeds of future conflict over their role as collaborators.

The second key aspect of colonialism was economic growth and development, including industrialization and technological modernization that transformed the structure of the economy. Some scholars suggest that Taiwan underwent its own Meiji Restoration under Japanese rule.[11] Japanese goals on Taiwan differed little from those of European imperialists in their own colonies — the island was to become a cheap source of raw materials and labor, and a market for manufactured goods. This required that economic competition be restricted from within (the Taiwanese) and without (other nations). High tariffs enabled the Japanese to control the island's resources and limit it as a market for European and American goods. Colonial rule redirected trade from China to Japan — about 85 percent of the island's exports, mainly raw materials and agricultural products such as sugar, camphor, tea, coal, and fruit, went to the home islands. Japanese businesses also blocked the expansion of Taiwanese economic power.[12] *Zaibatsu*, large conglomerates of corporations based in Japan, worked closely with the colonial administration. For example, zaibatsu ensured high profits by forcing Taiwanese farmers, who harvested sugarcane on land leased from Japanese companies, to sell the cane at fixed prices to Japanese-controlled mills.[13] The colonists also dominated the economy of the island through state-sanctioned monopolies on products such as tobacco, opium, salt, and camphor.[14]

Economic development provided opportunities for many Taiwanese, thus connecting their personal success to that of the colonial endeavor. Japanese rule brought industrialization to Taiwan, primarily in mining, transport, textiles, food processing, communications, and manufacturing. Local labor was key to building the economy — railroads, ports, roads, generating plants, factories, and mills. The island's elite found employment as low and mid-level managers in these facilities, and also dominated small and medium-sized enterprises on the island, serving as suppliers and local agents for the zaibatsu.[15] Some also were given the right to sell or distribute state monopoly goods as an inducement to support the regime. Islanders expanded their own enterprises as the empire's economy grew. In his examination of colonial rule on Taiwan, Chen Ching-chih noted that "by 1939, the Taiwanese owned 85 percent of the enterprises employing 5 to 49 workers, 74 percent of those employing 50 to 99 workers, and 38 percent of those employing 100 to 199 workers, and only 3 percent of those employing more than 200 workers."[16] Industrialization accelerated during the 1930s and early 1940s in order to support Japan's war effort.[17] In fact, the economy of Taiwan was more industrialized in the late 1930s than at any other time prior to the mid-1960s.[18]

The island became the base for the empire's expansion into South China and Southeast Asia, which accelerated the economic boom caused by World War I.[19] For example, many of the manufactured goods shipped from Taiwan to China were actually produced in Japan. Similarly, Taiwan's financial infrastructure was created as much for Japan's larger imperialist ambitions as for the island itself. The Taiwan Bank, which acted as a central bank on the island, opened offices in China in 1918.[20] Under the governor-general's leadership, the Hua'nan Bank, which concentrated on expanding investment from Taiwan into South China, was created in 1919 in Taibei. The Japanese also set up other enterprises, such as the Southeast Asia Warehouse Company, to build their presence and influence in the region.

Regional trade and investment became a strong impetus for cooperation between Japanese and Taiwanese. The colonizers relied upon the islanders' long-established business contacts and worked through the "cover" of Taiwanese, who were more readily accepted by Chinese throughout the region. Wealthy islanders thus found profit and employment in Japanese-created institutions, and also established their own enterprises.[21] For example, prominent Taiwanese from the central part of the island formed the

Zhanghua Bank, and in 1926, islanders established the Datong Trust Company, the largest firm owned and staffed by the Taiwanese.[22] After 1945, untangling the mixture of Taiwanese and Japanese assets became a contentious issue between islanders and the Nationalist government.

Japanese economic policies gradually restructured Taiwanese society.[23] The island's population became more urban, although the majority remained farmers. The proportion of the population engaged in agriculture declined from 70 percent in 1905 to approximately 59 percent in 1940, while those employed in industry increased from 7 percent to 13 percent and in services from 23 percent to 27 percent.[24] Life changed also for those who remained in the countryside after the Japanese undertook land reform in the early part of the century. This program sought to weaken Taiwanese landlords and clear the way for the purchase of land by Japanese individuals and firms. However, some wealthy Taiwanese landlords who cooperated with the new regime remained powerful, especially in the central part of the island. Landowners obtained bonds in exchange for land, thus tying their fate to that of the colony. By the 1930s, the percentage of owners, part-owners and tenants stabilized around 31 percent, 32 percent, and 37 percent respectively. Ultimately, however, a small number of individuals and Japanese corporations controlled about half of the farmland (5.7 percent of the landowners held about 50 percent of the land).[25]

The third pillar of Japanese rule was a system of education designed to create a loyal population with skills to support the colonial economy.[26] Although at the turn of the century there were three major systems of education on Taiwan — traditional Confucian, Christian missionary, and Japanese — the last dominated by the 1920s.[27] Primary school enrollment of Taiwanese youth increased from 21 percent of males and 4 percent of females in 1917 to 81 percent and 61 percent respectively by 1943.[28] Instruction concentrated on topics such as Japanese language, arithmetic, sewing, manual arts, and morals.[29] Taiwanese and Japanese studied at separate schools until the 1940s. Opportunities for education above the high school level often meant travel to Japan, and were available only to a select group who usually came from the families of landlords, businessmen, or professionals. In 1922, 2,400 Taiwanese were studying in Japan; by 1942 this had increased to 7,000.[30] The two most important fields were medicine and education. The Japanese discouraged the study of topics they felt likely to spur political activity such as law, history, and literature.[31] The colonial administration also established the first modern institutions of higher education on the island. Taihoku (Taibei) Normal School trained thousands of the island's teachers and Taiwan Imperial University grew from 20 Taiwanese students in the 1930s to about 170 by 1944.[32] The majority of the students, however, were the children of Japanese residents.[33]

Forming a Taiwanese Political Elite

The Taiwanese political elite, formed within the context of colonial policies and the implicit deal between it and the state, stood apart from the rest of society by virtue of its education, social status, wealth, and access to the state. Members of the elite thought of themselves as Taiwanese, that is, their relationship with the state was based primarily, although not exclusively, on an islandwide identity. Their interests and attention, in other words, were islandwide, rather than confined to a single region, city, or county. In particular, their concern was with Taiwan's relationship with the central government and its representative on the island, the governor-general.

The elite engaged in politics by writing, publishing, participating in organizations, and serving in elected or appointed posts. These prominent Taiwanese, born during the last years of Qing rule or the first decades of the colonial era, would draw on their colonial experience in their post-1945 political activity, especially in their drive for local autonomy.[34]

From the perspective of the Japanese, those who held leading positions in Taiwanese social networks and business enterprises represented a "subelite" since they occupied a position below the national elite that controlled the central government.[35] These Taiwanese could also be defined as a political elite, but not necessarily a governing or positional elite. In other words, although they were involved in politics and attempted to shape government policies, they did not necessarily hold formal elected or appointed posts.[36] They typically worked as doctors, journalists, teachers, managers in trade or light industry, or landlords. Most had education above the high school level, often in Japan. A hallmark of the Taiwanese elite was that its members continued to play a multiplicity of influential roles as they had during the Qing.[37] For example, a person might be a Japanese-trained doctor from a wealthy landlord family who organized petitions for expanded self-government. The line between economic and political power often blurred as many township heads and other local officials participated in the monopoly system, obtaining licenses to sell or distribute goods such as tobacco, camphor, and wine.[38] These roles were mutually reinforcing. Based on their economic power, members of the elite obtained the education needed to write and publish materials advocating their interests and the resources to organize and fund political associations. In turn, their ability to represent Taiwanese interests to the state strengthened their elite status.

Reflecting the contradictions of the colonial experience, the elite's relationship with state and society was simultaneously adversarial and cooperative. Prominent islanders had a coincidence of interests with the state in preserving order and promoting economic development. The colonial regime provided material progress and protected the status of these Taiwanese by blocking radical social change. If these benefits did not always create a compliant elite, the government harassed, arrested, or bankrupted those who appeared to advocate the interests of the Taiwanese too forcefully. This relationship put wealthy islanders at odds with many laborers and farmers, who sought higher wages or prices for their products, leftists who advocated class struggle, and those who strongly opposed Japanese rule. At the same time, members of the elite needed the support of their fellow islanders in order to legitimize their political agenda of limiting the power of the government and reducing institutionalized discrimination. Taiwanese who became too supportive of the state lost legitimacy with the populace.

The contours of the elite and its relationship with the colonial administration became clear after the short-lived resistance of 1895. Prominent Taiwanese had three options: flee to the mainland, avoid political activity and contact with the state, or cooperate with the new regime.[39] Those who fled were often among the wealthiest, with close ties to the Qing state. Many returned when it was clear the island was calm and their assets were protected.[40] Some remained on the mainland and eventually enjoyed successful careers with Jiang Jieshi's Nationalist government or with the Guomindang. Upon their return to the island in 1945 they too became part of the political elite. Unlike other prominent Taiwanese, however, their influence depended less on their social roles or economic influence and more on their formal state or party posts, characteristics of a positional elite.[41]

The new administrative system absorbed most of the Qing-era elite as unofficial local organs became tied to the colonial structure.[42] At the same time, the Japanese attempted to refocus traditional loyalties from the Chinese to the Japanese imperial house. For example, during the early years of Japanese rule, the governor-general emphasized that those who remained on the island owed loyalty to the Meiji Emperor because he now held the mandate of heaven.[43] The 1920s marked an important transition as a new generation began to supplant the older, Confucian-educated elite. Those who had been prominent during the late Qing lost influence through simple attrition. After the Japanese built a centralized and standardized bureaucratic administration, they no longer sought the trappings of Confucian legitimacy to gain support. They also feared the affinity many older Taiwanese had for the mainland could still spark anti-Japanese sentiment. For these reasons, they reduced the power of local notables by replacing them with Japanese or Japanese-educated Taiwanese.[44] Moreover, economic development fostered by the colonial regime rewarded technical skills and management ability, not Confucian education.

Colonial education, especially study in Japan, also played a key role in shaping the elite. Although examinations at all levels of the system created a meritocracy in theory, the cost of higher education meant that children of wealthy families represented a disproportionate number of students at that level. Thus, although there may have been change in the education and employment experiences of the island's elite, many prominent families survived the transition. Even with higher education, islanders could serve, but not lead, the island's development, and they encountered many barriers to career advancement. For example, in the 1930s only six of Taiwan's 1,074 public schools had Taiwanese principals. Within the colonial administration Taiwanese bureaucrats were usually limited to posts at the township level or below.[45] Even those in relatively important jobs at the end of World War II held their posts on an acting basis.[46] Exceptions to this were the handful of Taiwanese appointed to an islandwide advisory assembly beginning in 1921 and the three given membership in the House of Peers in exchange for their service to the Japanese government. One of those three, Gu Xianrong, is an excellent example of a Taiwanese who worked with the Japanese and obtained economic benefits as a result. A merchant, Gu accepted the Japanese takeover in 1895. He grew wealthy after being given responsibility for much of the island's salt monopoly, a position he soon parlayed into greater wealth through other commercial enterprises.[47]

Above all, the colonial administration sought to channel the islanders' energies into economic, not political, pursuits.[48] Economic change and career opportunities for educated Taiwanese led to a more urban elite. Fewer of the wealthy islanders were exclusively landlords, though many maintained investments in land or homesteads in more rural parts of the island.[49] The changing nature of the elite became clear in the makeup of the local self-government organs designed to advise the administration. By 1937, half of the members were businessmen or merchants, and 19 percent were doctors. Landlords or farmers made up only 13 percent.[50] The result of these changes was that businessmen became important figures in the island's political history.[51]

Besides implementing economic and education policies that fostered an elite, Japanese rule steadily strengthened a Taiwanese identity in several key ways. Compulsory education built a common language and economic development eased transportation and communication throughout the island. Greater interaction between the various ethnic and linguistic groups of Han Chinese on the island strengthened a common identity.[52] Colonial rule also created a shared experience of discrimination. The Japanese even helped build a Taiwanese identity by naming, and thus defining, islanders. Terms ranged from extremely derogatory, such as *Shinnu*, "Qing slaves", to merely descriptive, *Hontōjin*, "people of this island." These factors dampened pre-1895, mainland-derived, divisions based on Hakka or Minnan ethnicity and loyalty to one's clan or hometown.[53]

Although scholars today agree that a Taiwanese identity grew more important during colonial rule, the essence of that identity is hotly debated. Since history and the nation are closely intertwined, in order to legitimize Taiwanese independence today, one must find an islandwide identity in the past, and define it as a national identity. On the other hand, to delegitimize Taiwanese nationalism, one must portray the islanders' identity as local, provincial, or ethnic—a subset of China and less important than Chinese nationalism. Claiming that the island's colonial-era elite sought a middle ground somewhere between Taiwanese nationalism and assimilation into the Japanese nation, as this study does, serves few political agendas.

Was the Taiwanese identity "merely" an ethnic identification, or a sign of an imagined community and nationalism along the model developed by Benedict Anderson? Some observers have based their claim of Taiwanese consciousness on Anderson's model of nationalism in Indonesia under Dutch colonial rule. The increased use of the term *Taiwanren* (Taiwanese), particularly during the 1920s, is connected to a nationalist movement strongly influenced by United States President Woodrow Wilson's ideas on self-determination. According to this argument, colonial rule, which brought better communication and industrialization, was key to creating a Taiwan consciousness. Others see Taiwanese as an ethnic, not a national, identity. Wang Mingke of the Academia Sinica, who has written about Taiwan in the context of collective memory and ethnic identification, sees ethnicity as based on cultural nepotism (assumed blood ties) but shifting through collective memory. Changes in the social environment can change ethnic identity. Wang posits that Japanese attempts at assimilation in fact strengthened Taiwanese identification with the mainland's culture.[54]

What many contemporary scholars deem Taiwanese consciousness (*Taiwan yishi*) in fact represented a shifting mixture of competing values.[55] It was defined often in a negative manner: Taiwanese was neither Chinese nor Japanese. Many literate, politically active Taiwanese came to view their island as "Asia's orphan" (*Yaxiya de gu'er*), cast off by China and accorded second-class status by Japan. A famous novel of the same title, written by Taiwanese author Wu Zhuoliu during the final years of Japanese rule, is a case study in the difficulties the islanders had in defining themselves.[56] The vicissitudes of the novel's protagonist, Hu Taiming, are closely modeled after Wu's own experiences, but symbolized the fate of many educated youth under colonial rule. During his study in Japan, Hu found his resistance to the Japanese awakened by the travails of his fellow Taiwanese students. Yet, mainland Chinese cursed him for his ties to the Japanese.[57] In the end, Hu, unable to stand the competing pressures for his loyalty, becomes mentally unbalanced. The islanders' political activity reflected this uncertain identity and ambivalence toward the colonial experience.

The Elite's Political Agenda

In a pattern common to colonies, some of the people most privileged by the system — in the case of Taiwan, the very elite that obtained education, wealth, and status under the Japanese — became its most visible critics.[58] The forces of economic modernization, colonial education, and dictatorship under the governors-general that shaped the island's elite also influenced its political agenda. Other important factors included the political environment in Japan, Sino-Japanese relations, and international ideological currents such as Wilsonianism and Marxist-Leninism. In this context, the Taiwanese organized themselves on an islandwide basis, an activity that Japanese governors-general discouraged.

Reflecting the contradictions of the colonial experience, assimilation and autonomy became the two main strategies to deal with Japanese rule.[59] When the concepts of state and nation are examined separately, the Taiwanese combination of these two is not so incongruous as it might at first appear. Both assimilation and autonomy, under the banner of local self-government, were methods to increase the islanders' influence within the Japanese state. Both were nonviolent, reformist programs designed to limit the power of the governors-general. The elite's discussion of both strategies reflected the seemingly insurmountable barriers to becoming part of the Japanese nation. Supporters of assimilation hoped to avoid the question of nation, which the Japanese had tied to long-term cultural and linguistic change, and instead advocated reform of the colonial regime. Politically, assimilation sought to extend the administrative structure of the home islands to Taiwan, an approach some Taiwanese hoped would permit greater local autonomy than did the colonial system.   Advocates of greater local self-government, in contrast, emphasized the island's special characteristics, its enduring differences from Japan. They believed Taiwanese were not and could not become part of the Japanese nation.

Supporters of assimilation and advocates of greater autonomy (some individuals would seek both) wanted to abolish the institution of the governor-general. The former wanted the island placed fully under the Japanese constitution as a "regular" prefecture, thus removing the need for a governor-general. The latter extolled the ability of the Taiwanese to manage the island's administration more effectively than the could a governor-general. In the 1910s and early 1920s, assimilation dominated Taiwanese political discourse, but thereafter, reflecting new ideas of self-determination from outside Taiwan, the changing nature of the island's elite, and growing discontent with assimilation, advocacy of local self-government predominated.

The Japanese, who were never united on how to rule the island, shaped Taiwanese political aspirations and activities by setting the terms of debate and defining what was politically viable.[60] With few exceptions, Japanese residents of Taiwan opposed both assimilation and self-government out of fear either would jeopardize their privileged position on the island.[61] In Japan, the struggle to determine colonial policy usually pitted military and business interests against intellectuals, party politicians, and civilian bureaucrats. Debates in the home islands over colonial policy involved less immediate or material concerns, and were influenced by the policies of other imperial powers, events in other Japanese-controlled areas, such as Korea, and trends of domestic politics. Taiwan served as a laboratory for other parts of the empire, and provided another forum for Japanese to engage in political conflicts that began in the home islands. In particular, discussion of the political powers to be granted to the Taiwanese or the applicability of the Meiji constitution to the island was often a cover for struggles between the Diet, governors-general, and the colonial bureaucracy (the Bureau of Taiwan Affairs, then the Ministry of Colonial Affairs) in Tokyo.

Politicians and bureaucrats in the home islands consistently upheld assimilation as a goal of the colonial endeavor. The ideological foundation for their position was that cultural, social, and economic assimilation was a prerequisite for political change.[62] Japanese scholars and opinion makers like Naito Konan argued that Japan had first to achieve the social and cultural transformation of Taiwan by eradicating "backward" customs, ideas and loyalties.[63] "Improving" the islanders, which meant making them into Japanese, was also a chance to demonstrate colonial benevolence and superiority, as well as to ease the imposition of foreign rule.[64] In 1914, a few Japanese on the island, inspired in part by Itagaki Taisuke, attempted to turn their ideals of transformation into reality by forming the Taiwan Assimilation Society (Taiwan dōkakai; Chin., Taiwan tonghuahui).[65] Many Taiwanese eagerly joined, but the governor-general broke up the organization after only two months.[66] He and most colonists opposed an organization of Taiwanese and Japanese liberals discussing the reform of colonial policy.

Despite its brief life, this organization provided a forum for views on the methods and goals of assimilation. The colonizers tended to see assimilation as beginning with cultural change and ending with Taiwanese becoming part of the Japanese nation. According to this view, islanders would have to prove they were part of the national community before they could be given more influence in the state. Islanders, as we have noted, instead focused their attention on the state, and in particular on reducing the power of the governors-general.[67] Another significant difference was that the Japanese often defined Japanization, assimilation, and modernization synonymously. Taiwanese separated the concepts.[68] In the economic realm, the Taiwanese elite was eager to be part of the colonial system and enjoy the fruits of an expanding economy. Culturally, however, most islanders either did not wish to or could not become Japanese. When they did combine assimilation and modernization, islanders tended think of representative government, not administrative efficiency, as the hallmark of an "advanced" people. Finally, historian Mark R. Peattie points out that Itagaki Taisuke conceived of the Assimilation Society as a way to build racial harmony in the region, which would in turn facilitate the expansion of the empire.[69] There is little evidence that these ideas resonated among the Taiwanese.

The political career of the prominent businessman and landlord Lin Xiantang illustrates how Taiwanese endeavored to separate cultural and political assimilation. Lin, born in 1881 in Taizhong, skillfully expanded his family's investments from landholding into many different fields, following the development of the colonial economy.[70] He also engaged in political activities such as writing, publishing, organizing, and lobbying. Lin advocated limiting the powers of the colonial government and expanding his role and that of other prominent Taiwanese in the island's administration. He went to Japan and met sympathetic intellectuals and officials, like Itagaki, where he explained complaints about the powers of the governor-general. Lin's eager participation in the Assimilation Society was a reaction to pent-up frustration over the powers of the governor-general and discrimination against Taiwanese, not a sincere urge to become Japanese.[71] Through fifty years of Japanese rule, Lin never learned to read or speak the colonizers' language and never abandoned his membership in a variety of organizations devoted to the study of traditional Chinese culture.

The colonial administration ultimately dampened the drive for assimilation not by repressing it, but by co-opting it. In 1918 Tokyo decided on a long-term policy of assimilation (dōka; Chin., tonghua) to transform Taiwanese into Japanese culturally and eventually make the island into a prefecture of Japan. The governor-general's office called the latter step the "extension of the interior" (naichi enchō), meaning that the political institutions, and presumably the constitutional rights of citizens, that existed on the home islands would gradually be introduced to the island. In the 1930s, the authorities attempted to step up the rate of assimilation, which they now described as kōminka (literally "turning into a subject of the emperor"; Chin., huangminhua).[72] Taiwanese were rewarded for adopting Japanese surnames, engaging in Shintō worship, using only the Japanese language, and joining organizations designed to promote loyalty and regimentation such as the Imperial Subjects Public Service Society. In reality, by dominating the process of assimilation, the governors-general prevented it from unfolding in a manner the Taiwanese wished. The colonial administration consistently placed loyalty to the emperor, long-term cultural change, and finally wartime mobilization before political reform.

The state's approach to assimilation offered islanders scant hope of weakening, much less removing, the institution of the governor-general. Furthermore, the official assimilation policy served to justify discrimination, since "Japanization" in language and culture became a standard to measure loyalty to Japan. The state's attempt to limit the use of Mandarin Chinese and Taiwanese, and to promote Shintō, was enforced in such a way that islanders associated it with a host of other policies regarded as unfair or overly strict.[73] Some Taiwanese pragmatically contended that assimilation was not in the interests of Taiwanese. Even if the island became a prefecture of Japan, based on its population the island's inhabitants would only elect thirty representatives to the Diet, not enough to influence colonial policy.[74] Others emphasized the immediate barriers to assimilation and the deeply rooted nature of Chinese culture on the island, both of which of course compounded the difficulty of becoming part of the Japanese nation. For example, in 1914 Taiwanese intellectual Cai Peihuo was fired from his job for his political activity, including advocating assimilation. He then went to Japan with the help of wealthy Taiwanese such as Lin Xiantang, where, like many other overseas students, his views changed. He came to see the assimilation policy as a means to perpetuate domination of the Taiwanese. In 1920 Cai wrote that assimilation remained his highest ideal, but assimilation of a special type: natural, not man-made. Man-made assimilation, based on government policies, was very difficult. Natural assimilation, on the other hand, would surely, albeit it slowly, emerge if and when the islanders themselves saw it to be in their self-interest. This posed a challenge to the Japanese: assimilation would occur only if the colonizers made their culture attractive to the Taiwanese. In effect, Cai was deferring the question of the role of the colonized in the nation in order to emphasize the need to change their relationship with the state.

Expanded Autonomy within the Empire

Although assimilation remained official policy, and some Taiwanese sincerely sought to become Japanese, by the mid-1920s the search for self-government dominated political discourse. The elite pressed for greater autonomy at all levels of government. First, Taiwanese endeavored to change the island's relationship with the central government and its representative on the island, the governor-general. Second, they wanted to expand their influence over the administration at the city, county, and town levels. Calls for local self-government made explicit Taiwanese skepticism toward the assimilationist program and the possibility of ever joining the Japanese nation.

Colonial policy on local self-government in Taiwan grew out of Japan's experience in the home islands. The Town and Village Code, City Code, the Code for Urban Villages and Rural Prefectures, the County Code, and the Meiji constitution of 1890 set the pattern for relations between the central government and localities in Japan.[75] As articulated by one of the most influential framers of local administration in Japan during the Meiji era, Yamagata Aritomo, local self-government was not to be autonomous but a tool to improve administration by efficiently implementing policies from the central government, without hindrance from political parties.[76] Thus, local self-government (*chihō jichi*; Chin., *difang zizhi*) represented an extension of the central government's power, not a dilution of it or competition with it.[77] Yamagata and the Home Ministry decried the fact that towns, cities, and prefectures had become arenas of partisan politics.[78] Further, Japanese leaders sought to limit the franchise.[79] Clearly, the greater autonomy the Taiwanese advocated not only exceeded what the governors-general were prepared to grant, it would have exceeded the power allowed localities in Japan. The Japanese never seriously envisioned devolving political power; instead they sought to build a more effective and efficient state. At most, self-government meant local bodies implementing policies, not initiating them.[80] Time and again the Japanese reiterated that assemblies they would establish were to be advisory or consultative organs (*shimon kikan* or *shijun kikan*). In addition, the Japanese sought to limit reforms to the lowest level of the administrative hierarchy possible, emphasizing that local self-government meant the neighborhood, village, town, and city. On Taiwan, this meant that the Japanese rejected transforming the relationship between the central government and the island as a whole, which would have meant modifying the role of the governor-general.

Local self-government in Taiwan also became bound up in rivalries between civilian and military officials. For example, the question of local self-government and the role of the governor-general became entangled in a dispute over whether the Meiji constitution was applicable to Taiwan. Scholars and politicians who argued that the constitution applied to colonies reasoned that the office of the governor-general was unconstitutional and should be abolished. In practice, the constitution applied to the island only to the extent the Japanese state, through the governor-general, wanted it to.[81] Reflecting the reduced role for the military in the Taishō era, in 1919 the experienced bureaucrat Den Kenjirō became the first civilian governor-general.[82] His appointment was part of a larger drive by party politicians and civilian officials in the home islands to subordinate the police and military to civilian authority. Upon arrival, Den stated that Taiwan had advanced sufficiently that military control was no longer required. He raised Taiwanese hopes for reform by adding that, just as in Japan, military and civilian authority should be separated and the role of police in local affairs reduced.[83] He did not, however, seek to modify the basic political framework that severely limited local autonomy.

In 1920, Den began to reform the administrative system throughout the island, of which local assemblies formed a small part.[84] To his way of thinking, local self-government and assimilation worked together. The islanders had been sufficiently assimilated, and thus could be presumed adequately loyal to the nation, that they could be promised a larger role in managing local affairs — eventually. Den reasoned that Taiwanese could not immediately enjoy the same laws as the home islands because of differences in language and customs. The Taiwanese needed to be educated first. Because Taiwanese customs and loyalty were "improving," they could look forward to enjoying constitutional rule, as the Japanese did. All that was required was assimilation into the Japanese nation.[85]

Den created assemblies at the city, county, street, and neighborhood level and established an islandwide body, the Taiwan Governor-General's Consultative Assembly (Taiwan sōtokufu hyōgikai) in 1921.[86] The reforms were much less significant than they first appeared. The colonial administration selected all assembly members, most of whom were prominent Japanese residents or officials.[87] The governor-general, as chairman of the assembly, could dissolve it at will.[88] Members could only question officials — they lacked legislative power and control over budgets and administration. The content of the islandwide assembly sessions reflected the Japanese interest in discussing issues of economic, not political, significance. For example, the three sessions held in late 1921 took up roads, business law, compulsory education, and how to petition to higher authorities against the decisions of lower-level (often Taiwanese) bureaucrats.[89] This pattern continued throughout the life of the assemblies.[90]

Growing dissatisfaction with these powerless assemblies in the 1920s and 1930s spurred Taiwanese to agitate for greater self-government. Just as a Taiwanese identity did not necessarily equate to nationalism, the drive for self-government cannot be called an independence movement. Advocates of self-government sought a middle ground. Emotionally charged terms such as collaborator, sometimes used to describe those who favored assimilation, or nationalist, to label those who advocated independence, oversimplify the position of most Taiwanese. In fact, they blended ideas of assimilation and autonomy. For example, some islanders defined full self-government as attaining the same level of local or prefectural autonomy as they believed existed in Japan — in effect, political assimilation. Others cited their successful assimilation in the realms of language and culture as justification for expanded self-government. Almost without exception, however, Japanese standards for assimilation were far above what islanders envisioned as necessary preconditions for political reform.

An unanticipated result of the Japanese attempt to channel the Taiwanese into economic pursuits was that businessmen became key leaders of political movements on the island. Pragmatism constrained the drive for reform, as prominent Taiwanese knew they could not overturn colonial rule and did not expect China to regain the island. They also had developed strong economic ties to Japan and its empire. The Taiwanese elite thus wanted greater local autonomy and economic benefits while preventing radical change, especially if it involved weakening their dominance over the bulk of Taiwanese society.[91] For example, many businessmen considered the political activities of educated youth radical and threatening to their livelihood. During the 1920s and early 1930s Taiwanese political organizing went through a series of cycles wherein moderates, usually wealthy, formed groups that were then taken over by those seeking fundamental change in the social or economic order, or were more antagonistic toward Japanese rule. The founders would then split off and establish a new organization.[92]

An alternative to the reformist programs of assimilation and self-government was radical social and political revolution led by the Communist party. Communism, however, never became a major force on Taiwan due to Japan's effective repression coupled with its ability to provide some measure of material progress and stability, thus undercutting support for economic or social change. There was, however, a small Communist movement on the island. The radicalization of some Taiwanese students in Japan or the mainland during the 1920s was key to the creation of the Taiwanese Communist Party (TCP). The TCP, organized in Shanghai in 1928, became a branch of the Japanese Communist Party (JCP) while seeking guidance from the CCP (Chinese Communist Party). The Taiwanese party was constantly torn between CCP, JCP, and Taiwanese factions. Some who had joined the TCP drifted away for ideological reasons. For example, Lin Rigao, who became an important leader in Taiwan immediately after retrocession, had left the party earlier because he felt that the emphasis on class struggle was misplaced — the most important enemy was Japan, not rich Taiwanese. The Japanese were very effective in arresting TCP members on the island and the party almost completely disappeared by 1937. After World War II, Communists on Taiwan remained weak and faction-ridden.[93]

Moderate Taiwanese had little more success. The Taiwan Cultural Association (Taiwan wenhua xiehui), created by Lin Xiantang and Jiang Weishui in 1921, sought to preserve Taiwanese culture, increase local autonomy, and reduce the monopoly powers of Japanese corporations. It became torn by conflicts between older businessmen and Japanese-educated youth. As more vocal youth came to control the association, it was abolished by its founders in 1927. Jiang Weishui and other prominent Taiwanese such as Cai Peihuo then formed the Taiwan Renewal Society, which soon became the Taiwan Masses Party (Taiwan minzhongdang), the only legal political party of the Japanese era. By 1930, the party had as many as 800 members, primarily lawyers, doctors, and businessmen, in seventeen branches. This reformist group advocated expanded self-government and a reduction of Japanese domination of the economy, but like other Taiwanese organizations, it was hobbled by rivalries between those who favored greater political representation and limiting the power of the state and those who wished to remedy social and economic inequalities faced by peasants and laborers.[94] The Japanese banned the party in 1933.

Agitation against Law 63 and its successors, which gave the governor-general his sweeping powers, was an important impetus for the movement for greater self-government during the early 1920s. Wealthy Taiwanese landlords, businessmen, and doctors dominated this reformist effort, which became known as the Home Rule Movement or Petition Movement.[95] Leaders of the Home Rule Movement stressed that the Taiwanese were loyal to the Japanese empire but possessed a distinctive culture, language, and history, which warranted some measure of local autonomy.[96] This position reflected their determination to expand their role in the political structure of the state, if not the community of the nation. They rejected the self-government institutions established by Governor-General Den as "false," "half," or "in name only."[97] Between 1922 and 1934 they presented fourteen petitions for self-government to the Japanese Diet.

That prominent Taiwanese usually justified their political demands by emphasizing the special characteristics and customs of the people of Taiwan suggests they tacitly, if not explicitly, rejected assimilation.[98] Many, influenced by the ideals of Wilsonianism, discussed the global trend of self-determination and often raised Ireland's and India's tempestuous relationships with Great Britain as a warning of the consequences of stifling reforms. Lin Xiantang's own statements used the example of Ireland's conflict with England to justify Taiwan's need for special local representation.[99] From this perspective, reform was a buffer against demands for more radical and violent action — local self-government would prevent a nationalist movement, not spark it. In fact, the Petition Movement members took pains to emphasize that they were working through the structure of Japanese law to request the assembly and were not seeking independence.[100]

Yang Zhaojia, an associate of Lin Xiantang, illustrated how the island's elite attempted to shape colonial rule. Yang wrote that the Taiwanese, having lived under "incomplete" self-government, had become more and more vocal in their calls for reform.[101] He compared the Taiwanese level of education and wealth with that of Korea and stated that islanders were at least as capable of participating in politics. Reform was also a symbol of modernity. Yang stressed that self-government was in tune with global ideological currents; it formed the basis of constitutional rule that enlightened nations practice.[102] As the Taiwanese envisioned it, increased autonomy was part of a teleological process — the culmination of educational, material, or political progress. All they wanted, he explained, were local groups, separate from the administration of the governor-general, that managed their own affairs. The key was that elected representatives should control public services and possess power over resources and budgets.[103]

Taiwan League for Local Self-Government

Even as dissatisfaction with the colonial regime grew, the loosely organized Petition Movement made little progress. Moderates were thrown into disarray by police harassment and pressure from younger Taiwanese to be more aggressive. By the late 1920s, the Taiwanese Cultural Society had split, the government had suppressed leftist peasant and worker groups, and the Masses Party had alienated wealthier and more conservative Taiwanese with its growing attachment to class conflict. And, finally, some islanders were satisfied with the self-government organs created by the Japanese in the early 1920s.[104] In this environment, a group of prominent islanders formed the Taiwan League for Local Self-Government (Taiwan chihō jichi renmei; Chin., Taiwan difang zizhi lianmeng) in 1930.[105] The league's standing committee consisted largely of wealthy Taiwanese from the central part of the island; they elected Lin Xiantang as their chairman. These men contended that they were best able to manage the internal affairs of the island — they *should* have a greater role — and that their wealth and education warranted this role — they *could* bear this responsibility.[106] Most members continued to follow a moderate path: they did not wish to overthrow Japanese rule and realized they could not lead a successful nationalist revolution in any case. Documents from the league made clear its reformist strategy: they spoke of using only legal means, educating the people about self-government, avoiding factionalism, and applying a democratic spirit.[107]

The league stressed that it had one, overriding goal: expanded local self-government.[108] It criticized the governor-general's appointments to the local assemblies (which included both Taiwanese and Japanese), arguing that without popular elections and decision-making power, these people were no more than puppets.[109] At the neighborhood, city, prefectural, and islandwide levels, the league sought popularly elected assemblies that were to have real decision-making power and control over their own finances.[110] However, league members also made more specific requests in line with their reformist proclivities and personal financial interests. For example, they lobbied for compulsory schooling that would include instruction concerning self-government, for economic relief including assistance to rural small and medium-sized businessmen, and for fewer controls over sugar sales. They pointed out that greater autonomy would encourage people to participate in political life and awaken their sense of responsibility. Most importantly, reforms would prevent the further radicalization of youth and a possible violent revolution, something both the Japanese and the Taiwanese elite wished to avoid.

As had been the case with the Petition Movement, the league struggled to gain support from Japanese officials, intellectuals, and politicians.[111] For example, Lin Xiantang worked with Taiwanese in Japan in order to bypass the governor-general and influence the central government directly.[112] The league even sought members among the Japanese, but few joined. To many colonizers, the self-government movement had the "flavor" of Taiwanese nationalism.[113] They feared the assemblies envisioned by the league would be the first step in making Taiwan independent.[114] Some noted that, since the majority of the people on the island were Taiwanese, the Japanese residents would suffer in any election. The Japanese response to the threat of expanded Taiwanese autonomy was frequently cloaked in the language of assimilation. One publicly stated reason for resistance to change was that the Taiwanese were not ready for self-government due to their lack of Japanese language ability or education.[115]

Conflict among the Taiwanese hampered the league as well. The Masses Party prohibited its members from joining other political groups — clearly an attempt to limit membership in the newly formed league. This caused many moderates to quit the party, thus giving leftists more influence over it.[116] The Masses Party also attempted to make self-government a more important part of its platform, thereby increasing pressure on the league to take a stronger stand on the issue.[117] In particular, the party called on members of the local assemblies to resign immediately.[118] On this question, the league, which had some members who served in the very assemblies it sought to reform, was understandably ambivalent. The difficulties facing the league became abundantly clear after it held its first major public meetings in the late summer of 1930. Rowdy members of peasant and worker groups attempted to disrupt the meetings and, inevitably, the police were in attendance.[119]

Despite these problems, the Taiwanese appeared closest to success in the early 1930s. In 1931 Japanese politicians introduced a resolution in the Diet to speed the implementation of local self-government on the island. The resolution stated that since 1895 Japan had concentrated on the material, not spiritual, development of Taiwan. Nonetheless, today the Taiwanese had become sufficiently sophisticated to warrant political reform. The duty of Japan, the most advanced Asian country, was to lead others to constitutional government.[120] On the specific powers that reformed self-government might entail, the resolution was unclear. The Lower House approved the measure, but it was soundly defeated in the more conservative House of Peers. In truth, the Taiwanese faced indifference as much as opposition, since the administration of Taiwan was never an important political issue in Japan except insofar as many Diet members were interested in increasing their influence over the governor-general. Furthermore, frequent cabinet changes in Tokyo made it difficult for islanders to cultivate support in the government.

As with the earlier assimilationist movement, the governor-general diverted pressure for change by acceding to a few demands and taking firm control of the pace and scope of reforms. In 1932 a new governor-general, Nakagawa Kenzō, began to move gradually toward reform of the local administration and assemblies. Like Den Kenjirō, Nakagawa justified change by combined notions of assimilation and self-government. To him, expanded self-government was a temporary measure to compensate for the failure of assimilation. Nakagawa contended that there remained too many differences between the Japanese and Taiwanese races to allow immediate assimilation. Since Taiwan was a colony, expanded self-government was the best policy at this time.[121] In other words, a short-term policy to give islanders slightly more influence in the state was an integral part of the long-term goal of making Taiwan part of the Japanese nation.

The gap between Taiwanese and Japanese notions of self-government remained. The colonizers wanted assemblies to assist in the implementation of policy, not to take the initiative in policy making or to stand separate from the state. Furthermore, reform was not intended to change, much less challenge, the powers of the governor-general or his administration. Nakagawa warned that the Taiwanese needed to avoid "twisting" the meaning of self-government or forgetting the spirit of governmental supervision. Japan had many problems with China, Nakagawa continued, and the people and officials of the empire must unite during this time of crisis to preserve order. Most tellingly, he emphasized that it was more important that the Taiwanese know their duties than their rights.[122]

Additional reforms announced by the governor-general in January 1935 marked the apex of self-government under Japanese rule.[123] Under the new system, Taiwanese and Japanese voters on the island were to elect half the assembly members at all levels. (All candidates had to be approved by the governor-general, however.) As before, however, the assemblies had no power except to interpellate colonial officials, and also as before, they could be dissolved at any time by the governor-general. In the November elections, turnout of eligible voters (Japanese and Taiwanese male taxpayers over the age of twenty-five) was greater than 90 percent in all counties. Of about 3,700 seats, 3,000 went to Taiwanese (either through election or appointment). Taiwanese dominated the lower levels (neighborhood and city assemblies), while representation was split evenly at the higher levels. The biggest difference was that those *selected* had previously served in local assemblies, while those *elected* may have been involved in political activities in the past, but now were in official posts for the first time.[124]

The reform of self-government organs, coupled with increasing repression by the state and divisions among islanders, put the league in a difficult position. Reform brought uncertainty: should Taiwanese work through the new assemblies or reject them and demand further change?[125] Shortly before the reforms were implemented, Lin Xiantang and other prominent members of the league lobbied the governor-general for more powerful assemblies. Others, however, found the reforms satisfactory and hence believed the league had served its purpose.[126] Reform also led to more open criticism of the sitting representatives, something many of the league's leaders had avoided. The league's uncertainty was reflected in its simultaneous endorsement of candidates for the elections and its statement that the new system was unsatisfactory. Because of internal rivalries, a special committee established in 1935 to debate the league's fate could not reach any resolution.[127]

In the increasingly oppressive atmosphere of Japan's march toward war with China and then with the Western powers, the Taiwanese had few opportunities to press their demands.[128] In order to justify cracking down on political activity, the Japanese claimed that the empire had entered an "extraordinary period."[129] Under pressure, the league, which had been adrift since 1935, disbanded. By the time full-scale war broke out on the mainland in July 1937, the colonial authorities had banned even the most moderate political organizations.[130] The attempt of the Taiwanese to find a path between assimilation and independence had failed. The importance of this movement, however, lay in the pattern it set for interaction with a central government and the development of ideas to justify expanded autonomy. The drive for greater self-government would resurface in political discourse after 1945.

Wartime

Between the late 1930s and the end of World War II, the contradictions of colonial rule — shared struggle and virulent Japanese nationalism, industrialization and wartime deprivation, decreased discrimination and forced labor — became most apparent. To mobilize the Taiwanese for the war effort, the Japanese rigorously suppressed dissent and touted their record of providing material progress and relative stability.[131] Their propaganda to the bulk of the population — farmers and laborers — emphasized loyalty to the emperor, pan-Asianism, and the benefits of the Greater East Asia Coprosperity Sphere.[132] To the elite, the governor-general offered greater status and authority, such as political posts, and the promise of greater equality with Japanese residents and officials on the island. Increasing pressure for assimilation had already been felt in the wake of growing international tensions after the invasion of Manchuria in 1931. With the start of all-out war with China in 1937, the Japanese redoubled this effort at cultural, social, and linguistic transformation. This reflected the need to build support for the war throughout the empire and to more clearly separate Taiwanese from Chinese. Thanks to its relatively compliant population and its strategic location, the island became a key staging and supply area for the war in southern China and Southeast Asia.

Most prominent Taiwanese participated in the war effort as loyal, albeit second-class, subjects of the empire.[133] Although thousands of Taiwanese were drafted into the military, many others joined willingly.[134] This support, whether wholehearted or not, would come back to haunt islanders after the end of the war, when the Nationalists reestablished Chinese control of the island. Taiwanese themselves recognized this dilemma. For example, in his oral history, historian Lin Hengdao summed up the effects of colonial rule, listing the negative aspects (forced Shintō worship, conscription, and so on) and the positive (modernization, improved standards of living, and Japan's respect for the rule of law). Lin concluded that many Taiwanese had believed mistakenly that they and the Japanese were engaged in a common struggle.[135] Contradictory feelings about the Japanese extended to the personal level as well. Although author and journalist Wu Zhuoliu blamed the colonial police and military for killing more Taiwanese than did United States bombing, he also wrote of the good relations he had with many Japanese, such as scholars and reporters, who formed a literary group during the last years of the conflict.[136]

Only a few Taiwanese openly opposed their colonial masters or felt the pull of their Chinese ancestry and fled to areas of the mainland not occupied by the Japanese. About 1,000 islanders joined Nationalist government or party organizations, many in the wartime capital of Chongqing.[137] These Taiwanese, who became known as "Half-Mountain people" (banshanren), were an important link between the island and the central government when they returned to Taiwan after retrocession.[138] Many of them, however, were torn between loyalty to their native place and to the Nationalist state, which had provided them status and careers. The Half-Mountain people, the Nationalists, the Communists, and the United States were unable to develop an armed resistance movement or sabotage the war effort on the island.

Late in the war, life for the Taiwanese became more difficult as the island mobilized to repel a possible Allied invasion.[139] From 1943 to the end of the war, American attacks against Japanese shipping cut off access to markets and equipment necessary for the island's industry.[140] Officially reported rice production declined by 50 percent in the last years of the conflict.[141] Rice shortages sparked a flourishing black market as the strains of war weakened the law and order that had been a source of great pride for the Japanese. Tensions rose in 1944 and 1945, as Taiwanese heard rumors of Japanese plans for mass arrests and executions of suspected spies in the event of an Allied attack. The United States invasion of the Ryukyu Islands marked the high point of tensions: Many islanders feared that they would be forced to resist the Americans to the death.[142]

As was the case throughout areas they occupied, when the Japanese faced defeat they implemented measures to increase local support. The government in Tokyo selected three Taiwanese, including Lin Xiantang, for membership in the House of Peers and announced plans for Taiwanese representation in the Diet.[143] Japanese and Taiwanese youth were permitted to attend the same schools. And in 1945, the governor-general announced plans for equal salaries and treatment for Taiwanese and Japanese officials on the island. The regime justified all this with the argument that although the islanders were not Japanese, they were subjects of the emperor. Thus, facing defeat, the Japanese had begun to adopt the Taiwanese position: political and administrative change before cultural assimilation. The island's elite gained the promise of a greater role in the Japanese state without having proven its ability to become part of the Japanese nation. The same military setbacks that spurred these measures, however, prevented their implementation.

On August 15, 1945, the Taiwanese dutifully turned on their radios — they had been told by Japanese officials to expect an important announcement. They strained to hear the Shōwa Emperor announce that the time had come to "endure the unendurable." After fifty years, the empire had collapsed and the Taiwanese were no longer second-class citizens of Japan. But would they become first-class citizens of China?

3 Retrocession and the Debate over Taiwan's Place in China

Between late 1945 and early 1947, the legacy of Japanese domination and the immediate difficulties caused by Nationalist misrule spurred a lively debate over Taiwan's relationship with the nation of China and the state of the Republic of China. With reasoned argument, rhetorical sleights of hand, and unconsciously selected images, the Taiwanese constructed a political discourse that recalled positive aspects of the colonial experience (stability and economic growth, for example) while simultaneously downplaying the "problem" of collaboration with the Japanese.[1] The Taiwanese felt their colonial-era political activity and their relatively high levels of education and economic development warranted a loose relationship with the central government, a view articulated through calls for expanded local self-government. This, they hoped, might insulate them from what they defined as the defects of the Chinese mainland. Their experience under the colonial regime had also given them a standard of efficient and rigorous government that the Nationalists, corrupt and inept as they often were, simply could not meet. On these points, Taiwanese were generally in agreement. The framework of leftist/Communist versus rightist/Nationalist, so prevalent in discussions of politics in modern China, obscures the broad consensus among prominent islanders on Taiwan's place in the Chinese nation and the Nationalist state.

A problem for the historian is to determine what the Taiwanese "knew" had occurred during colonial rule or what they had experienced personally, as opposed to the history they constructed in public through speeches, oral histories, and essays. It is difficult, if not impossible, to know to what extent islanders consciously ignored the negative aspects of Japanese domination in order to further their political agenda. Nevertheless, that so many Taiwanese said or wrote similar things on the positive aspects of colonial rule, the defects of the Nationalist provincial administration, their differences from mainland China, and the resulting need for expanded self-government indicates that these ideas rang true to their fellow islanders.

The Nationalists came to Taiwan with a completely different understanding of local self-government, provincial autonomy, and Taiwanese responsibilities toward China. Their perspective grew out of a historical experience that Taiwanese knew little of, including the 1911 Republican Revolution, provincial independence movements, warlord conflicts, anti-Communist struggles, and Japanese brutality. The leaders of the Nationalists, Sun Zhongshan, then Jiang Jieshi, were certain that only a highly centralized state under their control could protect China. The regionalism and chaos of the warlord era had convinced them that provincial prerogatives stymied China's economic development and political unity. They also associated provincial powers, particularly when conceived in terms of federalism, with China's weakness in the face of imperialist aggression. To the mainland officials dispatched to the island in late 1945, limiting the power of provincial elites was entirely necessary in order to build the Nationalist state and strengthen the Chinese nation.

Taiwanese Prepare for Reintegration

Between Japan's surrender on August 15, 1945 and the formal establishment of Nationalist authority on October 25, islanders confronted their colonial legacy in the context of the impending political transition. A few Taiwanese attempted to declare the island independent, while others occupied Japanese property, sought to preserve public order, and prepared for the new administration. Islanders also began to detail their expectations for Nationalist rule. In each of these activities, the colonial experience shaped the relationship between Taiwanese and their new government.

Upon hearing the Shōwa Emperor's acceptance of the Potsdam Declaration, the Taiwanese were elated that the war had ended. This joy, however, was tempered by defensiveness and divisiveness.[2] Some islanders felt uneasy over their future in the Chinese nation and the treatment they might receive under the new government.[3] As one wrote, "The pitiful Taiwanese day after day watched the weather in Chongqing [the Nationalists' wartime capital] with happiness, concern, laughter, and tears."[4] Soon the island's elite confronted their history of cooperation with the Japanese even as other Taiwanese released pent-up hatred of the colonial regime. Doctor, political activist, and son of a traditional Chinese scholar, Han Shiquan reported on the events of August 1945 in Tainan, an important city on the southeast coast of the island.[5] He divided his fellow citizens into four groups. First were those who had helped the Japanese rule (*wei hu zuo chang*, given aid to the evildoers). These people suddenly became ardent and vocal Chinese patriots. Several sources allege that many islanders, including criminals, exaggerated their anticolonial activities while those who had been tortured by the Japanese or otherwise truly suffered preferred to remain silent.[6] Second were Taiwanese with a conscience who stayed indoors out of shame for their past association with the colonial regime. Third were those loyal to China who had opposed Japan. They eagerly used the opportunity to grasp for political power. Finally, the masses (*yiban minzhong*) went wild with joy as they released fifty years of accumulated hatred.[7] The Taiwanese directed their violence against the police, both Japanese and Taiwanese, but generally left alone those who did not react to taunting.[8] Further, hostility toward the colonial administration did not translate into blanket hatred of all Japanese. Personal ties that had developed over fifty years led many Taiwanese to commiserate with departing Japanese friends.[9]

A few Taiwanese with close ties to the colonial government rejected reunification. With the encouragement of Japanese military officers, one Gu Zhenfu and a handful of other islanders organized a short-lived movement to declare the island independent from China. In what is sometimes called the August 15 Independence Movement (*ba shiwu duli yundong*), Taiwan Headquarters Chief of Staff Isayama Haruki called together sixteen prominent Taiwanese and offered support for independence.[10] This offer sprang from a wish to make life difficult for the victorious Allies more than from a sincere interest in the Taiwanese or their welfare.[11] Governor-General Andō Rikichi quickly put an end to the scheme, reasoning that it could endanger the 400,000 to 500,000 Japanese on the island and anger the United States. Besides, such a step went against his orders from Tokyo.[12] This aborted move for independence seemed to confirm the mainlanders' worst suspicions about Taiwanese loyalties.[13]

Other islanders sought redress for colonial-era injustices by occupying land they claimed the Japanese had taken years ago or by attempting to seize other property, even colonists' homes.[14] Much of this property had been confiscated by the colonial government or sold to Japanese enterprises at unfair prices over the previous fifty years. Like everything else involving the legacy of colonial rule, countless individual agendas clouded the issue. Ownership was often unclear because at war's end many Japanese businessmen put their properties in the names of Taiwanese associates who were not necessarily the original owners.[15] Some Japanese gave their property to Taiwanese friends or sold it at bargain prices. Adding to the confusion was the fact that the colonial administration had occasionally given land, perhaps taken from islanders, as a reward for public service or loyalty to the regime. Furthermore, much of the disputed property had become more valuable because of Japanese investment — could a Taiwanese who lost crop land twenty years ago now recover the land as well as the sugar refinery that had been built on it?[16] Finally, many claims were simply unfounded. Some mainlanders felt that those who obtained property at the end of the war had profited from Japanese rule, and were thus tainted by an "original sin" (*yuanzui*).[17]

As the initial shock and confusion of Japan's sudden surrender wore off, prominent Taiwanese sought to guide the decolonization and reintegration. Their immediate goal was to preserve order during the temporary political vacuum, an endeavor for which the colonial police had little enthusiasm. Concerns over public order in late 1945 were reminiscent of the elite's anxieties during last major transition, in 1895. In both instances, wealthy Taiwanese seemed to fear poor and unemployed islanders as much as the new authorities.[18] Political leader, landlord, and businessman Lin Xiantang and other well-known figures in central Taiwan offered to help the Japanese maintain stability during this time of uncertainty.[19] These men worked closely with young Taiwanese, many of whom had Japanese military training, to keep order.[20] This highlighted the cooperative relationship between islanders and their colonizers, as well as the Taiwanese role in the colonial army. The Taiwanese role in Japan's colonial empire became a heated political issue after 1945.

Publicly, most Taiwanese enthusiastically supported reunification under the Nationalist government. A mania for learning Mandarin Chinese (*Guoyu*; literally, the "national language"; known in the West as "Mandarin"), the officially sanctioned dialect of the Nationalists, swept the island. Acceptance of Sun Zhongshan's political ideology became an important symbol of loyalty to China and confidence in the future under Jiang Jieshi's Nationalist government. For example, journalist and novelist Wu Zhuoliu discussed the need to transform Taiwan into a model Three-Principles-of-the-People (*Sanmin zhuyi*) province.[21] By early September, youth began to organize Three Principles of the People Youth Corps in their communities. Besides serving as a forum for learning about China and showing support for the Nationalists, these groups also helped maintain public order. Ironically, many members of corps had gained their first experience with mass mobilization and military training under the Japanese.

To promote reintegration, prominent Taiwanese formed the Preparatory Committee to Welcome the National Government.[22] Participants included Lin Xiantang, his protégé and Japanese-era advocate of self-government, Ye Rongzhong, and others who were simultaneously cooperating with the Japanese to maintain order. They led activities to showcase support for the new government, such as distributing Nationalist flags and banners, met newly arrived mainland officials, and encouraged the study of Mandarin Chinese. Smaller versions of this committee sprang up in communities throughout the island. Setting a pattern for the post-retrocession period, how-

ever, most of these Japanese-era political leaders quickly found they had little influence with the Nationalists. At the invitation of the Nationalist government, members of the committee traveled to the wartime capital of
Chongqing in September 1945. Even before they arrived, the central government had, without consulting them, determined the staffing and policies
for Taiwan's provincial administration.

The Nationalists, led by the highest ranking official sent to the island,
Chen Yi, took power following a ceremony in Taibei on October 25, 1945,
a date thereafter known as Retrocession Day (*Guangfujie*). The term "retrocession" (*guangfu*) carries with it strong political implications by stressing
the restoration of Chinese sovereignty over lands temporarily seized by foreigners. Thus, guangfu presupposes the legitimacy of the Chinese government's rule over Taiwan.[23] With retrocession, the Chinese nation and the
Nationalist state had come to Taiwan.

Local Self-Government and Federalism
in Republican China

Taiwanese would discover that their political aspirations represented
the road not taken in the competition for power between the central government and the provincial and lower-level governments in Republican China
(1911–49). Islanders sought greater autonomy than was acceptable to the
Nationalists, who felt that they had settled this issue on the mainland twenty
years before retrocession. While the Taiwanese connected local self-
government to expanded autonomy, the Nationalists tied it to administration, performing the tasks deemed necessary by the central government. The
Nationalists portrayed loyalty to any political entity other than the nation,
or to any movement outside of the Nationalist Party, as divisive, "feudal"
(*fengjian*), parochial, and anti-Chinese. In particular Sun Zhongshan, then
Jiang Jieshi, attempted to make the Nationalists' centralization efforts synonymous with the welfare of the Chinese nation. They were successful to the
extent that, as Prasenjit Duara writes, "the two N/nationalisms have been
fused and moralized."[24] Contemporary observers and historians have generally followed the lead of the "winners" in this conflict, focusing upon the
nation and its centralization efforts over provincial prerogatives.[25] They have
tended to accept the version of history put forth by the centralizers — that
federalism or local autonomy stood opposed to the interests of the Chinese
nation.

In China, the relationship between federalism and local self-government
was in contention throughout the first half of the twentieth century. Some
thinkers considered federalism an aspect of local self-government, meaning

that provincial autonomy vis-à-vis the central government would mirror the relationship between the province and the city or county. Each level of this hierarchy would have clearly specified powers and obligations. Others defined federalism solely in term of relations between the province and the central government. Still others conceived of "local self-government" as merely administration below the provincial level. The Nationalists followed the last definition in constructing their rule on the mainland, then on Taiwan.

In his study of local councils during the late Qing period, Roger Thompson analyzes the various meanings given to self-government (*zizhi*).[26] In its final years, the Qing envisioned *difang zizhi* (local self-government) as a system to facilitate China's gradual transition to constitutional monarchy. Qing officials expected — just as the Nationalist would later want — gentry to learn about the new local councils, then participate in elections. Often zizhi was explicitly tied to centralization, the antithesis of *zizhu* (autonomy).[27] Reformers outside the government saw local self-government as a way to unify China from the province upward. Around the turn of the century, Japan became a model of successful political and material modernization, even for anti-imperialist Chinese. The Japanese conceptualized local self-government as a way to depoliticize local administration, transforming raucous political competitors into quiet bureaucrats. For the first half of the century, Taiwanese experienced Japanese conceptions of local self-government as interpreted to suit the needs of the colonial regime. After retrocession, Taiwanese reencountered some of the same ideas, this time as translated through the political agendas and struggles of late imperial and Republican China.

Zizhi became such a ubiquitous term that it had meaning only when put into a specific historical context. Although centralization emerged victorious, four major groups in Republican China — traditional Confucian elites, warlords, non-Communist reformers, and the Nationalists — each with varying motivations and levels of commitment, promoted their own conceptions of local self-government or federalism. Much of the centralizers' criticism of these groups and their agendas was entirely correct. Local self-government often represented little more than an excuse for rural elites to maintain power and block central government initiatives.[28] During the late Qing, gentry, inculcated with the ideals of Confucianism, sought to protect their influence in the fengjian tradition. They accepted the sovereignty of the imperial state, but did not want it present in their communities, nor did they seek to become permanent bureaucrats. Elites at the town, county, and provincial levels protected their own class interests, thus preserving their social status and economic power, while performing "government" services by organizing people in their communities for tasks such as maintaining order, repairing public works, and assisting the poor. Their influence waned steadily throughout the Republican period. Nevertheless, later supporters of local self-government on the mainland and Taiwan would have great diffi- culty divorcing themselves from the perception that they served the interests of prerevolutionary elites.

In the beginning of the Republican era, however, federalism and local self- government were relatively respectable. As the Qing dynasty collapsed in 1911 and 1912, an alliance of traditional rural elites and urban revolution- aries declared their provinces independent from the central government in Beijing. The drive to keep local infrastructure out of the hands of foreign- ers, nationalist antipathy toward the Manchu regime, and the lack of effec- tive central authority justified their actions. Dissatisfaction with Yuan Shikai, the Qing general turned president of the weak Republican govern- ment, became another incentive to limit the power of the central government. Supporters of provincial autonomy were not, however, wedded to the idea of provincial independence. Rather, they sought to use the provinces as build- ing blocks of a unified Chinese republic.[29] After Yuan's death in 1916, the Beijing government ruled China in name only, as warlords came to control provinces and entire regions. These military strongmen, who were most influ- ential during the years 1916 to 1928, grasped at any idea that would ration- alize their rejection of the Beijing government's authority.[30] Federalism became tainted by its connection with the warlords, who were blamed for blocking China's modernization and leaving it impotent before Western and Japanese imperialists.

Those who wished to limit the power of the central government struggled to prove that federalism and local self-government were not simply excuses for warlord power or rural conservatism. These doctrines could be part of coherent programs to govern China that were promoted by moderates influ- enced by political thought from Western Europe and the United States.[31] Frustrated by the lack of progress toward China's unification and political modernization after 1911, urban intellectuals and liberals turned to the provincial level or below to implement reforms they could not apply at the national level.[32] For many non-Communists outside the Nationalist ranks, federalism and local self-government formed part of a scheme to divide power at all levels of government. They tied doctrines of autonomy to their goal of a multiparty democracy, and in so doing often portrayed themselves as a reformist alternative, or "Third Force," between the Nationalists and Communists. To them, federalism, a type of local self-government, implied a relatively loose relationship between provinces and the central government. The division of powers and responsibilities between the provinces and cen- tral government could be replicated in the relationship between each province and the counties and smaller political jurisdictions it contained.

Reflecting the ultimate success of the Nationalists in controlling the discourse on central-provincial relations, historians usually accept that local self-government and federalism were completely different phenomena. According to this notion, the former focuses on the county level and below while the latter defines the relationship between provinces and the central government.

Generally unarmed in a militarized China, and often out of touch with the vast majority of their poor and less-educated countrymen, politicians who supported expanded autonomy for the provinces found themselves relegated to minor parties. They struggled against the belief that anything that constrained the power of the central government was detrimental to the Chinese nation in its fight against warlords and imperialists. For example, according to the scholar Su Yunfeng, the federalist movement in Hubei Province during the 1920s faced four formidable challenges: the opposition of the central government, warlord invasions, poverty and a lack of popular education and support, and factionalism among its leaders.[33] The only factor missing in post-retrocession Taiwan was warlords.

When Sun Zhongshan and his followers were weak and controlled a single province, or even less, they accepted federalism and expanded local self-government. However, this was a short-term tactic — a fallback position when the Nationalists were unable to make progress toward their long-term goal of a centralized, bureaucratic state.[34] As the Nationalists became more powerful, they increasingly emphasized centralization. As historian Philip Kuhn writes: "It is clear that Sun viewed both democracy and local self-government not as independent values, but as essential prerequisites to the supreme goal of national integration and strength. Self-government was to inculcate national consciousness, not local separatism."[35] Sun and other revolutionaries had in fact called for a federal system of provinces as early as 1895. After 1911, in the wake of Yuan Shikai's increasing power, Sun and other leaders promoted the federal model in order to limit Beijing's influence. This appeared to be an orderly way to reunite the provinces of China that had declared independence after the 1911 Wuchang Uprising.[36] After 1916, the Nationalists found themselves dependent upon shaky alliances with warlords for survival. In this environment, federalism or a high level of local self-government provided warlords with a rationalization for their relative autonomy even as it gave the Nationalists a framework for national unification.[37]

The 1920s was a key transitional period leading to the triumph of centralization over federalism and local self-government. Early in the decade, the image of federalism suffered from its connection with attacks against Sun and his regime. Strongman Chen Jiongming, under the banner of federalism, stymied Sun's attempt to create a central government in southern China in the early 1920s.[38] Historians today may evaluate Chen as a leader who "never entertained the idea of provincial independence. He embraced the federalist cause because it permitted him to build the province as the basis of the nation."[39] The Nationalists, however, placed him squarely within the ranks of the warlords. The 1922 split between Chen and Sun marked the point when "progressive forces" turned away from federalism.[40] The Nationalists' temporary flight from Guangdong Province fired hostility toward any form of provincial autonomy, and made this doctrine even more difficult for moderate political activists to promote. Sun's statement, "On no account can we again allow the misleading principle of federation to serve as a charm to protect the militarists in their seizures of territory," became a mantra to the Nationalists.[41] They returned to Guangdong determined to build a strong central government backed by military power. Here, federalism and local self-government became clearly separate, the former becoming an anti-n/National excuse to weaken the Chinese nation and the latter a method of centralization and state-building.

The alliance of the Nationalists and Communists in January 1923 marked another step in weakening any alternative to a strong, centralized state.[42] The rise of the Chinese Communist Party and its conflict with the Nationalists became the most important issue in China's domestic politics. On the question of local self-government and federalism, the Nationalists and Communists were more alike than different. Essentially, they struggled over which of them would create and control China's central government, consigning the advocacy of federalism to small political parties that had no independent military power or financial base. Both major parties accepted the need for local self-government, but redefined it in their own interests. They agreed that it would be limited and would serve the state-building efforts of the central government. After retrocession, the Taiwanese would find that their aspirations for expanded autonomy were submerged by the larger struggle between these mainland antagonists.

The Northern Expedition of 1926 to 1928 gave the heirs of Sun Zhongshan an opportunity to realize their goal of centralization. As their military forces moved north from their base in Guangdong, through a combination of military victories, intimidation, and alliances with warlords, the Nationalists vastly expanded the area under their control and became the most legitimate national government China had enjoyed since 1911. In this position of relative strength, the Nationalists attempted to eradicate federalism and limit local self-government by relegating it to the county (*xian*) level.[43] Their understanding of local self-government grew from radically different assumptions than those held by the Third Force moderates. The latter were influenced by the United States, with its emphasis on individual rights and divided powers between branches of government at the central, state, and local levels. Nationalist experts on local self-government drew inspiration from the Japanese, who had widely read German texts. To them, local self-government became a method to extend central authority to the local level. Administration was to be separate from partisan politics, and local assemblies were not to possess legislative powers. In this scheme, self-government would establish the state at the local level, not serve as an alternate source of legitimate political power to balance or compete with the central government.[44]

On paper, the Nationalists seemed to be building a nationwide, centralized, bureaucratic system. However, continuing friction between the central government and the provinces, and the survival of alternative visions of the national polity, impeded centralization. These conflicts also formed the background to the Nationalists' approach to Taiwan and the February 28 Incident, when islanders briefly revolted against the provincial administration. For example, the conflict between the elite in Zhejiang Province and Jiang Jieshi's government in the late 1920s revealed similarities to postretrocession Taiwan. Many supporters of autonomy were part of the Third Force of reformist intellectuals or remnants of traditional rural elites, a group not much different from Taiwanese businessmen and landlords turned self-government activists. What historian R. Keith Schoppa deems the "perception of [Zhejiang's] capability for autonomy," including province-wide professional organizations and improved transportation and communication networks.[45] Schoppa notes, "Provincial autonomy was sought as the means to provincial security and integrity, to prevent [Zhejiang] from being sucked into warlord struggles and — an important corollary — to prevent consequent social disturbances."[46] The Taiwanese, as we have noted, sought autonomy after 1945 for essentially the same reasons, except they wished to avoid the turmoil of civil war rather than warlord conflicts. Like the provincial elite of Zhejiang, wealthy Taiwanese worried that larger conflicts could precipitate local social upheaval.

Zhejiang's experience is particularly pertinent for Taiwan because the island's future administrator, Chen Yi, was governor of Zhejiang during the Northern Expedition. In fact, Chen became entangled with issues of provincial autonomy in 1927, when he controlled Zhejiang as an underling of warlord Sun Chuanfang. The provincial elite urged Chen to accept a new constitution and prevent the Nationalist forces from entering the province. According to them, federalism meant that loyalty to the province would contribute to a strong Chinese nation. They did not seek independence, rather they hoped to blunt the Nationalists' drive for centralization. Prominent leaders called for a new government that would permit only those from the province to govern its people, force all militarists to leave the province, require provincial military forces to remain in Zhejiang, and put local military units under the command of a provincial committee. Zhejiangese, however, lacked sufficient military power and ideological legitimacy to win this level of autonomy. Chen determined that the Zhejiang plan was hopeless since the Nationalists had already begun to invade the province.[47] He threw his support behind Jiang Jieshi and his regime, thus beginning his career with the Nationalists and ending one province's drive for autonomy.

In Guangxi too leaders argued that provincial stability and prosperity resulting from a high level of local autonomy would build a strong China. In the early 1930s General Bai Chongxi, an important figure in the so-called Guangxi Clique, attempted to reconcile provincial and national loyalties by combining them. He claimed that "the reconstruction of [Guangxi] serves as the basis for the restoration of the Chinese people," a statement quite similar to those the Taiwanese made about their province. The attempt of leaders such as Li Zongren and General Bai to make Guangxi into a "model province," and to stress zizhi as one of the province's "Three Principles of Self-reliance," raised issues that Taiwanese would revisit after 1945.[48] The downfall of the Guangxi Clique, and its absorption into the Nationalist regime, in the mid-1930s represented a major victory for the Nationalist government.[49] Opposition to strong central control over provinces, however, continued. It was only in 1945 that the last major provincial-level rival to the Nationalists, Long Yun in Yunnan, was overcome. Thus, by 1945 Jiang and the Nationalists had successfully overpowered, absorbed, or intimidated a variety of provincial elites. Each victory served to legitimize further centralization under the Nationalists. Therefore, after retrocession it seemed to the Nationalists that the Taiwanese were attempting to reignite a debate over provincial autonomy that had been settled on the mainland.

Nevertheless, as war drew to a close, Jiang's regime had to contend with a variety of non-Communist revolts against its authority, particularly in border areas.[50] In early 1944, the Nationalists put down a short-lived uprising in northern Sichuan after rioters in one district attacked the Smuggling Investigation Bureau and the local tax office. Slogans used by Sichuanese included "Implement Self-Government for Sichuan Province." During their resistance, local citizens formed the Sichuan People's Self-Government Corps (Sichuan minzhong zizhituan).[51] Citizens from Gansu rose in revolt against the Nationalists' military draft and grain requisitions. And in late 1946, Xikang (formerly a province straddling the border between today's Sichuan and Tibet) was wracked by an uprising involving as many as 50,000 people. Then, throughout 1947, the Nationalist confronted a challenge in the far west, as ethnic minorities in Xinjiang fought Han Chinese. The Nationalists used a combination of negotiation and force to settle these incidents, setting a pattern they would repeat in Taiwan in early 1947.

Even as the Nationalists struggled with the Communists, postwar reconstruction, and local uprisings, they sought to codify their centralization efforts through a new constitution. In early 1946, China's political system was one of many issues the Nationalists and Communists disputed at the Political Consultative Conference (PCC; Zhengzhi xieshanghui), a body consisting of representatives of those two parties and most of the minor parties, organized for the purpose of reconciling the Nationalists and Communists and revising the constitution. The PCC was superseded by the National Constitutional Assembly (Zhixian guomin dahui) in November.[52] This body, boycotted by the Chinese Communist Party and a collection of liberal democratic organizations known as the Democratic League, quickly completed a draft of the constitution, which was promulgated on January 1, 1947 and went into effect on December 25 of that year.[53]

Jiang Jieshi had sought a constitution that would guarantee a strong chief executive and limit local self-government, in particular by blocking provincial autonomy. Non-Communist moderates advocated the province as the basic unit of self-government and wanted each province have its own constitution.[54] However, the constitution as adopted embodied the Nationalists' program of extending the reach of the central government, not sharing powers. It did provide for "Principles for Provincial and County Self-Government" (*Sheng xian zizhi tongze*) to be developed by the central government, which would authorize these jurisdictions to pass their own self-government laws.[55] The constitution also permitted the election of provincial governors, something denied the Taiwanese under the Taiwan Provincial Administrative Executive (Taiwansheng xingzheng zhangguan), an appointed official with great discretionary power.[56]

The Nationalists' version of local self-government on both sides of the strait owed much to Li Zonghuang, who held a variety of central government posts in the late 1940s and authored many books on local self-government and administration.[57] Li's ideas were legitimized by none other than the "Father of the Nation," Sun Zhongshan. Li wrote that in 1918 Sun instructed him to study Japan's system of local self-government during his time there. This, according to Li, gave birth to what became his life's work. In many respects, Li and other, like-minded Chinese wanted China to emulate Japan's highly centralized system.[58] In fact, Japanese politicians and intellectuals had a great deal of influence over the early Nationalist leaders, although given the anti-Japanese animosity in China, the Nationalists took pains to obscure this in later years.[59] Li, who served as the first provincial governor of Yunnan after quasi-warlord Long Yun was removed from power in 1945, was one of the founders of the Chinese Local Self-Government Study Society (Zhongguo difang zizhi xuehui), established in 1945. In 1949, Li revived the this organization in Taibei. None of its leading members was Taiwanese.[60]

Li shaped many of the constitution's provisions on the division of powers between the central government and provinces and lower levels of government. He worked to prevent the adoption of any form of provincial self-government when the draft constitution was debated in the National Assembly. The county, he wrote, was to be the unit of local self-government. Here he was merely echoing the words of Sun Zhongshan: "Xian wei zizhi danwei" (The county is the unit of self-government). Li also rejected the idea of provincial constitutions.[61] This marked an important step in redefining local self-government downward, pushing the relationship between the province and central government out of the political discussion. Nationalist commentators wrote that the relationship between the center (*zhongyang*) and province would be of two types: cooperative (*hezuo*) and supervisory (*jiandu*). In the former, the center and province were like elder and younger brothers; in the latter, they were like father and son. "Cooperation" did not involve questions of sovereignty or divided powers, but rather concerned the division of administrative responsibilities. The province was to be an administrative jurisdiction of the center, not a unit of local self-government.[62]

The Nationalists Prepare for Retrocession

The expansion of the Sino-Japanese war into a broader conflict involving the United States and Western European nations raised Chinese hopes of recovering Taiwan. After the Cairo Conference of November 1943, United States President Franklin Roosevelt, Generalissimo Jiang Jieshi, and British Prime Minister Winston Churchill stated their intention of returning Taiwan to China.[63] Simultaneously, the Nationalist government stepped up its preparations for the restoration of Chinese sovereignty over the island.[64] To this end, in April 1944, the Taiwan Investigation Committee (Taiwan diaocha weiyuanhui), chaired by Chen Yi, former governor of Fujian Province, was established within the Central Statistical Bureau.

Chen would become a key figure in the troubled relationship between the Nationalist state and the Taiwanese. Born into a merchant family in Zhejiang in 1883, Chen studied in Japan, where he came to know intellectuals such as Lu Xun and Cai Yuanpei. In the early 1920s Chen worked for warlord Sun Chuanfang, who made him governor of Zhejiang. Chen switched his allegiance to Jiang Jieshi, then leading the Northern Expedition, in 1926. He was briefly arrested by Sun, but freed thanks to the intercession of Jiang and the assistance of Ge Jing'en, who would become an important official under Chen on Taiwan. In 1934, Chen he was named governor of Fujian, a post he held until 1941. During his tenure, he was accused of both corruption and clandestine trading with the Japanese. Nevertheless, in 1942 Chen continued his rise and took the post of secretary-general of the Executive Yuan.[65] Perhaps the most favorable evaluation of Chen Yi was that he was a good man who loved his country but selected bad people to serve under him. Some historians used the phrase "xin you yu, li bu zu" (the heart is willing, but ability is lacking) to describe him.[66]

A significant facet of the postwar planning effort was the Half-Mountain people, islanders who had moved to the mainland during the colonial era and worked with the Guomindang or the Nationalist government. As many as 100,000 Taiwanese lived in China's coastal cities during the early 1940s, although only about 1,000 actually became involved in the Guomindang or its mass organizations. Most Taiwanese who lived in Japanese-occupied areas of China were merchants, soldiers, students, and low-level officials in the occupying administration. These people appeared to have few emotional or political ties to China. Half-Mountain people formed the Taiwanese Revolutionary Alliance (Taiwan geming tongmenghui), a loose coalition under Nationalist control, in the early 1940s.[67] Foreshadowing friction between the Nationalists and the Taiwanese, the alliance was held together more by anti-Japanese sentiment than a shared vision for postwar Taiwan.[68] Only a few Guomindang stalwarts in the alliance, some of whom were also members of the Investigation Committee, obtained influential positions in the postwar administration. The alliance faded from sight as the war ended.

Taiwan was not a major issue in war-weakened China.[69] For mainlanders, the most important national issues in the years 1945 to 1947 were the race between the Nationalists and Communists to control areas formerly occupied by the Japanese, negotiations between these two parties, the resumption of civil war, and the onset of massive inflation and financial instability. Because of growing conflict with the Communists, the needs of mainland reconstruction, and factional competition within the Guomindang and government ranks, officials in Nanjing paid little attention to China's newest, smallest, and least populous province.[70] Nationalist policies toward Taiwan were broadly similar to measures adopted for the rest of occupied China, and the regime's defects in Taibei differed little from its shortcomings in Shanghai, Nanjing, or Beijing.

The goals of Jiang's government involved both the state and the nation — seeking to decolonize and reintegrate Taiwan by erasing Japanese influence and bringing the island under the economic, political, and cultural sway of the central government.[71] The Nationalists hoped to exploit the island's wealth and industrial base for postwar reconstruction and the struggle against the Communists. Toward this end, in August 1945 they established an administrative system unlike that of any other province in China, the Taiwan Provincial Administrative Executive Office (Taiwansheng xingzheng zhangguan gongshu). Chen Yi became administrator and commander of the Taiwan Garrison. Chen, working through the Executive Office, had direct control over the administrative, military, judicial, and regulatory

organs on the island. The system gave officials great latitude to act with little input from local citizens or ministries of the central government. Although
this system was not intentionally modeled after the colonial era's Law 63,
its similarities to the Japanese administration sparked resentment among the
Taiwanese.[72]

The Nationalists' economic policies were intended to tie the island more
tightly to the mainland.[73] This effort was complicated by rivalries between
Chen Yi and the central government's National Resources Commission, an
organization designed to coordinate China's postwar economic recovery.
Chen and the commission held similar views on the need for the state to play
a dominant role in the economy, but Chen generally was more concerned
than the commission about limiting the damage to the island's economy from
chaos on the mainland.[74] This approach also benefited Chen by increasing
his own influence over functionaries sent by the Nanjing government.
Across the strait, the National Resources Commission emphasized that
Taiwan should develop light industry, but that investment should be carefully targeted to avoid building economic self-sufficiency on the island.[75]
Chen Yi and central government officials settled the dispute over control of
the island's economy in April 1946 when they agreed to divide control over
Taiwan's industries. Larger enterprises were generally placed under the
authority of the National Resources Commission and smaller enterprises
were to be exclusively the responsibility of the provincial administration.[76]
Regardless of the division of power between provincial and central governments, Taiwanese were relegated to the sidelines. Nationalist policies, as well
as conflicts over their implementation, meant that neither the scope nor pace
of industrial recovery would satisfy the Taiwanese.

Taiwanese found themselves trapped in Guomindang intraparty power
struggles as cliques and individuals around Jiang Jieshi vied for government
and party posts.[77] Although factional infighting exists under any regime, it
was endemic among the Nationalists. Bureaucrats and party members val-
ued expanding the influence of their clique over the implementation of government policies. Official positions translated into political power and also
into wealth through corruption and power over monopolies, United States
aid, and tax revenues. In 1945, Taiwan represented territory not yet controlled by any Guomindang clique.[78] Thus it was an especially fertile ground
for infighting. Even the selection of Chen Yi as administrator grew from his
ties to a political faction, the so-called Political Science Clique. His underlings in turn formed factions.[79] Mainland cliques opposed to Chen had their
own representatives on the island who tended to heed their factions' leaders rather than the administrative hierarchy.[80] Chen Yi's most persistent rivals
came from the C-C Clique, which alleged Chen and his government harbored
leftists.[81]

The arrival of the first Nationalist forces suggested how the colonial legacy would spark antagonism between the government and the Taiwanese. On October 5, the staff of the Taiwan Provincial Garrison Command Advance Command Office (Taiwansheng jingbei zongsilingbu qianjin zhihuisuo) flew to the island and on October 17, about 3,000 troops landed by sea. Mainland-born Nationalists, like the head of the Advance Command Office, Ge Jing'en, admitted that the reception was ambivalent. Ge wrote that newly arrived soldiers received a warm welcome, but that the streets were largely empty, shops were closed, and the atmosphere was lonely (*qijing*).[82] Many Taiwanese, implicitly comparing the Nationalist forces to the Japanese military, noted the mainland troops' poor equipment and lack of discipline.[83]

The Colonial Legacy and Taiwan

Within the context of the legacy of their Japanese-era political activity and the Nationalists' drive for centralization, Taiwanese sought to shape their relationship with the mainland government and its representatives on the island. They almost uniformly professed loyalty to the ideal of a united China, but differed considerably on the role of the Taiwanese in the provincial administration and the relationship between province and central government. The documentary materials show the Taiwanese accepted the legitimacy of Nationalist rule, but also felt the island deserved different treatment from the other provinces. Islanders held high expectations of an expanded role in governing the island at the time of retrocession — the rights they thought came with full citizenship in a nation. Their immediate concerns over Nationalist misrule, corruption, and ineptitude, defined by memories of Japanese rule, strengthened the drive for reform. The goal of that reform, expanded autonomy, represented a return to a political movement from the pre-retrocession era.[84]

Mainlanders agreed that fifty years of Japanese rule had made Taiwan very different from the other provinces of China, but it was precisely because of those differences that they believed Taiwan should be subject to even tighter control. As had been the case under colonialism, the central government made membership in the nation a prerequisite for reform of the state.

How could the Taiwanese claim to have benefited from foreign domination while avoiding any negative effects or influences that might impede their reintegration into China? After 1945 the clash between the collective memory of the Japanese era and the reality of Nationalist rule became a major point of contention between the state, which presented itself as synonymous with China, and the Taiwanese. Even the few Taiwanese within the Nationalist ranks expressed concern over reintegration. For example, Huang

Chaoqin, a prominent Half-Mountain person, wrote that the new administration must maintain the standards of law and order and material development set by the Japanese.[85] Articles in newly established newspapers called
for the Nationalist government not to take the Taiwanese lightly and challenged the new administration to manage the island's resources as efficiently
as had the former regime.[86] Some Taiwanese stressed that they were already
familiar with modernization and understood effective government from their
experience under the Japanese.[87] Others were more blunt. One anonymous
article declared that the Japanese knew the value of the island as a "treas-
ure house." It warned that although the Taiwanese were not seeking independence from the mainland, the island could become an entirely self-sufficient nation.[88]

Islanders utilized a variety of rhetorical tactics to articulate expectations
of their role in forging the island's political future. For example, essayists
often resorted to the image of the family to describe China: Taiwan was a
little brother separated from his family for fifty years, or a child abandoned
by his parents. The image of the child abandoned was of course a rebuke to
China because it suggested mainlanders were at fault for the island's colonial ordeal, not the Taiwanese. The idea of Taiwanese as children also demonstrated how eager and joyful islanders were to rejoin China.[89] The brother
imagery highlighted the need to involve islanders fully in governing Taiwan.
The younger brother's experience of slavery, one essay stated, made him love
his family even more than its other members did. However, as the parents
have sent an older brother to rule, friction is inevitable. Family peace and
renewal require that the family sometimes listen to the younger brother.[90]
Before and after retrocession, islanders emphasized that they possessed a special understanding of their island and therefore they must be deeply involved
in its political life.[91]

After interviewing three well-educated Taiwanese (a newspaper publisher,
a professor, and an engineer), an American intelligence officer wrote an excellent summary of how many prominent islanders felt about returning to
China:

Now, they said the Formosans want to become part of China. If possible, the educated class believe that it would be best if Formosa could become one of China's
provinces because the island is too small alone to have any kind of voice in world
affairs. The reason for the desire of a union with China is that the 6,000,000
Formosans have the same sentiments and background as the Chinese and know the
exact villages and places in Fukien [Fujian] Province, China, where their ancestors
came from. The educated Formosans do not particularly want the island to become
a "colony" of China but hope that it can be a province of China with the Formosan
people handling their own government. The three men said it was their belief that
the Formosans would eventually prefer to have native Formosans handling the gov-

ernment of Taiwan instead of having officials coming over from China who had little or no knowledge of exact conditions on the island.[92]

In an essay on the history of Taiwan, Zhejiang-born Zhou Xianwen outlined the problem of the colonial legacy. According to Zhou, some observers claimed Taiwan was more advanced than the mainland due to developments during the 1895-to-1945 period. Others responded that the legacy of Japanese rule required complete reform of the island. He concluded that Taiwan's special characteristics, based on fifty years of experience under foreign control, were not the sole cause of its problems — the island must join with the mainland while avoiding China's defects.[93] He did not provide specifics on how to resolve this dilemma, which goes to the heart of the Taiwanese conflict with the mainland-based Nationalist government.

The mainlander-dominated government interpreted the Japanese legacy to suit its own purposes. The Nationalists sometimes explained how they would improve upon the accomplishments of colonial rule. An editorial in a newspaper run by the provincial government, *Taiwan xinshengbao* (Taiwan New Life), credited the Japanese with improving education and promoting economic development on the island. At the same time, it declared that the culture of Taiwan, although not low by world standards, was not equal to the fatherland's (*buru zuguo*). The solution: increased contact with the mainland.[94] Another editorial acknowledged Taiwan's advances in education, industry, agriculture, and transportation under the Japanese. It compared the island to Sichuan Province, traditionally said to be a land of plenty (*tianfu*). The editorial concluded, however, that under Chen Yi's able leadership, Taiwan was now in good hands.[95] Thus, the Taiwanese were to continue to follow, not lead, in the island's development. The new administration also confronted the Taiwanese collective memory. For example, an English-language monthly magazine entitled *New Taiwan Monthly* stated that discontent with Nationalist rule stemmed from idealization of the past and a lack of understanding of the massive civil war on the mainland.[96]

For the most part, though, the government did not discuss Japanese influence as much as wield it as a political weapon. In light of Nationalist control of Taiwan, "Chinese" often meant little more than acceptance of Jiang Jieshi's government and specific policies of the provincial administration. It would be hard to overestimate the political sensitivity of the colonial legacy at this time. The discourse on the effects of Japanese rule and those who were influenced by colonial rule was shaped by the fully understandable hatred for those who had devastated China, reinforced by racism formed from traditional Chinese worldviews and modern nationalism.[97] Many mainlanders portrayed the Taiwanese as defective because of their Japanization (*Ribenhua*), which was often discussed in terms of enslavement (*nuhua*).[98]

They complained that Taiwanese knew little of the mainland or its culture and were biased against mainlanders — or worse, that they disdained China.[99] Those who benefited from their ties to the Japanese were particularly suspect. For example, the Nationalist-controlled press mentioned that among the various types of traitors (*Hanjian*) were those who had helped the Japanese military "loot" Taiwan.[100] Here, however, "traitor" seemed so broadly defined as to include anyone who became wealthy under Japanese rule.

While the colonial rulers of the island had defined "modern" as that which was Japanese, Nationalists such as Chen Yi defined it in terms of the political ideology and system espoused by the Guomindang. After retrocession, however, the Nationalists propaganda focused upon cultural and ideological development as Guomindang members could not make a credible claim that mainlanders were bringing modernization in the material sense. The mainlander-dominated government combined the ideas of modernization, patriotism, and loyalty to the state. For example, Chen Yi lambasted criticism of his policies as "feudal."[101] In particular, he dismissed resistance to his program of state control over the economy as selfish and backward. Nationalists such as Li Yizhong, chairman of the Guomindang Provincial Committee, claimed that Japanese rule had fostered "feudal" loyalties to the family and native place. After the war, he claimed, many Taiwanese remained mired in backward ideas and had failed to develop a sense of loyalty to China. This meant that islanders required extensive education.[102]

Some Nationalist charges were entirely valid — many islanders had cooperated with and benefited from colonial rule or assisted the Japanese in their invasion and occupation of China. Furthermore, a few islanders had supported independence at war's end. Other Taiwanese returned to the island and sought to cover up their wartime work for the Japanese in Manchuria or the Wang Jingwei puppet government. Yet the Nationalists had limited credibility on this issue, because islanders knew that many mainlanders had joined puppet regimes as well.[103] Chen Yi's personal history also undermined the Nationalists' criticism of Taiwanese "Japanization." Chen had studied in Japan and taken a Japanese concubine. In the late 1930s, as governor of Fujian, he had failed to vigorously support resistance to the Japanese. Indeed, he had dispatched several missions to the island that publicly praised colonial rule for its modernization of Taiwan.[104] Chen's appointment in late 1945 was hardly a sign that ties to the Japanese represented a permanent blight to one's career.

For the Taiwanese, cooperation with the Japanese was an aspect of colonial rule they hoped to forget, something to be excluded from the collective memory and political discourse during the post-retrocession era. When they did confront the issue, prominent and wealthy islanders defined collaboration in very narrow terms. They did not wish to connect their personal wealth, status, and education under colonial rule with collaboration, even though many mainlanders did. Rather, assistance to the Japanese military or police, not material success, was collaboration. Some Taiwanese did admit, however, that mainlanders' distrust stemmed from the Japanese use of islanders as spies or thugs on the mainland. In particular, criminals often cooperated with the Japanese military police (*Kenpeitai*) during the war — these were the true collaborators. Such people clearly had no particular feeling of kinship with China or loyalty to the Republic of China, but were not representative of the Taiwanese either.[105] In his memoirs, Taiwanese publisher and politician Wu Sanlian provided several justifications for cooperation with the colonial regime. First, China had abandoned Taiwan; islanders certainly had not asked to be part of Japan. Second, Taiwanese had no weapons or other means with which to resist colonial rule. Third, although Taiwanese merchants had done business with the Japanese on the island, on the mainland, and throughout Southeast Asia, as merchants they had to do business with anyone who came to their door.[106]

Some Taiwanese constructed their own narrative of colonial rule by vigorously rejecting the idea that they had been incurably infected by Japanese education or culture. Recalling resistance to colonial rule formed a key part of this effort to legitimize their participation in politics. At the end of the war, Li Wanju, who had worked with the Nationalist government on the mainland in anti-Japanese organizations, argued that the islanders had not been Japanized by their colonial experience. To the contrary, he complained that mainlanders did not understand that the Taiwanese had withstood assimilation by their colonizers and so had preserved the superiority of the Chinese race.[107] Taiwanese publications criticized the newly established Taiwan Provincial Propaganda Committee (Taiwansheng xuanchuan weiyuanhui) for incessantly (*kaikou bikou*) insisting that islanders had received slave education and were not prepared to enjoy the same sort of constitutional government as the rest of China.[108] An editorial in the newspaper *Minbao* charged that the epithets "enslavement" or "slaves" represented the sort of insult that turned the island's people against outsiders. Mainlanders did not realize that the Taiwanese had resisted foreign domination, particularly the autocratic rule of the Japanese governors-general, as vigorously as possible.[109] As a Taiwanese scholar has pointed out, the Nationalists could not accept that the colonial-era movement for self-government represented resistance to Japanese rule, even though the Taiwanese clearly saw it this way.[110] Based on the standards set by the bloody struggle against the Japanese on the other side of the strait, mainlanders were dismissive of the Taiwanese claim of unarmed resistance.

Islanders wielded many images and rhetorical techniques to legitimize their

participation in governing the island and criticism of the state. Some appro-
priated the theme of colonialism by reaching back to Manchu rule of
China — another instance of imperialism — and comparing it to Japan's
domination of the island. Poet and democracy activist Wang Baiyuan
asserted that the Taiwanese did not absorb Japanese thinking any more than
Manchu rule poisoned the minds of mainland Chinese. Taiwan was very
orderly, he claimed, and should be easier to rule than other recovered areas.
Thus, the island was ideally suited for modern democratic development. Yet,
Wang decried, some mainlanders saw Taiwan as their colony.[111] Thus, as
mainlanders, it was the Nationalists who had been infected by colonialism.
An editorial in *Renmin daobao* stated frankly that the prejudices of Taiwanese and mainlanders prevented their mutual progress. Although they
were all Chinese ("sons of the Yellow Emperor"), many of those from outside the province felt superior and looked upon Taiwan in the same manner
as the British treated India.[112] An anonymous article in the short-lived magazine *Xinxin* analyzed the terms used by many mainlanders to describe themselves (*neidiren*, people of the interior) and islanders (*Taiwanren*, Taiwanese),
and pointed out that the same framework had been used by the Japanese.[113]
In effect, mainlanders stood accused of adopting the mind-set of colonial rule
by placing Taiwanese outside of the nation.

By invoking the image of Taiwan as abandoned by China in the 1895
Treaty of Shimonoseki, Taiwanese turned the history of colonialism against
the Nationalists. As a result, islanders were "released" from any obligation
of national loyalty to China. Editorials and poems published in early 1946
declared that China had sacrificed Taiwan and that islanders quickly came
to see armed resistance to the Japanese was futile.[114] One Taiwanese refuted
accusations of collaboration by stating that the fatherland (*zuguo*) had cast
them away.[115] Essayists also pointed out what they saw as the mainlanders'
lack of attention to Taiwan during the fifty years of Japanese rule. Many literate, politically active Taiwanese still viewed their island as "Asia's orphan,"
a place without a true "national" home.[116] Others wrote that the fatherland
historically had shown little interest in Taiwan; after 1895 the Taiwanese had
no nation and no family (*wu guo wu jia*).[117]

Besides accusing Chinese of apathy toward Taiwan's fate — in many ways
a defensive strategy — Taiwanese also began to connect postwar political
instability on the mainland to misrule on the island — a more aggressive
approach. Provincial assemblyman Wang Tiandeng wrote that the Guomindang and the Communist Party were using the nation's youth to kill their
fellow countrymen and wreak destruction. This conflict, along with inflation and the Republic of China's sinking international position, harmed
Taiwan and hampered its economic recovery.[118] Another assemblyman
wrote that the mainland's problems had prevented economic reconstruction,

and led to corruption, nepotism, crime, and declining sanitation on the island. China's difficulties, he concluded, would not be easy to remedy soon.[119] General concerns over Taiwan's place in China combined with specific criticisms of the state to produce a drive for greater autonomy from the mainland government. For example, essays in *Taiwan pinglun* (Taiwan Commentary) urged islanders to avoid the whirlpool of party struggles on the mainland and instead to make Taiwan into a model province of local self-government.[120]

Islanders also tied the failures of the Nationalist state to a broader critique of the Chinese nation. Here, the Taiwanese portrayed the mainland as backward, in many ways the opposite of the Nationalists' view. A Taiwanese wrote that the Nationalists' difficulties in governing the island stemmed from the unequal levels of development on each side of the strait. Taiwan, unlike the mainland, was economically advanced and its people had the mentality of an industrial society, including orderliness and respect for the law.[121] Some members of the elite saw the mainland as still feudal, even as the island had advanced into the industrial age during Japanese rule. Specifically, nepotism, which was rampant in the provincial administration, was portrayed as a remnant from a stage of historical development through which the island had already passed. Taiwanese depicted corruption as part of the mainland's defective political culture.[122] In mid-1946, an editorial relayed a litany of complaints about the incompetence and dishonesty of the new administration, and concluded that the fundamental cause was the mainland's lack of the basic conditions for good government: talent, skill, and capital.[123]

Another tactic was to place the island in the context of Japanese rule *and* Chinese political ideology. According to the Principle of Democracy, one of the Sun Zhongshan's Three Principles of the People, the foundation of Nationalist ideology, China was to pass through three stages of political development — military rule, political tutelage, and finally democracy or constitutional rule. The Taiwanese conception of the final stage included two parts: protection of individual rights and the devolution of many powers to the provincial level or below. For example, an essay in *Taiwan pinglun* made clear that local (*difang*) self-government included the provinces and the central government, as well as lower levels of the administrative hierarchy. The author used the early works of Sun to bolster his interpretation, which the Nationalists rejected in the 1940s.[124]

Only by proving their national loyalty and demonstrating the island's relatively high level of education and economic development could islanders justify the greater autonomy they hoped would come with the third period of Sun's plan. Taiwanese accepted the basis of this teleological construct, but turned the Nationalist understanding of the colonial legacy on its head. Emphasizing the island's "uniqueness" became a key way to explain how foreign domination could justify political reform in Taiwan, even ahead of other provinces. For example, an islander stated he told mainlanders of Taiwan's unique qualities. Islanders thoroughly understood democracy and human rights — ideas transmitted from Europe through Japan to Taiwan.[125] Written under the pseudonym of I Love [My] Land (Wo Ai Di), an essayist in *Xin Taiwan* advocated intensive study of the cultural history of Taiwan. The author claimed that this was the vital base for any self-government, which must grow from an understanding of the special character of each area.[126]

It proved difficult to highlight Taiwanese uniqueness, which justified reform of the state, without appearing to challenge the Nationalists and the nation. A November 1945 essay by Xie Nanguang, a Taiwan-born leftist who worked with the Nationalists on the mainland, neatly summed up the islanders' ambivalence about the mainland and their expectations of Taiwan's special place in China.[127] Xie used the Three Principles as a foil for his case. First, the Taiwanese were ready for a high level of self-government and democracy because of their education and experience with political organization during the Japanese era. Second, Taiwan's developed economy was well-prepared to implement Sun's idea of People's Livelihood. Third, the island could serve as a test case for the Principle of Nationalism by leading the races of East Asia in living in harmony. Xie concluded with a plea for mainlanders to understand Taiwanese aspirations, which had been frustrated under the Japanese. He urged the Nationalists to bring to the fore their differences from the defeated colonial masters.[128]

Although Qiu Niantai, a prominent Taiwanese who became a Nationalist official, would have opposed Xie's social and economic policies, he too cited the colonial era to justify political reform. Qiu argued that Taiwan was not only suitable for a high level of self-government but could in fact become a model province. Taiwan had won political legitimacy based upon its half-century of resistance to colonial rule and had achieved remarkable material progress (albeit stemming from Japanese investment). No other province of China could make these claims. The Taiwanese could not be considered disloyal, Qiu claimed, since China had cast them out in the Treaty of Shimonoseki. Furthermore, during the Japanese era the Taiwanese had formed many organizations for expressing the popular will and resisting the colonizers. Finally, the island's well-developed industry, agriculture, and transportation — all positive results of the colonial era — deserved special protection by the government.[129]

Despite a wide range of ideas and emphases, the uncertainty of retrocession disappeared in 1946 as Taiwanese sought to reconcile their vision of the island's historical development with the ideal of national unity. A group of leading political figures spoke about their concerns with representatives of *Taiwan pinglun* in August of 1946. Lin Xiantang noted they could do nothing to influence the growing conflict between the Nationalists and Communists. In this environment, he suggested a federation of provinces (*liansheng*) would be the most effective system to govern China. This had the advantage of letting people select their leaders and be ruled by their own provincial representatives. He and others took pains to stress that they did not seek to exclude those outside the province. As was often the case with Taiwanese, however, he was not clear on how to resolve this apparent contradiction. Lin went on to state he understood that the concept of liansheng had been often connected to mainland warlords like Chen Jiongming and Sun Chuanfang.[130] However, the liansheng he sought left diplomatic, military, and financial powers in the hands of the central government. Administration, transportation, education, and production would be managed at the provincial level and below. Others in the group, like Lin Zhong, a Taiwan-born Guomindang and government official, followed a familiar pattern and used political and economic progress under colonial rule to argue for reform. Lin stressed the need for "complete" local self-government, since the island was clearly ready for it.[131]

The Taiwanese and the new government were on a collision course. What many notable islanders wanted — expanded self-government — and how they justified these requests — progress that had occurred during the colonial era — diametrically opposed Nationalist goals and perceptions of Taiwan's place in the nation and state. Neither side wholeheartedly welcomed the other. Instead, each increasingly viewed the other as backward and feudal: to the Nationalists, the Taiwanese were tainted with collaborationism and a willful refusal to rejoin the fatherland; to the Taiwanese, the Nationalists were corrupt and repressive.

In 1946, this conflict generally stayed within the realm of political debate among government officials and the island's elite. But by early 1947 events began to spin out of control as worsening economic conditions and police oppression spurred large segments of the island's urban population to violence against the state.

4 The February 28 Incident: The Climax of Taiwanese Political Demands

The February 28, 1947 Incident and its aftermath represented a conflict between decolonization and reintegration, when the legacy of Japanese rule and the drive for local self-government clashed with the centralizing mission of Jiang Jieshi's Nationalist regime.[1] Nationalist incompetence and misrule caused the short-lived uprising, but long-term Taiwanese political goals shaped its denouement. Unemployed youth, workers, students, peddlers, and small businessmen briefly wrested control of Taiwan from the provincial administration. The island's elite suddenly found itself caught between the mainlander-dominated state and Taiwanese society. They had not initiated armed resistance against the Nationalist Chinese. In fact, the elite moved to limit violence and to restore order, then to press for reforms under the broad rubric of local self-government. As they engaged in negotiations with the provincial administration, islanders expanded their demands to the extent that they threatened to change Taiwan's ties with the central government. Because some islanders resorted to force, the Nationalists saw calls for reform as a movement to overthrow the state and reject the Chinese nation. After a week of increasing tensions, mainland reinforcements massacred thousands of Taiwanese, both those involved in the uprising or subsequent negotiations, and others unfortunate enough to be on the streets.

This response illustrated that the island had become part of Nationalist China — a much more violent place under a state that portrayed dissent as inimical to the well-being of China. Decolonization made a quantum leap forward as those who had invoked the memory of the Japanese era to justify political activity were removed from public life or chose to leave politics. Subsequently, the state dominated discourse over the scope, timing, and powers of local self-government.

The Taiwanese and the Nationalist Administration

The Taiwanese considered both the Chinese and Japanese regimes exploitative, but deemed the new government particularly dishonest, incompetent, unpredictable, and inefficient. Suzanne Pepper, in her review of the Nationalists' takeover of occupied China in late 1945 and early 1946, noted four major problems: inability or unwillingness to punish collaborators; corruption; ineffective measures to rebuild the economy; and "condescending attitude adopted by returning officials."[2] The last three were amply evident in the Nationalist administration of Taiwan. The first point, however, is more difficult to assess in regard to Taiwan because of its complex colonial legacy. Policies on important issues such as the disposition of Japanese assets and economic reconstruction, cultural reintegration and language, and political participation engendered disappointment, frustration, then resistance.[3] The Nationalists did nothing to dispel the ambivalence of Taiwanese toward the colonial experience.[4] Because so many islanders soon came to see few major differences between the Japanese and the mainland Chinese economic and political systems, they began to discuss Nationalist rule as a form of colonialism.

The island faced two difficult economic transitions in late 1945: from the Japanese to the Chinese orbit, and from wartime mobilization to peacetime reconstruction.[5] The Nationalists inherited an industrial infrastructure worn down from the demands of Japan's war effort and American bombing. The most damaged areas included harbors, housing in coastal cities, sugar refineries, and communication and transportation facilities. Work on repairs ceased upon surrender, as Japanese technical experts and managers began to return home, and spare parts for equipment became difficult to obtain.[6] Agricultural production, insufficient in late 1945, remained inadequate because of a lack of fertilizer.[7] Food shortages and unemployment worsened as hundreds of thousands of Taiwanese who had been soldiers, laborers, students, merchants, and low-level bureaucrats in China, Japan, and Southeast Asia were repatriated. In such a situation, any government would have had a difficult time managing the island's resources. The Nationalists magnified these problems by connecting Taiwan to the mainland's economy even as the latter struggled, then failed, to recover from the war.

Taiwan's experience differed from that of other recovered areas in the degree, if not the form, of state intrusion.[8] Chen Yi molded the overall economic strategy set in Chongqing to fit his own ideas on the need for government control of Taiwan's resources.[9] In particular, he emphasized those aspects of Sun Zhongshan's ideology that favored national capital over private investment, thereby laying the base for conflict with Taiwanese businessmen. Since the nation and government belonged to the people, Chen argued, state enterprises were inherently good. He identified support of his policies with patriotism, thus leaving the Taiwanese little room for dissent. Chen attacked opposition to his economic measures, stressing that such critics held the "traditional ideology of the gentry." He asked, "The government should not make money, but merchants should? How can you say this? The money the government earns is for the benefit of the people, but the money earned by merchants goes into private pockets."[10] Chen's approach suggested that he saw the Taiwanese as backward, not advanced, because of colonial rule, a view completely at odds with the islanders' understanding of their recent history.

Nationalist policies proved a bitter disappointment to the island's elite as the new regime seemed better at seizing Japanese assets than at managing them or at encouraging Taiwanese capitalists to flourish.[11] Measures implemented by Chen Yi collided with the attempt by Taiwanese businessmen to expand their enterprises into areas formerly controlled by Japanese firms or the colonial government.[12] The state confiscated but did not reopen many factories; some were even moved to the mainland.[13] The provincial administration established trade bureaus to manage commerce between the island and the mainland as well as with the outside world. Businessmen large and small could not compete with state firms or trade freely with either old buyers in Japan and its former colonies or new ones on the mainland.[14] Monopolies had long been a grievance of the Taiwanese; the hope that Chen would abolish them after the war was soon dashed.[15]

In the competition between Taiwanese and mainlanders to control colonial-era assets, the disposition of Japanese property, especially homes, became a contentious issue. Simply put, the state's legal claim conflicted with what many Taiwanese portrayed as a moral claim. According to Nationalist law, all Japanese property now belonged to the government; transactions between islanders and Japanese that had been made at the end of the war were invalid.[16] Many Taiwanese, however, laid claim to land that had been confiscated or sold to the Japanese during the previous fifty years.[17] Corruption complicated this issue as some mainlanders took advantage of their power and positions to obtain disputed property. The colonial legacy became part of this conflict. A Taiwanese observed later that, "When a Chinese with some influence wanted a particular property, he had only to accuse a Formosan of being a collaborationist during the past fifty years of Japanese sovereignty."[18] For years, islanders filed lawsuits and petitions — unsuccessfully — in an attempt to obtain or hold onto property they felt was rightly their own.

Corruption and crime magnified the problems stemming from government policies.[19] Bribery was pervasive: for example, acquiring import-export licenses required payments to newly arrived officials.[20] Taiwanese joked about passing the Five-Part Imperial Exam (*wuzi dengke*), referring to the five things officials craved: gold, automobiles, rank, homes, and women.[21] Corruption was particularly offensive to the Taiwanese, who came to recall fondly the rule of law under the strict, yet predictable, police state of the Japanese.[22] Profiteering by Chen Yi's underlings galled the island's business leaders.[23] According to Chen Fengyuan, a successful businessman under both Japanese and Nationalist rule, the term for the mainland's takeover (*jieshou*) was replaced by a homonym meaning "to plunder." Chen also complained that corrupt officials monopolized former Japanese assets and that public security had declined — two areas of particular importance to prominent islanders, who had substantial property to protect and who dealt frequently with government officials.[24] Taiwanese blamed mainlanders, particularly soldiers, for the general breakdown of law and order on the island and the extortion of shopkeepers.[25] Poor relations between the Nationalists and the Taiwanese grew out of thousands of small acts. For example, soldiers from the mainland were accused of taking almost all the bicycles on the island.[26] Mainland criminal groups from China's coastal cities also gained access to the island, and after 1945 gang activity, especially extortion and bank robberies, increased in the cities.[27] Although the Taiwanese tended to focus their anger upon mainlanders, it is clear that regional networks of Japanese and Taiwanese criminals also existed.[28]

Retrocession did little to stem the decline in living standards that had marked the final years of Japanese rule. Taiwanese endured inflation, unemployment, food shortages, disease, and a declining infrastructure.[29] Chen Yi's attempt to insulate Taiwan from the ravages of inflation on the mainland failed, and prices rose in proportion to the plunge in value of the central government's currency (*fabi*) and growing recognition of the Nationalist China's instability.[30] Unemployment resulted from the lack of industrial recovery, magnified by the demobilization of many youth who had served as laborers or soldiers for the Japanese.[31] State monopolies on goods such as tobacco, alcohol, salt, and matches proved unable to meet the needs of consumers. Grain and housing shortages also harmed most Taiwanese. Attempts to control grain prices and sales proved ineffective. Hoarding and profiteering by merchants and officials, both Taiwanese and mainlanders, exacerbated these difficulties.[32] Finally, public health and sanitation declined. A cholera epidemic hit southern Taiwan during the summer of 1946, the incidence of malaria and leprosy increased, and bubonic plague reappeared for the first time since 1919, thus creating another basis for comparing Japanese and Nationalist Chinese rule.[33] Reflecting their increasing discontent with mainlanders, Taiwanese blamed newly arrived soldiers for bringing disease.[34]

Culture and language constituted another problematic aspect of decolonization and reintegration. The government sought to eradicate Japanese

influence and Sinicize the Taiwanese through a process of cultural reconstruction (*wenhua chongjian*), Sinicization (*Zhongguohua*), or "fatherlan-
dization" (*zuguohua*).[35] Toward this end, Chen Yi used organizations like the
Three Principles of the People Youth Corps, the Taiwan Office of Translation
and Compilation, and the Association for Improving Taiwan Culture. The
goals of the last included spreading the spirit of the Three Principles of the
People and democratic political thought, reforming Taiwan's "enslaved" (*bei
nuhua*) culture, assisting the government by spreading official pronouncements, and promoting the study of *Guoyu*.[36] This organization, made up of
prominent Taiwanese and government officials, illustrated the dual nature
of Nationalist policies involving the islanders' place in the Chinese nation.
The association lurched from berating Taiwanese for their colonial legacy to
welcoming them back into the fatherland.

The Taiwan Office of Translation was headed by Xu Shouchang, an associate of Chen Yi, who felt the state should foster national loyalty among the
Taiwanese through art and literature. The Taiwanese were to be "modernized" by bringing them their own May Fourth Movement and New Cultural
Movement to sweep away the influence of Japanese colonialism and Chinese
feudalism.[37] Xu promoted the writings of Lu Xun, an icon of China's youth
and one of the leading authors of the mainland's New Culture Movement.[38]
For several reasons, the program had little success. At the most basic level,
Xu's project, built on the assumption that the mainland had a modernizing
mission on the island, was diametrically opposed to the understanding of
modernization held by many Taiwanese. Islanders tended to see their society as advanced and orderly, and focused on modernization in the economic
or material realm, an area where they also compared quite favorably with
the mainland. There were other difficulties as well. First, there was limited
interest in Lu Xun, as many Taiwanese gave cultural change a much lower
priority than economic recovery. Second, some interpreted Lu Xun's works
as a critique of the mainland and its culture. Thus they served as much to
turn Taiwanese intellectuals against China and its representatives, the
Nationalist government, as they did to build ties.[39] Finally, the Taiwanese
received mixed messages from the Nationalist state because of its ideological and factional rivalries. Xu's work to promote the thought of Lu Xun conflicted with much of the Guomindang's official ideology, which centered on
the Three Principles of the People.[40]

Language became a point of conflict between the Taiwanese and the new
administration. Over fifty years Japanese had become the language of the
island's elite, even replacing the common Chinese dialects (*Taiyu*, also
called *Minnanhua*, and *Kejiahua*, the dialect of the Hakka) among the better educated.[41] Since language was a key facet of the Nationalists' Sinicization
program, the provincial administration under Chen Yi strove to increase the

use of Guoyu by establishing in April 1946 the Taiwan Provincial Committee for the Promotion of Mandarin.[42] Although most Taiwanese enthusiastically studied their new language — whether out of patriotism, a drive to profit in the China market, a release of curiosity stifled by the Japanese, or simple self-interest is difficult to say — the government's approach encountered obstacles. The state vastly overestimated the speed at which Taiwanese could learn Mandarin well enough to discuss political issues or read and write official materials. Even in the 1946 meeting of the Taiwan Provincial Consultative Assembly (Taiwansheng canyihui), translation was required as few representatives could speak "standard Mandarin."[43]

Language competence became a symbol of one's "Chinese-ness" and national loyalty, and thus the use of Japanese turned into a "political problem."[44] To mainlanders, the inability to speak, read, and write the official language suggested backwardness and a lack of patriotism.[45] An editorial in a Taiwanese publication stated that mainlander complaints about islanders' "Japanized" culture actually stemmed from a language gap. In other important areas of culture, the piece continued, islanders met the highest standards.[46] Taiwanese became especially upset when the ability to communicate in Mandarin became a symbol of political and educational development required for the implementation of self-government or the holding of official posts.[47] Nevertheless, the government moved ahead with its attempts to restrict the use of Japanese. On the first anniversary of retrocession, periodicals using the colonial language were banned. The state's credibility weakened, however, when Taiwanese realized that many newly arrived mainlanders could not speak understandable Mandarin — they brought with them the plethora of China's regional dialects.[48]

The print media represented another problematic aspect of cultural policy that sparked discontent among islanders. Actually, the press enjoyed greater freedom immediately after retrocession than at any other time prior to political reform in the 1980s. First, the Nationalists were no more adept at manipulating the media than at managing the economy or promoting the use of Guoyu. Second, Nationalist officials did not immediately seek to control all media. When the depth of Taiwanese discontent became clear in 1946, many Nationalist officials seemed genuinely surprised at the criticism they received.[49] Even *Taiwan xinshengbao* (Taiwan New Life), a newspaper owned by the provincial government, enjoyed relative independence in 1946.[50] Chen Yi had stated that freedom of the press would be protected in accordance with law, but that he hoped reporters would cooperate with the provincial administration, disseminate government decrees, and help build a new Taiwan.[51] By mid-1946, however, the limits of Chen's tolerance became increasingly clear, as reporters and editors were harassed, sued, or arrested. For example, tea merchant, newspaper publisher, and member of the

Provincial Assembly Wang Tiandeng was arrested for "undermining public confidence in authority."[52]

Elite Aspirations Denied

The weakness of elected assemblies and the mainlanders' domination of the provincial administration frustrated the Taiwanese. Retrocession had appeared to present an unprecedented opportunity for participation in public life, which had been severely restricted by the Japanese. However, Taiwanese obtained appointments to only three of the first twenty-three posts for county magistrates and mayors, and one of the twenty-one highest posts in the provincial government.[53] In mid-1946, none of the eight heads of administrative offices and only twenty-two of the top 296 government officials on the island were Taiwanese.[54] Moreover, islanders made up only a small portion of mid-level officials in the various departments.[55] Opportunities for employment and influence at all levels declined after the war as the bureaucracy shrank from 85,000 persons (including Japanese and Taiwanese) in 1944 to 44,000 in 1946. The Nationalists sent about 28,000 officials to the island. In the end, about 36,000 Taiwanese lost their jobs in the change of administrations.[56]

The limited powers of the consultative assemblies did not meet Taiwanese expectations. In late 1945, the Nationalists' willingness to create assemblies appeared to fulfill Taiwanese expectations related to local autonomy. While the administrator system was unique, the assemblies established on the island were little different from institutions in the mainland provinces. The central government had published the general outline for consultative assemblies (canyihui) at the provincial level and below in 1944.[57] As a handbook on administration made clear, "The provincial government is no more than a branch of the central government located in the province. . . . From the perspective of history, the province has always been an administrative district of the central government and not an entity for local self-government." The limited power of the assemblies, particularly at the provincial level, flowed naturally from these assumptions.[58] In 1946, provinces established consultative assemblies whose members were elected by county and city assemblies.[59]

On Taiwan, the first registration of candidates occurred in February 1946. At the lowest level, 36,966 candidates vied for 7,771 posts on village and town councils. They, in turn, elected 523 county and city representatives in March and April. These representatives then elected thirty provincial assemblymen apportioned among the eight counties and nine cities on the island.[60] Reflecting the continuity of personnel between the Japanese and Nationalist eras, of 1,180 candidates for the Taiwan Provincial Consultative Assembly in 1946, 400 had been involved in the colonial-era assemblies, which had fewer seats.[61] As had been the case prior to retrocession, the limited powers of the local and islandwide bodies left the Taiwanese dissatisfied. Although all assembly members were elected directly or indirectly, their powers had changed little from the colonial era — they could make suggestions, present petitions, or question officials, but had no direct control over budgets, official appointments, or policies. Nonetheless, these assemblies provided an important forum for the political elite to express their growing disaffection with the government.

The Provincial Consultative Assembly's first meeting on May 1, 1946, immediately revealed discontent with Chen Yi and the Nationalist government. Many Taiwanese favored the selection of colonial-era political leader Lin Xiantang as chairman of the assembly.[62] Lin represented the interests of the island's elite, attacking discrimination against Taiwanese, official monopolies, unemployment, corruption, and the inadequate funding of education.[63] However, Lin's prior involvement with the Japanese did not endear him to the Nationalists. With government support, Huang Chaoqin, a Half-Mountain Taiwanese appointed mayor of Taibei in early 1946, became chairman. After a brief uproar over Huang's selection, the thirty representatives settled down to discuss the island's future.[64] Assembly members requested elections for mayors and county heads (which were appointed posts at that time) as well as expanded powers for assemblies at all levels — town, county, city, and province. They wanted the assemblies to have powers over local administration, including budgets and staffing. Assemblymen also wanted a regular provincial government and the abolition of the institution of the administrator, a clear separation of civilian and military powers, the abolition of trade and monopoly bureaus, and the promotion of more Taiwanese into administrative posts.[65] Mindful of their position as elected representatives, they also raised issues of direct importance to less-wealthy islanders, such as food shortages and unemployment.

The assembly became a forum to draw together many different strands of the Taiwanese political agenda. Members attempted to connect economic development to expanded self-government within the framework of the Nationalists' political ideology. One representative raised the issue of Taiwan's material progress during the colonial era, asking the head of the Civil Administration Department, "According to Sun Zhongshan's teachings, the order of each province's implementation of local self-government depends upon the conditions in each location. This province is more advanced than others, so why cannot Taiwan carry it out first?" Others, like Gaoxiong's representative Guo Guoji, whose anti-Japanese activities and arrest during the 1930s first brought him into the public eye, stressed the middle ground of self-government that many of his peers were seeking. Guo charted a course between independence and complete assimilation by attempting to illustrate how self-government was part of building a better China: "The Taiwanese advocate ruling themselves. Because Taiwan is part of the territory of China, and the Taiwanese love their nation and native place, self-government and self-strengthening are natural requests and logical hopes." Like many other politically active Taiwanese, however, Guo confronted the negative aspects of the Japanese legacy. Even as he advocated self-government, he was careful to invoke the memory of resistance against colonial rule, declaring that Taiwanese had not been slaves of the Japanese.[66]

Here, Guo was responding to the Nationalists who believed the Taiwanese, because they had worked with the Japanese colonizers, were ipso facto collaborators. Many Nationalists questioned the qualifications of Taiwanese for holding official posts because of their lack of Mandarin Chinese and administrative experience.[67] Taiwanese, particularly those who had no contact with the Nationalists prior to retrocession, chafed at the number of mainlanders and Half-Mountain people given high posts. Archival material hints at the tense environment for both Taiwanese and newly arrived mainlanders even into 1946, as accusations of collaboration with the Japanese led to investigations of government employees.[68] Those islanders who managed to keep their jobs faced institutionalized discrimination. As had been the case during the colonial era, there was a salary differential between the Taiwanese and officials sent by the central government.[69] Islanders who remained employed threatened to strike during the summer of 1946 because of low pay and the lack of promotions.[70]

Two months before the February 28 Incident, the Taiwanese learned of the Nationalists' version of self-government as defined by the revised constitution. Simply put, the highly unpopular administrator system was to remain in place, and even the severely limited local self-government permitted on the mainland would not come to Taiwan in the near future. In January top officials in the provincial administration publicized a three-year plan for local self-government.[71] It called for the election of county heads and mayors, but few other significant changes. Officials took pains to stress that the plan and the constitution were compatible with one another.[72] In reality, the three-year plan represented an outline of how the constitution would not immediately apply to Taiwan, as it did on the mainland. While consultative assemblies on the mainland were to be replaced by "regular" (albeit still relatively powerless) bodies, the island's system would not change immediately.

The notion of special characteristics, an idea vital to the Taiwanese promotion of greater local autonomy, came back to haunt the island's elite.[73] The state made the colonial legacy an explicit part of the debate over the island's preparedness for constitutional rule and the system of self-government that would accompany the constitution. As had been the case prior to 1945, the state expected Taiwan to join the cultural community of the nation before enjoying political reform. This was articulated using Sun Zhongshan's three-stage plan for China's political development: military rule, then political tutelage, and finally constitutional government. Under the new constitution, the mainland was to move into the third stage while Taiwan remained in the second. Chen Yi stated that Taiwan, as a newly recovered area (*guangfuqu*), would require a period of political tutelage to catch up with the mainland. He thought islanders needed to develop respect for the law, even though this was an area where Taiwanese claimed to be ahead of mainlanders. He also declared the county would be the unit of local self-government while avoiding discussion of the province's special status.[74] A commentator, almost certainly a mainlander, in the newspaper *Xinshengbao* wrote that implementation of the constitution must take into account the island's deficiencies. For example, Taiwanese education, although widespread under the Japanese, had focused on technical or professional fields instead of the humanities (*renwen jiaoyu*) that were vital for grasping the meaning of democracy. Further, the Taiwanese did not yet sufficiently understand the mainland.[75]

The elite's hope that the island's colonial-era experience might warrant greater autonomy than that accorded to mainland provinces was dead. The United States ambassador to China, J. Leighton Stuart, reported that a major cause of the February 28 Incident was the announcement that the constitution would not come into effect on the island until 1949.[76] Now, Taiwanese seemed willing to settle for the same treatment as other provinces. Even before the crisis of early 1947 many Taiwanese participated in meetings and petition drives to request that the central government and the administrator speed the timeline for new elections.[77] Members of the Provincial Consultative Assembly such as Guo Guoji attacked the three-year plan, stating that the constitution had no provision for delaying the election of mayors and county magistrates.[78] Other prominent islanders pointed to section 11 of the new constitution, which called for the election of provincial governors — an issue Chen Yi studiously avoided.[79] These debates over the nature of local self-government could have continued in the press and consultative assemblies but for a crisis that gave the elite an opportunity and obligation to turn rhetoric into action.

Simmering Tensions Explode

More ominous than this moderate movement for expanded autonomy was the gap between the elite and much of urban Taiwan, especially small merchants, laborers, and unemployed youth. In the central part of the island, people talked of "three hopes" (*san xiwang*). First came hope (*xiwang*), which existed from the time of Japan's surrender through the arrival of the Nationalist administration two months later. Next was lost hope (*shiwang*), which grew from the dismal performance of the new government. Finally came hopelessness (*juewang*) which set in once people realized "the future was black."[80] A short poem published in *Xin Taiwan* summed up how many Taiwanese felt about the events of 1945 and 1946:

> American bombing startled heaven and moved the earth,
> the news of retrocession led to boundless joy,
> the Nationalist takeover was debauchery,
> the government was sinister and dark,
> and the people appealed to heaven and earth.[81]

Poor Taiwanese, suffering from the lack of food, shelter, and health care, did not so much discuss China and the Nationalist government as disdain them. Sun's *Sanmin zhuyi* (Three Principles of the People) was mocked as *canmin zhuyi* (immiserate the people–ism) or *sanmian quli* (grasping benefits from all sides).[82] Taiwanese began calling corruption "Sun Zhongshan" because Sun's face was on the currency that so many officials demanded as bribes.[83] Complaints degenerated into insults. Some islanders said that the dogs (the Japanese) had left, but the greedy and uncultured pigs (mainland Chinese) had come.[84] By mid-1946, newspapers reported brawls between mainlanders and islanders as living conditions worsened.[85]

By early 1947 the problems of reintegration and postwar dislocation led to simmering discontent in the cities, towns, and villages of Taiwan. As a Taiwanese wrote later, "We entered 1947 without even a bit of the hope that comes with springtime, as the situation worsened day by day."[86] The incident could have occurred in late 1946 or early 1947, as several short-lived outbreaks of violence occurred between the government and islanders around New Year's.[87] Because they took place in rural areas, however, they did not spread. Despite the islanders' pride in their sense of law and order, Taiwanese society was becoming increasingly violent due to crime, poverty, unemployment, and poorly disciplined police and soldiers. Weapons — some left over by the Japanese, and others brought from the mainland — were plentiful. One prominent Taiwanese lamented that the general level of violence on the island had increased since retrocession: "It even reached the point that husbands and wives fighting would pull out guns to threaten one another, or [people would] even shoot those only suspected of a crime. . . . This was really the fuse for the February 28 Incident."[88]

Formidable problems on the mainland not only worsened the difficulties faced by islanders, but also diverted the central government's attention from rising tensions on Taiwan. In January 1947, United States General George

Marshall abandoned his effort to mediate between the Nationalists and the Communists and returned to Washington. On February 1, the Beijing-Tianjin railway link was temporarily cut by the Red Army, and on February 23 the Communists resumed their offensive along the Sungari River in northeast China. The Nationalists later considered January 1947 to be the beginning of the Communists' "all-out rebellion."[89] As a consequence of the expanding civil war, as well as its own corruption and mismanagement, the Nationalist government began a two-and-a-half year slide toward collapse. Political instability spurred inflation, and on February 16 all transactions using gold and foreign currency were banned.[90]

As the Taiwanese had feared, crises on the mainland reverberated across the strait.[91] In January 1947 the government announced it would begin conscription of Taiwanese youth later that year.[92] At the same time it found control of the economy slipping through its fingers. When the authorities were willing and able to enforce price controls on commodities such as rice, shortages from hoarding arose. When they did not implement controls, inflation soared. On February 14 Taibei's rice market closed after a small riot. A crowd of 4,000 marched to the nearby city government offices, holding banners reading "Ask the government to hold down rice prices."[93]

On the evening of February 27, six police officers attempted to arrest a women selling cigarettes illegally in Taibei.[94] A policeman struck the woman, an angry crowd gathered, and violence broke out after an officer fired his weapon, killing a bystander. The next day, 2,000 to 3,000 Taiwanese marched to the Monopoly Bureau Headquarters, and hundreds moved on to Chen Yi's office.[95] Besides protesting the beating and shooting, islanders complained of unemployment, food shortages, inflation, political repression, and corruption. That afternoon, a soldier or police officer at the office fired into the crowd, sparking an islandwide uprising. Vandalism and violence against police, soldiers, bureaucrats, and any mainlander unfortunate enough to be on the streets spread beyond Taibei.[96]

The provincial administration had badly underestimated the willingness of Taiwanese to transform their discontent into concrete action. Incident turned into uprising as urbanites and government forces battled over buildings, railroad stations, and police stations in large towns and cities. Taiwanese gained control of most of the island since Nationalist soldiers, almost exclusively young draftees from the mainland, had little stomach for a fight.[97] Many mainland officials and businessmen abandoned their posts and stayed home throughout the crisis.[98] In some cities, officials and police sought safety together in local military outposts. Railroad, telephone, and telegraph traffic throughout the island ground to a halt in the first days of March. After two or three days of conflict, the situation calmed, although occasional shots were still heard in Taibei.[99]

This crisis was not simply a revolt against the state. Many different groups used the opportunity created by the temporary power vacuum to pursue their own agendas.[100] For example, while educated youth sought immediate political and economic reform, secret society and gang members took advantage of the chaos for personal profit. Urban workers and youth wanted economic recovery and jobs. Youth who had received Japanese military training reconstituted their old units in many of the island's cities and took to wearing their old uniforms, singing wartime songs, and sporting swords. This naturally served to justify the suspicions of mainlanders that the Taiwanese had been "Japanized." Ironically, many of these youth had joined the Three Principles of the People Youth Corps after retrocession. Just as they had done immediately after Japan's surrender, these young men helped maintain public order.[101]

As had been the case under Japanese rule, the elite's political agenda placed them between the state and Taiwanese society. They sought the restoration of order and reform of the provincial administration, but found themselves dragged into a maelstrom by the actions of less wealthy Taiwanese. In fact, Taiwanese politicians had frequently raised the problems of poor and homeless islanders in the town, county, and islandwide consultative assemblies. Their solution, however, was reform to facilitate greater Taiwanese control of the island's resources. In late February and early March, prominent islanders often attempted to limit violence between Taiwanese and mainlanders. For example, Xie E, one of the few Taiwanese women involved in politics at that time, tried to calm islanders through a broadcast that suggested soldiers had not fired on the crowd on February 28.[102] Lin Xiantang personally protected Yan Jiagan, a Nationalist official, from angry Taiwanese.[103] In another instance, some Taiwanese sheltered the Taizhong county magistrate from an angry crowd that wanted to cut off his nose.[104]

The Elite Takes Charge

Though few of the elite participated in the initial violence or anticipated that the Nationalists would lose control of the island, they suddenly found themselves negotiating between the state and Taiwanese society. This role took a tangible form through committees to resolve the Incident. On March 1, members of the Taibei City Council hurriedly organized the Committee to Investigate the Case of the Arrested Smuggler (Qisi xue'an diaocha weiyuanhui) to bring calm to the city and seek punishment of the policemen responsible for the conflict. They invited other important political figures, including representatives to the national and provincial assemblies, to participate. The Taibei committee dispatched a delegation to meet with Chen Yi and request that he lift martial law (which had been declared on February 28), release arrested islanders, prevent Nationalist troops from indiscriminately shooting or beating civilians, and form a committee with representatives from the government and the people (*guanmin*) to settle the incident.[105] Chen Yi responded positively, promised to punish anyone in the police force guilty of crimes, and delegated five officials to join the committee. This group became known as the February 28 Incident Resolution Committee (Er erba shijian chuli weiyuanhui).[106] The organization in Taibei was duplicated throughout the large towns and cities of the island. The committees often cooperated with local youth to maintain order, much as the elite had done immediately following the Japanese surrender.[107] In addition to taking over the functions of the police, the committees began to restore communication and transportation, in many ways replacing Chen Yi's administration.

The February 28 Incident revealed no single Taiwanese agenda, but rather a multiplicity of contending views and interests. Prominent islanders involved in the incident fell into several general categories. First were Japanese-era leaders of the movement for local self-government who had been elected to post-retrocession assemblies. They accepted Nationalist rule, but wanted major reforms. When confronted with the takeover of the island by their less wealthy neighbors, they sought to limit violence against mainlanders and head off possible retribution. Although they quickly came to see the crisis as an opportunity to press for moderate political change, they were also obliged to become involved. If they did nothing they would weaken their claim to political influence. Thus, to serve their own interests and meet the expectations of their fellow islanders, they came to dominate the island-wide and other large resolution committees.[108] Next were those who wanted to remove Nationalist rule, even as they accepted that Taiwan was part of China. Their goals, which included political and economic reform, often focused on the needs of peasants and workers, and seemed to support a position close to that of the Communists.[109] These leaders were generally not islandwide figures, but were prominent in particular towns or cities. Third, a small group of younger men sought independence or a United Nations trusteeship for the island.[110] Finally, each of these three groups contained individuals simply out to benefit personally or to enjoy a few minutes of fame. A Taiwanese author sympathetic to islanders' demands admitted that the incident attracted "lovers of the limelight" (*aichu fengtou*), braggarts (*chui niupi*), and hypocrites (*xuwei*).[111]

The government was no more unified than were the Taiwanese. It seemed to waver between two approaches toward the crisis: pacification (*anfu*) and division (*fenhua*).[112] The former meant attempting to negotiate with important islanders to reach a peaceful resolution of the crisis; the latter, dividing the Taiwanese by hoping violence would turn people to the government to restore order and by threatening retribution. The military tended to take a harder line, and there is evidence that some officers planned from the outset of the incident to use force. Recriminations over the origins and handling of the incident also provided opportunities for cliques in the Nationalist government and party to press for the removal of rivals. This infighting worsened an already chaotic situation.

The Taiwan Garrison Command had declared martial law on February 28, but Chen Yi rescinded it the next day. Officials seemed to accept the mediation of some Taiwanese during the first few days of March. For example, near Tainan Taiwanese were unsure initially whether the branches of the resolution committees had the sanction of Chen Yi and the government. Many later remarked bitterly that Chen changed his view of these committees after enticing Taiwanese to join them and speak out in the expectation of reform.[113] Some Taiwanese wrote later that local police officials actually asked leading islanders to help guide youth in order to keep the peace.[114] On March 3, General Ke Yuanfen, chief of staff under Chen, promised the island-wide resolution committee that Nationalist troops would be off the streets of Taibei that day. He stated that students and other youth would be permitted to play a role in maintaining public order, thus basically accepting the situation that had existed since March 1.

The immediate opportunity presented by the incident and the long-term advocacy of self-government combined, as the Taibei committee expanded its membership and goals.[115] The committee soon included prominent members of local, provincial, and national assemblies, representatives from student and other groups, and delegates appointed by Chen Yi. Its standing committee included many leading members of the Provincial Consultative Assembly such as Lin Xiantang, Li Wanju, Wang Tiandeng, Huang Chaoqin, and Guo Guoji.[116] The representatives met with Chen during the first days of March, each time moving further toward urging fundamental political reforms under the rubric of self-government.[117] They restated earlier requests related directly to the incident as well as demands similar to those articulated during the Japanese era and in the post-retrocession period. Although some political leaders, particularly Half-Mountain people, attempted to moderate Taiwanese demands, passions were running high. By March 4, the government officials participating in the resolution committee were no longer welcome.[118]

The Taiwanese became less interested in justifying expanded autonomy than in elucidating what they expected of it. After a disorderly public meeting on March 6, the resolution committee drafted a General Outline for Resolution (*Chuli dagang*). The first part of this document provided a comprehensive overview of the defects of Nationalist rule as defined by island's elite. The litany of complaints included the use of force to cheat or oppress islanders, the failure to protect human rights (*renquan*), the decline of freedom of speech and the press, financial collapse, inflation, factory closings, poverty in the villages, and unemployment. The General Outline concluded that because of these basic problems, the Taibei incident had grown into an islandwide movement.

The General Outline included thirty-two specific requests for reform (*Sanshi'er tiao yaoqiu*; often translated as the "Thirty-two Demands") that reflected the connection between the incident and long-term political aspirations.[119] The Thirty-two Demands were divided into two main sections: the first, devoted to "Resolving the Present Situation" (*Duiyu muqian de chuli*), that is, solving the problems spawned by the actual incident (seven items); and the second, entitled "Resolving Basic [Problems]" (*Genben chuli*), devoted to military and political reform (three and twenty-two items, respectively). The quest for expanded self-government formed the driving force behind the basic resolution section. Foremost of the proposed political reforms was making the province, not the county, the highest level of local self-government, a position many islanders had taken since late 1945. As a corollary, the General Outline called for transforming the Taiwan Provincial Consultative Assembly into a Taiwan Provincial Assembly (Taiwansheng yihui). The name change would signal that Taiwan was no longer to be singled out for "special treatment."

The General Outline incorporated Taiwanese aspirations for participating in the provincial government, reducing state control of the economy, and limiting the impact of the mainland's civil war. Under the broad heading of "letting Taiwanese rule Taiwanese" (*Tairen zhi Tai*), islanders demanded to hold the most important posts in the provincial administration.[120] The document also called for the direct election of mayors and district magistrates; assurances that the top police officials would be islanders; greater Taiwanese representation in the justice system; the abolition of the propaganda, trade, and monopoly bureaus; guarantees of freedom of speech, press, and assembly; and a promise that Taiwanese would not be drafted and sent to fight on the mainland.[121] It asked that military police (*xianbing*) be authorized to arrest only soldiers, not civilians, and that new elections be held for all levels of assemblies, suggesting that the drafters of this document were confident of the support of their fellow islanders.

In making their case for reform in March 1947, the islanders on the resolution committees reiterated an approach dating back to the colonial era as they combined elements of assimilation and autonomy. Their call for expanded self-government emphasized how this was compatible with the political structure and ideology of the Nationalist government. The General Outline made clear that most members of the resolution committee were moderates who accepted the overall framework of reintegration into the Chinese nation. The elite claimed that fundamental reform would prevent another, perhaps even more serious, calamity in the future, and it did not challenge Chinese sovereignty or Nationalist legitimacy. Despite the violence of the February 28 Incident and the extensive changes contemplated by the Thirty-two Demands, islanders were not seeking independence. Rather, they linked their agenda to the national narrative of Chinese political development, arguing that expanded local self-government would realize the ideals of Sun Zhongshan's own plans as stated in his 1924 General Outline for National Reconstruction (*Jianguo dagang*). In effect, they suggested that their aspiration for greater autonomy made Taiwan more a part of China, and fulfilled, not repudiated, Sun's nation-building dream.

As late as March 6, Taiwanese leaders could feel satisfied with their efforts. They had maintained order on most of the island and had restored transportation and communication. The government appeared receptive to requests for reform. The provincial administration had retreated from its three-year plan for local self-government. Chen Yi promised to petition the central government to establish a regular provincial government. He also agreed to direct elections of county magistrates and mayors by July 1947.[122] The provincial administration, however, could no longer keep pace with rising Taiwanese expectations. Furthermore, Chen Yi had to contend with a central government that knew little and cared less about the nuances of Taiwanese political aspirations.

Islanders, emboldened by their newly achieved power, moved beyond the requests they had made during the Japanese era. Political leaders also had to respond to pressure from below, as urbanites and youth who actually took control of the island's towns and cities expected immediate, tangible results for their efforts. Ten additional far-reaching demands were added to the General Outline, including the immediate abolition of the administrator's office and Garrison Command, and greater Taiwanese control over the military forces on the island.[123] These steps would have given islanders influence over the provincial administration and fundamentally changed the relationship between the province and the central government. Yet, Taiwanese remained careful to acknowledge the ultimate legitimacy of the Nanjing government.

The revised document even touched upon sensitive issues of colonial rule. Taiwanese asked for the release of those arrested on suspicion of war crimes or collaboration, and for the reformed provincial government take responsibility for the disposition of Japanese property. If they had acquiesced to these requests, the Nationalists would be accepting some key Taiwanese assertions about the Japanese legacy. First, they would be acknowledging that islanders had not been collaborators, and thus were not disloyal to China.

This represented an important justification for expanded local self-government and the elite's participation in governance. Second, they would also be acknowledging that the wealth generated by colonial rule belonged to islanders and that Japanese assets were actually Taiwanese property that had been unjustly confiscated over fifty years.

Just as the government had underestimated the anger of the Taiwanese a few days before, now islanders courted disaster. When Provincial Consultative Assemblyman and head of propaganda for the resolution committee Wang Tiandeng, chairman of the Provincial Consultative Assembly Huang Chaoqin, and other prominent islanders presented their requests for reform to Chen Yi on March 7, the administrator became visibly angry. Many members of the committee feared that they had overstepped themselves and that military reinforcements were already en route from the mainland. The next day they repudiated much of the previous day's statement, especially the sections that called for Taiwanese control of the police and military. They also claimed that their requests had not been discussed thoroughly and acknowledged that the government had met their initial calls for police restraint. Although most of the committee emphasized that order had been restored and that they wished to contain the incident, a few Taiwanese outside the committee called for armed struggle against the Nationalists.[124]

The Nationalists' Response

The state responded to the challenge presented by the uprising and demands for reform with overwhelming force. On the morning of March 8, the first Nationalist military reinforcements arrived in the northern port city of Jilong. As these forces moved southward toward Taibei, fighting broke out with Taiwanese. Over the next two days, thousands of soldiers landed in Jilong and on the south coast at Gaoxiong. They reasserted the government's control by indiscriminately shooting anyone on the streets. Martial law was declared throughout the island on March 9. On March 10, Chen Yi announced that the resolution committees had become part of the revolt and were now illegal. He also ordered all workers to return to their posts and shopkeepers to open for business, implemented price controls, and outlawed meetings or the collection of money for any purpose.[125] Since Taiwanese were poorly armed and lacked a unified command, resistance collapsed quickly. Furthermore, most prominent islanders never sought a pitched battle with mainland forces.

The Nationalists began to earnestly exploit the incident for their broader ends of eliminating opposition. Even as the island returned to Nationalist

control, the government embarked upon a movement to "exterminate traitors" (*sujian*) by rounding up Taiwanese who may have offended anyone in
the government. This was accompanied by the "clearing of the villages"
(*qingxiang*) campaign, where soldiers and police hunted down individuals
who had fled the cities when Nationalist troops returned.[126] In at least some
areas, the military offered rewards for Taiwanese who secretly turned in their
fellow islanders for participating in the incident.[127] Tight controls on communications and travel were imposed. All but three government-approved
newspapers were banned, and soldiers and police ransacked the offices of
other newspapers.[128] The fear of future terror kept the Taiwanese on the
defensive. Police took photos and business cards from the homes they
searched, and arrested visitors to residences under surveillance. Taiwanese
became reluctant to talk with each other, much less criticize government policies or officials.[129]

The Nationalists' oppression, however, was no more systematic than any
of its other activities. There existed an unnerving element of chance in the
arrests and executions of early 1947. For example, a Taiwanese member of
the National Assembly, Lin Lianzong, was arrested by military police at a
friend's home and subsequently disappeared. The police apparently had no
idea who he was until he gave them his business card, perhaps in the hope
that his relatively prominent position would protect him.[130] Leading political figures often labored under the assumption that they served as useful
mediators between the Nationalist state and Taiwanese society, even though
the Nationalists clearly had decided that they and violent urbanites were one
and the same. Many islanders, such as Wang Tiandeng, were arrested without a struggle, as they did not expect to be the object of the government's
wrath.[131] Wang, a vocal critic of the provincial administration and an advocate of greater autonomy, was taken by plainclothes police and killed by a
stream not far from the current site of the Academia Sinica on the northeast
edge of Taibei.

Leaders in Nanjing saw the takeover of the island by Taiwanese as nothing less than a rebellion. They evaluated the resolution committees in the context of thirty years of struggle against provincial rivals. Officials on Taiwan
reinforced these perceptions. They downplayed the crisis, then exaggerated
it, in order to cover up their own inability to prevent the conflict or reach
compromise with the Taiwanese.[132] However, what transpired on Taiwan in
1947 was unlike the earlier experiences of revolts and resistance on the mainland in at least two respects: the Taiwanese had directly confronted local
Nationalist forces and defeated them, and the central government had the
troops available to crush the Taiwanese and thus had no need to seek a negotiated settlement.

Personal humiliation also played an important role in sparking the brutal crackdown. For example, an account of the incident by Peng Mengji (known as the Butcher of Gaoxiong for his bloody role in reestablishing Nationalist control of this city) mentioned the taunts hurled at him and his unit by Taiwanese youth: "Can your cannons fire? We doubt it. Can Chinese troops fight? We also doubt it."[133] Nationalist military leaders had been forced to retreat, or even hide, from youth with Japanese military training. This embarrassment gave them an incentive to paint the incident as an organized, anti-Chinese revolt, thus justifying their initial retreat and then their brutal counterattack. Though Jiang Jieshi promised there would be no retaliation by the military, in light of the Nationalist military's history of indiscipline, it was naive to expect no violent retribution.[134]

Estimates of the number killed range from unbelievably low (500) to absurdly high (100,000).[135] Those with close ties to the Nationalist government claim lower figures for the dead and injured, while supporters of Taiwan independence and critics of Jiang's regime insist on higher numbers.[136] The rough consensus among scholars is 10,000 killed and 30,000 wounded.[137] Although discovering whether 5,000, 10,000, or more died is an important way of understanding the scope of the massacre, knowing who was killed helps make clear the incident's effect on later political activity. As soldiers spread terror through the island, they crushed the Taiwanese as a political force able to advocate change outside the Nationalist state or Guomindang party structure. The elite's struggle to position themselves between the Nationalists and the bulk of the island's population failed. Instead, the government saw as one the elite, urbanites who took up arms, and even Taiwanese who stayed home throughout the crisis. All were part of a rebellion against the state.

The incident and its aftermath had a greater impact on the island's elite than did retrocession. Many of the most vocal critics of the state and promoters of expanded self-government, usually prominent figures from the Japanese era, died, fled, or were frightened into silence.[138] For example, two members of the Provincial Consultative Assembly were killed and five others arrested, while four members of the Taibei City Council died and nine were jailed. Others killed included lawyers, professors, teachers, landlords, merchants, and journalists. Because of their political activity under both Japanese and Chinese rule, these were among the best educated and most prominent islanders.[139]

Throughout the spring of 1947, the Nationalists made clear that the Japanese legacy was a dangerous liability jeopardizing the political standing and even the personal safety of all Taiwanese. The state moved ahead with decolonization, at gunpoint. Chen Yi outlawed Japanese-language publications and phonograph records, and ordered the confiscation of military uniforms, flags, and other items from the colonial era.[140] Editorials in the tightly controlled press ranted that those who had called for democracy in early March 1947 were despicable, self-serving traitors. Some evil conspirators, the editorials warned, remained hidden.[141] Many Taiwanese who had avoided involvement in the incident parroted the Nationalist line, and denounced the lingering influence of the Japanese era and the old elite for their "collaboration."[142]

The Nationalists Define February 28

In the spring of 1947, Taiwan became part of the mainland's political history, as the ideas, priorities, and problems of Republican China came to dominate the island. The Nationalists' interpreted the February 28 Incident to have been the result of the Japanese legacy and Communist conspiracies, with some traditional parochialism thrown in.[143] When the Nationalists did admit that declining standards of living or misrule contributed to the crisis, they usually placed such problems in the context of errors by individual officials rather than systemic failures. This strange concoction justified the arrests and deaths of islanders, set the terms of future political discourse, and paved the way for the imposition of new government controls. The incident also revealed the shifting priorities, and fears, of the Nationalists. From retrocession until March 1947, the government's propaganda concentrated on the theme of the alleged baleful influence of Japanese rule. After the incident, it shifted to the issue of Communism. One source, for instance, specifically blamed the incident on young Communist agitators who had received Japanese military training.[144] The discussions of Communism actually reflected the Nationalists' growing panic as they faced an increasingly powerful foe on the mainland, not the reality of the incident. In this sense, the "problem" of Communism came to Taiwan in 1947, but with few actual Communists. The Nationalist's solution, an authoritarian police state, logically followed from the "discovery" of Communism on Taiwan. Ultimately, it is impossible to know to what extent the Nationalists truly believed Communism led the opposition and to what extent they used it merely as an excuse for crushing resistance to their rule.

The Nationalists began writing a history of the incident even as troops were reasserting control over the island. Although the evidence suggests troops were ordered to the island in the first few days of March, the Nationalists' public statements claimed that the demands of the resolution committee — especially to reign in the military — made the crackdown unavoidable. The Nationalists sometimes spoke of the long-term (*yuanyin*) and short-term (*jinyin*) causes of the incident. The former consisted of defects of the Taiwanese: Japanese education, unrealistic expectations of the

Nationalist government, and Communist conspiracies. The latter were material problems of the post-retrocession period: food shortages, inflation, and mistakes by government officials.[145]

Three evaluations of the incident by prominent Nationalists show slight variations on the overall themes of a pernicious colonial legacy and Communist conspiracy. Yang Lianggong, head of the Supervisory Yuan for Fujian and Taiwan, reported on the incident for the central government. According to him, the two central causes of the uprising were Taiwanese misunderstanding of the fatherland and the poisonous Japanese legacy.[146] Yang singled out for blame criminals, youth with Japanese military training, students, Japanese who remained on the island, and Communists. He also pointed to "evil politicians" and former members of wartime groups created by the Japanese — a clear reference to the Taiwanese political elite.[147] Yang wrote that some on the February 28 resolution committees had not controlled troublemakers among their fellow representatives.[148] His evaluation made clear that prominent Taiwanese had failed to situate themselves as mediators between the Nationalist regime and islanders.

Bai Chongxi, former leader of the Guangxi Clique and minister of national defense in 1947, was dispatched by Jiang to Taiwan to report on the incident.[149] His evaluation was more balanced than most; for instance, he accepted that reform was necessary. Bai's slightly more benign view of the incident and Taiwanese demands for expanded local self-government stemmed from his background in Guangxi, the fact that he personally had not been embarrassed by the short-lived takeover, and his dislike of Chen Yi. Bai saw four causes of the uprising: the effects of Japanese education, the Japanese wartime support of "dangerous" people, the economic dislocation caused by the war, and the lack of opportunities for Taiwanese to participate in politics.[150] He noted colonial education "gave Taiwan Chinese the wrong idea about their own fatherland, the government, the people, and the national army."[151] He made several suggestions that indicated he was aware of the Thirty-two Demands: first, abolish the administrator's office and make Taiwan a regular province, with elections for county magistrates and mayors; second, place more Taiwanese in government posts at the provincial level, and treat Taiwanese and mainland officials equally; third, decrease the scope of public enterprises; and finally, disband illegal groups connected to the incident, but handle everyone connected with the incident leniently.

General Ke Yuanfen, who as head of the Taiwan garrison played a leading role in the crackdown, explained his understanding of the impact of colonial rule in an essay written in 1989. Although written long after the incident, his version of events illustrates how the dual themes of the Japanese legacy and Communism dominated the Nationalists' understanding of the islanders. Ke admitted that Taiwan, thanks to fifty years of colonial rule, was far more modernized than was the mainland. The refusal of the mainlanders to recognize this, Ke also admitted, was a cause of dissatisfaction among the islanders. Also, the chaos in China after the war naturally made Taiwanese recall the stability of Japanese rule. However, Ke echoed a familiar theme in arguing that islanders had experienced half a century of slavery under colonialism. While most Taiwanese were patriotic Chinese, some had joined the Imperial Rule Assistance Society during the colonial period, or secretly gained Japanese property at the end of the war, or served as soldiers for the Japanese. He listed collaborationist gentry (*yuyong shenshi*) and landlords as the main tools of the Japanese.[152] His sweeping definition of "collaborator" encompassed the vast majority of prominent Taiwanese since almost all of them had cooperated to some degree with the colonizers, had sons drafted into the Japanese military, or had reclaimed property from the Japanese at the end of the war. General Ke also illustrated the Nationalists' approach to local self-government — namely, there were no acceptable programs outside what the government presented. He wrote that self-government was an important aspect of Taiwanese political activity, but added that the incident had been manipulated by Communists and evil politicians. In particular, he cited the Self-Government Youth Alliance (Zizhi qingnian tongmeng), a relatively minor group, as a Communist-controlled organization.[153]

In fact, the role of the Communists in the February 28 Incident was negligible, although they themselves exaggerated it, thus reinforcing the Nationalists' biases.[154] The Communists welcomed the uprising since it diverted the Nationalists' resources and provided a propaganda coup. Their version of events emphasized the anti-Nationalist nature of the incident and downplayed the significance of calls for expanded provincial autonomy. For example, a contemporary pro-Communist newspaper article declared that the islanders were glad to be part of China, but had the same grievances against Jiang's regime as did mainlanders.[155] The Communists situated the islanders' animosity toward the Nationalists within the larger struggle on the mainland, in effect placing the Taiwanese and their political activity into Mao Zedong's narrative of national awakening and social revolution. Although there is no indication of a strong Communist presence on the island through 1947, United States observers suggested that the February 28 Incident and Nationalist weakness on the mainland would lead to Communist infiltration of the island.[156]

Today there exists little evidence to back up the contention that Communists or the ideology of Communism played a major role in the crisis of February and March.[157] Communists had been brutally suppressed by the Japanese, and colonial propaganda and military training certainly did not inculcate islanders with an affinity for the international socialist movement.

Furthermore, the merchants and landowners on the resolution committees had no interest in allying with, much less promoting, a mainland-controlled party devoted to violent social revolution. The most visible Communist leader was a woman named Xie Xuehong, who organized some youth and led short-lived resistance to the Nationalists in central Taiwan.[158] The Communists later claimed that a "people's government" had been created in Taizhong on March 2, 1947, and that it had organized an armed force to fight the Nationalists.[159] Alleged representatives of "Taiwan compatriots who participated in the 'February 28' Uprising" claimed that the Communists supplied support and instruction by radio.[160] In reality, the few Communists residing on Taiwan failed to attract a large following.[161] Because many Taiwanese hoped to avoid involvement in the mainland struggle, they were not inclined to support either side in the civil war. That Communists, mainly members of the Taiwanese Communist Party founded during the Japanese era, participated in the incident does not prove that Communism as an ideology was important. In other words, the Taiwanese Communists involved in the incident were as much Taiwanese as Communist.[162]

By the end of 1947, the incident began to disappear from public discourse. As the Nationalists confronted the possibility of retreat to Taiwan, they became less interested in discussing this potentially explosive incident. For example, in a speech in December 1947, Peng Mengji, who had been accused of ordering the slaughter of thousands of islanders, stated he did not want the incident discussed further. He complained that a small group of people were "deliberately or accidentally" (*youyi wuyi*) raising the incident and that this was "regrettable."[163] In the language of post-incident Taiwan, this meant that those broaching the issue risked arrest. Having created a history of the incident, the Nationalists sought to freeze it and prevent further discussion.

Conclusion

The February 28 Incident was a watershed in Taiwan's modern political history. Decolonization essentially came to a close in early March 1947. At that point, many of the Taiwanese most likely to use the Japanese-era experience as a basis for evaluating the Nationalists and promoting expanded self-government were killed or cowed into silence. Now, the state dominated debate over the colonial legacy and thus prevented Taiwanese reference to it as justification for political reform. After the incident, the Nationalists combined limited reforms with increasing repression to solidify their rule. Subsequent changes in the political and economic spheres came from and through the state, not as a result of initiatives from the Taiwanese themselves. The events of early 1947 also marked the conclusion of debates over provincial-central relations in Republican China. The centralizers, represented by the Nationalists, had won. And in their victory, any hope for islandwide self-government, for which the Taiwanese had yearned throughout the colonial occupation, was dashed.[164]

The incident is fascinating on two levels. First are the facts, what actually happened on Taiwan in February and March of 1947. Second is the way the incident illustrates the impact of history upon politics and vice versa. Paul Cohen, in his research of the Boxer Movement in China, examines how political context influences the memory of important events. "Certainly, mythologizers start out with *an* understanding of the past," Cohen writes, "which in many (though not all) cases they may sincerely believe to be 'correct.' Their purpose, however, is not to enlarge upon or deepen this understanding. Rather, it is to draw on it to serve the political, ideological, rhetorical, and/or psychological needs of the present."[165]

Understanding the background to the incident requires examining two opposing agendas: the Nationalists' drive for centralization and the Taiwanese movement for greater autonomy. On the mainland, the Nationalists created a history to legitimize their drive for a strong central government and to attack supporters of federalism or any other system of local autonomy. On the island, the collective memory of the Japanese era shaped standards for effective governance that the Nationalists proved unable to meet, and provided a model for seeking expanded autonomy.

The interpretation of specific events such as the February 28 Incident highlights the political uses of history in modern China.[166] Cohen posits that Chinese historians have found it difficult to free themselves from mythological constructions of the Boxer Movement because they "raised, in the most dramatic way, what has very possibly been the central issue of cultural identity in the last century or so of Chinese history: the ambivalence with respect to the West."[167] Just as this ambivalence became the core issue of Chinese identity, the February 28 Incident became the most important single event in shaping the central issue of Taiwanese identity: the troubled relationship with the mainland and the mainlander-dominated government. The incident also suffered from distortion — willful and unconscious — to serve political ends. Beginning in March 1947, the mainlander-dominated government controlled the interpretation of the incident.[168] The Nationalists' understanding of history — their centralization efforts on the mainland, the colonial legacy on Taiwan, and the growing challenge of Communist power — were the lens through which they viewed the events of early 1947. The connection between history and politics on Taiwan would be further accentuated when the Nationalists began to implement their version of local self-government in 1948.

5 Nationalist Consolidation and Local Self-Government, 1948–1950

In the final years of the 1940s, the Taiwanese witnessed a great contradiction: the regime led by Jiang Jieshi crumbled on the mainland while simultaneously consolidating its hold over the island. Through a combination of authoritarianism and reform, the Nationalists achieved a higher level of control in Taiwan than they had ever enjoyed in any province on the mainland. At the same time, Taiwan became a "regular" province as the Nationalists abolished the administrator system and recruited more islanders into official posts. Many Nationalists saw the island as a laboratory where they could implement programs, such as local self-government, that they had been unable to carry out on the other side of the Taiwan Strait.

Even as the Nationalists strengthened their regime on the island, the mainland slipped from their grasp. From 1948 to 1950, Jiang's government endured military defeat, administrative collapse, and economic chaos. Taiwan faced an influx of approximately one and a half million refugees with all its attendant problems, including inflation, housing shortages, and declining morale. The refugees carried with them history, political goals, and ideology that grew out of their mainland experiences. Based on the conviction that Communism and "Chineseness" were incompatible, the Nationalists transformed the image of Taiwan from a province tainted by Japanese influence to the last redoubt preserving the essence of China. The colonial legacy receded into the background as issues, parties, and personalities from the mainland came to dominate the island's politics. Even the relatively tame opposition the Nationalists tolerated — mostly in the form of small political parties that had migrated from the mainland — tended to reflect a "Chinese" point of view. Few politicians dared to emphasize an agenda centered on the interests of islanders, such as increasing the power of provincial-level institutions or improving the quality of life.

Limited Reform, Growing Repression,
and a Cowed Elite

Nationalist policies toward Taiwan immediately after the February 28 Incident reflected a confluence of currents: a recognition of the need for reform, the arrival of new personnel, a response to outside interests and pressures, and the success of violent repression in March and April 1947. Islanders won a slightly larger public role in the provincial government, but little actual influence over policies. They were intimidated by the government's violent crackdown in response to the incident. Debates in the Provincial Consultative Assembly and articles in the press became exceedingly cautious. Discussion of issues such as the disposition of Japanese property, economic policy, and corruption also demonstrated the new atmosphere. As the civil war turned against the Nationalists, the provincial administration increasingly became absorbed in finding and crushing Communism. In order to participate in public life, Taiwanese had to prove that they were untainted by "Japanization" or by Communist ideology.

A more sympathetic government seemed in the offing in April 1947 when Nanjing announced that Dr. Wei Daoming would replace Chen Yi.[1] Wei's selection represented both a public relations gesture and a compromise between Nationalist factions. In March and April, recriminations over the February 28 Incident intensified infighting in the Nationalist government and party ranks.[2] Enemies of Chen Yi on the island and on the mainland attacked his handling of the incident.[3] The American Department of State, which was now was paying more attention to the island, expressed concern over the quality of Chen's rule and the brutality of the crackdown after the incident.[4] The United States government encouraged the Nationalists to emphasize the rhetoric, if not the reality, of reform — an extension of reform efforts on the mainland. Even the pro-Nationalist press acknowledged that Wei's selection was based in part on his diplomatic experience with the Americans.[5] Wei had been ambassador to the United States between 1942 and 1946, and was generally respected by American officials. Jiang Jieshi hoped to use Wei's contacts in Washington to gain support for his faltering government.[6] The promotion of officials with ties to the Americans set a pattern on Taiwan that would be repeated with Governor Wu Guozhen and General Sun Liren in the early 1950s — their presence "proved" the Nationalists' intentions of implementing reform even though they had little actual power.

In their governance of Taiwan, the Nationalists increasingly looked like their colonial predecessors: both promised economic development and law and order in exchange for political dominance. Wei stated that, as governor, he would strive to move Taiwan "from stability to prosperity" (*zai an-*

dingzhong qiu fanrong). Only through peace, he declared, could there be prosperity and wealth.[7] In mid-1948, a *Gonglunbao* editorial said that, compared to the mainland, Taiwan enjoyed stability (*anding*). As for prosperity (*fanrong*), however, Taiwan had made only slight progress over the past year.[8] This attention to public order and economic growth reflected the state's goals, as well as the success of the police and military in intimidating the Taiwanese.

The provincial government moved ahead with limited reforms, many of which General Bai Chongxi had suggested during this visit. Most significant was the reform of the islandwide administration. Wei took power as governor (*zhuxi*, also translated as "chairman") of a provincial government like any on the mainland; the reviled administrator system had been abolished. In theory, the powers of the governor were much less than those of his predecessor. Upon Wei's arrival in mid-May, he announced four conciliatory steps: lifting martial law, concluding the "clearing villages" campaign, removing controls over communications, and implementing currency reform to limit inflation.[9] These actions indicated not only Wei's relatively liberal views and the need to please the Americans, but also the fact that there was no chance of renewed resistance by the Taiwanese. The Nationalists also acted in two other areas to gain support. First, they improved health care. A program of compulsory vaccinations, effective quarantines, and improved sanitation brought an end to plague and cholera after 1948.[10] Second, they relaxed slightly the prohibition on speaking and publishing in Japanese. Use of the colonial language, however, remained politicized.[11]

Wei undertook several measures to increase the Taiwanese elite's participation, if not actual power, in the provincial government. Islanders held more posts in the bureaucracy and state-controlled enterprises. In May, the government established the Taiwan Provincial Government Committee (Taiwansheng zhengfu weiyuanhui) to provide advice on the administration of the island. Seven of its fourteen members were Taiwanese, six of whom had been members of assemblies at the city, county, provincial, or national level.[12] Some of the Taiwanese members had started their political career with the Nationalists on the mainland before retrocession, then served in elected assemblies on the island in 1946. They tended to be moderates who had not played leading roles in the February 28 Incident resolution committees. However, in its lack of authority, the Provincial Government Committee closely resembled the advisory assemblies established in the 1920s by the Japanese governor-general. The Provincial Government Committee had no formal power and little informal influence over the state, and its members could not name their subordinates or staff the committee.

Governor Wei never lived up to his early promise as a reformer, and in the end he made little impression on the provincial administration. He was considered an outsider with few friends in any Guomindang clique and little support from Nanjing.[13] Holdovers from the previous administration often did not cooperate with Wei.[14] Many Nationalist officials involved in the debacle of early 1947 had escaped with their reputations and influence undamaged. This weakened the governor's ability to modify earlier policies or remove personnel from their posts. For example, Chen Yi held the post of senior advisor to Jiang Jieshi, then served as governor of Zhejiang from July 1948 to February 1949.[15] The Butcher of Gaoxiong, General Peng Mengji, remained on Taiwan as a military commander under Governor Wei and his successors, Chen Cheng and Wu Guozhen (K. C. Wu). The continuing careers of these men ensured that the Nationalists would not change their evaluation of the February 28 Incident, or the resulting political repression. This also reduced islanders' trust in the provincial government and the governor.

Wei and his government also proved unable to solve many of the economic problems that had contributed to the February 28 Incident. Growing chaos and uncertainty on the mainland led the central government to devalue the Nationalist currency (fabi), which in turn destabilized Taiwan's economy.[16] Much of the damage to infrastructure caused by United States bombing in 1944 and 1945 awaited repair while the government devoted its attention and dwindling resources to fighting the Communists on the mainland. Corruption remained common, and a lack of technical experts to replace the repatriated Japanese slowed the pace of industrial recovery and kept the unemployment rate high.[17] The United Nations Reconstruction and Rehabilitation Administration, which had provided assistance with economic recovery, disbanded in December 1947, thus reducing the availability of aid.

Politically, the bloody aftermath of the February 28 Incident made clear the penalties for running afoul of the Nationalists. Despite Wei's pronouncements upon his arrival, the de facto, if no longer de jure, restrictions on freedom of speech and of the press remained. Also, arrests and trials of "reds" — as many of the critics of the government were labeled — continued.[18] The central government clearly set the tone for the island's politics. For example, upon returning from a visit to Nanjing in December 1947, Governor Wei announced that much of the criticism of the Nationalists on Taiwan came from the Communists and independence activists under the sway of the Japanese.[19]

Although there was occasional violence between Nationalists and Taiwanese, organized resistance or revolts approaching the scale of those of early 1947 did not recur. Thousands of prominent islanders had been killed or imprisoned in March, April, and May of that year. Others spent weeks after the incident on the run, hiding from the police and military. Islanders carried out delicate negotiations with the government in order to return home. Many hoped that by reporting to civilian officials they could avoid arrest and the imprisonment or execution that often followed. Taiwanese accepted publicly the Nationalists' interpretation that the incident and demands for reform were a rebellion, but they downplayed their personal role in any illegal activities. They engaged in *zixin* (turning over a new leaf, or literally "self-new," connoting admitting errors and making a fresh start) by explaining that their activities were neither pro-Communist nor anti-Nationalist. The courts found some islanders legally guilty but not at fault—an ambiguous verdict that kept the elite off balance. For example, in at least one case the courts described the accused as a blind follower (*mangcong*) who had been forced to take part in (*bei po canjia*) the February 28 Incident.[20] The Nationalists were determined to prevent a repeat of early 1947. The police and military used mass detentions, primarily of educated youth, in early 1948 to prevent protests or commemorations of the incident.[21]

The June 1947 session of the Provincial Consultative Assembly illustrated the new political climate. Just over half of the thirty members attended; others were dead, under arrest, or afraid to appear in public.[22] In contrast to the contentious sessions of 1946, the meetings of 1947 were subdued and attracted little public interest.[23] A few islanders cautiously attempted to hold the government to its earlier promises. For example, assembly member Han Shiquan wanted to know when Taiwanese arrested in March would be released. He complained that local officials had not followed the central government's directive to act leniently.[24] However, in general criticism of the government was muted and requests for change were made with much less vigor than before the incident.[25] In July 1948, an editorial stated that, in order to be taken seriously, members of the Provincial Consultative Assembly needed to avoid empty talk and raising issues that were impossible to solve.[26] Now, islanders tended to focus on individual officials and their actions, not on "big" issues such as the structural defects of Nationalist rule or the island's place in the Republic of China. For example, assemblymen attacked the head of the Transportation Bureau and his subordinates for fostering an atmosphere of corruption and exclusion of Taiwanese "one hundred times worse than the plague."[27] The solution the assemblymen offered, however, was the removal of specific officials, not systemic reform.

The elite was hampered not only by its weakness vis-à-vis the state, but also by its lack of unity. For example, although Taiwanese remained concerned about the role of mainlanders and the government in the island's economy, they could not agree on what to do about it. They complained that, for various "mysterious" (*mo ming qi miao*) reasons, the government sold the island's products at low prices to mainland buyers. They also urged that public enterprises, other than mines with direct military importance, be privatized.[28] The press noted some progress in increasing Taiwanese investment in the match and chemical industries, but pointed out that printing companies had been sold to mainlanders.[29] On the other hand, Li Wanju, vice chairman of the Provincial Consultative Assembly and one of Taiwan's most prominent non-Guomindang political figures, pointed out that the Taiwanese lacked the capital to purchase these state enterprises. Thus, selling major companies like the Taiwan Sugar Corporation to private investors would only increase the economic influence of outsiders.[30]

One newspaper editorial hinted at the atmosphere after the February 28 Incident, writing that disputes over the disposition of Japanese property had been transformed from a hot war (*re zhan*) to a cold war (*leng zhan*). Though less was said in public, people still submitted requests for assistance in recovering property to the city and provincial assemblies, while a special committee established to sort out these claims made little progress.[31] Here, too, the Taiwanese were divided over what course to follow. Some islanders, and many mainlanders, felt those who had obtained Japanese property immediately after the war were speculators and those who held on to such property were politically connected or simply corrupt.[32] For example, Han Shiquan wrote that some islanders pressured him to request that October 15, 1945 be the cut-off date for the transfer of Japanese property. He noted, however, that many law-abiding islanders had missed an opportunity for great profit because they had not purchased property at war's end. Thus, he supported the August 15, 1945 deadline.[33] In early December 1948, the Taiwan High Court upheld an earlier ruling by a Tainan court invalidating all transfers of Japanese property made after August 15.[34] This meant that property sold by the Japanese to Taiwanese after the surrender announcement belonged to the Nationalist government.

Mainland Collapse and Taiwan Consolidation

After mid-1948, trends that began in the wake of the February 28 Incident — mainland domination over the island's politics, limited top-down reform, and the growing police state — accelerated because of events across the Taiwan Strait. Reeling from military defeat, inflation and economic instability, administrative chaos, and dissipating morale, the Nationalists lurched toward collapse on the mainland.[35] As in early 1947, the effects of this crisis spread immediately to Taiwan. Over 1.5 million refugees poured into the island during 1949 and the first half of 1950, exacerbating inflation, crime, unemployment, and housing shortages. Not only the quantity, but also the quality of refugees became an issue. Islanders complained that "Taiwan was number three" (*Taiwan di san*), meaning that it was the third most desirable destination. The wealthiest and most influential refugees, so the Taiwanese claimed, moved to the United States; those a step down in wealth and power went to Hong Kong.[36] Editorials stated the island needed "high quality refugees" (*gaodeng nanmin*) to contribute to Taiwan's political and economic development.[37]

Taiwanese novelist Wu Zhuoliu described the end of the 1940s as a chaotic and phantasmagoric time.[38] Doctor, writer, and political activist Wu Xinrong, exemplifying the hopelessness felt by many islanders, wrote that his ideology had become "three no-ism" (*san bu zhuyi*) — do not go out, do not ask about worldly affairs, and do not try to understand the logic of life.[39] The rampant inflation of the late 1940s devastated Taiwan. The order of the day became "spend money as soon as you get it" (*you qian chu qian*).[40] Prices quadrupled for some commodities between September and October of 1948. Even the Nationalist press had to admit that the chaos on the mainland led to "panic purchases" of food.[41] Mainlanders for their part blamed islanders for some of these problems, grumbling that Taiwanese speculators were making a great deal of money from the new arrivals.[42]

Other than a few merchants, everyone on the island — Taiwanese and mainland immigrants alike — suffered in the late 1940s. Taiwan was isolated from mainland markets and other, potential markets, such as Japan, had not recovered from the war.[43] Another problem was skyrocketing housing prices as wealthy mainlanders fled to the island.[44] Some Taiwanese even moved from Taibei back to their less expensive hometowns or villages.[45] During the summer of 1948, the Nationalists made their first serious attempts to restore economic stability to Taiwan, but they met with only limited success. For instance, the authorities strengthened regulations against hoarding grain, and in October stopped exporting food and other commodities from the island in order to ease shortages and relieve inflation.[46]

By early 1948 Governor Wei, by all accounts an ambitious man, had become frustrated by his lack of real power and inability to replace officials left over from the Chen Yi administration. For example, he told the Americans he wanted to remove General Peng Mengji, who was forging a close relationship with Jiang Jieshi's son, Jiang Jingguo. The American consul general suggested to his superiors that the United States make explicit its support for Wei.[47] The governor came into conflict with Nanjing over economic policy, particularly concerning his attempts to limit the impact of the mainland's problems on the island. For example, Wei requested permission to detach Taiwan's currency from China's national currency, then called the Gold Yuan, but the central government refused.[48]

Tensions increased throughout 1948. In late November Wei, bitter because of Nanjing's lukewarm support, discussed with American officials the possibility of breaking completely from the mainland. Diplomats reported that "Wei made [an] extraordinary proposal or feeler. . . . He suggested that Taiwan be severed from the mainland politically, develop its own economy, and welcome American investment and loans."[49] In early December 1948 American diplomats discussed the advisability of Wei and American-trained General Sun Liren establishing their own regime on Taiwan.[50] American interest in this option was tempered by doubts about Wei's ability to carry it out. Leaders in Washington gave him little chance of success, and the Department of State ordered officials in Taibei not to discuss with Wei the possibility of forming a government independent of Jiang.[51] Implicit in all this was the assumption that the Taiwanese would be ruled by a mainlander-controlled government made up of Nationalists (or renegade Nationalists).

In a testament to its political impotence, the provincial elite stood on the sidelines even as instability again threatened the island's ties with the mainland. In the late 1940s, rumors abounded about possible foreign intervention on the island in collusion with mainlanders or Taiwanese. Scenarios included Taiwanese independence with United States support, a United Nations trusteeship, or even the return of the Japanese.[52] As early as August 1947, Special Envoy to China General Albert Wedemeyer reported to the secretary of state: "There were indications that Formosans would be receptive toward the United States guardianship and United Nations trusteeship. They fear that the Central Government contemplates bleeding their island to support the tottering and corrupt Nanking machine and I think their fears are well-founded."[53] Officials in the Department of State maintained discreet contact with Taiwanese who wished to make their island independent from China by overthrowing the mainland-dominated government.[54] Yet the possibility of independence depended on events across the strait, not on the island itself. In December 1947 American officials considered supporting an independent Taiwan only if the Nationalist government collapsed on the mainland and could not control the island.[55]

Wei's discussions with the Americans, fears of Taiwanese separatism, and the disintegration of the Nationalists on the mainland drew Jiang Jieshi's personal attention to the island. In December 1948, Jiang suddenly announced the removal of Governor Wei and, on January 5, 1949 replaced him with General Chen Cheng, who was also appointed commander of the Garrison Command and chairman of the Guomindang Provincial Committee.[56] Chen had come to the island in late 1948, supposedly to recuperate from an illness, but rumors were rife that his true intention was to reconnoiter the island as a final redoubt for the Nationalists.[57] Chen, sometimes called Jiang's "trump card" from his close connection to the Generalissimo, became an extremely important figure in the early history of the Republic of China on Taiwan.[58] He further consolidated Nationalist rule, helped build an effective police state, prepared for Jiang's arrival, began to implement a program of local self-government, and oversaw rent reduction and land reform. Later, he served as premier and vice president.[59] In private, Taiwanese complained about his wide-ranging powers over state, military, and party organizations, and often compared him to the Japanese governors-general.[60]

In light of the apparent hopelessness of Jiang's regime, the Americans decided to make several approaches to Chen Cheng that bypassed the central government. In January 1949, the Department of State reported to the National Security Council that the main obstacle to Chen stabilizing the provincial government was the interference of the Generalissimo.[61] As a result, in March American officials were instructed to discuss the possibility of aid "designed to assist development [of a] viable, self-supporting, economy [on] Formosa."[62] Contact was to be with Chen Cheng, not representatives of the crumbling central government or the Taiwanese.[63]

Despite American meddling, the island remained under Jiang's control.[64] Chen would not or could not limit the number of soldiers and bureaucrats fleeing the mainland.[65] Jiang was confident enough of his power to replace Chen and install a relative liberal in Taiwan's highest provincial post. With this change, Jiang hoped to shore up American support, as he had done with Wei Daoming's appointment in 1947. Former mayor of Shanghai Wu Guozhen (K. C. Wu) replaced Chen as governor on December 21, 1949, while Chen became director of military affairs for southeast China. The new governor proved more popular, but ultimately much less powerful, than his immediate predecessor.[66] Wu, like Wei, encountered factionalism and hostility within the provincial government and had little influence over policy. Furthermore, and unlike Chen Cheng, Wu held no high-ranking posts in the military or party and lacked influence over much of the government bureaucracy.[67]

Three interrelated factors kept Taiwanese separatists and the Americans from cooperating. First, many Americans saw Jiang Jieshi as the only figure with any chance of preserving a unified, non-Communist China. In effect, they accepted and approved of the Nationalists' political agenda for China both before and after the regime's defeat on the mainland. For example, in mid-1948, an American official in Nanjing wrote that "it may conceivably get so bad that the Gimo may, by one means or another, be removed from the scene. Yet the Gimo seems to be the only element holding this vast country together, and should he go there would be a very strong chance that we would see a return to regionalism, making the pickings much more easy for the Communists."[68] Even as the Nationalists collapsed on the mainland, they continued to enjoy the support of strongly anti-Communist politicians and publicists in the United States. Most Americans accepted, or simply did not address, the Nationalists' political agenda for Taiwan. Second, the United States felt publicly obliged to uphold the status of Taiwan as a territory returned to its rightful ruler after World War II.[69] For example, the Central

Intelligence Agency stated that although technically Taiwan's fate was not final until a peace treaty was signed with Japan, the Cairo and Potsdam Declarations made independence unlikely.[70] The United States was not eager to become embroiled in an issue of China's territorial integrity — a problem that could only invite comparisons to the era of unequal treaties.[71] Third, officials in the Department of State described the Taiwanese as "politically immature" and unlikely to overthrow the Nationalists.[72] Islanders who openly favored independence tended to be young (age fifty or less), and commanded little influence on the island through social networks or business enterprises. Islanders also had more specific "defects." American military intelligence officials in Tokyo revealed that many Taiwanese in Japan had entered that country illegally and that "the activities of the League [Formosan League for Reemancipation, a small pro-independence group based in Tokyo] in Japan are financed by large-scale penicillin smuggling."[73] United States leaders never simultaneously found the will and the opportunity to remove Jiang, much less build a viable alternative to him among the Taiwanese.[74]

The "Nationalization" of Taiwan

With the influx of refugees having little interest in or knowledge of Taiwan, and with the imposition of government policies designed to strengthen authoritarian rule, the themes, organizations, and personalities of mainland politics came to dominate the island. Wielding slogans such as *kang Ri kao shan, kang luan kao hai* (To resist the Japanese, rely on the mountains; to resist chaos, rely on the sea) the Nationalists portrayed the island as a vital base for a great national crusade. Building on images of Ming resistance to the Qing and the more recent struggle against the Japanese, they cast the conflict with the Communists in nationalist terms. Jiang's regime portrayed itself as engaged in a life-and-death struggle against an alien ideology, Communism, promoted by foreigners, the Soviets. The attempt to make Taiwan an idealized version of Republican China influenced the composition of elected assemblies and political parties. As the Nationalists built the Chinese state on Taiwan they could not create on the mainland, they remained largely oblivious to the islanders' political aspirations.

The Nationalists brought the "problem" of Communism to the island, despite the absence of Communists. Although they had begun to regularize the repression of Taiwanese political activity in the name of fighting Communism during Wei Daoming's tenure, the process expanded greatly under Chen Cheng and Wu Guozhen. The number of arrests and executions increased through 1949 and 1950, marking the start of what became known as the White Terror.[75] The Nationalists implemented a variety of measures that had little impact on the war-torn mainland but were very important on Taiwan.[76] For instance, in April 1948, the central government announced the "Temporary Provisions for the Period of Mobilization for the Suppression of Rebellion." This essentially suspended the constitution and gave the president dictatorial powers. Fearing mainland refugees were leftists influenced by the Communists, if not actual underground members of the party itself, the police paid a great deal of attention to issuing and inspecting the identity cards of Taiwanese and refugees.[77] Beginning on May 20, 1949, the island was placed under martial law. In June, a surprise nighttime census was undertaken, leading to the arrest of many recent arrivals wanted on the mainland for suspicion of ties to the Communists.

The Nationalists expanded the scope of what was considered a "crime" to include a wide variety of ill-defined activities, such as "spreading rumors, and propagandizing for bandits." Some teachers who had come to the island immediately after retrocession to teach Mandarin Chinese had discussed the conflict between the Nationalists and Communists — this led to the arrest of them and their Taiwanese students in 1949 and 1950.[78] The Taiwanese, already frightened by the results of February 28, were not so much the target of Nationalist policies, but the by-product of political and military conflict on the mainland. A Taiwanese dissident who spent years in prison, Li Zhenzhou, later wrote that propaganda about crushing the "Communist bandits" and recovering the mainland had little connection to the Taiwanese. Rather, these themes represented a way to boost the morale of mainlanders who had left families and hometowns behind.[79]

The combination of anti-Communist ideology and the White Terror became the overriding political problem for islanders. Wu Zhuoliu wrote later, "The so-called 'red' question was a huge problem after retrocession and a cause of calamity for islanders. Actually, most of the 'reds' had fled early on, and those wearing the 'red' hat were not Communists, but opponents of government policies."[80] The shortage of actual Communists, however, did not deter the government from arrests and intimidation. Li Zhenzhou wrote that the Nationalists were a minority who could rule only by force. To the police and military, "it was worth it if there was one conspirator or unsatisfied element (buman fenzi) among the one hundred, one thousand, or even ten thousand they grabbed."[81] The drive to supervise and punish became systematized and bureaucratized, and spread to reach almost all islanders, but particularly intellectuals. Public security personnel took posts in workplaces and schools to report on political views and activities. All organizations had to register with and obtain the approval of the government. Anti-Communist hysteria reached absurd heights. Wu Zhuoliu was even cautioned about using red on the cover of his books.[82]

There existed a gray area between legal and illegal activity that the Nationalists interpreted according to the political climate of the moment. For example, the government outlawed publications such as *Das Kapital*, but many of the materials deemed illegal in 1949 had been tolerated in 1946, during the peace talks between Nationalists and Communists. Perhaps the most effective tool to govern the Taiwanese was not tangible, such as written laws or squads of police, but the fear caused by uncertainty and ambiguity. An editorial entitled "Opposing the Government and Commenting on Politics" discussed the scope of tolerable debate. "Opposing" threatened the existence of the nation's people, and equated to support for the Communists or that which benefited them. "Commenting," done in the interest of the people, merely pointed out errors of the government.[83] The police and military determined the difference between opposing and commenting. Some Taiwanese were charged with "financing bandits" (*zifei*), a crime which one prisoner later related was the result of a small loan to a man who was later executed as a Communist.[84] Anti-Communist laws were used to suppress a wide range of activities. One particularly well-known case occurred in 1949. Yang Da, a writer and leftist political activist under the Japanese and the Nationalists, wrote an editorial promoting better relations between islanders and mainlanders and pointing out deficiencies in the Nationalist administration. As part of his call for reconciliation, he urged the release of those arrested after the February 28 Incident. For this, in April 1949 he was sentenced to twelve years in jail.[85]

Aside from intimidating the population, the Nationalists effectively "tamed" institutions such as the Taiwan Provincial Consultative Assembly. After the February 28 Incident, an increasing percentage of the assembly members were Half-Mountain people, Taiwanese whose political careers were tied to the Nationalists, not the Japanese-era movement for expanded self-government on the island. The assemblies at all levels remained little more than forums for questioning government officials and presenting petitions.[86] The Nationalists changed the nature of the Consultative Assembly by adding six appointed representatives in December 1947. This measure, which islanders had never requested, allowed the China Youth Party (Zhongguo qingniandang) and the Democratic Socialist Party (Minzhu shehuidang) each to appoint three representatives.[87] Both of these parties were part of the mainland's Third Force of small parties favoring liberal democratic reforms for China, and had little popularity on Taiwan. Most of the six additional representatives were Taiwanese, but they had been educated or had lived on the mainland.[88] In March 1948, the government added a special representative for aborigines. The Nationalists organized supplementary elections in 1948 to replace assembly members who had died or resigned for other posts. Each of these changes diluted the influence of prominent Taiwanese leaders from the colonial era.

Educational and cultural institutions also reflected the Nationalists' agenda. The government placed mainlanders, such as the eminent scholar Fu Sinian, in leadership positions at Taiwan's colleges and universities.[89] Although some of these educators, like members of the Democratic Socialist and China Youth Parties, were not supporters of the Nationalists, their criticism of Jiang's regime was in the context of democracy for China, not specific problems on Taiwan or the relationship between the province and the central government. The government closely supervised Taiwan's schools and colleges and did not hesitate to arrest "subversive" university students.[90] In the realm of publishing also, political discussions became dominated by mainlanders and the issues that interested them. Almost all of Taiwan's pre-February 28 publications disappeared. New magazines and newspapers took their place, but these were increasingly managed by mainlanders as private enterprises, or by the government, military, or Guomindang.[91] In transforming the character of newspapers and magazines on the island, as important as overt censorship were harassment, onerous regulations, and the arrival of mainlanders with financial resources. The most important themes now became anti-Communism and recapturing the mainland, not the governance of Taiwan.

The Nationalists also employed scholarship to show how the island was an integral part of China, politically and culturally. Toward this end, the provincial government established the Taiwan Provincial Gazetteer Office (Taiwansheng tongzhiguan) in 1948.[92] A committee of mainlanders and prominent Taiwanese who had weathered the storm of arrests and intimidation managed the office. The first issue of their journal made clear that the organization and its publications were established to remedy the alleged distortions of history created by the island's former colonial masters.[93] The island's settlement by Han Chinese, Zheng Chenggong's resistance to the Manchus in the late 1600s, Taiwanese resistance to Japanese colonialism, and the Nationalists' attempts to restore Chinese rule represented the safest (and most common) subjects of historical inquiry. These topics dealt with Taiwan's contribution to the Chinese nation. Running through many of the essays published by the Provincial Gazetteer Office was the assumption that the interests of the Chinese nation, the Nationalist state, and the province of Taiwan were one and the same.

To Jiang Jieshi and the non-Communist world, Taiwan became synonymous with China as provincial and national administrations increasingly overlapped. As early as 1947, visits by top central government officials began, marking the province's rising profile on the national scene. On December 30, 1948 American officials in Nanjing reported that Jiang Jieshi's personal files were being secretly moved to Taiwan, indicating the Generalissimo's eventual plans.[94] Some magazines even joked that the island was becoming the "Switzerland of the East," a safe haven for prominent Nationalists.[95] In the face of military defeat, economic collapse, and social chaos, on January 21, 1949, Jiang resigned as president.[96] He left the mainland debacle to Vice-President-turned-Acting-President Li Zongren. After "resting" for three months in his home province of Zhejiang, Jiang spent the next nine months in Taibei and Tainan, with short visits to Guangzhou, Chongqing, Manila, and Seoul.[97] In reality, he retained his influence through personal ties to military commanders, the loyalty of Guomindang members, and control of financial resources. Jiang's reconsolidation of power and the career of his son, Jiang Jingguo, became closely intertwined on Taiwan.[98] In late 1949 Jiang entrusted his son to transfer the government's gold reserves to the island.[99]

Taiwan's relatively small size appeared well suited to the Generalissimo's highly personal style of leadership. The creation of a Political Action Committee (Zhengzhi xingdong weiyuanhui, eventually renamed the National Security Council) in July 1949 was the first step in rebuilding his authority. The committee included Jiang Jingguo, Peng Mengji, and others close to Jiang, but no allies of Acting President Li Zongren. It was formally inaugurated on August 20 at a meeting on Yuan Shan, just north of Taibei.[100] This small group gave Jiang and his son close control over the wide range of secret police and intelligence services on the island, which furthered their goal of "nationalizing" the province. In December 1949, the Nationalist government moved formally to the island. After about thirteen months of "retirement," Jiang resumed the presidency on March 1, 1950. He reestablished his power over the central government with relative ease. Like many of Jiang's non-Communist rivals, Li Zongren ended up in the United States. By the time the Korean War began in June 1950, Jiang also held the posts of director general (*zongcai*) of the Guomindang and commander-in-chief of the armed forces, giving him the top positions in the state, party, and military.[101] That his personal purview, the Republic of China, and Taiwan were one and the same shaped politics on the island for the next three decades.[102]

Local Self-Government for China on Taiwan

The implementation of local self-government demonstrates how a national mission came to dominate the island's provincial politics. After the February 28 Incident, the Nationalists continued to reject provincial autonomy, whether defined as federalism or as part of local self-government, but began to promote limited reform at the city, town, and county levels.[103] This did not mean, however, that Taiwanese could now question their ties to the nation of China or those who claimed to represent it. Instead, local self-government marked the completion of state-building that could not be accomplished on the other side of the strait. Publicly, the Nationalists set forth the main motivations for implementing local self-government: to stabilize Taiwan as a base for recapturing the mainland, to fulfill Sun Zhongshan's teachings by creating a model Three Principles of the People province, and to promote economic development.[104] Above all, local self-government became an aid to the government in transforming islanders into an idealized version of Chinese citizens who would serve the nation and its protector, the Nationalist government.

The Nationalists simultaneously created rules to manage political activity and made clear that they would ignore those rules when they saw fit. The local self-government system for Taiwan grew out of the 1947 constitution, which mandated that the central government prepare guidelines for self-government in the provinces. Guidelines were duly adopted in 1948, after which each province was free to adopt local self-government laws for itself and the counties under its jurisdiction.[105] Nonetheless, the central government under Jiang Jieshi, by invoking the Temporary Provisions or martial law, could override any legislation on local self-government.

The Nationalists enlisted several official and quasi-private groups to promote their program of local self-government. Preparatory discussions and propaganda began in 1948. In July the Taiwan Provincial Local Self-Government Association (Taiwansheng difang zizhi xiehui) was created under government auspices. Chaired by Weng Qian, deputy chief of the Civil Administration Office (Minzhengting), it included government officials and provincial leaders of the Guomindang, as well as the commander of the Taiwan garrison. Over the summer, the government established branch offices throughout the island. The pace of preparation for reform accelerated in 1949. Based on Governor Chen Cheng's slogan of "the people are supreme, the people's livelihood comes first" (*renmin zhi shang, minsheng di yi*), local self-government and economic reconstruction were to be the top priorities of his administration.[106]

Another important organization was the Taiwan Provincial Local Self-Government Research Society (Taiwansheng difang zizhi yanjiuhui). This group included local elected leaders and experts from the government. Seven of its twenty-nine members were mainlanders, including the chairman, Hebei-born Zhang Lisheng, who had been minister of the interior and a Guomindang functionary on the mainland.[107] The society concluded its work in December, when it presented a blueprint for local self-government on the island.[108] The Chinese Local Self-Government Study Society, led by the influential Li Zonghuang, also helped shape policies on the mainland and the island. In 1949, he revived the Study Society after moving to Taibei.[109]

Justifying Nationalist authority and implementing specific policies such as local self-government required that Taiwan fit into the history of political development in Republican China. Because the Nationalists wanted Taiwan to represent all of China, Zhang Lisheng, Li Zonghuang, and Weng Qian each discussed local self-government as though it were being implemented throughout the nation, not simply in its smallest, and perhaps least typical, province. For example, part of Li's justification for local self-government on the island grew from his periodization of history on the mainland. First, he wrote, was the dark period (*hei'an shiqi*), when an autocratic monarchy prevented the establishment of democracy. During this time the people's knowledge was undeveloped, politics was corrupt, and local strongmen powerful. This lasted until the 1920s, when Sun Zhongshan began to publish his writings on local self-government, most importantly the General Outline for National Reconstruction. This marked the germinal stage (*mengya shiqi*). Although the Nationalists had unified the country, internal revolts and external pressure prevented them from implementing local self-government. Finally came the period of maturity (*chengzhang shiqi*), which began in 1938 when the Provisional National Assembly (Linshi quanguo daibiao dahui) discussed plans for self-government at the county level in preparation for constitutional rule.[110] That the laws and rules of prewar China had limited relevance to Taiwan was of no interest to Nationalist experts, who were determined to create a history of inevitable progress toward their program of local self-government. To Li, reform on Taiwan would mark the culmination of almost fifty years of struggle against warlords, Communists, and imperialists.

Nationalists involved with local self-government emphasized their long and arduous struggle to regain the island for China, once again underlining the connection between specific policies and national loyalty. They also sought to strengthen the perception of a historical bond between Republican China and Taiwan, thus further legitimizing Nationalist state-building. The lack of a history of concrete actions between 1895 and 1945 to remove the Japanese did not deter mainlanders from discussing the Nationalists' efforts. Li Zonghuang wrote that when the Xing Zhong hui (Revive China Society), a precursor to the Guomindang, was formed in 1894, Sun Zhongshan made one of its goals the restoration of Chinese sovereignty over the island.[111] Later, Jiang Jieshi continued this national mission. In the words of Wu Tiecheng, secretary-general of the Guomindang, "Taiwan's restoration was the jewel of fifty years of Guomindang-led national revolution, the Chinese people's eight-year war of resistance [against Japan], and the blood and sacrifice of patriotic martyrs from Taiwan's restoration movement."[112]

In the face of Communist victory, Taiwan became the base for national preservation and a test case for policies the Nationalists had been unable or unwilling to implement on the mainland. The Nationalists refashioned Taiwan's image from what it had been in the immediate post-retrocession period, namely a province to be rescued by the mainland and a land populated by newly freed slaves of colonialism. Officials were now determined to prove that the Nationalists' program of local self-government was both authentic — "Chinese" — and practical — viable on the island. For example, Li Zonghuang declared that the Nationalists' system of self-government grew out of Chinese history and society, and was completely unlike the earlier Japanese assemblies.[113] He wrote that the Taiwanese, as descendants of the Yellow Emperor, were rich in the ideas of nationalism and self-government.[114] Since retrocession, he added, islanders had been eager to be part of Sun's grand scheme for local self-government.[115] Li claimed that local self-government was a vital instrument for restoring the Chinese people and resisting outside aggression.[116] Ironically, now that mainlanders had only one province to work with, they appeared to accept tacitly, though they could never acknowledge publicly, a key aspect of the ideology of federalism — that China could be strengthened from the provincial level upward. Li portrayed building a prosperous Taiwan as advanced preparation (*zhangben*) for building a new China.[117] Zhang Lisheng also repeated the new mantra of Taiwan as a fortress for the restoration of "our" race, a conservative and patriotic people.[118]

In reality, however, local self-government was to be built from the top down, and was to be a privilege to be earned by meeting the central government's standards. Various Nationalist experts had slightly different interpretations of the conditions necessary for reform. Weng Qian, chairman of the Taiwan Provincial Local Self-Government Association, thought the island had met the preconditions for reforms set forth in the 1920s by Sun Zhongshan: public order, a household census, widespread education, and convenient transportation.[119] Some of these strengths, which the Taiwanese had touted before the February 28 Incident in order to justify their own version of expanded local self-government, stemmed directly from colonial policies. However, the Nationalists so dominated Taiwan that they could raise certain aspects of Japanese rule without fearing questions about their legitimacy: it was the Taiwanese who could not discuss the issue freely. Li Zonghuang divided the prerequisites for limited local autonomy into two main categories: security and finance. The former did not present a problem, he wrote, since Taiwan was well ordered as a result of Japanese rule. In the realm of finance, the goal was self-sufficiency (*zigei zizu*) for local self-government organs. Here, various administrative levels on Taiwan had not prepared themselves sufficiently, since counties, cities, and towns still relied on funds from the central government.[120] In reality, this did not present a barrier to the Nationalists' program because financial dependence was a fundamental way the central government maintained its hold over lower administrative levels.

Accepting that Taiwan was worthy of China's system of local self-government, what exactly would the new system entail? Given the Nationalists' view of the reforms as a tool to accomplish central government tasks at the local level, local self-government certainly did not represent an invitation for local initiative. To lay out the Nationalists' position, Li Zonghuang asked, then answered, the key questions concerning local self-government. Local governments would manage, not govern.

What is the definition of local self-government?

Local self-government is local people, according to laws and regulations of the nation, managing (*guanli*) local affairs.[121]

What is the goal of local self-government?

The goal of local self-government is the realization of a new China, based on the Three Principles of the People; that is, to become rich, strong, healthy, and content (*fu, qiang, kang, le*).

What is the essence of local self-government?

To be not only a political unit, but also an economic unit. In other words, the essence of local self-government is the combination of politics and economics.

What is the most important component of local self-government?

Economics is the most important part of local self-government: seven of the . . . fourteen tasks [of local government] focus on economic reconstruction.[122]

Other Nationalists agreed that local self-government included economic as well as political aspects: Government by the people (*minzhi*) represented a way to support the people (*yangmin*) in vital areas such as food, clothing, housing, education, and recreation.[123] In fact, the Nationalists consistently encouraged islanders to engage in economic pursuits while stifling their political activity. The most meaningful reforms would be in the realm of material development, land reform, for example.

The Nationalists' local self-government would not modify the relationship between the province and the central government. The province would supervise (*jiandu*) and direct (*zhidao*) the promotion of local self-government in each county.[124] But this reform, the tightly controlled press stressed, must in no way weaken the island's links to the central government.[125] Zhang Lisheng emphasized that Sun Zhongshan had made the county the unit of local self-government in his 1924 General Outline for National Reconstruction and that this had been codified in the 1947 constitution. Zhang reflected a common belief of the Nationalists: if given autonomy, provinces could not be trusted to remain loyal to the central government. He attacked the federal system, connecting it to plots to keep China weak and divided.

Zhang argued that making the county the unit of local self-government, while giving the province the right to supervise, was the best way to prevent the breakdown of national order as had happened early in the Republican period.[126] Li Zonghuang wrote in the mid-1950s that local self-government (*difang zizhi*) should not be confused with local sovereignty (*difang zizhu*). Zizhu was a form of separatism tied to warlords and federalism, and thus forever tainted.[127]

Local Self-Government and the Taiwanese

Throughout the discussions and implementation of local self-government, Taiwanese remained on the defensive. Just as advocates of federalism and provincial self-government on the mainland early in the century had to disassociate themselves from warlords and traditional rural elites, islanders felt the need to avoid unwanted connection with independence activists and the Japanese legacy, as well as with student protesters and Communist-front groups. By portraying provincial self-government, federalism, and independence as identical, the Nationalists made county-level reform the only acceptable choice. For example, the indictment of Gu Zhenfu and four others in July 1947 for their role in the short-lived independence movement immediately after Japan's surrender used the terms independence (*duli*) and self-government (zizhi) interchangeably.[128] Islanders had to be on guard to avoid having their own aspirations for greater local autonomy anathematized in this way. Li Zonghuang pointed out that "end the civil war, remove American troops, and implement democratic self-government" were themes bandied about by leftist students.[129] Self-government became further tainted when it was tied to Xie Xuehong, the communist leader who had led the short-lived armed resistance to the Nationalists in central Taiwan after February 28. After fleeing the island in May, Xie helped established the Taiwan Democratic Self-Government League in December 1947 in Hong Kong, and served as its chair. This organization did not represent the Communists' ultimate views on local self-government, but rather was an attempt to build a united front against Jiang Jieshi.

Local self-government and the colonial legacy remained connected — by legitimizing the Nationalists' reforms and limited autonomy. In 1946 and 1947, the Nationalists had tended to emphasize the differences between Taiwan and China in order to explain the "defects" of islanders and justify limits on local self-government. From 1948 onward, the government showed a greater willingness to accentuate the "Chineseness" of islanders, even during the colonial era. The government increasingly used the image of resistance to the Japanese as a device to link the island and the mainland, making Taiwan's experience a subset of Chinese political history. The Japanese legacy represented little threat to Nationalist legitimacy because no Taiwanese dared use it to criticize the government.

The Nationalists seemed unable to conceive of provincial autonomy without making the leap to nationalism. Just as many mainlanders had feared provincial self-government because they connected it with independence, now they decided that the advocacy of greater islandwide autonomy during the colonial era represented a Chinese nationalist movement designed to remove the Japanese. For example, Li Zonghuang emphasized that Taiwan had no self-government under the Japanese and that local assemblies were simply items for the use of the Japanese emperor (*yuyongpin*). He wrote that the Taiwanese possessed a Chinese national consciousness and spirit of seeking self-government despite colonial domination. He made Taiwanese political activity and organizations part of the mainland's anti-Japanese struggle, contending that islanders had resisted throughout fifty years of slavery. The cruel lesson of colonialism made Taiwanese especially receptive to local self-government under the Nationalists.[130] However, Li's interpretation had a major problem: the Taiwanese drive for expanded self-government was a reformist movement built around the acceptance of Japanese rule, not Chinese nationalism. Both the Nationalists and the Taiwanese, however, shared an interest in "forgetting" the latter's cooperation with the Japanese.

The Nationalists did not present a completely united front when discussing local self-government in the context of Japanese rule. Taiwan's colonial experience still served on occasion as a way to attack the island's elite and to justify the central government's domination of the discussion and content of reform. Some pro-Nationalist publications suggested that implementing local self-government was difficult because prominent Taiwanese did not really represent the island's people. One author pointed out that the majority of Taiwan's elected representatives were landlords or merchants, with little in common with their fellow islanders. The structure of the island's society stemmed from the colonial administration, which was defined as "feudal." Because landlords had dominated the movement for greater self-government on the island, further political training and education were needed.[131] Other mainland writers stated that Taiwan was still in the germinal stage of development for local self-government. This was blamed on the Japanese, who had prevented the Taiwanese from gaining political experience.[132] These essays made clear the Nationalists could still interpret the colonial legacy in a way that was hazardous to islanders.

The Taiwanese elite had no choice but to conform to the terms of political discourse set by the Nationalists. Islanders emphasized that their vision of local self-government in no way supported independence, and that their proposals fit with the currents of Chinese political development. For example, in 1948 the Taiwan delegation to the National Assembly requested the rapid implementation of reform. At the same time, the delegation was careful to deny it was seeking a United Nations mandate to replace Nationalist rule.[133] Taiwanese political leaders, including many in the Provincial Assembly, sent a petition to Jiang Jieshi upon his election as president in April 1948 asking for greater local self-government, but stressing that their intentions were patriotic: the self-government they sought was completely in accord with the constitution, it was not an attempt to leave the nation (*tuoli guojia*). Their motivation for supporting local self-government, they explained, was to participate in the nation's politics, contribute to life on Taiwan, and help China become rich, strong, healthy, and happy. They were not requesting anything like what the Philippines or Burma enjoyed, nor were they seeking a system of assemblies similar to those that had existed under colonialism.[134]

Most Taiwanese political leaders accepted the Nationalists' attempt to connect Taiwan to mainland politics, even as they pushed carefully for reform. Li Wanju, vice chairman of the Provincial Consultative Assembly and a leader of the China Youth Party, wrote that a relatively high level of self-government was an effective way to fight the Nationalists' greatest enemy, the Communists. He stated that China should not suffer the divisiveness of federalism nor the autocracy of a highly centralized system. In particular, power concentrated in the hands of one government, one party, or one person was dangerous. Li suggested that the best system equally divided power (*junquan*) between central and local levels. He also wrote that historically a concentration of power had not kept China unified, citing the maxim "the empire, long united, must divide" (*he jiu bi fen*). To Li, overcentralization diminished the ability of localities to resist internal chaos or outside invaders. The success of alien dynasties such as the Liao, Jin, Yuan, and Qing was the result of an imperial system that allowed no self-government, and thus prevented people from organizing to defend themselves.[135] This veiled criticism of Jiang and his regime marked the outermost limit of acceptable dissent during the White Terror.

After February 28, islanders advocated moderate expansion of local self-government.[136] For example, Han Shiquan asked when elections would be held for county magistrates and mayors, something that had long been part of the Taiwanese political agenda. He claimed that the current guidelines for county magistrates and mayors led to the appointment of men who did not understand the island's "special characteristics" (*teshu*). This in turn inflamed public opinion.[137] He praised some of the reforms implemented over the preceding months, such as ending the administrator system, lifting martial law, abolishing the trade bureau, reorganizing the monopoly bureau, and assuring a better food supply.[138] Provincial leaders requested no more than to have mainland policies implemented on the island. For example, islanders were irritated that elections had been held in Xinjiang for mayors and county magistrates. In late 1948, Provincial Consultative Assembly member Guo Guoji stated that, of China's provinces, Xinjiang was the most culturally backward, yet it held elections in 1946. Taiwan was China's most advanced province, he stated, but still awaited elections. Provincial officials replied that the central government had given Xinjiang permission and that they had no power to decide such matters.[139]

Taiwanese came closest to articulating the real motive behind the Nationalists' program of local self-government when they complained that officials delayed reform out of fear islanders had not received enough training and so might elect "bad" people.[140] The system was designed to transform Taiwanese into loyal Chinese, not empower them. The state placed local self-government in the context of a broader program of "citizenship training" and the newly promulgated constitution of the Republic of China.[141] Li Zonghuang summed up the Nationalists' goals when he wrote that local self-government should "manage, teach, cultivate, and protect" (guan, jiao, yang, wei).[142] Islanders would be taught to be the kind of citizens the Nationalists had wanted to lead on the mainland. The Taiwanese would have to earn the state's version of local self-government by assimilating into the Nationalist Chinese political order. The process started with meetings sponsored by the Civil Administration Office to train cadres.[143]

The Self-Government Association and Chen Cheng made ideological training a key part of the preparations for local self-government. The association called for education in Sun Zhongshan's teachings on local self-government and the constitution, and dissemination of "correct" (zhengque) ideas about democracy. Branches of the association throughout the island were to help prepare and educate islanders. In particular, Chen stated that the lack of local self-government training caused the failure of earlier elections ("failure" seemed to be a code word for Guomindang candidates losing elections). This represented a great source of frustration for the national revolution.[144] Weng Qian stressed the need for the training of local self-government cadres. Even as he voiced the familiar Nationalist refrain that local self-government formed the basis of democratic rule, he explained how important it was to reshape how the Taiwanese thought about politics.[145]

The actual implementation of the new system of local self-government was anticlimactic. A special session of the Provincial Assembly met in January 1950 to discuss the upcoming reform. Assembly members met with government officials, military leaders, as well as the chairmen of county and city assemblies on the island.[146] Beginning in April 1950, the government began to accept and implement proposals from the Self-Government Association. On April 5, 1950, Governor Wu announced that elections for mayors and county magistrates would be held soon. Candidates, however, were subject to government approval. Openly anti-Nationalist politicians were either under arrest or knew not to run for office. In early July 1950, the implementation of local self-government began officially with the elections to the Hualian County Assembly. Over the next few months, elections were held in the rest of the counties and cities throughout the island.

In December 1951, the Taiwan Provincial Provisional Assembly (Taiwansheng linshi yihui) was established.[147] Huang Chaoqin, the Half-Mountain Taiwanese elected as chairman, saw the assembly as a moderating force between the Taiwanese and the government, not as a legislative body. He stressed that the people and government must show a tolerant spirit toward one another. The assembly's activity would center on interpellation.[148] Regardless of Sun Zhongshan's outline for local self-government, the provincial and lower levels all depended on the central government for funds. While the new system permitted the election and recall of members, it did not have two key powers spelled out by Sun in his oft-quoted General Outline — the right to initiate laws (chuangzhiquan) and the right of referendum (fujuequan).[149]

In sum, the Nationalists' program of local self-government was not "local," because it was designed to further a national agenda rather than solve provincial or county problems. It was not "self," because the Taiwanese themselves had little role in its formulation or implementation. Finally, it was not "government," since it provided no autonomous local power. Local self-government on Taiwan did represent, however, the successful extension of the central government's administration and ideology to the provincial level and below.

Conclusion

Examining the implementation of local self-government complicates our understanding of two widely accepted dichotomies: Communist/Nationalist and mainland/Taiwan. Historians of Republican China have generally accepted that mass mobilization and political participation represented important factors in the Communists' victory and the Nationalists' defeat on the mainland.[150] Simply put, the Communists were inclusive and able to liberate and utilize popular energies, while the Nationalists were exclusive and sought to suppress them. Some scholars focus on Mao Zedong's gift for harnessing anti-Japanese sentiment or peasant nationalism, meeting the peasants' economic needs, or organizing an effective government that appealed across class lines.[151] Those who investigate the pre-1949 Nationalists often highlight the regime's inability to gain or maintain support on the mainland, creating a mirror image of Communist success. Scholars offer another mirror image of the Nationalists on the mainland and on Taiwan by concentrating on how the regime changed or improved because of the lessons learned in defeat across the strait.[152]

Local self-government suggests a more nuanced picture. First, on questions of political structure and relations between province and central government, the Communists and Nationalists were more alike than different. Both parties' perspectives were shaped by the chaos of China's warlord era, and both sought to build a powerful central government with weak provinces and counties. In this regard, their ultimate goals, if not short-term tactics, were the same. Second, the Nationalists' approach to participation was not simply negative, but was riddled with contradictions. The Nationalists had tolerated, or even encouraged, a variety of mass movements and political organizations on the mainland, including the Blue Shirts, the New Life Movement, the Three Principles of the People Youth Corps, the Renewal Movement, student and intellectual groups, and small non-Communist political parties.[153] Jiang Jieshi had initiated some of these activities, but turned against them when they went from serving the central government's interests (as he defined them) to questioning or criticizing the regime. There existed a fundamental tension in the Nationalists' approach to the citizens they governed. The regime wanted public involvement, but could not accept the "price" of participation any more than the Communists could, that is, harsh criticism, electoral competition, and local autonomy.

Taiwan's experience with local self-government represented an excellent example of the Nationalists' approach to political activity — an extension of long-term trends on the mainland. The Nationalists brought to bear a broad array of methods to control the discourse and policies concerning local self-government. They wrote a constitution, laws, and regulations to maintain a dominant central government, and to limit local, particularly provincial, autonomy. They also built a police state after the February 28 Incident that grew into the White Terror. These measures made the Taiwanese elite more malleable to the Nationalists' interests. If all else failed, the suspension of the constitution and martial law allowed Jiang to override any potential opposition. On Taiwan, the regime could concentrate its attention, as well as its police and military resources, much more effectively than it had ever been able to do across the strait.[154]

As important as written laws, powerless assemblies, and the threat of violence was ideology. Jiang wanted to create a citizenry that would always choose to do that which served the interests of the central government and, by extension, the nation. As far back as 1946, Chen Yi had stated, "Currently, our most critical task is Sinicizing Taiwan, making Taiwanese customs, thought, and language gradually return to that of Chinese people."[155] By 1948, refugees from the mainland saw Taiwan as the place where they could implement and prove the efficacy of their policies. It was not the Nationalists who changed, but "China," that is, the relatively small area of Taiwan that now represented the Republic of China. To central government leaders, the Taiwanese would have to think and act in accord with the Nationalists' priorities, which they equated with the welfare of China. In light of this "nationalization" of Taiwanese politics, the island's elite came to realize that the safe way to discuss local self-government was in the context of building a strong China and struggling against Communism. This marked a great success for the Nationalists' citizenship training and propaganda and created the framework for relations between Taiwanese and the state for the next forty years.

Ironically, Jiang's consolidation of power and the Nationalists' domination of Taiwan facilitated the return of the Japanese. Although it was not politically expedient to say so in the 1940s, many Nationalists admired the Japanese system of military and police, which had proven quite successful on Taiwan and the mainland at exterminating Communists. Although Jiang used arms supplied by the United States, he relied heavily upon training from a so-called White Group of retired Japanese military officers.[156] These advisors began arriving in Taibei in late 1949 and in the spring of 1950 they helped create and manage the Yuan Shan Training Institute located north of Taibei. United States Ambassador Karl Rankin suggested that affinity for the Japanese was based on "the view that Japan may well again develop into the dominant power in the western Pacific."[157] Both General Peng Mengji (who served as director) and Jiang Jingguo were influential in this school.

Overall, Jiang Jingguo was more closely connected to those who had studied in Japan, such as General Peng, than to returned students from the United States. This is not to suggest that there was widespread amity for the Japanese as a people. However, since the 1894–95 Sino-Japanese War and the Russo-Japanese War of 1905–5, many Chinese had hoped to replicate Japan's development experience. Peng's background, in personal and educational terms, indicated that he had no particular affection for America or its ideals. Even as the Nationalists decried Japanese influence among the Taiwanese, they turned to the former colonial rulers for assistance. The Japanese served to balance the Americans, who seemed uncertain whether they were trying to remove, reform, or simply abandon Jiang. Observers in the Department of State understood the important role of the Japanese and their supporters: "In playing Tokyo and Washington as two separate, competing entities, the Generalissimo openly shows favor to Tokyo's personnel and almost equally ignores and undercuts accredited United States Government officials. . . . At the same time he is careful to restrict the contacts of the Tokyo personnel to those individuals who are properly indoctrinated and under strict control."[158] The Nationalists firmly controlled this outside influence. Japanese activities were limited to military advice and they did not delve into the realms of culture, education, or politics. Under the Nationalists' authoritarian rule, islanders were "insulated" from contact with their former colonial master.

6 *Taiwan's Elite Transformed*

Although the violence surrounding the February 28 Incident and the White Terror have attracted a great deal of attention, economic measures, propaganda, and programs such as local self-government also shaped Taiwan's elite and its relationship with the Nationalist state and Chinese nation.

The relationship between prominent Taiwanese and the Nationalist government was shaped by a complex mixture of individual personalities, educational background, economic interests, and experiences and alliances formed during colonial rule, reinforced by government policies designed to foster a compliant elite.[1] A useful framework for examining reactions to Nationalist rule was provided by Taiwanese author Wu Zhuoliu. He presented four ideal types: opponents, idealists, transcendentals, and compromisers.[2] "Opponents" (*dikangpai*), such as Communists and independence activists or those otherwise deemed subversive by the state, had been either killed or imprisoned by the late 1940s, or had fled to the mainland (Communists) or Japan (independence activists). The concept of "opposition," however, is problematic because what many of the islanders executed by the Nationalists espoused differed little from the agendas of others who survived this tumultuous era. Other Taiwanese remained active in politics by promoting reform within the limits set by Nationalist rule even as they rejected membership in the Guomindang. These "idealists" (*lixiangpai*) hoped to bring about peaceful change as careful critics of the regime. They could also be called the loyal opposition, although their loyalty may have been prompted as much by fear as by political conviction. Idealists survived thanks to a combination of luck, personal connections, and a clear history of anti-Japanese activity during the colonial era. On Taiwan in the late 1940s, opposition often meant a dead idealist.

Many of the most important leaders from the Japanese era hoped Nationalist rule would mean the realization of their long-cherished political goals. Frustrated with their lack of influence under the new regime, they simply abandoned politics. These "transcendentals" (*chaoyuepai*) devoted themselves to their professional careers or retired from public life completely. Finally, "compromisers" or "accommodationists" (*tuoxiepai*) advanced their political careers by working with the Nationalists during the War of Resistance against Japan and immediately after retrocession. This group generally accepted the Nationalists' vision of Taiwan's place in the nation of China and the administrative structure of the Republic of China, and by extension the mainland-derived system of local self-government. Some islanders, particularly Half-Mountain Taiwanese, enjoyed long and successful careers in the regime. Others attempted to build a relationship with the Nationalists after retrocession, but found themselves distrusted by both the Taiwanese and the government.

The state had strategies to eradicate, isolate, suborn, or foster those who fit into each of these four ideal types. Although the Nationalists often treated the Taiwanese with great brutality, they did not manage the transformation of the island's elite solely through the use of force. Almost all prominent islanders had the opportunity to participate actively in the regime. For those who did so, the state and party responded by fostering their political careers and material well-being. As in the colonial era, Taiwanese could obtain employment in the administration and benefit economically through their association with the government, but not enjoy real influence over policy. In other words, they could compete for central government benefits, but were not permitted to shape the system that distributed them. Local self-government became a tool for managing the island's elite. From the Nationalists' perspective, local self-government illustrated their willingness to reform and strengthened their control of the island. Their ability to manipulate elections and keep local jurisdictions weak assured dependence upon the Guomindang and central government. Local self-government also served as a safety valve for Taiwanese energies and a method of indoctrinating islanders.

Opposition Real and Imagined: Wang Tiandeng

There existed two faces to opposition on Taiwan: real—those who declared their determination to overthrow the government, and manufactured—those who sought nonviolent change, but were deemed threats by the Nationalists. Communists and independence activists represented the most intractable, yet least influential, opponents to the rule of Jiang Jieshi. Because of oppression from above and lack of support from below, Communists and separatists alike had little chance of overthrowing the Nationalists. Furthermore, neither Communism nor Taiwanese nationalism addressed the aspirations of most prominent islanders. Other Taiwanese, however, who were neither Communists nor separatists, were still treated as opposition. The Nationalists changed their definition of opposition over the period from 1945 to 1950. In particular, after the February 28 Incident and during the White Terror some islanders were treated as opponents even though they had not modified their political position significantly since 1946. This issue is further complicated as historians supporting Nationalism (the ideology of the Guomindang as interpreted by Sun Zhongshan, then Jiang Jieshi), Communism, or independence had their own motives for creating traitors or martyrs, depending upon their point of view.

Tea merchant and elected representative Wang Tiandeng (1901–47) illustrates the difficulty inherent in rigidly applying the categories of Communist or independence activist. Wang's death at the hands of Nationalist police served as a warning to Taiwanese about the power of the state, and also made him a martyr to both leftists and independence activists. Born in the Taibei suburb of Xindian, Wang became a prosperous businessman under colonial rule, and opened offices in northeast China and Manchuria during the 1930s. He rose in stature among his fellow merchants to become chairman of the Taiwan Tea Guild in 1945. Like many of his peers, Wang sought expanded local autonomy within the confines of the Japanese empire. Although he was a relatively strident member of the Taibei branch of the Taiwan League for Local Self-Government, Wang did not call for armed resistance or the island's return to China.[3] In what almost became a rite of passage for young islanders, he was arrested briefly by the Japanese for his political activity.

Wang's high hopes at the time of retrocession soon turned to disappointment. He was caught up in the widespread enthusiasm for the political participation that had been suppressed by the Japanese.[4] Like many other prominent islanders, he became a member of the Guomindang and cooperated closely with Half-Mountain Taiwanese working with General Chen Cheng and the Three Principles of the People Youth Corps.[5] Wang was in the Guomindang but not of it — he was technically a member even though his views increasingly put him at odds with the mainlander-dominated party. This became clear in his journalistic endeavors. He became active in publishing as director (*shezhang*) of *People's Report* (*Renmin daobao*), a newspaper critical of the Nationalists until it was forced to close in the summer of 1946. Wang then helped organize *Freedom* (*Ziyoubao*), a newspaper published sporadically until shut down permanently by the government after the February 28 Incident. Wang's attacks on corruption and defects of the provincial administration did not endear him to Administrator Chen Yi.[6]

As had been the case under colonial rule, Wang was a participant in political activity, thus serving to legitimize the regime, and a strong critic of it.

In March 1946 he was elected to the Taibei City Consultative Assembly, then in April to the first Provincial Consultative Assembly. The new assembly member used the standards created by colonial rule to judge and criticize the Nationalists, writing that "The good people of Taiwan still do not dare hope for real governance under the Three Principles of the People, they only hope for a little rule of law. . . . [They also] hope that the system of not daring to disrespect the rule of law [that existed] under Japanese imperialism can continue."[7] Wang became one of the most outspoken members of the assembly, and frequently championed expanded local self-government. His goal, increasing the role of islanders in governing the province and limiting state control over the economy, was shared by many other Taiwanese. His attitude became clear in the first session of the assembly. Most assembly members largely repeated platitudes about the need for cooperation between the government and the people. Wang, however, presented very specific proposals: the election of local officials, an end to corruption, and an assembly with veto power over decisions concerning government business enterprises. He also urged that only Taiwanese represent the island in the National Assembly.[8] Wang had other reasons for conflict with the Nationalists, since he became embroiled in disputes related to his financial interests. He was a rival of the younger brother of Nationalist General Ge Jing'en for control of the Taiwan Provincial Tea Company.[9]

Wang saw his chance to turn his political rhetoric into concrete action in early 1947. He played a leading role in the islandwide February 28 Incident Resolution Committee, served as its propaganda chairman and spokesman (*xuanchang zuzhang*), and helped present the famous Thirty-two Demands to Administrator Chen Yi. As Nationalist reinforcements arrived in Jilong, many people urged Wang to flee Taibei. He apparently did not expect to be arrested or killed, and hesitated to take a train to family property in Pingdong in southern Taiwan. Military police picked up Wang and another prominent Taiwanese, Chen Xin, telling witnesses that they were taking the men to meet a friend in the Nationalist military. Wang was soaked in gasoline and burned to death.[10] According to Chen Yi's statement, Wang was arrested for joining in an armed rebellion and attempting to start a new nation while on the islandwide February 28 committee.[11] No one in the government has ever admitted ordering or participating in his murder.

Wang's son would later remark that some people claimed his father was a Communist and others said he supported independence.[12] Actually Wang's vision of the island's relationship with China and the Nationalist state did not fit into any simple category of Communist, Nationalist, or independence advocate, but rather took elements from each. His critique of Nationalist misrule and corruption often found him in the company of Communists. Although his economic interests hardly made him a proponent of violent class conflict, his work in the Youth Corps and newspapers put him in close contact with journalists and political activists later discovered to have been Communists. Whether Wang was aware of the political affiliations of his friends is difficult to substantiate. In the eyes of many Nationalists, Wang was hopelessly compromised by colonialism. Mainlanders often associated advocates of expanded local self-government, such as Wang, with separatism and the Japanese legacy. For example, a Nationalist military commander, Ke Yuanfen, specifically labeled some Taiwanese, such as Wang, "Japanese-era collaborators."[13] Wang's business ties with Gu Zhenfu, who was involved in the short-lived plot with Japanese officers to declare the island independent in August 1945, did not help matters.

Wang and others promoted greater autonomy in order to save Taiwan from the chaos of a war-torn China and a tottering Nationalist state, but did not seek independence. They had also wanted an administration free of corruption, and moderate social and economic reform. His "opposition" in Nationalist eyes was as much a product of their rage after the February 28 Incident as of his actual activities or ideas. Wang's views did not differ greatly from many Taiwanese who were fortunate enough to avoid arrest or execution. Over the next four decades, however, there was little room for anyone whose agenda could not be clearly classified as Communist, Nationalist, or pro-independence.

Cautious Critics:
Tiger Generals Guo Guoji and Li Wanju

Other Taiwanese managed to work within the political system established by the mainland regime; they were not in the Guomindang, but accepted Nationalist rule of the island. These individuals were idealistic enough to criticize the government and advocate change, but pragmatic enough to understand the grave dangers of taking too strong a position against the Nationalists. Furthermore, many shared a strong antipathy toward the Japanese that manifested itself as Chinese nationalism. Such careful critics of the regime never favored revolution or violence against the Nationalists, yet faced the constant threat of being seen by the government as "red" or as supporters of independence. Many of them had views similar to those killed or arrested, but through luck, caution, or personal connections managed to survive. The Nationalist government accepted the participation of these moderate outsiders in order to bolster its claim to being a democracy, but had no intention of actually modifying any policies at their behest.

Cautious critics included Taiwan-based politicians and mainland-based democracy advocates. The former gained support from the grassroots through elections to assemblies. They tended to have solid anti-Japanese credentials, thus defusing the potentially delegitimizing taint of colonial-era collaboration. For example, Guo Guoji, the anti-Japanese activist who represented Gaoxiong in the Provincial Consultative Assembly after retrocession, was arrested briefly after the February 28 Incident and left the Guomindang shortly thereafter. Guo never questioned the Nationalists' ultimate sovereignty, but remained one of the their most visible critics into the 1960s. Many mainland-based dissidents had been involved in the third-party movement in Republican China. Their political activity — promoting Western ideas of liberal representative democracy and attempting to blend these with Sun Zhongshan's Three Principles of the People — centered on China more than Taiwan. A good example of these dissidents is Li Wanju, who built his early political career on the mainland and then became a leader of the democracy movement on Taiwan. Li's experiences represent the roots of later opposition parties on the island, which combined the rhetoric of democratic reform from the mainland's third-party movement with issues and concerns of local Taiwanese politics. In the 1950s, Taiwanese called Guo and Li two of the "Five Tiger Generals" (*wu hu jiang*), the politicians most critical of the Nationalists.[14]

A strong personality tempered by prudence shaped the political career of Guo Guoji (1900–70). Born into a small landlord family in Pingdong County, Guo's interest in politics dated from encounters with discrimination in high school. Guo, however, did go to Tokyo and studied law at Meiji University, becoming one of the few islanders to enter this field. His interest in China seemed to be part of his response to Japanese oppression. After graduation, he traveled to the mainland and even approached the weak Beijing government to ask for help for the people of Taiwan.[15] In Tokyo, he became a secret member of the Guomindang in 1926. He was also an active member of Taiwanese student organizations in Japan, and upon his return to the island in the 1929, he joined the Taiwan Masses Party (Taiwan minzhongdang). One of his strengths was a sense of drama and combativeness. During the colonial era, he earned the nickname Big Cannon Guo (Guo Dapao) from Lin Xiantang for his outspoken opposition to the Japanese.[16] In and out of jail during the 1930s, in 1942 his political activity led to a ten-year prison sentence. He was freed shortly after the war.

After retrocession, Guo followed a political agenda little different from Wang Tiandeng's. In 1946, he became a Guomindang cadre, and was elected to the Gaoxiong Consultative Assembly, then to the Provincial Consultative Assembly. As a biographical dictionary points out, Guo's politics represented a competition between three competing ideologies: China-ism, Taiwan-ism, and Gaoxiong-ism (*da Zhonghua zhuyi, da Taiwan zhuyi, da Gaoxiong zhuyi*).[17] Guo tried to maximize government benefits for his Gaoxiong constituents and to obtain greater self-government for Taiwan, which he conceived of as helping China. In his opening statement about his hopes for the provincial body, Guo presented one of the longest lists of specific requests, rivaled only by Wang's. He wanted to increase the islanders' role in the military defense of the island, assist the aborigines, make Tainan into a major naval base and build an airport there, and employ more islanders in government, regardless of their Chinese-language ability.[18] In other forums, he went beyond suggestions for policy changes into strong criticism of Nationalist misrule and corruption, which quickly earned him the enmity of Administrator Chen Yi. Guo even attacked some of his fellow islanders, complaining about the release from prison of some Taiwanese who had been charged with war crimes.[19] Although this may have antagonized some islanders, it did have a positive result: it helped to neutralize the issue of the colonial legacy by making Guo more anti-Japanese than many mainlanders.

Unlike Wang Tiandeng, Guo did not play a major role in the February 28 Incident or in the resolution committees. Nevertheless, the incident marked a major turning point in his career. Because his political views had created enemies among the Nationalists, Guo was supposedly the target of shoot-on-sight orders after the incident. After using go-betweens, he surrendered and spent over 200 days in jail.[20] In early 1948 Guo was found not guilty of encouraging rebellion. The remarks by the judge, published in a newspaper, made it difficult to tell whether Guo had committed a crime or not: "You are a member of the Provincial Assembly, with the responsibility for leading the Taiwanese. Speaking and acting have a close relationship. Although you took no particular action in last year's February 28 Incident, your earlier views and speeches had many inappropriate aspects."[21] This verdict was as much a warning as a vindication. Subsequently, Guo had few friends in official circles and none among the Nationalists.[22] He left the Guomindang.

Immediately after his release from jail, Guo devoted himself to protecting fellow islanders and blunting the police power of the state. He called for the right of assembly members to speak freely as well as for guarantees for their physical safety. For example, he asked that Lin Rigao, an assembly member arrested after the February 28 Incident, be freed from custody in order to attend meetings and receive medical treatment for tuberculosis. Guo complained that no judgment had been made in Lin's case, but he was being held out of suspicion that he would flee the island. Guo's solution was an innovative one: he suggested the assembly act as guarantor.[23] In a more general vein, he urged the implementation of the jury system for criminal trials. This, he declared, was a sign of an enlightened country, and would reduce corruption while ensuring fair judgments. Guo also sought better treatment of prisoners.[24]

Expanding Taiwanese influence in the island's administration and promoting local self-government remained Guo's long-term priorities. In mid-1948, he made a series of requests of Governor Wei Daoming: implement local self-government, cultivate local talent, protect freedom of speech, remove corrupt and incompetent officials, and retain Taiwanese officials in their posts.[25] Guo clearly irritated Governor Wei and other officials. When answering one of Guo's questions about government policies and local self-government, Wei stated that the assemblyman wanted the central government to give Taiwan special attention and treatment (*zhuyi yu youdai*). This, Wei averred, was unreasonable since the island was well treated, receiving more fertilizer than other provinces despite its relatively small population, for instance.[26] Guo constantly requested changing the Provincial Consultative Assembly into a regular assembly with greater powers. He also called for the election of the island's governor.[27] In early 1950, Guo asked Governor Wu Guozhen about the role of the province in local self-government. Wu quickly reminded him that the province was to help implement local self-government, but that any provincial self-government could only be determined by the central government.[28] Guo even dared to raise the issue of the Taiwanese language (*Minnanhua*), stating that islanders and their representatives should be allowed to use their local dialect.[29] This request, like most of Guo's others, was ignored.

Guo was not openly anti-Nationalist; that would have been unsafe. Instead, he tried to expand the Taiwanese role within a system he had little prospect of changing. For example, he never rejected the islanders' participation in the military, but instead urged that young men be given greater opportunities for advancement in the navy and air force.[30] He sought to increase the influence of Taiwanese who lacked strong, long-term ties to the regime (not coincidentally, people like himself). In 1949 Guo complimented the government for giving Taiwanese seventeen of twenty-three places on the provincial committee, but asked rhetorically if the individuals selected by the regime were the best available. Simply increasing the number of islanders was not enough, he emphasized: the government needed to choose people who would enjoy popular support.[31]

Many of Guo's statements fit closely with the Nationalists' own propaganda and placed him safely in the realm of Chinese nationalism. Even as Guo asked about the reform of county boundaries, a prerequisite to new elections, he stressed that Taiwan was part of China and was not seeking independence. Guo listed what he saw as the island's contributions to China: anti-Qing resistance in the 1600s, the fight to prevent cession to Japan in 1895, the struggle for return to China during fifty years of colonial rule, and efforts to help refugees from the mainland.[32] He also publicly criticized the United States and Great Britain for alleged plots to foster Taiwan's independence, declaring that the island was an indivisible part of China.[33]

Guo struggled with a difficult balancing act. While his statements about Taiwan as part of China proved his patriotism to the Nationalists, his personality and interest in local issues gained support from the Taiwanese people. Guo worked harder than most members of the Provincial Consultative Assembly to maximize the government benefits available to his constituents, proving the adage that "all politics is local." For example, in 1948 he urged the government to expand military schools and armaments factories near Gaoxiong, pointing out that this would increase the ability of the province to defend itself.[34] Guo also called for the repair of schools damaged by United States bombing, provisions for night classes to help students who had dropped out, and the establishment of a university in Gaoxiong.[35] On another occasion, he complained that land occupied by the government at the end of the war had been promised as a future park, but had been rented by a police organization to vendors.[36] He expanded this into a more general critique of police treatment of islanders, complaining that the police had many bad habits, such as a propensity for violence, and did not respect the people's rights.[37]

Guo represented the outermost limit of political activity acceptable to the Nationalists. He built on his early reputation as a fiery speaker, and presented a great contrast to the usually colorless politicians approved by the Nationalists. Guo's electioneering slogans included "grant that I may die gloriously in the assembly hall." He tried to turn his lack of Guomindang membership to his advantage, stating that "party members concentrate on secretly helping one another; those outside the party concentrate their efforts on openly providing relief [to the people]."[38] Ironically, his tough questioning of officials was blamed for the death of esteemed mainland scholar Fu Sinian in late 1949. Fu, then serving as president of National Taiwan University, collapsed during an argument with Guo in a meeting of the Provincial Consultative Assembly. Guo regretted the death, which was unrelated to events in the assembly chamber, but added that Fu was like a gladiator who had died in the arena.

Despite his high profile, Guo had no influence over government policies and struggled constantly to remain in office. In fact, elections under the system of local self-government implemented in the early 1950s harmed him, as the Nationalists brought the full force of vote buying, patronage, intimidation, and control of the media to bear against him. He lost the indirect election for the first Provincial Provisional Assembly. For the next six years, Guo built alliances and developed his own electoral machine through tireless campaigning. Although the Nationalist-controlled press prevented mention of his candidacy during the 1957 campaign, he was still elected in

Taibei.[39] He lost again in 1963, but won in Gaoxiong in 1968. During the last few years of his life, he suffered from bowel cancer, and died in 1970. Big Cannon Guo had been a consistent, albeit minor, thorn in the side of the Nationalists. His brand of brash political theater and attention to the needs of his constituents, however, set a pattern for later opposition.

A frequent ally of Guo, Li Wanju (1902–66), helped to connect China's third-party movement to Taiwan, presenting another facet of the "Nationalization" of the island's politics. Li moved to the mainland as a youth to attend Shanghai's National People's University.[40] He later traveled to France to study sociology, then returned and became a professor in Shanghai. Li possessed solid anti-Japanese credentials. Whatever his feelings about the Nationalists or Communists, he had personal reasons to oppose the Japanese. His father died when he was nine, and his mother committed suicide when he was eighteen, allegedly after being hounded by colonial police and tax collectors.[41] Li supported the Nationalist government, particularly in its anti-Japanese struggle, but did not join the Guomindang. He researched international issues with the government's National Military Affairs Committee during the War of Resistance, and traveled to Hong Kong and Vietnam to gather intelligence for the Nationalist government. He became a leader of the Taiwanese Revolutionary Alliance (Taiwan geming tongmenghui), a broad anti-Japanese coalition on the mainland consisting of Taiwanese members of the Guomindang and small political parties such as the China Youth Party. He also published the *Voice of Taiwan* (*Taiwan minshengbao*), a newspaper that encouraged resistance to the Japanese and discussed plans for postwar Taiwan. Li was tolerated by the Nationalists because his presence "proved" the regime was democratic and multiparty, and helped to build a broad anti-Japanese coalition.

Without a common enemy, Li and the Nationalists gradually became adversaries. After retrocession, one of Li's chief accomplishments stemmed from his wish to create an alternative to the Nationalist-controlled media. He returned to Taiwan in order to take control of news organizations for the government. Li became editor-in-chief of *Taiwan New Life Daily* (*Taiwan xinshengbao*), the paper supported by the provincial administration. Under his leadership, however, the paper frequently published criticism of the Nationalists and their policies. Conflicts over wages and editorial policy were rife, and Li faced the difficult task of managing both the Chinese and Japanese editions. The staff represented a microcosm of political conflict on the island. Newly arrived reporters from the mainland, many Half-Mountain Taiwanese, were paid twice as much as holdovers from the colonial era.[42] Li also brought some members of the China Youth Party with him to the paper.[43]

In 1946 it appeared that Li was destined to hold a variety of highly visible, if not extremely influential, posts. He was elected to the first Provincial Consultative Assembly and became its vice chairman. He became the longest serving member of the provincial body, from 1946 to 1966. Li was also elected to the National Assembly, but neither he nor the rest of the Taiwanese delegation had any significant influence there. His political interests grew from his career on the mainland and had less to do with the Taiwanese in and of themselves and more with democracy for China. For example, in 1946 Li stated that his goals for the Provincial Consultative Assembly were twofold: to represent the people and to supervise and assist the government. He especially emphasized that the assembly must ensure that the government operated lawfully and in the interests of the people. However, he never actually mentioned Taiwan in his statement.[44] Some of the issues he raised dealt with the control the Guomindang exercised over other parties, such as his China Youth Party. For example, Li complained that school officials forced students to join the Three Principles of the People Youth Corps.[45]

The February 28 Incident marked the decline of Li's limited influence as the Nationalists became much less tolerant of criticism. He played no significant role during the incident, perhaps because his experience on the mainland had taught him how the government would react to the uprising. Moreover, in 1947 organizational changes made him virtually powerless at *Xinshengbao*. He left to establish *Gonglunbao*, which he managed for thirteen years. This paper offered careful criticism of the Nationalists and provided a forum for the legal opposition. Li continued to focus on democratization and rule of law for China, while avoiding the topic of Taiwan's relationship with the mainland. Li's concerns with judicial and police reform often coincided with Guo Guoji's interests. They jointly asked that only police, not the military, be authorized to make arrests; arrests be made with warrants; that the government provide information on why individuals were arrested; that corporal punishment be prohibited; and that judicial independence be respected. In order to legitimize their calls for reform, Guo and Li carefully framed their requests in terms of "opposing Russia and resisting communism" (*kang E fan gong*), thus covering themselves with the cloak of Chinese nationalism.[46]

Li, however, was never so critical of the Nationalists that he was threatened with death or imprisonment. His moderation was clear in a 1950 speech before the Provincial Consultative Assembly, where he discussed the importance of reform for the governance of the island. In light of Taiwan's role as a vital base for recapturing the mainland, however, he accepted that changes would be delayed. Li stated his hope that the province would hold elections soon and lauded the elections at the lower administrative levels as a good sign.[47] Nevertheless, his complaints and requests, and his lack of Guomindang membership, led the government to make sure that he was not elected vice chairman of the Provincial Provisional Assembly in 1951. Although Li left the Chinese Youth Party, he remained close to the mainlander-dominated reform movement and to dissident intellectuals such as Hu Shi and Lei Zhen.[48] In his last years, Li suffered many political defeats and humiliations at the hands of the Nationalists. A combination of prominent Taiwanese and mainlanders, including Li, Lei Zhen, Guo Yuxin, and others, attempted to establish a Chinese Democratic Party in 1960. The Nationalist government quickly disbanded their organization and imprisoned Lei Zhen. In 1961 Li Wanju's *Gonglunbao* was fined for discussing the mainland's wartime collaborationist Wang Jingwei regime in a way that offended a member of the Guomindang's Central Committee. This caused Li to lose the newspaper. Weakened by age and diabetes, he died in 1966.[49]

In concrete terms, Guo and Li accomplished little: one can point to few laws changed or prisoners released due to their efforts. They were tolerated because they represented no threat to the political order and because their activities allowed the Nationalists to claim that "Free China" was a democracy. Their importance lay in the future: they were precursors to later, and more effective, opposition. A combination of Guo's emphasis on the specific needs of islanders and Li's rhetoric of democracy would come to characterize the *dangwai* ("outside the party") movement and the Democratic Progressive Party.[50]

Japanese-Era Reformers Abandon Politics: Lin Xiantang and Han Shiquan

In the five years following retrocession, many of the important leaders from the Japanese era simply abandoned politics. These "transcendentals" came to concentrate on their professional careers or retired out of frustration with their limited influence under the Nationalists. Although they had high expectations for the island and their own political careers in 1945, they grew disillusioned over the next few years. The Nationalists *preferred*, but did not require, the support of these prominent Taiwanese. Being denied real power, these Taiwanese responded not by building a mass movement to demand reform, much less engaging in violent revolutionary activity, but simply by withdrawing from politics. They could not organize effective, peaceful opposition because the Nationalist police and military proved effective in controlling dissent. And they did not countenance violent opposition since their class background — many of them were landlords or merchants — led them to fear social chaos and violence from below as much as oppression from the state. Trapped between the Nationalist state and Taiwanese society, they chose to leave the political arena.

Lin Xiantang (1881–1956), one of the most important political figures of the Japanese era, became a prominent transcendental. Finding himself marginalized after retrocession, with little influence over the state and increasingly overshadowed by Taiwanese with stronger ties to the Nationalists, Lin chose to withdraw from public life and move to Japan.[51] He had made the accommodations necessary for success under colonial rule, but seemed lost in the more tumultuous world of Nationalist Chinese politics. Lin was born near Taizhong into a wealthy family of landlords and merchants. His experience epitomizes the contradictions of the colonial era. Lin enjoyed wealth, prestige, and stability while enduring discrimination and experiencing frustration with the power of the governors-general.[52] His financial interests expanded from land holdings into modern banking institutions and regional trading networks. Lin participated in the colonial regime by accepting membership in the advisory organs created by various governors-general. When the Japanese sought to increase local support during the final years of the war, they promoted important Taiwanese such as Lin. For example, he was made a local leader of the Imperial Subjects Service Society (Kōmin hōkōkai), an organization designed to build loyalty to the empire, and in April 1945 he became the third islander named to the House of Peers, but never traveled to Japan to participate. Such honors came back to haunt him after the war.

Lin was never a firebrand, but rather a well-educated gentleman more likely to use quiet persuasion than mass mobilization. According to one who knew him, his education gave him the traditional Confucian outlook of a scholar. Lin had a lifelong affinity for traditional Chinese culture and never learned to speak Japanese.[53] This cultural connection to the mainland, however, did not translate into concrete action in support of Chinese nationalism or the Nationalists. The effectiveness and brutality of Japanese rule, his wish to avoid violence, and the unlikelihood of reunification with China all constrained Lin's political activism. He was characterized by a friend as someone who had a fiery temper and strong sense of righteousness in his youth, but then mellowed.[54] Some islanders even criticized Lin as reactionary. Ye Rongzhong, an associate of Lin, wrote that although some felt Lin was not sufficiently active or adamant, he did as much as he could given his style of leadership and the constraints of Japanese rule.[55] Lin was characterized as a pragmatist (*xianshi*) who understood the limits of what could be accomplished under colonial rule.[56]

Lin worked within the colonial system even as he sought to change it. He promoted Chinese culture and education for Taiwanese youth, but also flirted briefly with the promotion of assimilation into Japan, and then turned to supporting expanded autonomy for the island within the colonial empire. He served as the chairman of many organizations and helped found or support publications that promoted nonviolent reform, including the Taiwan People's Party (Taiwan minzhongdang) and the Taiwan Local Self-Government League.

In late 1945, Lin appeared to be on the right track for the impending political transition. Like almost all of the Taiwanese discussed in this chapter, he joined the Guomindang and was elected to the Provincial Consultative Assembly. Lin was also elected to the Political Consultative Conference in 1946. Because of his long-term ties to the Japanese and lack of allies in the Nationalist ranks, however, he had limited access to leaders in Nanjing or Taibei. Chen Yi's administration did not meet Lin's expectations.

Lin's retreat from politics took place over four years. The first sign of conflict came in early 1946, when the provincial government briefly listed him as a suspected traitor because of his long relationship with independence activist Gu Zhenfu and the Japanese. Qiu Niantai, an important Taiwan-born official, quickly interceded with the government to help Lin avoid any legal difficulty, but damage had been done. The next conflict came in the newly elected Taiwan Provincial Consultative Assembly, where the Nationalists engineered Lin's defeat by the Half-Mountain Taiwanese Huang Chaoqin for the assembly's chairmanship.[57] After this, Lin seemed to accept that his influence was waning. In mid-1946, he stated that he only wanted to serve his native place, but as an old person, his strength was limited. He emphasized that he had spent decades under colonial rule fighting for liberation. Lin now hoped that superior youth and "sharp newcomers" (xinjin qirui) would "apply the whip."[58] Huang Chaoqin, representing the Nationalists, seemed simultaneously to honor and pity Lin. The new chairman placed Lin in the position of elder statesman, a man whose best accomplishments were behind him. Huang called Lin part of the qianbei (previous, or elder, generation), and himself part of the houbei (later, or younger generation).[59] The Nationalists were making clear that Lin's political career was drawing to a close.

The chaos and violence of early 1947 accelerated Lin's withdrawal from public life.[60] He was a moderate during the February 28 Incident, and even helped protect a mainland official from an angry mob of islanders. In 1947 and 1948, as the Nationalists tried to gain his support by bringing him into the administration without surrendering any power to him, his titles became more prestigious and less meaningful. He became a member of the powerless Taiwan Provincial Committee in 1947, and in 1948 he was named chairman of the newly formed Taiwan Provincial Gazetteer Office. The one bright spot was that the official he protected in early 1947 helped arrange for his chairmanship of one of the largest financial institutions on the island, Zhanghua Bank. His actual influence, however, never matched this title.

Beginning in the late 1940s, Lin was hurt financially by grain purchase programs, rent reduction, and land reform.[61] Governor Chen Cheng, backed by a growing police power, was a strong advocate of land reform. Chen, with the cooperation of Half-Mountain people, used land reform to attack wealthy Taiwanese and those who had worked with the Japanese.[62] He also wielded land reform to drive a class-based wedge between Taiwanese, giving poorer islanders a concrete reason to support the Nationalists.[63] Many landlords and capitalists, the members of the elite who had enjoyed some measure of independence from the state due to their wealth, were devastated by the reforms implemented in the early 1950s.[64] The stocks in the four large companies that were given to large landlords as compensation made a few very rich, but tied their fate to that of the Nationalists. On the other hand, many small and medium-sized landlords were wiped out.[65]

Lin's declining influence, the pain of the February 28 Incident, rural economic policies, and his age spurred him to move to Japan in 1949. One author wrote that Lin felt that the lack of real local self-government was history mocking (*chaofeng*) him.[66] His public approval was still sought by the regime, which dispatched emissaries to urge him to return. However, Lin complained of his losses from rent reduction and seemed to fear returning.[67] His last years were his saddest, as he remained in Japan even after the death of his younger brother in 1954 and second son in 1955. An educated gentleman to the end, he spent his final years reading Buddhist texts.[68] Although he was not a supporter of the Nationalists, his nonviolent and moderate political agenda meant that he never represented a threat to Jiang's rule.

Lin's career illustrated the political decline of a loosely organized group of prominent islanders sometimes called the Taizhong Clique. These men had been involved in the Taiwan Cultural Association and Taiwan Assembly Petition Movement in the 1920s and early 1930s. Many were landlords with relatively high social standing in Japanese-era Taiwan.[69] The Taizhong Clique was not popular with Chen Yi, who berated them for their alleged collaboration with the Japanese and their capitalist proclivities. They responded with criticism of provincial administration, focusing on the problems of corruption, the breakdown of law and order, and poor management of the economy. These moderates did not play a major role in the violence of early 1947, but the bloody aftermath spurred many of them to leave politics. By the time the Nationalists implemented local self-government and rent reduction, the Taizhong Clique was disappearing. Most dropped out of the public eye, left the island, or died of old age.

The life of Japanese-trained doctor and political activist Han Shiquan included professional accomplishment, public service, and political frustration. Han attempted to serve as a bridge between the Taiwanese and the government by becoming a member of the Guomindang and running for office. However, he chafed at his lack of influence in the aftermath of the February

28 Incident and left politics to focus on his medical work. Han was of a slightly younger generation than Lin, although he faced many similar problems. He was a beneficiary and victim, a critic and collaborator, under Japanese rule. Han received a modern education in medicine, established one of the few private, Taiwanese-managed, hospitals on the island, and gained a reputation for treating those unable to pay.

Han's political life under Japanese rule followed a familiar pattern. The colonial system sought to foster technical experts, doctors, and teachers who would serve the empire while avoiding politics. This policy did not prevent political activity, but instead led to reformist movements led by engineers, doctors, and teachers. Born after 1895, Han developed Lin's critique of colonial rule without the elder man's strong cultural ties to China. Like many of his peers, in 1921 he joined the Taiwan Cultural Association formed by Lin Xiantang and Jiang Weishui. Han was jailed for two months in 1923 for his involvement in work to create a provincial assembly. In 1927, he joined Jiang Weishui and the Masses Party rather than support those who advocated more sweeping social and economic change.[70] When the Japanese tightened their hold over Taiwan in the mid- and late 1930s, Han retreated from public life.

The doctor's experience with Nationalist rule was similar to that of Wang Tiandeng, Guo Guoji, and Lin as enthusiasm turned to disappointment. He assisted with the Nationalist takeover and the establishment of the Guomindang party office in southern Taiwan. The Tainan assembly elected him to the Provincial Consultative Assembly in April 1946. His centrist orientation became clear when he faulted both the government *and* his fellow representatives for the ineffectiveness of the assembly. He blamed officials for lack of sincerity in fulfilling requests made by the assembly, but also admitted that assembly members raised difficult issues and were too confrontational with each other and the government.[71] During the February 28 Incident, Han tried to prevent violence by all sides.[72] Because of his cooperation with officials during the incident, he enjoyed slightly more latitude than most islanders to criticize or cajole the government. Han tried to limit the government's brutality and to assure the protection of human rights, particularly through the new constitution. For example, he wanted to know when arrests and trials related to the incident would be concluded. Finally, he decried that islanders were still not treated equally to mainlanders and complained that economic conditions had continued to worsen.[73]

Han took a stance that was not at all unusual among prominent Taiwanese when he accepted the state's program of local self-government, but wanted to implement it quickly and completely. For example, he queried provincial officials as to why local finances remained dependent on higher levels of government and stated that the financial independence of each administrative unit would increase its effectiveness.[74] In 1948 he asked repeatedly when the Legislative Yuan would pass the laws necessary to allow for local self-government and new elections.[75] Later that year, Han argued that the province should proceed with local self-government since the national legislature seemed unable to pass the laws required by the constitution.[76] Upon Governor Wu Guozhen's arrival in late 1949, Han renewed his campaign for local self-government.[77] There is no evidence, however, that Han's pressure had any bearing on the timing or content of subsequent reforms.

Although conscientious in his duties to the Provincial Consultative Assembly (he attended all but two of 153 meetings over five years), Han became increasingly discouraged and turned more to his medical work, particularly the Red Cross.[78] He failed in his attempt to gain election to the National Assembly in 1947. In defeat, he blamed people with money and connections for stymieing his campaign. Afterward, Han proposed changes in the election laws, but decided never to run for office again.[79] According to Cai Peihuo, a prominent Taiwanese intellectual, the exact reasons for Han's withdraw from public life were not entirely clear. Cai suggested that the criticism of Han for his perceived support of the government during the February 28 Incident was one important factor. Han proved unable to adapt to the new political environment that came with the restoration of Chinese sovereignty.[80] By 1953, a biographical dictionary of prominent islanders did not include Han.[81]

Han's experience was not atypical. For example, Wu Zhuoliu noted that, as during the Japanese era, many people decided to concentrate on their work. Wu explicitly called for islanders to avoid political or military affairs, and instead focus on industrialization and building the nation.[82] Wu did not even vote in National Assembly elections of 1947, reasoning that since only nineteen of over 1,800 members would be Taiwanese, there was no use in voting.[83] Wu Xinrong, author and political activist, wrote that after the February 28 Incident he buried himself in medical work to boost his spirits.[84] Han Shiquan and others like him did not hinder the Nationalist cause because they never created a viable alternative to Jiang's regime, nor did they organize effective resistance. In a more positive sense, they provided important professional and technical skills for the island's economic development.

An Accommodationist Prospers: Huang Chaoqin

As was the case under Japanese rule, when discussing the Taiwanese relationship with the Nationalists, words such as "compromise" and "accommodation" evoke strong reactions. Nevertheless, some prominent islanders depended almost entirely on ties to the government rather than on social networks or landed wealth for their political and material well-being. Many of these Taiwanese forged their relationship with the Nationalists before retrocession (often in Chongqing), becoming the so-called Half-Mountain people. Because their economic interests on the island were relatively limited, many of these people had little to lose by leaving the island to seek their fortunes with the Nationalists during the colonial era and they were unlikely to resist land reform after retrocession. For example, Huang Chaoqin (1897–1972) built a successful career with the Nationalists on the mainland and became one of the highest-ranking Taiwanese in the Guomindang and the government in the 1950s. He consistently echoed the Nationalists' views on the island's place in China and the Republic of China, as illustrated by his discussions of local self-government.

Born in Tainan, Huang inherited an affinity for China from his father, who taught him Chinese. In 1916 he traveled to Tokyo to continue his education. Although the Nationalists often claimed Japanese "slave" education turned the Taiwanese against China, Huang, like many Half-Mountain people, was educated first in the colonial system. Huang found life in Japan, with its relatively open political environment and contact with ideas of national self-determination from the West, politically stimulating. Unlike many of his peers, however, he often put his political activism in the context of China, not simply Taiwan and its relationship with Japan. Huang was a frequent contributor to Taiwanese magazines and newspapers in the 1920s and 1930s, writing about such topics as the need for Chinese-language reform and Japan's Twenty-one Demands upon China. Ironically, while in Japan Huang became drawn into the history of Republican China. For example, he assisted several important visiting mainlanders, including the warlord Zhang Xueliang, by serving as translator during their visits to Japan. He also traveled to the mainland, where he witnessed the political and cultural ferment of the May Fourth Movement. In 1923, Huang and his wife went to America. He obtained his master's degree in political science from the University of Illinois, and expanded his circle of acquaintances among mainland Chinese in the United States.

After returning to the mainland, Huang made China, not Taiwan, the object of his political activity. He joined the Guomindang, because, as one of his essays in *Taiwan minpō* (Chin., *Taiwan minbao*) explained, only this party had a program for China.[85] Huang's career with the Nationalists began in the Foreign Ministry, and was marked by a steady, if unspectacular, rise in rank and responsibility. Perhaps the key to his success was not the strength of his convictions or decisiveness, but his ability to recognize political trends and avoid giving great offense to anyone powerful. He represented exactly what the Nationalists wanted from the Taiwanese: loyalty to Jiang Jieshi and his son, and willingness to put the needs of China, as defined by the government, before those of the island. He became part of factional rivalries in the Nationalist ranks, and was often connected to the Political Science Clique of bureaucrats and technical experts.[86] In order to continue his work, he renounced his Japanese citizenship, one of the few Taiwanese to take this step. He had a future with the Nationalists, as illustrated by his participation in the Central Party Training Corps for high level cadres.

During the last years of the war, Huang became involved in planning for the Nationalist takeover of Taiwan. He joined the Taiwan Investigation Committee in Chongqing, and authored several books about the island.[87] Huang's writing suggested a man trying to reconcile the interests of the mainland's government and the island's people. His essays immediately prior to retrocession urged the Nationalists to take a relatively benevolent stance toward the Taiwanese and the colonial legacy. He acknowledged the material progress achieved under colonial rule and cautioned the Nationalists to maintain the standards set by the Japanese. In particular, he warned that officials sent to the island must perform as competently as their predecessors. Furthermore, he wrote, the mainland government must trust that islanders are loyal Chinese and make Taiwan a model province.[88] But after his return to the island, Huang shifted his position slightly, and clearly put Taiwan into a position subordinate to the mainland. He invoked his Chinese identity and accurately pointed out that the mainland had suffered the hardships of war far more than the island had in the recent past.[89] Although this statement was undoubtedly true, Huang's public acknowledgment of this fact signaled his willingness to accept the Nationalists' version of Taiwan's history and the colonial legacy.

Administrator Chen Yi appointed Huang mayor of Taibei, a post he only held for a short period before being elected to the Provincial Consultative Assembly. With the support of the provincial administration, he was chosen as chairman of the assembly by its members. Questions about Huang's election sparked a public dispute over whether Lin Xiantang had been pressured to remove himself from contention. The Taibei assembly voted to recall Huang during the ensuing public uproar. He felt it necessary to deny that he had been "bought" by Chen Yi.[90] Huang claimed he had talked to Lin before the election and had received the elder leader's blessing. He then resigned, blaming the chaotic nature of democracy on the island, particularly in the assembly, as well as the attempts to recall him over the Lin Xiantang issue.[91] After a series of meetings with Lin and others, Huang announced that he had been convinced to return.[92] He served as chairman of the Provincial Consultative Assembly and then of the Provincial Provisional Assembly (later transformed into the Provincial Assembly) until 1963. Nevertheless, Huang struggled against charges that he had used his close ties to the Nationalists in order to intimidate Lin. This incident marked the beginning of a trend that would last for decades — Huang had become a lightning rod for criticism of all Half-Mountain Taiwanese.

Huang at least obliquely acknowledged that his mainland experiences sparked conflict with other assembly members. He stated that since he had been trained by the Nationalists about democracy, his ideas and those of his fellow islanders in the assembly often differed.[93] Unlike many of his fellow assembly members, Huang expected the body to discuss and educate, not criticize or legislate. In particular, he called for tolerance (*rongren*) and cooperation (*hezuo*) between the people and the government.[94] Huang envisioned his role as chairman as one who facilitated meetings and presented members' views to the government. He focused on maintaining proper procedures for managing the assembly, but rarely expressed his own opinions.[95] Although he attended almost all assembly meetings, Huang was conspicuous for his lack of resolutions, petitions, or interpellation of officials. When he did raise issues, they were usually national in scope and utterly uncontroversial. For example, in late 1947 he presented a resolution urging the central government to pressure Japan to surrender sovereignty over the Liuqiu (Ryukyu) Islands to China. He justified this by emphasizing that the language, culture, and customs of those islands were not the same as Japan's.[96] Why the inhabitants of this archipelago should be part of China, however, he did not say.

Huang sought to project an personal image best summed up by the title of his biography, *A Biography of Huang Chaoqin: Love of Country and Native Place (Huang Chaoqin zhuan: Aiguo, aixiang)*.[97] Huang wanted to take a middle position on most issues. Like Han Shiquan, he blamed conflicts during the first sessions of the Provincial Consultative Assembly on both government errors and Taiwanese misunderstanding of democracy. The people expected too much, he said, but he also admitted government policies had failed.[98] Ultimately, however, when Huang had to choose between the Nationalist government and Taiwanese society, he sided with the former. Huang participated in the February 28 Resolution Committee and attempted to limit violence by the Taiwanese and the government. When events spun out of control in the second week of March 1947, Huang clearly backed the Nationalists. He was never arrested or harassed over his role in the incident. Overall, Huang's position shifted with the political winds — his support of the Nationalists became stronger as the regime grew less willing to tolerate dissent on the island. In the session of the Provincial Consultative Assembly following the incident, Huang accepted Governor Wei Daoming's goal of moving from stability to prosperity (*zai andingzhong qiu fanrong*), and added that the government must lead sincerely and the people must follow orders.[99] Huang was content to follow the state's program of local self-government. He even worked to lower expectations about the Provincial Consultative Assembly by accepting that this body was only transitional and as such had limited power. He was not a strong voice for speedy or comprehensive reform.[100]

Perhaps no work better summarizes Huang's views than his essay "China's Revolutionary Movement and Taiwan," in a collection of articles intended for citizenship training.[101] This essay repeated the Nationalist view of the island's place in the state and nation by highlighting the common political history and destiny of people on both sides of the strait. Implicit in it was the assumption that the fate of the Guomindang was synonymous with that of the Chinese nation. Nationalists leaders such as Sun Zhongshan, Huang wrote, had long struggled to reunite Taiwan with China. Politics on the island thus formed part of China's revolutionary movement. During the colonial era, Taiwanese came to the mainland to join the Nationalists, and were deeply influenced by Sun's, then Jiang's, leadership. In the wake of the Nationalists' defeat on the mainland, Taiwan had returned to the vital position it held in the mid-1600s as the last redoubt of the Chinese nation against a foreign invader. The essay concluded that Taiwan had a glorious mission to complete China's revolutionary struggle.[102] In other writings, Huang repeated the familiar Nationalist theme that Taiwan was the "base for the restoration of our race" (*minzu fuxing de jidi*). He also compared the beleaguered Nationalists to Zheng Chenggong: both represented Chinese loyalists struggling against alien invaders.[103] He said little about what the Nationalists would do for Taiwan, as though the island was only important as it related to the mainland.

Huang, as a Taiwanese "winner" in this mainlander-controlled state, illustrates how politics on the island remained competitive, but not terribly meaningful. By the early 1950s the colonial-era leaders of the Taizhong Clique had largely disappeared. Younger politicians with no ties to the Nationalists prior to retrocession, sometimes known as the Ah Hai Clique, had been arrested or killed, or had chosen to leave politics. The islanders who survived and remained active in provincial affairs after the February 28 Incident, the White Terror, and land reform formed factions made up almost exclusively of loyal Guomindang members with few discernible differences in their political views. For example, after 1953 most members of the Provincial Assembly were divided into two cliques, both beholden to the Nationalists. One, led by Huang Chaoqin, traded on its political capital based on relationships with more powerful mainlanders, and also influence in four large companies (mining, cement, paper, and lumber) placed under public ownership as well as three major banks (Zhanghua, Hua'nan, and Diyi). The other, led by Lin Dingli, made up a larger part of the provincial body, but possessed less influence as individuals.[104] Huang and Lin were constantly in conflict, so much so that the central government stepped in at least once to limit their rivalry.[105] For the most part, however, the

Nationalists tolerated these disputes, because both factions depended upon the Guomindang and state for their influence and presented no threat to the regime. Taiwanese could compete within the system if they did not seek major reform of it.

Chairman Huang enjoyed the benefits, both economic and political, available to prominent supporters of the Nationalists. For example, his service was rewarded with positions in various state corporations. Most notably, he became director of a former Japanese bank, the Taiwan Commercial and Industrial Bank (today the First Commercial Bank of Taiwan). Huang had been involved in taking over this bank for the Nationalists after Japan's surrender. He played a key role in the construction and management of the Grand Hotel, Taiwan's most luxurious hotel when it opened, in cooperation with Madame Jiang Jieshi (Song Meiling). Because of his long history of anti-Japanese activism, he was entrusted to serve in various groups, such as the Sino-Japanese Economic and Cultural Association, involved in improving relations with Japan.

Huang remained chairman of the Provincial Assembly until 1963. He was so secure in that position that he was successful in the 1957 and 1960 elections even though he was in Japan at the time.[106] Jiang Jingguo became a key patron of Huang, and oversaw his steady promotion. Huang's career peaked in the 1950s when he became a member of two of the most powerful organizations in the Nationalist state and party, the Central Advisory Committee (Zhongyang pingyi weiyuanhui) and the Standing Committee of the Guomindang Central Committee.[107]

Throughout his career, Huang Chaoqin remained a solid, and stolid, follower of the mainlander-dominated government. He had in abundance the qualities and skills needed for a Taiwanese to enjoy political success under the Nationalists: a long relationship with the Guomindang, a willingness to put Chinese prerogatives before Taiwanese interests, and an eagerness to follow central government dictates.

Conclusion

Postwar Taiwan is difficult to categorize: is it a nation, a province, or some combination of the two?[108] The case studies of Taiwanese reactions to Nationalist rule contained in this chapter raise still another possibility: a colony. Although even the suggestion of colonialism is politically sensitive, colonialism merits discussion because it captures the complexity of the Taiwanese interaction with the Nationalists and forms part of the ideological underpinning for the independence movement today.[109] Since retrocession, when islanders compared Japanese and Nationalist policies, aspects of colonialism were not defined in any abstract sense, but by the similarities between the pre- and post-1945 administrations.

One common way of describing colonial rule is the model of core and periphery. The metropole is the core, which dominates and exploits the less developed periphery. A variation of this model is the notion of internal colonialism developed by Michael Hechter. Essentially, Hechter places the core-periphery paradigm within one nation-state; in his case study, the Irish, Welsh, and Scots within the United Kingdom. He writes that a "spatially uneven wave of modernization over a state territory creates relatively advanced and less advanced groups."[110] Hechter points out that the core has economic dominance and political control, and practices "national discrimination on the basis of language, religion or other cultural forms."[111] The core uses its political power to maintain its advantages, much as a colonial power seeks through direct or indirect rule to dominate a colony. "Disadvantaged groups," Hechter notes, "are likely to demand that decision-making be 'localized' so that their special problem might become appreciated and therefore taken into account in the allocation process."[112] This describes the goals of the Taiwanese elite.

However, to describe Taiwan as a colony or internal colony under Nationalist rule is problematic. First, this peripheral island was more advanced economically than the mainland. Second, immigrants from the mainland after 1945 were more exiles than colonists. Furthermore, the government struggled to prove that the local population was culturally, politically, and historically one and the same with mainlanders. The Nationalists never thought of themselves as colonizers, and in fact based their legitimacy on a claim of restoring Chinese rule to the island. This idea was even embedded in language, as retrocession (*guangfu*) became the term used by the Nationalists to describe their takeover of the island after the war. To the Nationalists, three factors "proved" Taiwan was not a colony: international law (the Cairo Declaration returned the island to China), intent (mainlanders did not seek to make Taiwan a colony), and policies (government measures were designed for the entire nation). Specific programs such as local self-government represented the fulfillment of long-term goals for China, not a specific colonial policy.

Nevertheless, when examining the island's elite, the model of Taiwan as a colony has some validity. The various positions taken by Taiwanese vis-à-vis the Nationalist state, and the divisions among prominent islanders, had many similarities to the pre-1945 colonial experience. As these case studies illustrate, most islanders found ways to reconcile their personal, professional, and political aspirations with the reality of Japanese, then Nationalist, control without resorting to violence.[113] This is not to gloss over the brutality of Jiang Jieshi's police state. The fate of Wang Tiandeng, for example, was an example of how violent mainlander rule of Taiwan could be. However, the authoritarianism of the Nationalist regime constituted just one of many factors that shaped the provincial elite's relationship with the government. Continuing a trend initiated during the Japanese period, many islanders participated in an impotent system of local self-government even as they tried to reform it. Although the Nationalists *preferred* to have the support of islanders, they were *satisfied* if Taiwanese simply avoided all political activity and did not openly oppose the regime, as exemplified by the experiences of Han Shiquan and Lin Xiantang. The Nationalists never matched the Communists' drive to transform individuals, and unlike the mainland experience after 1949, apathy was a viable and safe option for individual Taiwanese. Before and after 1945, islanders were encouraged to use their professional and technical skills to promote economic development while avoiding politics. Elites under both regimes found that material incentives gave them a reason to accept political domination.

Taiwanese author Wu Zhuoliu likened supporters of the Nationalists, particularly Half-Mountain people, to those who had helped the Japanese occupy the island in the late 1890s.[114] Mainlanders, particularly Jiang Jieshi and his son Jiang Jingguo, became vital patrons of those wishing to advance their careers, just as the Japanese governors-general in their day had patronized ambitious and compliant Taiwanese. For example, the career of Huang Chaoqin illustrated how political connections could be a means of gaining influence over economic organizations such as banks. Huang inherited many of the economic privileges that the Japanese had given prominent Taiwanese such as Lin Xiantang. Taiwanese like Huang were welcomed by the Nationalists. They could participate in politics and compete against one another through factions if they did not try to bring about systemic change or challenge the Nationalists' legitimacy.

Terms like assimilation and independence do not convey the complexity of the Taiwanese understanding of their place in China and the Republic of China. Most islanders hoped to find a modus vivendi that fell between these two ends of a continuum — usually articulated as a drive for expanded local self-government. In the same way, the term colonialism is too simple and does not fully explain the reality of Nationalist policies on the island, even if the Taiwanese elite *reacted* like a people living under colonial rule. Perhaps this lack of clarity is to be expected in postwar Taiwan. The advocacy of local self-government, itself an ambiguous concept whose meaning shifted over time, corresponds to this situation just as nationalism can be a reaction to "pure" colonialism. Ultimately, Taiwan is best understood by examining the complex interaction of all three of these seemingly contradictory elements: nation, province, and colony. After the Nationalists' defeat on the mainland, Taiwan represented a nation with a state that insisted it was a province, and the Taiwanese were a people whose political activity suggested they were living in a colony. Ironically, the real colonizers were the Han Chinese immigrants to the island during the late Ming and Qing periods who had conquered Taiwan and subdued the aboriginal peoples — the first Taiwanese. This fact, like so much of the island's history, was conveniently forgotten by Han Taiwanese and mainlanders alike.

7 Conclusion and Epilogue

The years 1945 to 1950 were the most tumultuous in Taiwan's history. The period was marked by high expectations for retrocession, disappointment with Nationalist misrule, struggles over the Japanese legacy and decolonization, a violent uprising by many Taiwanese and a brutal response by the state, the chaos of Jiang Jieshi's retreat, and the consolidation of a mainlander-dominated authoritarian regime through measures such as local self-government. The Taiwanese political elite — relatively wealthy, Japanese-educated, moderate reformers who found themselves part of a militarized and poor nation — proved dangerously out of step with the major political trends of late Republican China. They had not engaged in armed struggle against their colonial masters under the banner of Chinese nationalism, and were thus tainted with collaboration in the eyes of mainlanders. Nor did they respond to Japanese rule by seeking independence for Taiwan. Under the Japanese, and then the Nationalist Chinese, the Taiwanese elite attempted to maximize its autonomy within a larger political entity.

As uncomfortable as it may have been for all those involved, the Taiwanese relationship with the Nationalist state between 1945 and 1950 blended the political conflicts of Republican China and the legacy of colonial rule. Islanders recalled the efficient and effective, if repressive, colonial administration as they navigated their way through this extraordinarily difficult period, and soon determined that the new state failed to meet their standards of acceptable governance. After the eight-year War of Resistance, mainlanders did not want to confront the positive aspects of Japanese rule and usually dismissed islanders' attempts to hold the government to colonial-era standards. To supporters of Jiang's regime, criticism by Taiwanese represented anti-Nationalist (and, to their mind, antinationalist) sentiment stemming from the "poisonous legacy" of colonialism. Furthermore, the Nationalists were convinced that expanded provincial autonomy threatened the nation. It was, they believed, no more than an excuse for warlords' avarice and a cause of divisiveness that only aided imperialism. Whatever the logic of the Nationalist position, it was buttressed by both the will and the ability to enforce state policy.

Although Taiwan became the focal point of China's unfinished civil war and part of the global Cold War, the Taiwanese stood on the periphery of the forces of Communism and revolutionary violence that swept the world during the twentieth century. Under the Japanese and then the Nationalist Chinese, the police effectively blocked the "importation" of Communism and prevented its indigenous development. In any case, few Taiwanese sought radical economic or social change. The provincial elite after all consisted of successful capitalists who ranked among the most prosperous people in the region. Because of state oppression and their own economic interests, these islanders had little sympathy for Communism or other violent revolutionary movements. In fact, their demands for expanded local self-government under Nationalist rule were spurred in part by the inability of the state to protect private property and to preserve public order.

The Taiwanese were unarmed, both militarily and ideologically, in Republican China. The latter half of the 1940s was a time of extremes, when the only viable political alternatives, the Nationalists or the Communists, engaged in a bloody civil war.[1] Based on their colonial-era experience, however, the Taiwanese had learned to pursue a moderate course of reform and local self-government. In addition, members of the islandwide elite feared the social forces that might be unleashed by uprisings against the state. Even the February 28 Incident demonstrated the elite's nonviolent approach to politics. If the incident signified more than provincial resistance to central authority, it was still less than a full-blown nationalist movement. In fact, prominent islanders often attempted to limit violence and protect mainland officials. They also used the opportunity afforded by the Nationalists' weakness to press for reforms that would increase the island's autonomy vis-à-vis the central government. These Taiwanese had badly miscalculated. Even as they negotiated with the provincial government and local military leaders, military reinforcements arrived from the mainland, crushing all opposition and massacring thousands.

Under the Nationalists, the Taiwanese sought to situate their province between independence, becoming a nation in their own right, and assimilation, becoming what they perceived to be a typical province of China. Taiwanese and the Nationalists struggled to shape the ideology of the province, the ideas and images that determined the relationship between Taiwan, the central government, and the nation. The regime wanted to make the islanders loyal to the Chinese nation, but also to limit their political activity to the provincial level and below. Here, the province was important only as it assisted the goals of administration and of building a strong central government, which in turn was deemed vital for the Chinese nation. The Taiwanese accepted the nation and the ultimate authority of the central government, but attempted to maximize provincial autonomy and limit the impact of mainland events upon the island. They attempted to define local self-government in such a way as to limit the scope of "national" involvement in what they saw as provincial affairs. To them, the island's relatively developed economy and educated population, both results of colonial rule, deserved protection from the nation's problems. To the Nationalists, Taiwan's advantages only increased its obligations to assist their national agenda of building, then preserving, China.

Because of the February 28 Incident and collapse on the mainland, the Nationalists refashioned Taiwan into a citadel for protecting the Chinese nation from Communism. The Taiwanese found themselves playing a small role in a national crusade against Communism. Mainland immigrants and their Republic of China led this effort to contain the Chinese Communists. Americans, Japanese, and others outside the island paid little attention to the Taiwanese because the islanders' "provincial" political agenda did not fit neatly into the Cold War context nor directly serve an anti-Communist agenda.

By 1950, the Nationalists dominated discourse concerning the Chinese nation, the mainlander-controlled government, and Taiwan Province. They implemented a system of local self-government that reflected their understanding of China's history, Taiwan's relationship with the mainland, and Sun Zhongshan's mission of national salvation. Jiang Jieshi and his supporters at last implemented on the island of Taiwan the highly centralized political system they had sought on the mainland since the 1920s.

Taiwanization: Islanders Take Control from the Inside

Defying the expectations of many Chinese, Taiwanese, and Americans, the regime that failed miserably on the mainland became a success, both by its own standards and those of many outside observers, on the island.[2] Jiang Jieshi obtained financial, diplomatic, and military backing from the United States as Taiwan became Free China, a vital link in America's containment structure. The Nationalist government put into practice economic policies that brought prosperity and an enviably fair distribution of wealth among both mainland immigrants and Taiwanese. Backed by United States aid and advice, the Nationalists implemented rent reduction and land reform, as well as import substitution then export-oriented policies that made Taiwan a major economic power.[3] The relationship between Taiwanese and the Nationalist state facilitated these measures. Because of the February 28

Incident and the White Terror, the island's elite, particularly Japanese-educated landlords, did not dare oppose government policies, even if such measures were not in its interest. As had been the case under colonial rule, the Nationalists permitted relative economic freedom even as they stifled political activity. Taiwan became home to thousands of small and medium-sized enterprises, thus providing an outlet for the islanders' energies. Taiwanese enjoyed the fruits of prosperity, including a rising standard of living, improved education, better health care, and low unemployment.[4]

Despite its accomplishments in the economic realm and the early success the Nationalists enjoyed at dominating Taiwan's elite, the regime appeared electorally endangered and ideologically adrift by the 1990s. No single event or individual sliced through the Gordian knot of Nationalist state and Taiwanese politics; rather it came undone in a variety of ways. First, the Nationalists' attempt to co-opt islanders by allowing them to participate in the state and the party enabled Taiwanese to take over the Guomindang and the Republic of China from the inside. Second, the oppression and brutality of the state pushed some islanders to oppose Jiang's government, and to reject explicitly its ideology. Third, economic progress changed society, enlarging and emboldening a reformist middle class. These trends had their roots in the relationship between the Taiwanese and the Nationalist state during the 1945 to 1950 period.

The Nationalists failed to freeze the relationship between the state and Taiwanese society as it existed in 1950. Even as the regime crushed dissent and manipulated local self-government in its own interest, it offered compliant islanders a place in the Guomindang and the government. Many of those who accommodated themselves to mainland rule discovered they could participate in local administration and engage in political competition among local factions.[5] Through their own efforts and the attrition of the mainland rulers, islanders gradually moved up in the ranks of the party and bureaucracy, displacing the aging mainland-born elite in a process known as Taiwanization (*Taiwanhua*). The leaders of the Half-Mountain Taiwanese, with ties to the Nationalists dating back to before the retrocession, also faded away. They had been a link between the Taiwanese, the mainlander-dominated state, and the Nationalists' national priorities. Over the course of four decades, Taiwanese, most of whom had never been to the mainland, came to control the Guomindang and government from the inside — thus making both institutions more amenable to the interests of the island's people.

Ironically, the Nationalists brought a government to the island that gradually became a forum for questioning their ideology of Chinese nationalism. By the 1980s, the province no longer represented the pinnacle of political participation for the Taiwanese, as islanders came to control the central government headquartered in Taibei as well. Even Taiwanese members of the

Nationalist Party rejected or ignored the image of Taiwan as a microcosm of China or as a base in a national struggle to retake the mainland. "Nationalism," the ideology of Three Principles of the People, anti-Communism, and loyalty to the Guomindang, declined in importance. In this environment the idea of a Taiwanese nation, legally and permanently independent from the mainland, gained prominence, if not clear dominance.

The regime's early success in restructuring and co-opting the island's elite created Trojan horses in its midst. The most notable example is perhaps Li Denghui (Lee Teng-hui), president of the Republic of China from 1988 to 2000.[6] Born north of Taibei in 1923, Li prospered under colonialism. His early education marked him as a future member of the elite, as he passed the difficult tests necessary to enter the predecessor of Taiwan Normal University. In 1943, Li traveled to Japan to study agricultural economics at Kyoto Imperial University, beginning a successful career in this field. Like many of his classmates, both Taiwanese and Japanese, he was drafted into the military, and made a second lieutenant in the army, but saw no combat. After the war, he returned to the island and continued his studies at National Taiwan University. Li's personal abilities enabled him to overcome the dangerous taint of Japanese education and colonial collaboration to become what the mainland regime wanted. He generally supported the government and the Guomindang, and provided valuable technical skills for economic development. Li stuck to professional and academic activities, and avoided politics, during the first decade of Nationalist rule. In the early 1950s he earned a master's degree in agricultural economics in the United States. Li returned to America and obtained his doctorate in the same subject from Cornell University in the late 1960s. After returning to Taiwan, his contribution to the Nationalist state continued to be more professional than political. He was a university instructor and worked for the China Village Restoration Committee (Zhongguo nongcun fuxing weiyuanhui). As a protégé of Jiang Jingguo, he appeared to be a "safe" Taiwanese to promote during the 1970s. In visible, yet relatively powerless, posts, he dampened criticism that the government was not promoting Taiwanese, yet did not appear to threaten the dominance of mainlanders or their ideology.

Li exemplified the results of Taiwanization. He quietly moved up the Nationalist hierarchy to become Jiang Jingguo's vice president in 1984, then president after Jiang's death in 1988.[7] The new president surprised many observers not only by remaining in office, but also by engineering the retirement of the mainland-born premier. Li consolidated his power, and was reelected in his own right in 1990 and 1996. In both rhetoric and action, however, he steadily drifted away from the mainlanders' vision of the Chinese nation and Nationalist state. For example, he sped Taiwanization by promoting islanders into key posts. He also broadened the democratic reforms begun under Jiang Jingguo, enabling the opposition party to gain strength. As Taiwanese moved to control the central government, the issue of provincial autonomy became less important. Li took on the difficult task of reconciling provincial and national governments, attempting to remedy a problem dating back to the late 1940s when the Republic of China and Taiwan Province essentially became the same territory. He supported reform to abolish the provincial government and assembly, thus combining the central and provincial governments. Perhaps most controversially, he was ambiguous at best on unification with the mainland, a fundamental tenet undergirding the Nationalists' legitimacy.[8]

Although economic, social, cultural, and political contacts with the mainland expanded dramatically during Li Denghui's tenure, the president antagonized Beijing with statements that cast doubt on his commitment to unification within the framework of "one China." Until his presidency, the official Guomindang policy had been that there was but one China and that Taiwan was a province of China. Both the Communists and the Nationalists insisted that they represented the sole legitimate national government of China. However, as president, Li acknowledged that the PRC represented the mainland, thus abandoning the ROC claim to be the sole legitimate government of China. He sought diplomatic recognition for the Republic of China on Taiwan, pushing the goal of reunification with the mainland into the distant future. Although Li stated that Taiwanese are culturally Chinese, he separated this from the question of national identity. In effect, Li and his supporters seemed headed toward Taiwanese independence.

Li expressed his ambivalence over unification most freely to foreign journalists, thus giving ammunition to those who associated separatism with outside interference. In a controversial 1995 interview with a Japanese writer, he voiced many of the themes and goals of critics of mainland rule of Taiwan. He argued that traditionally China had found Taiwan expendable — it was unwanted (*buyao*) and considered to be outside of civilization (*huawai zhi di*). Li even suggested that the Nationalists were a "regime from outside" (*wailai zhengquan*), as had been every government that held power on the island. His stance is best summed up by his promise to transform the ruling party into a Taiwanese Guomindang. However, like many of those seeking to build a Taiwanese consciousness on the island, he did not exclude mainlanders. Li declared that everyone residing in Taiwan who had come from the mainland or whose ancestors had come from the mainland was Han Chinese.[9]

Despite the uproar sparked by his 1995 visit to the United States, Li Denghui suggested his support for independence as the Republic of China. For example, in a November 1997 interview with an American reporter, he called Taiwan a sovereign, independent state (*zhuquan duli de guojia*).[10] In

July 1999 Li openly repudiated the one China principle in an interview with German correspondents, stating that the cross-strait relationship was "state to state" (*guojia yu guojia*), or "at least a special *guo yu guo* relationship."[11] He contended that because the ROC has been sovereign since 1912, there was no need to declare Taiwan independent.[12] He described the ROC on Taiwan as the political equal of the People's Republic based on the continuity of its government from the mainland — in effect hijacking the Nationalist state for a Taiwanese nation.

The original Nationalists, those born across the strait, found the policies and power structure created between 1945 and 1950 under attack. For example, language remained a political issue, but reflected the shifting balance of power on Taiwan. Politicians found that getting elected required speaking *Taiyu*, the dialect understood by most islanders. This marked a reversal from the immediate postwar period, when the state mandated Mandarin Chinese as the only acceptable language. Taiwanization threatened to marginalize mainlanders and their political agenda. Indeed, opposition to President Li within the Guomindang became known as the "nonmainstream faction" (*fei liuxingpai*). As the political power of Taiwanese expanded beyond the provincial level, the rhetoric of fighting Communism and reuniting with the mainland receded in importance. Politicians benefited little from discussing these "national" priorities. Mainlanders and their children who felt betrayed by the Taiwanization of the political system in general and the Guomindang in particular formed their own small political party (the New Party; Xindang) that adhered to the long-term Nationalist goals for the Chinese nation. In 2000, mainlander James Song formed the People First Party (Qinmindang), which has a similar platform.[13]

Triumph of the Ambiguous Moderates

As the Nationalist regime gradually succumbed to a takeover from the inside, it also faced a more overt opposition outside the government and party ranks. Taiwan's "economic miracle" created a social base for political change as professionals and business people returned to public life.[14] Beginning in the 1970s, many of the children of those who had abandoned political activity began to demand a more responsive government, less corruption, and greater attention to quality of life issues.[15] Some of these moderates became leaders in social movements devoted to environmental protection or women's rights, problems that had no place in the "old" Nationalist paradigm of anti-Communism and Chinese nationalism. This reversed the process wherein the "transcendentals" of the late 1940s, dis-

couraged by their lack of influence, abandoned politics for business or professional careers.

Because Taiwanization made the government less willing to use force to
stifle the opposition, and a growing middle class risked arrest in order to promote reform, organized alternatives to the Nationalists gained both popularity and legal sanction. Immediately after retrocession, Taiwanese learned
to focus on local issues, not national-level policies or systematic change to
the provincial administration. Unlike the Communist regime, however, the
Nationalists were never so brutal as to exterminate all opposition, and "careful critics" could participate as independent politicians or as members of the
tiny Third Force parties.[16] As old age reduced the remnants of the mainland-
based liberal reform movement, the opposition went through its own
process of Taiwanization. This reduced the interest in and rhetoric for reform
in the context of China, a place most of these activists had never been.

Taiwanese worked through the system created to serve mainlanders' interests even as they hoped to reform it. The heirs of the careful critics of the
Nationalist regime eventually became the open and organized opposition.
Despite imprisonment and harassment, in the 1970s non-Guomindang
politicians and intellectuals, dubbed *dangwai* ("outside the party"), grew
more vocal. They formed the Democratic Progressive Party (DPP; Minzhu
jinbudang) in 1986, which became the largest opposition party on the island.
Under the leadership of Jiang Jieshi's son and successor, Jiang Jingguo, the
government lifted martial law in 1987. The younger Jiang came to realize
that the Cold War approach of widespread oppression and limited participation for the Taiwanese was no longer viable. Wide-ranging reforms followed, including the relaxation of controls over the press, speech, assembly,
and political opposition.[17] In this environment, the DPP was able to work
within the political structure established by the Nationalists in the late 1940s,
and to expand its influence upward from towns, to counties, to the province,
and to national-level bodies. The party, bolstered by support from the growing middle class, made quality of life issues and corruption important parts
of its platform.

The most implacable opposition to the Nationalists' vision of Taiwan's
place in China and the Republic of China came not from the Communists,
but from the independence movement.[18] The relationship between the
Democratic Progressive Party and the issue of independence was and is complex. Perhaps many islanders rejected reunification in part because the
mainlander-dominated regime wanted it — questioning membership in the
Chinese nation is a way to question Nationalist legitimacy. Separatists
played pivotal roles in establishing the party and today provide some of its
strongest support. The DPP, however, made independence only one of many
issues in its platform, and its leadership has been divided over the priority

to be accorded to the question of national identity. Furthermore, DPP leaders found that electoral victory often required downplaying separatism, since many voters feared a military attack from the PRC if independence was declared. Nevertheless, the DPP has become the single most important forum for Taiwan independence (*Taidu*).

Regardless of the complexity of the Taiwanese experience during the years 1945 to 1950, Taidu activists have described this period as the imposition of colonial rule by mainlanders. Backers of independence have created their own narrative to demonstrate the island's differences from the mainland and to validate the yearning for separation from outside political entities, be they Chinese or Japanese. Scholars who favor independence have emphasized the need to study the island with less reference to the mainland, and certainly not to treat it as a case study for comparison with other provinces of China.[19] Most importantly, they have argued that China abandoned the island in 1895 and thus compromised any claim to sovereignty. Taidu advocates often claim a strong resistance to Japanese rule, but argue that this occurred without the support of the Nationalists and the Communists. In effect, resistance to colonialism indicated a nascent Taiwanese, not Chinese, nationalism.

Ironically, this Taiwan-centered history accepts one of Jiang Jieshi's key assertions — that the Nationalists represent China. Separatists combine Nationalist state and Chinese nation, but reject both. They eschew the term *guangfu* (retrocession) and instead use *jieshou*, which means "to receive" or "take over," and lacks the connotation of political legitimacy. Nationalist rule is classified as colonial, little different from the rule of the Dutch, Manchus, and Japanese before them. Taiwanese nationalists identify the February 28 Incident as a pivotal event in the island's history. In their version, conflict with Jiang's government was a nationalist struggle; there is little room for evidence that many islanders sought to reform, not remove, the Nationalists in 1947.[20] Until recent years, the Nationalists spoke of what happened on February 28 as an "incident" (*shijian*), implying an unexpected or unplanned event. Taiwanese independence activists, on the other hand, have often used the terms "popular uprising" (*minbian*) or "massacre" (*can'an*).[21] Some even called what happened on and shortly after February 28 a "holocaust."[22]

The political career of independence activist Peng Mingmin illustrates how the Nationalists seemed to create opposition to their regime and ideology. Born the same year as Li Denghui, Peng came from the relatively wealthy family of a Christian doctor. He seemed destined for a successful life under the Japanese but had contradictory feelings toward colonial rule. Peng enjoyed the material benefits and stability of the Japanese administration, but chafed at discrimination and attempts at forced assimilation.[23] After retrocession, Peng metamorphosed from colonial success story to politically apathetic professional to opposition activist. His discontent with Nationalist rule grew into a sweeping critique of the mainland, which he portrayed as backward, corrupt, and violent. Like many youth, he was swept up in the February 28 Incident, then went into political hibernation after the Nationalists reestablished their control of the island. In fact, Peng was a success under Nationalist rule, and became the youngest professor at National Taiwan University. In the 1950s he was a "transcendental": "In these years politics as such held no interest for me. I was concerned only with my own career and my writing."[24]

In the early 1960s, as Li Denghui was quietly working his way up the Guomindang hierarchy, Peng went from discontent to criticism of the state, then to an attack on the Chinese nation and the legitimacy of Nationalist rule. In 1964 he and a few friends attempted to publish "A Declaration of a Movement for Formosan Self-Salvation" (*Taiwan ziqiu yundong xuanyan*), calling for self-determination for the Taiwanese and an end to Nationalist rule. Peng was arrested, but his relatively prominent position enabled him to avoid execution or a long jail sentence. Constant harassment and surveillance, however, spurred him to flee Taiwan in 1970. From exile, he became one of the best known voices for the Taiwanese independence movement.

After the implementation of democratic reforms in the late 1980s, Peng returned to Taiwan and ran for president under the Democratic Progressive Party banner in 1996. Nothing better symbolized the continuing dilemma of state and nation on the island than the fact that a pro-independence politician competed for the presidency of the Republic of China.[25] Peng was continuing a political legacy dating back to colonial rule and the 1945–50 period by attempting to work through the state even as he tried to change it. He lost the election to incumbent Li Denghui because voters remained ambivalent over their future as a nation and unsure of Peng's ability to manage the day-to-day affairs of state. Islanders had a chance to make a clear declaration of their views on the nation, state, and province, but did not take advantage of it.

Li's final term as president ended in 2000, and the election that year marked a historic transfer of power on Taiwan. After a closely fought race, the opposition candidate, DPP standard-bearer Chen Shuibian, was victorious. Reflecting the growth of Taiwanese power on the island, over three decades Chen advanced from lawyer, dangwai activist, and local politician, to DPP leader, to mayor of Taibei, and finally to president of the Republic of China. With his declared aim of improving government services and democratic reform, Chen was the political heir of Guo Guoji and Li Wanju.

Chen's position on the mainland and the possibility of unification was pragmatic. In the year Chen was elected, the PRC issued a White Paper that made clear it reserved the right to use military force against Taiwan under three circumstances: a declaration of Taiwanese independence, the occupation of Taiwan by foreign forces, or an indefinite delay of talks on political unification. Before his election in March 2000, Chen began to back away from the plank in his party's platform that supported independence to a more ambiguous policy that in fact differed little from Li Denghui's approach. The new president, however, has frustrated Beijing. The PRC has derided his inaugural pledge of the "five no's" (not to declare independence, not to change the name of the country, not to put state-to-state relations in the constitution, not to promote a referendum on independence, and not to abolish the Guidelines for National Unification and the National Unification Council). Chen's refusal to announce his unequivocal acceptance of the one China principle has caused the mainland authorities and the Taiwan opposition alike to doubt his commitment to reunification.[26] Despite controlling the state, this president, like the island's elite in 1945, must reconcile a recognition of the mainland government's power with the drive to maximize autonomy.

Developments during the years 1945 to 1950 brought short-term success, but long-term failure, to the Nationalists and their Chinese nationalist ideology. For the Taiwanese, the events of those years meant the defeat of the movement for greater autonomy within China and the possibility of complete independence today. In building a highly centralized state through measures such as local self-government, the Nationalists enjoyed success from the late 1940s to the 1980s. They were in unassailable control of the island for decades. Yet, the Nationalists ultimately failed since they could not "contain" Taiwanese political activity to the provincial level. As islanders came to control the central government, the expansion of local self-government, the central issue of the 1945 to 1950 period, dwindled in importance. In building the Chinese nation on Taiwan, the Nationalists were even less successful. The island did not become a base for retaking the mainland, and most of the Taiwanese — even those who became Chinese Nationalists — did not become die-hard Chinese nationalists. Although the Taiwanese have taken over the state, the question of nation, whether Chinese or Taiwanese, awaits resolution.

Notes

1. Lan Dingyuan, "Luzhou wenji," 1.

2. Most Taiwanese came from provinces along the southeast coast of the mainland during the Qing dynasty (1644–1912), prior to the Japanese occupation in 1895. Traditionally, the Taiwanese have been divided into two main groups, Hokkien and Hakka. The former are mainly from the Minnan region of the province of Fujian, directly across the Taiwan Strait. (Minnan means south of the Min River, which cuts through Fujian.) They constitute about 85 percent of the Taiwanese population. They can be subdivided into two groups named for the areas of Fujian from which they hailed: Zhangzhou and Quanzhou. The coastal cities of Xiamen (Amoy) and Fuzhou were also important sources of migrants. The smaller group is the Hakka, also called Kejiaren (Guest People). These people came from the highlands of Guangdong Province, located immediately south of Fujian (especially from Chaozhou Prefecture). "Mainlanders" are Chinese who came to the island after 1945, the majority arriving between late 1948 and mid-1950 as the Nationalist government faced defeat at the hands of the Chinese Communists. Aborigines (*yuanzhumin*) comprised about 2 percent of the population. They are not Han Chinese, but are most closely related to the Austronesian peoples of island Southeast Asia. Through intermarriage and cultural assimilation, the distinctions among these groups have become less clear. Self-definition is often the only effective way to categorize the inhabitants of Taiwan.

3. The Republic of China (Zhonghua minguo) is also known as Nationalist China. This state was led by the Guomindang (the Nationalist Party), which in turn was guided by the ideology of Sun Zhongshan (Sun Yat-sen) called the Three Principles of the People (*Sanmin zhuyi*): Nationalism, Democracy, and People's Livelihood. The party was dominated by Jiang Jieshi after Sun's death in 1925.

4. Anderson, *Imagined Communities.*

5. Gellner, *Nations and Nationalism,* 7.

6. Hoston, *The State, Identity, and the National Question,* 3–4.

7. Gellner, *Nations and Nationalism,* 3–4. Max Weber defined the state as the formal administrative apparatus that monopolizes (or seeks to monopolize) the use of force in society. Theda Skocpol defines the state as "a set of administrative, policing, and military organizations headed, and more or less well coordinated by, an executive authority." Skocpol, *States and Social Revolutions,* 29. The state can also be understood as the political unit that is often (but by no means always) coterminous with the nation.

8. Duara, *Rescuing History from the Nation,* 10. Gertrude Himmelfarb could be

describing the framework of my study when she writes: "It is the function of the historian to show that nationality, like nationalism (and like the nation itself), has a history, changing over the course of time and varying from place to place, even taking different forms at the same time and place — providing the impulse, for example Little Englandism as well as imperialism, behind liberalism as well as conservatism." Himmelfarb, "Is National History Obsolete?" 142.

9. "Republican China" encompasses the period from the end of the last dynasty, the Qing, in 1912, until the establishment of the People's Republic of China (PRC) in 1949.

10. Between Taiwan and the mainland province of Fujian lie the Penghu Islands, a small archipelago also known as the Pescadores. To the northeast are the Liuqiu Islands (Ryukyu in Japanese), which have historically served as a stepping stone for Japanese interests in Taiwan. Southward are the Paracel (Xisha qundao) and Spratly Islands (Nansha qundao), which today are objects of competing claims by the PRC, Vietnam, the Philippines, Malaysia, Indonesia, and the Republic of China on Taiwan.

11. Ocean currents and weather patterns made it relatively difficult for sailing vessels to cross the Taiwan Strait to Taiwan. By way of comparison, Chinese knowledge of and settlement of Hainan Island dates from the Han dynasty (206 B.C.–A.D. 220), although Hainan is farther from the Chinese political and cultural heartland in the North China Plain. Another measure of the island's relative isolation is that the famous ocean expeditions to Southeast and South Asia led by Ming dynasty explorer Zheng He in the early fifteenth century never came to Taiwan.

12. The archaeological work of Kwang-chih Chang and others has shown contact with the mainland dating from the earliest sites discovered. This may, however, only indicate trade with the mainland, not Chinese settlement on Taiwan. Further, the mainland-based people in contact with Taiwan may not have been Han Chinese. They could be the people whom either intermarried with the Han people or migrated southward, away from the expanding Chinese empires on the North China Plain. Kwang-chih Chang, *Fengpitou, Tapenkeng, and the Prehistory of Taiwan*. The role of non-Han mainland cultures on Taiwan is an important part of discussions over the role of the Yellow River area as the sole source of what became known as Chinese culture. See Kwang-chih Chang, *The Archaeology of Ancient China*; and idem, "Chinese Archaeology since 1949."

13. Through gradually expanding trade and migration during the Song dynasty (960–1279), the Chinese began to settle the Penghu Islands, which served as a vital stepping stone for Han Chinese migration to Taiwan. Much of this early migration was the result of Mongol invasions from the north that pushed the population and political center of China southward during the Southern Song dynasty (1127–1279). By the thirteenth century, Taiwan had become part of the vibrant trade routes centered on the mainland entrepot of Quanzhou (Zayton). It was not until the late sixteenth century, however, that the Chinese came to the island in appreciable numbers. Pre-Ming records contain many names that may refer to Taiwan, but these references are often unclear, and it is difficult to know whether the authors are referring to Taiwan, Penghu, the Liuqiu Islands, or other islands off the southeast coast of China. The island were often described as home to ill-defined "Eastern Barbarians."

Chinese only had a clear idea of Taiwan's location and size in the seventeenth century. The term "Taiwan" probably came from the Minnan dialect pronunciation of Dayuan, the name for the area around today's Tainan now called Anping. By the late 1660s, "Taiwan" became widely accepted. This was confirmed when the island became a prefecture of Fujian. On early Chinese contact with and writing about Taiwan, see Lian Yatang, *Taiwan tongshi*, 1–21; and Guo Tingyi, *Taiwan shishi gaishuo*, 1–8.

14. On Zheng Chenggong, see Croizier, *Koxinga and Chinese Nationalism.*

15. The Manchus, non-Han peoples who conquered China in the mid-1600s and established the last imperial dynasty, the Qing, quickly adopted and adapted Confucian ideology and culture in order to buttress their rule of the Middle Kingdom. Following the Republican Revolution of late 1911, the dynasty officially ended with the abdication of the last emperor in 1912.

16. Fairbank, "Maritime and Continental in China's History."

17. For example, see Fairbank, *The United States and China*, part 1.

18. For example, problems such as "uncultured" migrant workers, violent conflict between ethnic and linguistic communities, and the difficulties of ruling a remote island province are detailed in Zhang Yuying, *Taiwan fuzhi*; and Liu Langbi, *Chongxiu Taiwan fuzhi*. For official views of Taiwan, see *ZhiTai migaolu*, a collection of essays and reports compiled by Ding Rijian during the 1860s. In it, Qing official Lan Dingyuan discusses the problems of frequent revolts, an uneducated population, greedy officials, widespread gambling, the impossibility of controlling immigration to the island, and the immigrants' depredations of the aborigines. Lan Dingyuan, "Luzhou wenji."

19. Fairbank called Maritime China "a peripheral region along the southeast coast." Fairbank, "Maritime and Continental in China's History," 9.

20. Conflict among the inhabitants of Taiwan was common during the Qing era. Contemporary scholar Lin Weisheng has investigated sixty conflicts of various types on Taiwan between 1721 and 1894. He writes that most conflicts stemmed from rivalries between those from different native places on the mainland. Next in importance were those arising from disputes between different clans (surnames, *xing*). Despite the relatively small size of the island, migrants settled in isolation from existing villages, bringing with them rivalries from the mainland. These communities then expanded until they clashed with others. Settlements on Taiwan had to band together to provide the protection and security the state could not. Lin Weisheng, *Luohanjiao.*

21. The idea of a coastal identity rising from these regional characteristics is problematic. Lynn White and Li Cheng examine competing and overlapping loyalties, and place them in three general categories: regional (Maritime China), national (China), and global (cosmopolitan). Lynn White and Li Cheng, "China Coast Identities."

22. For a more complete discussion of this issue and the debates between Li Guoqi, an advocate of *neidihua*, and Chen Qi'nan, a backer of *tuzhuhua*, see Chen Qi'nan, *Taiwan de chuantong Zhongguo shehui*, chap. 6; and Li Guoqi, *Zhongguo xiandaihua.*

23. Much of the information in this section comes from what is perhaps the best-known single-volume history of Taiwan from earliest times to 1895, Guo Tingyi,

Taiwan shishi gaishuo. See also Qi Jialin, *Taiwanshi*; and Lin Hengdao et al., eds., *Taiwanshi*. The landmark work by one of the most renown scholars of Taiwan's history, language, and customs is Lian Yatang's *Taiwan tongshi*. I am also deeply indebted to Professor Li Guoqi. In his graduate-level class at National Chengchi University, Topics in Taiwanese History, he raised and elucidated many of the issues discussed in this chapter.

24. Shepherd, *Statecraft and Political Economy on the Taiwan Frontier*.

25. Lian Yatang, *Taiwan tongshi*, 98–100; and Guo Tingyi, *Taiwan shishi gaishuo*, 93–96. On how these discussions relate specifically to Taiwan, see Guo Tingyi, *Taiwan shishi gaishuo*, 178–90.

26. On Taiwan's economic and political development during the late Qing, and the island's role in the history of the Self-Strengthening Movement, see Li Guoqi, *Zhongguo xiandaihua*.

27. Chen Ching-chih, "Impact of Japanese Colonial Rule," 28. Chen bases his assessment on the dissertation of Harry Lamley, "The Taiwan Literati and Early Japanese Rule."

28. The cession was formalized in the Treaty of Shimonoseki, signed in April 1895. An eyewitness account by a Taiwanese present during the Japanese takeover excoriates the Qing and bemoans the island's fate: "Since ancient times, nations have fallen. For a nation to fall, it must first abandon the people, who then abandon the government. To abandon the people, [the government] must first abandon land. Taiwan is an example of this, even though our ancestors have managed it for two hundred years." He goes on to lament that the Qing did not think the island worth fighting for. Written in 1906, this account predicts that the Qing were doomed because of their failure over issues like Taiwan. Huang Defu, *Taiwan zhanji*, intro. Japan's acquisition of Taiwan was opportunistic, as Tokyo had no grand imperial plan for the conquest of the island. See Edward Chen, "Japan's Decision to Annex Taiwan."

29. My use of the words "elite" and "group" rather than "class" reflects the fact that a strictly class-based analysis in the Marxist sense would tend to ignore the central role played by the state — both Japanese and Nationalist Chinese — as an independent force in forming the economic and social structures of the island.

30. For a discussion of the dominance of the narrative of the nation in history, see Duara, *Rescuing History from the Nation*, intro. and chap. 1.

31. Modern in this sense indicates the overall level of technological development, organizational forms, and worldview in Japan prior to World War II. This package of values and material change grew from the adoption of and adaptation from aspects of the societies, governments, and economies of Western Europe and the United States.

32. "Collective memory is an elaborate network of social mores, values, and ideals that marks out the dimensions of our imaginations according to the attitudes of the social groups to which we relate. It is through the interconnections among these shared images that the social frameworks (*cadres sociaux*) of our collective memory are formed, and it is within such settings that individual memories must be situated if they are to survive." Hutton, *History as an Art of Memory*, 78. One of the premier sociologists of memory, Maurice Halbwachs, wrote that "collective frameworks are . . . precisely the instruments used by the collective memory to reconstruct an

image of the past which is an accord with the predominant thoughts of the society." Halbwachs, *On Collective Memory*, 40.

33. Some scholars of federalism in Republican China point out that such a formula could be a way to promote the democratization of China as well as the reintegration of Taiwan. Both Hu Chunhui, author of a major work on federalism in early Republican China, and Leslie Chen (son of Chen Jiongming, a Republican-era regional leader and rival of Sun Yat-sen) have told me that their work can be used as a model or an attempt to rehabilitate federalism, the division of powers, and local self-government in China.

34. In this sense, examining the Taiwanese and their attempt to find a modus vivendi with the Japanese and Nationalist governments seems to fit perfectly with the ideas of the conservative French intellectual Raymond Aron:

Political thought is essentially an attempt to elucidate, from the study of societies, the goals to which one can aspire and the means most likely to reach them. Clearly, this investigation of what is possible is influenced by prior desires and preferences, desires and preferences that are also modified by the investigation itself. The outcome is never a moral or political imperative but an indication of the diverse possibilities (as to goals) and the degrees of probability (as to means).

Aron, *Politics and History*, 238.

35. Fitzgerald, *Awakening China*, 3.

36. The Communists can never admit that Nationalist rule was colonial, as this might tend to support separatism. The Communists, too, have had to wrestle with the difficult question of defining colonialism or some form of it in China. Guo Morou's conception of a semifeudal and semicolonial China proved to be useful for the Communists in light of the party's uncertainty over whether their nation was prepared for a bourgeois or proletarian, nationalist or class-based, revolution. Understanding Taiwan presents the same sort of difficulties.

37. The Taiwanese view can be summed up in a slightly different manner. Novels such as *Asia's Orphan* (*Yaxiya de gu'er*), written by Wu Zhuoliu during the Japanese era, show the complexity of Taiwanese identity — islanders were not sure where they belonged as they had been abandoned by China and given second-class status in Japan. Their political activity reflects this uncertainty. Wu Zhuoliu, *Yaxiya de gu'er*.

38. For example, see Lin Hengdao et al., eds., *Taiwanshi*. This work was produced by the Taiwan provincial government.

39. For example, Wang Xiaobo, in his collection of essays, writes that the United States promoted Taiwanese independence as part of its long-term drive to control Taiwan. Wang Xiaobo, *Zouchu Taiwan lishi de yinying*. The thirty-page introduction treats the U.S. role on Taiwan from the time of Commodore Matthew Perry through the Cold War.

40. The other parts of China were Hong Kong, which was absorbed by PRC in 1997, and Macao, which was absorbed in 1999.

41. Most famous in English is Peng Mingmin's *A Taste of Freedom: Memoirs of a Formosan Independence Leader*. In Chinese, Shi Ming's massive and well-known history of Taiwan stresses that the Nationalists had no more legitimacy to rule Taiwan

than did the Dutch, the Manchus of the Qing era, or the Japanese. Shi Ming, *Taiwanren sibainian shi*. See the author's intro. and pp. 5–8.

42. Early works set the pattern by discussing the island almost exclusively in a Cold War context. For example, see Bate, *Report from Formosa*; and Ballentine, *Formosa: A Problem for U.S. Foreign Policy*.

43. For example, see Kerr, *Formosa Betrayed*; and Mendel, *The Politics of Formosan Nationalism*.

44. The research commission created under the auspices of the Executive Yuan of the central government to study the February 28 Incident is an example of a more open attitude on the part of the government. In the public sphere, there has been an explosion of interest and publications about Taiwan's recent history. The most visible manifestation of this tide was the creation of an Institute of Taiwan History within the Academia Sinica, the premier research institution in the Republic of China. Other important organizations include the Taiwan Studies Center at the Taiwan Provincial Branch of the National Central Library and the Wu Sanlian Taiwan Historical Materials Center. For several interesting articles on recent trends in historiography of Taiwan, see the *Free China Review* 42, 3 (Mar. 1992), and the Special Section on Taiwan Studies in *Free China Review* 44, 2 (Feb. 1994). For an excellent Chinese-language overview of the changing nature of the study of Taiwan's history over the past forty years, see Zhang Yanxian, "Taiwanshi yanjiu de xin jingshen."

CHAPTER 2: CREATING A COLONIAL LEGACY

1. Between 1897 and 1901 the Japanese claimed to have arrested 8,000 "brigands" and killed 3,500. Yosaburo Takekoshi, *Japanese Rule of Formosa*, 90–91, 100.

2. Retreating Qing soldiers, many of whose leaders had already fled to the mainland, engaged in looting, as did some poor Taiwanese. A short-lived attempt by a few islanders to create a Taiwanese republic lacked both popular and elite support. On the failed republic, see Lamley, "The 1895 Taiwan Republic."

3. Some Taiwanese had hoped a coalition of European nations would oppose Japan's occupation in exchange for trade benefits, in effect, obtaining another Triple Intervention. None, however, was interested. A final factor in explaining the lack of Taiwanese resistance was that guerrilla warfare was difficult, because relations between aborigines, who lived in remote areas of the island, and the Taiwanese were often hostile. Throughout the Qing dynasty, Taiwanese and aborigines fought over land and water rights. The Japanese used the long-running rivalry for their own purposes. Aborigines and Taiwanese were kept separate and generally hostile to one another. The colonial rulers of the island effectively put themselves into the position of assisting aborigines through a system of reservations, education, and medical care, and of protecting the Taiwanese through police and military force. On the Japanese policy toward the aborigines, see Chai Chen-kang, *Taiwan Aborigines*; Government of Formosa, *Report on the Control of Aborigines in Formosa*; McGovern, *Among the Head-Hunters of Formosa*; Bigelow, *Japan and Her Colonies*; Yosaburo Takekoshi, *Japanese Rule of Formosa*; Timeline of Formosa, Records of the Office of Chinese Affairs; and Economic Conditions in Formosa, Apr. 30, 1920, United

States Military Intelligence on Japan, reel 16. All Department of State records in this work are from the National Archives, Record Group 59.

4. Yosaburo Takekoshi, *Japanese Rule of Formosa*, 10. Although the Japanese controlled the opium monopoly, they claimed to have reduced the number of addicts from 170,000 in 1900 to 18,000 in 1933. Hideo Naito, ed., *Taiwan: A Unique Colonial Record*, 242. By 1942, there were 2,441 Japanese-trained Taiwanese doctors on Taiwan. Chen Ching-chih, "Impact of Japanese Colonial Rule," 36–37.

5. The home islands — *nachi* (Chin., *neidi*), meaning "mainland" or "interior" — are the islands of Japan, excluding colonies and protectorates.

6. Wu Wenxing, *Riju shiqi Taiwan shehui lingdao*, 3. The governor-general answered directly to the premier.

7. The original law was replaced by Law 31 in 1907 and by Order Number Three in 1921. The powers of the governor-general changed relatively little over fifty years and "Law 63" became the term used most frequently for this system. On Japanese colonial policies and administrative structure, see Huang Zhaotang, *Taiwan zongdufu*; and Edward I-te Chen, "The Attempt to Integrate the Empire." *Sōtoku* (Chin., *zongdu*) is the governor-general, *sōtokufu* (Chin., *zongdufu*) signifies the governor-general and his administration.

8. Taishō democracy refers to the reign of the Taishō Emperor (1912–26) when political parties and the Diet (National Assembly) were relatively powerful in comparison to the military, the Privy Council, and the genrō (elder statesmen from the Meiji era). This period was marked by greater demands for public participation in politics.

9. Wu Zhuoliu, *Taiwan lianqiao*, 15–21.

10. Ibid., 21–23.

11. Following the overthrow of the shogunate by court nobles and samurai in 1868, administration of Japan was returned to the emperor, who adopted the reign name of Meiji (Enlightened Rule). The restoration marked the beginning of a wide-ranging modernization led by the central government. Li Xiaofeng, *Daoyu xin taiji*, 80.

12. See Lin Manhong, *Sibainian lai de liang'an fenhe*, 32–38.

13. Each conglomerate tended to concentrate on one product. For example, the Mitsui Corporation largely controlled the tea business of Taiwan. Economic Conditions in Formosa, Apr. 30, 1920, United States Military Intelligence on Japan, reel 16.

14. On the monopoly system, see Yosaburo Takekoshi, *Japanese Rule of Formosa*, chaps. 8–10. Opium, in particular, was controversial. Japanese policy toward opium appeared schizophrenic — simultaneously attempting to reduce its use (as a "civilized, modern" nation was expected to do) and to profit from its sale through a state monopoly.

15. "By the end of 1926, 57 of 150 major Taiwan-based banks and companies, each with [assets] of at least half a million yen, had Taiwanese listed as their institution's representatives." Chen Ching-chih, "Impact of Japanese Colonial Rule," 42.

16. Ibid. While Taiwanese expansion into finance, industry and trade is undeniable, exact figures are open to debate because the Japanese were not eager to high-

light their domination of the economy. Also, Japanese financial interests often worked through Taiwanese in order to avoid stirring up anticolonial feelings.

17. The Japanese sought to make the island a self-sufficient center for shipping and resupplying troops in Southeast Asia and southern China. These efforts intensified after 1943 as the Allies increasingly controlled sea lanes around the home islands.

18. Although the Nationalist government has assiduously emphasized the role of their economic policies in fostering the "miracle" of Taiwan's development, a growing body of research shows the importance of the Japanese era in laying the base for the island's postwar prosperity. For example, see Frank T. S. Hsiao and Mei-chu W. Hsiao, "Colonial Linkages in Early Postwar Taiwanese Economic Development." For a comprehensive analysis of Taiwan's economic development, see Samuel P. S. Ho, *Economic Development of Taiwan*. The same author places the island's experience in a comparative perspective in his essay, "Colonialism and Development: Korea, Taiwan, and Kwantung." As with studies of the mainland, there exists a lively academic debate over the genesis of modernization on the island. For the best review of theories explaining Taiwan's economic development, see Song Guangyu, "Lishi wenhua lun de tichu." According to Song, the commercial culture and trade networks that had existed on Taiwan since large-scale migration to the island in the 1600s were the keys to the island's modern economic development.

19. On Japan's hopes for economic expansion into South China and Southeast Asia, and Taiwan's role in this endeavor, see Kitayama Fukujirō, "Taiwan o kyūshin toseru." Kitayama claims the government of Japan and the people of Taiwan understood the importance of expanding economic ties with southern China and Southeast Asia.

20. Under colonial rule, Taiwan had its own currency issued by the Taiwan Bank, which was in turn subordinate to the central bank of Japan. Some of Japan's profit from the colonial endeavor came from its power to manipulate exchange rates between Taiwan and the home islands.

21. Ide Kiwata, *Riju xia zhi Taizheng*, 683–84.

22. Chen Ching-chih, "Impact of Japanese Colonial Rule," 41–42.

23. Wu Wenxing, *Riju shiqi Taiwan shehui lingdao*, 4.

24. Paul K. C. Liu, "Economic Development and Population in Taiwan since 1894," 8.

25. Grajdanzev, *Formosa Today*, chap. 5.

26. See Patricia Tsurumi, *Japanese Colonial Education*; and idem, "Colonial Education."

27. Traditional Confucian education, a legacy of the Qing rule, declined during the early decades of the twentieth century. In fact, rising nationalism on the mainland led the Japanese to discourage the study of Chinese language, history, and literature. As on the Chinese mainland, the spread of Christianity and Western imperialism were closely related, since it was the so-called unequal treaties of the mid-1800s that enabled missionaries to come to Taiwan. These included Spanish Dominicans, English Presbyterians, and the Canadian Presbyterian Mission. Both Presbyterian organizations offered medical care in order to gain converts. Christianity and Christian education were not major influences on Taiwan during the Japanese

era. By the late 1930s, Japanese pressure resulted in the closing or downsizing of Christian schools. On early Christian education, see Arnold, *Education in Formosa*.

28. Paul K. C. Liu, "Economic Development and Population in Taiwan since 1894," 11.

29. Patricia Tsurumi, *Japanese Colonial Education*, 239; Arnold, *Education*, 32.

30. Patricia Tsurumi, "Colonial Education," 292. In 1943, among Taiwanese who studied in Japan was the future president of the Republic of China on Taiwan, Li Denghui (Lee Teng-hui).

31. Patricia Tsurumi, *Japanese Colonial Education*, 255. Despite Japanese concerns that study of these topics would lead to resistance to their rule, many Taiwanese sought to use their education in order to become teachers or bureaucrats. The most important political movements under colonial rule were led by doctors, landlords, and businessmen. Chen Ching-chih, "Impact of Japanese Colonial Rule," 38.

32. Today, these institutions have been renamed National Taiwan Normal University and National Taiwan University respectively. They are among the most respected universities on the island.

33. Most of the Taiwanese at Taihoku University studied medicine.

34. On the formation of the elite under the Japanese, see Wu Wenxing, *Riju shiqi Taiwan shehui lingdao*; and Chen Ching-chih, "The Impact of Japanese Colonial Rule." Elite formation, colonial rule, and economic development in Taiwan and Korea were in may ways similar. Carter J. Eckert's work on the development of the bourgeoisie in colonial Korea examines the role of Japan in creating the social structure and infrastructure vital for future economic success. The history of the Korean elite under the Japanese, including assimilationist movements, attempts to preserve traditional culture, and co-optation by the colonial authorities, parallels Taiwan's experience. Eckert, *Offspring of Empire*.

35. There are many ways to define the elite and its influence. Chen Mingtong, in his examination of Provincial Assembly candidates during the 1946 to 1986 period, explains that the elite's influence stemmed from its power to control the distribution of resources, both personal (political power, social authority and personal resources) and nonpersonal (natural resources, capital, financial resources). Chen Mingtong, "Weiquan zhengti xia Taiwan difang zhengzhi qingying de liudong." On defining elites, see Welsh, *Leaders and Elites*.

36. Some studies of Taiwanese elites under Japanese rule, such as Chen Ching-chih's, utilize materials published with Japanese approval, such as biographical dictionaries. Although useful, these are not exhaustive lists of the island's elite. Individuals well-known or influential in public life because of their dissent or resistance to the Japanese were naturally excluded. Other scholars, such as Chen Mingtong, examine the elite under Nationalist Chinese rule. Looking at those elected into the Provincial Assembly, Chen examines the nature of Taiwan's elite and its relationship with the state. This excludes those who were influential but were unable to get elected, as well as those who influenced politics through unofficial channels such as cliques or personal relationships. For an analysis of a positional elite under Nationalist Chinese rule, see Chen Ching-chih, "The Impact of Japanese Colonial Rule"; and Chen Mingtong, "Weiquan zhengti xia Taiwan difang zhengzhi jingying de liudong."

37. The Qing era's "three positions in one body" (*san wei yi ti*) signified that a prominent individual might be simultaneously an official, a landlord, and a merchant. Chen Sanjing and Xu Xueji, *Lin Hengdao xiansheng*, 1–8.

38. Chen Ching-chih, "Impact of Japanese Colonial Rule," 33.

39. Acquiescence to Japanese rule or avoiding contact with the state did not necessarily mean retreat from public life. Many Taiwanese remained active in community activities involving education, religious institutions, and charities. On the elite during the early years of Japanese rule, see Lamley, "The Taiwanese Literati and Early Japanese Rule."

40. Wu Wenxing, *Riju shiqi Taiwan shehui lingdao*, 371. The Treaty of Shimonoseki allowed the inhabitants of Taiwan two years to leave the island if they wished to, though few did.

41. For example, the family of Qiu Niantai (1894–1967) completely rejected Japanese rule. Son of a Qing official on the island, Qiu was born in Zhanghua. His family fled to the mainland shortly after the arrival of the Japanese. Qiu became involved in several mining ventures in China, and was advisor to the Guangdong provincial government. In 1943, he became a member of the Guomindang's Taiwan Jurisdiction Office. In 1945, he returned to the island, where he eventually served as chairman of the Taiwan Provincial Guomindang Committee. See Tong Jianyan, ed., *Taiwan lishi cidian*, 123.

42. Wu Wenxing, *Riju shiqi Taiwan shehui lingdao*, 3.

43. Patricia Tsurumi, *Japanese Colonial Education*, 11.

44. Wu Wenxing, *Riju shiqi Taiwan shehui lingdao*, 371–72.

45. Chen Ching-chih, "Impact of Japanese Colonial Rule," 47.

46. Huang Zhaotang details the discrimination against the Taiwanese in employment, salaries, and education. The entire island had only four Taiwanese professors during the colonial era. Huang Zhaotang, *Taiwan zongdufu*, 241–45.

47. For a complete list of his contributions to the colonial regime and his business ventures, see Hara Kansyū, *Shin Taiwan no jinbutsu*, 710–14.

48. The Lin clan of Banqiao, now a suburb of Taibei, illustrates Japanese efforts to gain the cooperation of prominent Taiwanese. The colonial government protected the Lins' extensive property on the island, and urged family elders to return from Fujian, where they had fled in 1895. Although most of the clan returned to the island, they maintained their links with the mainland, providing financial assistance to the government of Fujian, where they maintained business interests. In order to ease the imposition of their rule, the Japanese urged the Lins to participate in local government. The clan's relative decline mirrored Japan's success at dominating Taiwan's economy and politics. Even as the clan diversified its holdings — reflecting the developing economy of the island — its relative wealth and influence steadily declined. After the Japanese consolidated their rule, they pressured the clan and other wealthy Taiwanese to sell off many of their more profitable enterprises. Chen Sanjing and Xu Xueji, *Lin Hengdao xiansheng*, 48–53.

49. Hui-yu Caroline Tsai's dissertation shows how the Japanese attempted to use the *hokō* (Chin., *baojia*) system, a system of shared responsibility originating in imperial China, to impose state control over the community and family. Over fifty years, prominent Taiwanese made their career through education and business in the cities,

not the *hokō* structure. Hui-yu Caroline Tsai, "One Kind of Control." See also Ching-chih Chen, "The Police and the Hokō System in Taiwan under Japanese Administration."

50. Chen Ching-chih, "Impact of Japanese Colonial Rule," 44, see also the chart on p. 45.

51. Chen Ching-chih has compared Taiwan's elite under the Japanese to other colonies, including Korea under the Japanese, India under the British, the Philippines under the United States, Indochina under the French and the Dutch East Indies under the Dutch. He concludes that Japan's colonies had a higher percentage of the population who could be called business people or professionals than did other colonies. According to a Japanese biographical dictionary published in 1943, about 54 percent of the Taiwanese listed were merchants. This was up from 38 percent in 1916. Ibid., 43, 47–51.

52. Japanese policy toward aborigines, however, was to keep them separate from Han Chinese.

53. This is not to suggest that the long-running rivalry between various groups of Chinese migrants, based primarily upon their place of origin on the mainland, disappeared completely under Japanese or Nationalist Chinese rule. However, the salience of these divisions decreased.

54. Jian Rongren, "Riben diguo de zhimin tongzhi yu Taiwan yishi de xingqi"; Wang Mingke, "Guoqu, jiti jiyi yu zuqun rentong."

55. "Although nationalism and its theory seek a privileged position within the representational network as the master identity that subsumes or organizes other identifications, it exists only as one among others and is changeable, inter-changeable, conflicted, or harmonious with them." Duara, *Rescuing History from the Nation*, 8. For example, Li Chensheng (1838–1924) illustrates the dilemmas of national identification during the early years of Japanese rule. Scholars Wang Junjie and Gu Weiying have used Li to illustrate the problem of dual (*er-yuan xing*) national identity under colonial rule. Li, who was born in Fujian into a Christian family, like many other immigrants came to Taiwan to avoid chaos on the mainland, in this case the Taiping Rebellion. Li began by promoting the sale of Wulong tea, then diversified into other goods, and ended up being one of Taibei's best-known merchants. Like many other wealthy residents of the island, in 1895 he cooperated with the Japanese in order to restore public order. He was a practical merchant and accepted Japanese rule, yet his writings, many of which were published in Fujian, show continued concern for developments on the mainland. Culturally, he remained Chinese. Wang Junjie and Gu Weiying, "Xin'en yu jiuyi zhijian." On the "idea" of Taiwan and a Taiwanese consciousness, see Yin Zhangyi, "Taiwan yishi de xingcheng yu fazhan."

56. Wu Zhuoliu was a prolific writer and journalist. His stories and reminiscences are important source material for understanding Taiwan's experience of oppression and ambiguity under both Japanese and Nationalist rule. Wu Zhuoliu, *Yaxiya de gu'er*; idem, *Wuhuaguo*; and idem, *Taiwan lianqiao*.

57. Wu Zhuoliu, *Yaxiya de gu'er*, 7–10.

58. Wu Wenxing, *Riju shiqi Taiwan shehui lingdao*, 373.

59. Zhou Wanyao, *Riju shidai de Taiwan*, 10. On Japanese-era political activity,

see Cai Peihuo et al., *Taiwan minzu yundongshi*; Lian Wenliao, *Taiwan zhengzhi yun-dongshi*; Zhou Wanyao, *Riju shidai de Taiwan*; and Wu Wenxing, *Taiwan shehui ling-dao jieji*. In English, see Kerr, *Formosa: Licensed Revolution and the Home Rule Movement*; and Edward Chen, "Formosan Political Movements under Japanese Colonial Rule." Douglas Fix's dissertation not only reviews the political activity of this era, but also the role of a growing Taiwanese vernacular literature. Fix, "Taiwanese Nationalism and Its Late Colonial Context."

60. Zhou Wanyao, *Riju shidai de Taiwan*, 36–45.

61. The landlord Yang Zhaojia acknowledged that some of the first calls for local self-government came from civilian Japanese officials in the late 1890s, including from the chief of the Taiwan High Court Branch. The judge and others who thought like him were quickly sacked by the governor-general. Yang Zhaojia, "Taiwan difang zizhi zhidu," 3–5. On the debates over colonial policy, see Zhou Wanyao, *Riju shidai de Taiwan*, 36–45.

62. On the assimilationist impulse among the Japanese, see Peattie, "Japanese Attitudes Toward Colonialism."

63. See Fogel, *Politics and Sinology*, 77–83. Naito's famous history of China, *Shinaron* (On China), traced long historical trends that, he believed, could culminate in the Middle Kingdom becoming a modern nation-state, building from local autonomous units into a "federate republic." Given Naito's relatively wide reader-ship, it is entirely possible that many of his ideas—in particular, that economic devel-opment and educational achievement are justification for political change—influ-enced some Taiwanese. Taiwanese, however, did not resort to Chinese history, and certainly did not reach back to the Song period (when mainlanders only had a dim idea that the island existed), to justify increased autonomy under colonial rule. They usually measured themselves according to standards set by the Japanese—often their ability to fit into the Japanese polity. Fogel, *Politics and Sinology*, 65–78.

64. This is a common pattern in colonization. For example, in 1871 Lord Thomas Babington Macaulay stated that "we must . . . do our best to form a class who may be interpreters between us and the millions who we govern; a class of per-sons, Indian in blood and colour, but English in taste, in opinion, in morals, and in intellect." Minute, as Member of Supreme Council of India, Feb. 2, 1871. Cited in Angela Partington, ed., *The Oxford Dictionary of Quotations*, 4th ed. (Oxford: Oxford University Press, 1991), 435.

65. Itagaki Taisuke was one of the young samurai who helped overthrow the shogunate. He played an important role in early Meiji state-building and was a leader of the movement for political reform.

66. Huang Zhaotang, *Taiwan zongdufu*, 136.

67. Cai Peihuo et al., *Taiwan minzu yundongshi*, 139. This book, a compilation of essays, mostly by participants in cultural, social, and political movements during the colonial period, is one of the best discussions of the political representation many prominent Taiwanese sought during the Japanese era. Many of the themes discussed in this book would continue after 1945.

68. Just as scholars today debate the extent to which modernization and Westernization are the same phenomenon, so too Taiwanese struggled to determine whether Japanization and modernization were one and the same. Scholars on

Taiwan have shown that "modern" meant much more than simply things (railroads or telephones, for example) or organizations (bureaucratic administration or corporations); it was also a way of thinking. For example, Lu Shaoli has researched the changing sense of time and standardization of schedules among islanders as part of the societal modernization that occurred under colonial rule. Lu Shaoli, "Shuiluo xiangqi."

69. Peattie, "Japanese Attitudes Toward Colonialism," 103.

70. Japanese documents stressed the importance of Lin and of the area around Taizhong, which was described as the intellectual and political center of Taiwan. Huang Zhaotang, *Taiwan zongdufu*, 135.

71. Cai Peihuo et al., *Taiwan minzu yundongshi*, 1.

72. On the *kōminka* movement between 1931 and 1937, see Cai Qintang, "Huangminhua yundong qian Taiwan shehui jiaoyu yundong de fazhan."

73. Wu Wenxing, *Riju shiqi Taiwan shehui lingdao*, 375–76.

74. Much of the information in these two paragraphs is from Zhou Wanyao, *Riju shidai de Taiwan*, 36–45.

75. These codes were promulgated before the constitution because Meiji leaders feared elected Diet members might weaken the central government by adopting legislation on self-government. Yasuo Takao, *National Integration and Local Power in Japan*, 53.

76. Gluck, *Japan's Modern Myths*, 192–93.

77. As noted by Yasuo Takao, in his overview of local administration of Japan:

The purpose of the Town and Village Code and the City Code which was stated in these Codes was as follows: The reformed local government system exists to assign national functions to the local entities. The people shall participate in it (the implementation of national functions) to reduce the intricacies of government. The people shall thus fulfil the proper work. The central government, however, shall hold the fundamental principles of government, give directions, and keep the substance of state government. The people shall share the responsibility of self-government and thus devote themselves to the public interests of the local entities.

Yasuo Takao, *National Integration and Local Power in Japan*, 52–53.

78. Ibid., 234–35. On Japan's centralized political system, see Quigley, *Japanese Government and Politics*, chap. 15.

79. Until universal manhood suffrage was implemented in 1925, the assemblies at the prefectural, city, and county levels (the counties were abolished in 1923) were elected by relatively wealthy taxpayers. Mayors were elected by the city or town assemblies, but elections required the ratification of prefectural governors, who were appointed by the central government.

80. Ide Kiwata, *Riju xia zhi Taiwan*, 693–85

81. On debates over the Meiji constitution and Japan's colonies, see Noboru Asami, *Japanese Colonial Government*, chap. 2.

82. Some of Den's relatively liberal policies included legalizing marriage between Taiwanese and Japanese (which had been occurring in any case) and abolishing caning as a punishment.

83. Ide Kiwata, *Riju xia zhi Taiwan*, 687–95.

84. The administrative jurisdictions of Taiwan, which formed the basis for the elected assemblies, changed frequently over fifty years.

85. Ide Kiwata, *Riju xia zhi Taiwan*, 693–94.

86. An earlier islandwide group had consisted solely of colonial officials, a pattern typical of colonial regimes. For example, beginning with the Indian Councils Act of 1908, the British began to permit assemblies similar to those the Japanese organized on Taiwan. The Dutch East Indies had the Volksraad, established in 1918. These bodies were partly elected and partly (or mostly) selected by the governor-general. Members, particularly at the upper levels, were often colonists. The colonial powers hoped such bodies would forestall nationalist movements. The assemblies were usually advisory and lacked the powers commonly associated with legislatures in the West. On Dutch rule in Indonesia, see Sutherland, *The Making of a Bureaucratic Elite*; and Furnivall, *Colonial Policy and Practice*.

87. Assembly members were selected by the next higher level. For example, the governor-general appointed those at the prefectural level, and prefectural heads chose members of the city assemblies. The local administrative head chaired and provided staff for the assembly in his jurisdiction.

88. Ide Kiwata, *Riju xia zhi Taiwan*, 699.

89. Ibid., 702–4.

90. For example, the 1930 session included discussions of Taiwan's economic role in South China and Southeast Asia, and industrialization on the island. "Pingyihui gaizheng yu zhengzhi shang houbu" (The Advisory Assembly and Political Reform), *Shinminpō* (Chin., *Taiwan xinminbao*) (July 5, 1930): 2.

91. On the economic class background of Taiwanese leaders, see Lian Wenliao, *Taiwan zhengzhi yundong shi*.

92. The same cycle can be found in other colonial regimes. For example, Mahatma Gandhi struggled to build a broad-based movement encompassing all economic classes and religions. This was hampered by the conflict between those who accepted British reforms in the 1910s and 1920s, those who wanted dominion status, and those who wanted immediate and complete independence from the empire. See Kumar, "From Swaraj to Purna Swaraj."

93. Ruan Meimei, *Yu'an jiaoluo de leisheng*, 63–68. Frank Hsiao and Lawrence Sullivan have written the most detailed English-language articles on the TCP. "A Political History of the Taiwanese Communist Party"; and "The Chinese Communist Party and the Status of Taiwan." See also Patricia Tsurumi, *Japanese Colonial Education*. The most detailed Chinese-language account is Lu Xiuyi, *Riju shidai Taiwan gongchandang shi*.

94. During the 1920s, the Taiwan Youth Association, which increasingly fell under the influence of students who had returned from Japan, urged peasants to protect their economic rights. The association fomented tax strikes and protests, such as that against Mitsubishi's plan to purchase large tracts of bamboo forests. In 1926 the Taiwan Farmers' Union, which came to be closely associated with its counterpart in Japan, was formed. Since the Taiwanese Communist Party was also tied closely to Japan at this time, a strong link between the Communists and the Farmers' Union is likely. The Farmers' Union was outlawed in 1931. Department of State,

Office of Intelligence Research; and Patricia Tsurumi, *Japanese Colonial Education*, 205.

95. See Kerr, *Formosa: Licensed Revolution and the Home Rule Movement*. A list of the financial supporters of the Petition Movement illustrates the leading role of Taiwanese landlords in the island's political life: landlords Lin Xiantang, Cai Enju, Chen Qichuan, Yang Zhaojia, Li Ruiyun. Other contributors were Lin Boshou (landlord and concrete company president), Luo Wanzhen (landlord), Lin Jietang (Lin Xiantang's younger brother), Lin Zibin (Lin's relative), Lin Gensheng (Lin's relative), Chen Xin (landlord), Wu Qiuwei (Tainan doctor), Gao Zaide (Tainan doctor), Han Shiquan (Tainan doctor), Wang Shoulu (Tainan doctor), Yang Liang (Xinju sugar refining), Lin Duxun (Zhanghua doctor), Yang Zhenfu (head of a granary society), and Qiu Dejin (Gaoxiong doctor). Cai Peihuo et al., *Taiwan minzu yundongshi*, 297–98.

96. Cai Peihuo et al., *Taiwan minzu yundongshi*, 110–11, 159. In 1906, the governor-general decreed that all Taiwanese were Japanese nationals. However, this had little impact upon the treatment of Taiwanese and the virtual dictatorship of the governor-general. Edward I-te Chen, "The Attempt to Integrate the Empire," 245.

97. Primary source material on the self-government movement includes Yang Zhaojia, "Taiwan difang zizhi zhidu" and hundreds of articles and editorials in magazines and newspapers published by the Taiwanese including *Taiwan*, *Taiwan minpō* (Chin., *Taiwan minbao*), and *Taiwan shinminpō* (Chin., *Taiwan xinminbao*). These newspapers often included both Chinese- and Japanese-language articles and essays. By the late 1930s, pressure by the colonial government bought about the end of publications using the Chinese language.

98. Cai Peihuo et al., *Taiwan minzu yundongshi*, 108.

99. Ibid., 175.

100. Ibid., 110–11, 159.

101. Yang Zhaojia, "Guanyu Taiwan difang zizhi lianmeng." Specifically, Yang complained that the current representatives were merely tools of the government. Yang Zhaojia, "Taiwan difang zizhi zhidu," 1–2, 14–15.

102. Yang Zhaojia, "Chuangli hou de zizhi lianmeng."

103. Yang Zhaojia, "Taiwan difang zizhi zhidu," 14–15.

104. Many of the elite who wanted to sit on these assemblies or obtain other posts curried favor with Japanese officials, "exchanging money for a position" (*yi jinqian huanchu diwei*). Criticism of this grew during the 1920s as the new elite began to replace the old. Wu Wenxing, *Riju shiqi Taiwan shehui lingdao*, 231–32.

105. As would be the case after 1945, the Taiwanese often used the adjective "local" (Chin., *difang*; Japanese, *chihō*) to describe the type of self-government they sought: autonomous assemblies at the islandwide level and below.

106. Cai Peihuo et al., *Taiwan minzu yundongshi*, 449–51.

107. Ibid., 452–54.

108. Yang Zhaojia, "Taiwan difang zizhi lianmeng."

109. Cai Peihuo et al., *Taiwan minzu yundongshi*, 450–64.

110. Ibid., 463–64.

111. Ibid., 445.

112. Ibid., 446–47.

113. Zhou Wanyao, *Riju shidai de Taiwan*, 165–70.

114. Huang Zhaotang, *Taiwan zongdufu*, 140.

115. Cai Peihuo et al., *Taiwan minzu yundongshi*, 480–81.

116. Ibid., 445.

117. For example, Wang Tiandeng, an important member of the relatively stri-dent Taibei branch of the league, was a young tea merchant who would become prominent in post-retrocession politics. Ibid., 478–81.

118. "Quangao xiehuiyuan tuici" (Urging Assembly Members to Resign), *Taiwan shinminpō* (Sept. 27, 1930): 4.

119. Cai Peihuo et al., *Taiwan minzu yundongshi*, 455–59.

120. Ibid., 461–62.

121. Ide Kiwata, *Riju xia zhi Taiwan*, 919–21.

122. Ibid., 931–34.

123. Wu Wenxing, *Riju shiqi Taiwan shehui lingdao*, 234–41.

124. Those elected were slightly younger than the appointees. Both groups included many who had studied in Japan. Ibid.

125. Cai Peihuo et al., *Taiwan minzu yundongshi*, 482–84.

126. Ibid., 476–77.

127. Wu Wenxing, *Riju shiqi Taiwan shehui lingdao*, 228.

128. Cai Peihuo et al., *Taiwan minzu yundongshi*, 490–91. For example, in 1935 Lin Xiantang was physically attacked by thugs under Japanese control after he returned from a tour of the mainland. This so-called fatherland incident was supposedly sparked by Lin's continued ties to the mainland. Lin and Yang briefly hid out in Japan.

129. For example, police often confiscated the league's written materials. Cai Peihuo et al., *Taiwan minzu yundongshi*, 470–76.

130. Huang Zhaotang, *Taiwan zongdufu*, 145.

131. On Japanese wartime mobilization, see Lai, Myers, and Wei, *A Tragic Beginning*, 26–49; and Huang Zhaotang, *Taiwan zongdufu*, 182–93.

132. The most important group was the Imperial Subjects Public Service Society (Kōmin hōkōkai). Other key organizations included the Citizens Volunteer Corps, Taiwan Producers Public Service Society, Greater Japan Women's Society, and Taiwan Youth League. On the island's administration and these organizations on the eve of surrender, see *Taiwan tōki gaiyō*.

133. A particularly contentious issue was Taiwanese service in the Japanese police and military on the mainland. Whether Taiwanese served for the money or out of loy-alty to the Japanese empire (or a combination of the two) is difficult to discern. See Lin Zhen, "Kangzhan shiqi Fujian de Taiwan jimin wenti."

134. After the Diet passed the National General Mobilization Law in 1938, many Taiwanese were drafted to work in military-related industries, often in Japan. Over 200,000 young draftees served in the imperial army and navy during the war, mainly in Southeast Asia. More than 30,000 Taiwanese died. Huang Zhaotang, *Taiwan zong-dufu*, 253. On the Taiwanese role in the Japanese military, see "Programs and Personnel of Japan on Formosa: Extracts from Short Wave Radio, Tokyo and Affiliated Stations from December 1941 to March 15, 1944," OSS/Honolulu, Apr. 19, 1944, United States Military Intelligence on Japan; and "Certain Aspects of the Formosan-Japanese Relationship," Allied Translator and Interpreter Section, South

West Pacific Area Research Report 223, Mar. 31, 1945, United States Military Translations of Japanese Broadcasts and Documents.

135. Chen Sanjing and Xu Xueji, *Lin Hengdao xiansheng*, 71.

136. Wu Zhuoliu, *Taiwan lianqiao*, 143–44.

137. Jacobs, "Taiwanese and the Chinese Nationalists," 85–86. Between 1940 and 1942, six groups of Taiwanese on the mainland allied to form the Taiwanese Revolutionist League, a loose coalition under Guomindang auspices. Presaging future conflicts between the Taiwanese and the Nationalist government, the league was held together by anti-Japanese sentiment, not a plan for postwar Taiwan. Taiwanese Independence Movements, 1683–1956, Department of State, Office of Intelligence Research.

138. The term "Half-Mountain people" is derived from a Taiwanese term for the mainland: the "Tang Mountains" (*Tangshan*). The term was not merely descriptive; often it was pejorative as well. Islanders tended to view those with close ties to the Nationalists as less "Taiwanese" and more responsive to the central government than to local needs. Taiwanese also often referred to mainlanders as *Ah shan* (literally, "little mountain") and to themselves as *Ah hai* ("little ocean").

139. Wu Zhuoliu, *Taiwan lianqiao*, 144–45.

140. Lin Manhong, *Sibai nian lai de liang'an fenhe*, 32–38.

141. Because farmers were forced to give up ever larger amounts of what they produced, it is likely that they reported less than they actually harvested. Nevertheless, all Taiwanese faced hardship during the closing years of the war. Food production was reduced further by a major typhoon and drought in 1944, and a shortage of labor and fertilizer.

142. Wu Zhuoliu, *Taiwan lianqiao*, 145–47.

143. Since America had cut the shipping lanes, none of the three was able to travel to Japan.

CHAPTER 3: RETROCESSION AND THE DEBATE OVER TAIWAN'S PLACE IN CHINA

1. These same problems of collaboration existed on the mainland. For example, see Poshek Fu, *Passivity, Resistance, and Collaboration*. One key difference was that the Taiwanese were formally part of the Japanese empire, not a puppet regime (as was the collaborationist government in wartime Nanjing). Also, the Taiwanese, unlike the mainland Chinese, enjoyed the benefits of economic development and stability brought by Japanese rule.

2. Taiwanese, like the Japanese, were shocked to hear the emperor's voice announce surrender. Some islanders believed that the broadcast was a fake. Others remembered that the sound quality of the broadcast was so poor that they were not sure what was said. For example, see Chen Sanjing and Xu Xueji, *Lin Hengdao xian-sheng*, 71–72; and Chen Yisong, *Chen Yisong huiyilu*, 291–93.

3. Wu Xinrong, *Wu Xinrong riji*, 3–7. Wu Xinrong, born in 1907 in Tainan, became politically active through the Taiwan Youth Association, which he joined while studying medicine in Japan. In addition to his involvement in many colonial-era organizations devoted to the study of Taiwanese history and literature, he also

participated in the local self-government organs created by the Japanese governor-general.

4. Chen Yisong, "Muqian jinji de zhengzhi zhu wenti." There are many examples of this ambivalent attitude. You Mijian, a Taibei native who studied in Japan before going to the mainland and serving in the Nationalist government, emphasized that confusion and uncertainty led to silence at war's end. You Mijian was born in 1897. He worked as an educator on the island, then graduated from Nihon University. He first traveled to Beijing in order to work in the publishing industry. You later went to Nanjing to teach at the Three Principles of the People Middle School, where he came into contact with Nationalist officials who guided his career in the central government. You was an important member of the wartime Taiwan Revolutionary League and the Taiwan Investigation Committee. He returned to Taiwan in late 1945 as a part of a committee investigating the island's finances. In early 1946, Chen Yi appointed him mayor of Taibei. You Mijian, "Wenxie de shiming."

5. Han Shiquan was born in 1897 in Tainan. After studying medicine at a school established by the governor-general, he spent the much of the colonial era in political activities (he was important in the Taiwan Cultural Society and the Taiwan Masses Party), as well as managing his own hospital.

6. Chen Sanjing and Xu Xueji, *Lin Hengdao xiansheng*, 76–77.

7. Quoted in Yin Zhangyi, *Chou nongyan, he liejiu, dasheng kangyi*, 210.

8. Chen Sanjing and Xu Xueji, *Lin Hengdao xiansheng*, 72–77.

9. Wu Zhuoliu, *Taiwan lianqiao*, 151.

10. Gu Zhenfu was the son of Gu Xianrong, a wealthy islander known for his cooperation with the Japanese. The elder Gu was rewarded with a variety of posts giving him economic benefits and prestige; in 1934 he became the first islander named to the Japanese House of Peers. As a result of their scheme for independence, Gu Zhenfu and others were arrested in 1946, and sentenced to short jail terms in 1947. For a generally sympathetic account of Gu and his father, see Shen Zijia and Zhang Jueming, *Gu Zhenfu zhuan*.

11. The case was slightly different elsewhere in the empire. The Japanese had held out the promise of independence in the Philippines, Malaya, and the Dutch East Indies in order to gain support during the final years of the war. See, for example, Legge, *Sukarno: A Political Biography*.

12. *Er erba shijian wenxian jilu* 1: 11–12.

13. Wu Zhuoliu, *Taiwan lianqiao*, 151.

14. Chen Sanjing and Xu Xueji, *Lin Hengdao xiansheng*, 72–74.

15. Petition from Society of Taiwanese (Formosan) Residents in Japan, November 20, 1945, Department of State, Records of the Office of Chinese Affairs.

16. Chen Sanjing and Xu Xueji, *Lin Hengdao xiansheng*, 76–77.

17. Ibid., 77–78.

18. Ibid., 72–74. Resistance to the Japanese takeover quickly degenerated into looting, leading wealthy Taiwanese to welcome the colonial forces.

19. See Ye Rongzhong, "Taiwan guangfu qianhou de huiyi." Ye was an assistant and confidant to Lin Xiantang, and later, after retrocession, became important in political and cultural circles in his own right.

20. There were reasons for some Taiwanese to dislike the police, both Japanese

and Taiwanese, at the end of the war. During the colonial regime, in addition to enforcing criminal codes, police managed household registration, price controls, and public sanitation. They also monitored Taiwanese political activity, and often harassed and arrested those seen as threats to the colonial administration.

21. Wu Zhuoliu, *Taiwan lianqiao*, 152–54.

22. A wide variety of small groups sprang up to greet mainlanders. For example, Hakkas organized to welcome their fellow ethnics from the mainland. Wu Zhuoliu, *Taiwan lianqiao*, 152–54.

23. Retrocession Day became an official, and controversial, holiday on Taiwan.

24. Duara, *Rescuing History from the Nation*, 198.

25. For example, R. Keith Schoppa writes: "For most historians of modern China, as with most twentieth-century Chinese, nation-building has been the central interest; as a result, provincialism has been seen as subordinate in value to nationalism." Schoppa, "Province and Nation," 661. As Duara notes, "In the end, the interplay of power politics and authoritative language enabled the hegemonic, centralizing nationalist narrative to destroy and ideologically bury the federalist alternative early in the history of modern China." Duara, *Rescuing History from the Nation*, 177–78.

26. The translations of English and Chinese terms do not always match perfectly. For example, *zizhu* is defined as "independent" in Mathews Dictionary. *Zizhi* is "self-government" and "self-control."

27. Thompson, *China's Local Councils*, intro.

28. "Local self-government was invariably connected with political programs that promised more than they delivered. It was a universally discussed component of twentieth-century political theory; but in practice was associated with all the evils of the age: the arbitrary exercise of power by rapacious local elites and petty functionaries; the ambitions of provincial warlords; and the preachments of a political party that promised democracy but delivered dictatorship." Kuhn, "Local Self-Government under the Republic," 257.

29. On provincialism around the time of the 1911 Revolution, see Fincher, "Provincialism and National Revolution."

30. Often called the "warlord era" in China, the period 1916 to 1928 was bracketed by the death of Yuan Shikai (in 1916) and the victory of the Northern Expedition, which brought the Nationalists to power (1928). It is usually considered to be the period when modern China, plagued by warlords and imperialists, was at its most disunified. The attempt to define the difference between warlord opportunism and federalism as a coherent plan for China has continued for decades. See Waldron, "Warlordism versus Federalism."

31. Hu Chunhui, *Minchu de difang zhuyi yu liansheng zizhi*, esp. 375–90.

32. Chesneaux, "The Federalist Movement in China," 135–36.

33. Su Yunfeng, "Liansheng zizhi shengzhong de 'eren zhi e yundong.'"

34. "The federalism of the Kuomintang [Guomindang] was purely tactical, a temporary retreat while awaiting a political situation more favourable to national unity." Chesneaux, "The Federalist Movement in China," 96.

35. Kuhn, "Local Self-Government under the Republic," 283.

36. Hu Chunhui, *Minchu de difang zhuyi yu liansheng zizhi*, 45–50.

37. For instance, in early 1921, Sun wrote that "if we want to solve the long-running dispute between the center and localities (*difang*), the only way is for each province's people to have complete self-government, with provincial constitutions and the election of provincial governors. If the center divides powers among the provinces, and each province divides power among its districts, then perhaps the divided nation can be associated through self-governmentalism (*zizhi zhuyi*) and once again united." Quoted in Xu Langxuan, *Zhongguo xiandaishi*, 100.

38. Chen has his defenders, including his son, Leslie H. Chen, whose works have attempted to show that "to dismiss all the federalist activities in the various provinces, such as Yunnan, Hunan, Hubei, Sichuan, Zhejiang, and others, as motivated by self-seeking provincial militarists or 'warlords' is not only unfair, but simply fraudulent." Leslie H. Chen, "Chen Jiongming," 34.

39. Duara, *Rescuing History from the Nation*, 195.

40. Ibid., 202. It is difficult to find sources that make this shift explicit. The Nationalists did not want to "remember" that they had seriously considered a federalist alternative for China. A 1937 work by Paul Lindebarger touches on the Nationalists' changing views. *The Political Doctrines of Sun Yat-sen*, 229–31.

41. Sun Yat-sen, *San Min Chu I*, 257. See also Leslie H. Chen, "Chen Jiongming," 28.

42. Chesneaux, "The Federalist Movement in China," 135–36.

43. Lindebarger, *The Political Doctrines of Sun Yat-sen*, 227–31.

44. Kuhn, "Local Self-Government under the Republic," 271–72. See also the discussion of Yamagata Aritomo in Gluck, *Japan's Modern Myths*.

45. Schoppa, "Province and Nation," 666–67. Schoppa's examination of elite activism in Zhejiang discusses the important effect of varying levels of economic development within a province upon views of central-local relations. However, Taiwan's size and its experience of economic development under Japanese rule makes such a "zonal" approach — to use Schoppa's terminology — less applicable to post-1945 Taiwan.

46. Schoppa, "Province and Nation," 673–74.

47. Ibid., 672.

48. On politics in Guangxi in the 1930s, see Levich, *The Kwangsi Way in Kuomintang China*.

49. Lary, *The Kwangsi Clique in Chinese Politics*, 194.

50. See Guo Tingyi, *Jindai Zhongguo shigang*, 758.

51. Hou Kunhong, "You jisi dao baodong."

52. On the development of the constitution, see Li Zonghuang, *Li Zonghuang huiyilu*, 273.

53. The final constitution eliminated provincial autonomy and continued the presidential system (many at the 1946 PCC had sought a cabinet system). Pepper, *Civil War in China*, 137–38.

54. Carsun Chang, *The Third Force in China*, 188–222, chap. 10.

55. Zhou Jixiang, "Xingxian yilai de Taiwan."

56. Chen Yi's full title was *Taiwansheng xingzheng zhangguan* (Taiwan Provincial Administrative Executive) *Zhangguan*, is often translated governor-general, but it is not exactly the same as the governor-general of the colonial era (Chin., *zongdu*;

Japanese, *sōtoku*). The translation of term *zhangguan* has been politicized. Those who wish to emphasize the legitimacy of Nationalist rule and its differences from the colonial era tend to use the term "administrator"; those who favor independence use "governor-general." This work uses administrator because it most closely fits the definitions offered in Chinese dictionaries.

57. For example, in 1946 he served as secretary to the Party and Government Administration Work Evaluation Committee (Dangzheng gongzuo kaohe weihuanhui). One of the best summaries of Nationalist views of self-government on Taiwan is Li Zonghuang's *Taiwan difang zizhi xinlun*, which contains many essays written in 1949 and 1950.

58. Li Zonghuang, *Li Zonghuang huiyilu*, 303–4.

59. On the Japanese and Sun Zhongshan, see Jansen, *The Japanese and Sun Yat-sen*.

60. Li Zonghuang, *Li Zonghuang huiyilu*, 310.

61. Ibid., 277–78.

62. On Nationalist thinking on this topic, see Shi Yangcheng, *Zhongguo sheng xingzheng zhidu yice*, 1.

63. "It is their [the Allies] purpose that Japan shall be stripped of all the islands of the Pacific which she has seized or occupied since the beginning of the First World War in 1914, and that all territories Japan has stolen from the Chinese, such as Manchuria, Formosa, and the Pescadores, shall be restored to the Republic of China." "Statement of Conference of President Roosevelt, Generalissimo Chiang Kai-shek, and Prime Minister Churchill, Cairo, Dec. 1, 1943," Department of State, Office of Public Affairs, *United States Relations with China*, 519. Hereafter cited as *United States Relations with China*. The Soviets had no objection to this agreement. On America's wartime policy toward Taiwan, see Gordon, "American Planning for Taiwan."

64. On the planning and implementation of the takeover of Taiwan, see Zheng Zi, *Zhanhou Taiwan de jieshou yu chongjian*. The Nationalists have constructed their own history that emphasizes the mainland government's constant concern for the recovery of Taiwan and careful planning for retrocession, as well as the role of Taiwanese in the anti-Japanese struggle. For example, see Zhang Ruicheng, ed., *Taiji zhishi zai zuguo de fu Tai nuli*; idem, ed., *Kangzhan shiqi shoufu Taiwan zhi zhongyao yanlun*; and idem, ed., *Shoufu Taiwan zhi chouhua yu shoujiang jieshou*.

65. On Chen's career, see Zhang Fumei, "Chen Yi yu Fujian shengzheng."

66. Dai Guohui and Ye Yunyun, *Aizeng er erba*, 61, 125.

67. Taiwanese Independence Movements, 1683–1956, Department of State, Office of Intelligence Research. The groups that allied included the Taiwanese Revolutionary Party, Taiwanese Independence Revolutionary Party, Taiwanese National Revolutionary Party, Taiwanese People's Revolutionary Federation, Taiwanese Youth Revolutionary Party, and Taiwan Guomindang Headquarters. See *Taiwan geming tongmenghui zonghui ganbu mingce*; and Junshi weiyuanhui, *Junshi weiyuanhui zhengzhibu*.

68. Based on an interview with an unnamed Taiwan-born official, United States Office of Strategic Services (OSS) reports stated that on Taiwan secret members of the Revolutionary People's League, an anti-Japanese organization closely tied to the

Nationalists, were divided into two broad factions: those who wanted "dominion status under China" and those (landlords and country gentry) who wanted independence. "Certain Aspects of the Formosan-Japanese Relationship," Office of Strategic Services, National Archives, entry 136, Calcutta-ND-INT-2, folder 641. See also Joint Army-Navy Intelligence Study of Formosa (Taiwan): People and Government, JANIS 87, June 1944, Library of Congress, microfilm 86–2087, part 8, x-13.

69. The most attention the island received from the central government occurred when Jiang Jieshi visited the island between October 21 and 27, 1946, and publicly praised Chen Yi. Ralph J. Blake, U.S. consul in Taibei, to J. L. Stuart, ambassador to China, Oct. 31, 1946, Department of State, Central Files, 894A.00/10-3146. All files with the 794 or 894 codes are from the Department of State Central Files, Record Group 59, held in the National Archives. Hereafter cited as Central Files.

70. The Nationalist capital was returned from its wartime location of Chongqing to Nanjing in late 1945.

71. On Nationalist goals, see for example Chen Mingtong, "Paixi zhengzhi," 257–59. Primary source materials on Nationalist plans for Taiwan include *Taiwan gongzuo gaijin yaogang*; Chen Wuzhong and Chen Guangtang, eds., *Taiwan guangfu*; Guo Yimin, *Shoufu Taiwan yijianshu*; He Taishan, *Taiwan zhanhou wenti*; and He Fengjiao, ed., *Zhengfu jieshou Taiwan shiliao huibian*.

72. Both the Japanese governors-general and Administrator Chen Yi were nicknamed *tu huangdi* (local emperors). On the similarities between Japanese and early Nationalist rule, see Huang Fusan, "The Japanese Legacy and Nationalist Chinese Response." Naturally, the Nationalists sought to emphasize the differences between the pre- and post-1945 regimes. For example, Chief of the Civil Administration Office Zhou Yi'e noted that his office's publications concerning the Nationalist administration were designed in part to highlight great changes in laws and regulations since October 1945. Taiwansheng xingzheng zhangguan gongshu [3], intro.

73. On central-provincial relations, particularly regarding national economic policies, see Kirby, "Planning Postwar Taiwan." As Kirby emphasizes in his recent article on the development of commercial law in Republican China, the Nationalists' management of the economy was focused on political ends — primarily "the strengthening of central government power." Kirby, "China Unincorporated," 44. For a comparison of Nationalist policy on the mainland and Taiwan, see also Kirby, "Continuity and Change in Modern China."

74. Kirby, "Planning Postwar Taiwan," 294. See also Chen Mingtong, "Paixi zhengzhi," 263–64.

75. Kirby, "Planning Postwar Taiwan," 293.

76. Ibid., 294.

77. See, for example, the struggle between the Political Science Clique (also called the Political Study Clique), which included many Japanese- and American-trained administrative and technical experts, and the virulently anti-Communist C-C Clique (name for the two brothers who led it: Chen Lifu and Chen Guofu), upon which Jiang Jieshi depended for control of the Guomindang. Eastman, *Seeds of Destruction*, 111–12.

78. Factions were a way of distributing political power and controlling resources through personal relationships. They grew out of shared experiences (such as edu-

cation or military service), place of birth, economic interests, political ideology, or a combination of the four. At the national level, Jiang Jieshi deliberately promoted competing factions to protect his own power by keeping potential rivals divided and off balance.

79. Most of Chen's subordinates had formed ties with him during his study in Japan or Germany, or during his tenure as governor of Fujian.

80. Chen Mingtong, "Paixi zhengzhi," 271–74.

81. Ibid., 253–55. See also Chen Mingtong, *Paixi douzheng*.

82. Ge Jing'en, "Lai Tai yinian de huigu."

83. Many accounts of the arriving troops are so similar that it is difficult to tell whether they come from personal observation or from collective memory. Huang Haibo, a Gaoxiong businessman, stated that many Taiwanese were eager to learn Mandarin Chinese, and warmly welcomed the Nationalist military. However, soldiers had a habit of shooting their weapons whenever they were displeased and did not pay full price for what they bought. *Er erba shijian wenxian jilu*, 13. Other sources claim the soldiers received a great welcome along the roads, though their appearance and discipline did raise questions among Taiwanese. See Wu Zhuoliu, *Taiwan lianqiao*, 152–54. Lin Hengdao remembered that everyone knew the Japanese had been defeated by the atomic bomb, not by China. Chen Sanjing and Xu Xueji, *Lin Hengdao xiansheng*, 74. The account written by Taiwanese independence activist Peng Mingmin is perhaps the must devastating: "With no attempt to maintain order or discipline, they pushed off the ship, glad to be on firm land, but hesitant to face the Japanese lined up and saluting smartly on both sides. My father wondered what the Japanese could possibly think. He had never felt so ashamed in his life." Peng Mingmin, *A Taste of Freedom*, 51.

84. On the colonial legacy, see Fix, "Taiwanese Nationalism in Its Late Colonial Context." Fix's work emphasizes the separatist aspirations of the Taiwanese and offers a useful counterpoint to this work's conclusions.

85. Huang Chaoqin, *Taiwan shouhui hou zhi sheji*, 1–2.

86. Editorial, *Xin Taiwan* 2 (Feb. 28, 1946): 1; Taiwan chongjian xiehui, "Wei Taiwan tongbao jiang ji ju hua."

87. Chen Sanjing and Xu Xueji, *Lin Hengdao xiansheng*, 80.

88. Zhe Ye, "Taiwanren de huhuan."

89. For examples, see Chen Yisong, *Chen Yisong huiyi lu*, 299.

90. "Chuangkan ci" (Inaugural Issue Statement), *Xin Taiwan* 1 (Feb. 15, 1946): 2. The same views can be seen in Shanghai, where Taiwanese students and merchants organized themselves and lobbied Nationalist officials for a speedy return to the island. They knew Taiwan, they said, and thus would be vital in its governance. Yin Zhangyi, *Chounongyan*, 229–30.

91. Jiang Weichuan, "Taiwansheng canyiyuan houxuan xuanyan (1)."

92. Strategic Services Unit, "A Report on Formosa (Taiwan) — Japanese Intelligence and Related Subjects," Office of Strategic Services, National Archives, XL 49553. The report's cover letter is dated April 12, 1946.

93. Zhou Xianwen, "Ruhe kan Taiwan?"

94. "Jianshe Taiwan xin wenhua" (Establishing Taiwan's New Culture), *Taiwan xinshengbao* (Nov. 6, 1945): 2.

95. "Taiwan de tedian" (The Special Points of Taiwan), *Taiwan xinshengbao* (July 5, 1946): 1.

96. Robert H. S. Lee, "Changes in Taiwan Attitudes."

97. On ideas of race and nation in modern China, see Dikötter, *The Discourse of Race in Modern China*.

98. Wu Zhuoliu, *Taiwan lianqiao*, 156–157.

99. Li Xiaofeng, *Daoyu xin taiji*, 94–105. In particular, the Taiwanese interest in the Provincial Assembly and the strong views of some of its members were portrayed as extremist and exclusionary of those from outside the province. "Sheng canyihui bimu" (Closing of the Taiwan Provincial Assembly), *Minbao* (May 16, 1946): 1.

100. Other types of traitors included those who use "pretty words to promote independence" and those who oppose "our government or disrupt society." "Zai lun jianju Hanjian" (Again Discussing Informing Authorities of Traitors Against China), *Taiwan xinshengbao* (Feb. 27, 1946): 2.

101. For an overview of Chen's views on feudalism, see Dai Guohui and Ye Yunyun, *Aizeng er erba*, 91.

102. Li Yizhong, "Lingdao shehui yaoyi."

103. *Er erba shijian wenxian jilu*, 9–10. The Nationalist government had to confront this issue on a much larger scale on the mainland, in particular with regard to the remnants of Wang Jingwei's puppet regime in Nanjing. Most of the puppet government leaders and functionaries were defectors from the Nationalist cause. The justification offered by Wang, and often used by others in his government after the war, for conciliation with the Japanese invader was that China was too weak and disunified to resist effectively. About 2,700 officials in Wang's government were executed and 2,300 were given life imprisonment (most were eventually freed). See Boyle, *China and Japan at War*, 331–35, 361.

104. For example, in late 1936, a group of officials under Chen Yi made a study tour of Taiwan and investigated its administration and industries. Although at the time Chen could not have known that all-out war would break out between China and Japan in 1937, that he sent a delegation to Taiwan indicated he at least tacitly accepted the legitimacy of Japan's occupation. Fujiansheng zhengfu, *Taiwan kaocha baogao*.

105. Chen Sanjing and Xu Xueji, *Lin Hengdao xiansheng*, 80–81. See also Lin Zhen, "Kangzhan shiqi Fujian de Taiwan jimin wenti."

106. Wu Sanlian, *Wu Sanlian huiyilu*, 104–6.

107. Li Wanju, "Taiwan minzhong bing meiyou Ribenhua." *Zhengjingbao*, the magazine in which Li Wanju published his article, began in October of 1945 under chief editor Su Xin, an anti-Japanese activist and leftist labor organizer who had been jailed by the Japanese in the 1930s. He fled to the mainland in the late 1940s.

108. Min-Tai tongxun shebian, *Taiwan zhengzhi xiankuang baogaoshu*, 24. Office of Strategic Services, National Archives, entry 173, box 11.

109. "Taiwan wei chang 'nuhua'" (Taiwan Has Not Been "Slavized"), *Minbao* (Apr. 7, 1946): 1.

110. Chen Fangming, "Zhanhou chuqi Taiwan zizhi yundong," 157.

111. Wang Baiyuan, "Gao waishengren zhugong."

112. "Waishengren wenti" (Problems with Those from Outside the Province), *Renmin daobao* (May 9, 1946): 1.

113. Su Shen, "'Neidi' yu 'neidiren.'"

114. Taiwan chongjian xiehui, "Wei Taiwan tongbao jiang ji ju hua." See also the fascinating poem by Lin Tangchuan, which is based on a classic pedagogical tool. Lin Tangchuan, "Xin Taiwan sanzijing."

115. *Er erba shijian wenxian jilu*, 10–11.

116. The term was popularized by Wu Zhuoliu's wartime novel, *Yaxiya de gu'er*.

117. Song Feiru, "Minzu zhuyi zai Taiwan."

118. Wang Tiandeng, "Niantou zhi ci."

119. Liu Zhuanlai, "Guangfu hou de huigu."

120. Li Chunqing, "Zhongguo zhengzhi yu Taiwan."

121. Wang Baiyuan, "Zai Taiwan lishi zhi xiangke."

122. Li Xiaofeng, *Daoyu xin taiji*, 30–35.

123. "Women dui Taiwan de yijian" (Our View of Taiwan), editorial reprinted in *Riyuetan* 14 (July 1, 1946): 7–10.

124. Xiang Ting, "Lun difang zizhi."

125. Chen Sanjing and Xu Xueji, *Lin Hengdao xiansheng*, 75–76.

126. Wo Ai Di, "Yu 'difang zizhi' tan dao xiubian 'Taiwan wenhuashi' de biyaoxing."

127. Xie later fled back to the mainland to escape arrest.

128. Xie Nanguang, "Guangming puzhao xia de Taiwan."

129. Qiu Niantai, "Renshi Taiwan fayang Taiwan." Qiu reiterated these points in many of his interviews and writings. See also idem, "Zhanming Tairen wu Hanjian." Qiu, born in Taiwan and educated in Japan, launched his political career in Guangdong Province. After retrocession, he became a member of the Guomindang Provincial Party Committee in Taiwan and held a variety of government posts there.

130. This observation may have been a jab at Chen Yi, who had been an underling of Sun before the Northern Expedition.

131. Lin Zhong, "Dui shichu fabiao zhengjian."

CHAPTER 4: THE FEBRUARY 28 INCIDENT

1. A sensitive issue in the historiography of Taiwan is how to refer to the events of early 1947: Incident (*shijian* or *shibian*)? Popular uprising (*minbian*)? Rebellion (*panluan* or *panbian*)? Massacre (*can'an*)? Each term carries with it political implications. For the purposes of this book, "incident" will be used. On this topic, see the translator's introduction in Yang Yizhou, *Er erba minbian*, 13–16. In Chinese, *shijian* often carries the connotation of an important event that is both unexpected and accidental (*oufa*). It tends to suggest that the Nationalists were not to blame for the events of February and March 1947. I use "incident" because I do not believe it carries with it the connotation of the English "accidental." By far the most comprehensive account of the incident in English is Lai Tse-han [Lai Zehan], Ramon H. Myers, and Wei Wou, *A Tragic Beginning*. The book by Lai et al. portrays the uprising as a tragedy stemming from a clash of worldviews. George Kerr, *Formosa*

Betrayed, and Peng Mingmin, *A Taste of Freedom,* provide first-person accounts by supporters of the island's independence. The Nationalist version of events is in the March issue of *New Taiwan Monthly* and in Taiwan News Service, *An Infamous Riot.* A Taiwanese separatist version is Thomas Liao, *Inside Formosa.* Another relatively well-known pro-independence history is Shi Ming, *Taiwanren sibainian shi.*

2. Pepper, *Civil War in China,* 9.

3. In fact, as early as September 1945, United States intelligence reports stated that "80% of civilian pop. very indignant over Chinese occupation" and "Very few Formosans want China overlordship." NR 8 Clark to Indiv. for Helliwell, 19 Sept, and NR 22 Clark to Indiv. Op-Secret. 231625C, Office of Strategic Services, National Archives, entry 173, box 11, folder 98. A report from March 28, 1946 mentioned "Taiwanese holding thoughts of organized revolt." Morgan to Indiv., Mar. 28, 1946, ibid., entry 140, box 47. The Office of Strategic Services (OSS) files contain a wealth of information on relations between mainland Chinese, Japanese, Taiwanese, and Americans from September 1945 to April 1946.

4. Chen Mingtong, "Paixi zhengzhi," 257–59.

5. This framework was pointed out in an editorial, "Zhong-Mei hezuo jingying: Taiwan luye" (Sino-American Cooperative Management: Taiwan's Aluminum), *Gonglunbao* (Feb. 7, 1948): 2.

6. At the end of the war, about 488,000 Japanese (322,000 civilians and 166,000 soldiers and sailors) remained on the island. Huang Yingzhe estimates that as many as 200,000 planned to stay on Taiwan indefinitely out of uncertainty about their future in Japan or personal ties to Taiwanese. By early 1946, however, these Japanese too began to return home. Huang Zhaotang, *Taiwan zongdufu,* 254–57.

7. In 1946 poor weather was also a factor, as a major typhoon hit the island in September, reducing agricultural production and damaging industrial facilities.

8. William Kirby writes:

> Taiwan then, was less the exception than the rule carried to a near extreme. Policies were pursued from a national agenda that was not one of "plunder" but of planned nationalization and economic "synchronization." The policies may have been ill-conceived and state industries ill managed; and certainly from that perspective "nationalization" seemed much more like "expropriation." Given Taiwan's initial place in national economic planning, which was one of relatively low priority, it is likely that Nationalist policies would result in a lowering of Taiwan's standard of living.

Kirby, "Planning Postwar Taiwan," 297.

9. Chen Yi and the Nanjing government were in frequent conflict over the management of Taiwan and its resources. It is difficult to determine whether Chen's desire to limit the central government's influence was truly based on his concern for the welfare of the Taiwanese or on factional rivalries among top Nationalist leaders. On Chen's views of economic development, see Zhang Fumei, "Chen Yi yu Fujian shengzheng"; and Liu Shiyong, "Chen Yi de jingji sixiang ji qi zhengce."

10. Ting Wenzhi, "Chen zhangguan lun 'guanliao ziben.'"

11. On the mainland, the relationship between the Nationalist government and business people was troubled as well. The Nationalists often resorted to "regulations"

and "taxes" that were little more than expropriation of private resources in order to fund state-building, particularly funding the military. See Eastman, *Seeds of Destruction*; idem, *The Abortive Revolution*; and Coble, *The Shanghai Capitalists and the Nationalist Government*.

12. "Now that the Japanese are to be eliminated, the Formosans anticipated an opportunity to return to full control and ownership of their private businesses." Conditions in Formosa, Mar. 15, 1946, Central Files, 894A.00/3-1546. See also Current Public Opinion in Formosa, Nov. 23, 1945, 894A.00/1-2846.

13. In August 1946, the *New York Times* reported that the Nationalists had seized 500 factories or mines, of which 300 were sold and 200 were nationalized. Lieberman, "Obstacles Delay Formosan Output." I cannot find evidence that any factory transferred to the mainland was reassembled or put back into operation.

14. American observers reported in March 1946 "Trade from Taiwan to Shanghai hampered by squeeze at both ends. Estimated ten per cent of profits goes to Chinese officials but rate varies with cargo." "Morgan to Indiv., March 28, 1946," Office of Strategic Services, National Archives, entry 140, box 47. Smuggling arose between Taiwan, Japan, Okinawa, and the Philippines, possibly as an attempt by Taiwanese merchants to avoid export controls and taxes. This represented a continuation of trade patterns from the colonial era. See the review of press reports in Central Files, 894A.00/5-2146; and *The China Weekly Review* of Apr. 20, 1946. See also Ralph Blake, U.S. consul in Taibei, to J. L. Stuart, ambassador to China, Oct. 31 1946, Central Files, 894A.00/10-3146.

15. In August 1946, United States officials reported that "economic paralysis has set in, attributed primarily to the policy of creating semi-official companies against which private enterprise cannot successfully compete." Memorandum from Blake to Stuart, Central Files, 894A.00/8-1246.

16. For a comprehensive collection of official decrees and other materials on the disposition of Japanese property, see He Fengjiao, ed., *Zhengfu jieshou Taiwan shiliao huibian*, chap. 2.

17. See the many petitions in the archives of the provincial government contained in the Academia Historica (Guoshiguan). For example, in November 1945 islanders from Taizhong attempted to regain land taken by the Japanese navy. Taiwansheng xingzheng zhangguan gongshu [1], Provincial Government Records, file no. 453/143.

18. Peng Mingmin, *A Taste of Freedom*, 54.

19. Li Xiaofeng, *Daoyu xin taiji*, 48.

20. See review of press reports in Central Files, 894A.00/5-2146. Frederick Wong in *The China Weekly Review* of Apr. 20, 1946. See also Memorandum from Blake to Stuart, Oct. 31, 1946, Central Files, 894A.00/10-3146.

21. *Er erba shijian wenxian jilu* 1: 13–14.

22. Li Xiaofeng, *Daoyu xin taiji*, 32–33.

23. United States Department of State documents provide some of the best information on the business connections of members of the Nationalist government. For example, during his tenure as governor of Fujian, Chen hired Yan Jiagan (also known as K. K. Nyien or C. K. Yen) as his assistant. Yan became communications director of the Taiwan Provisional Government. He also made his personal secretary, Jian Zhongji, Taiwan director of the China National Relief and Rehabilitation

Commission. Other Taiwanese Half-Mountain officials used their government posts for personal profit. Many of the top employees in the Taiwan government were closely connected to the China Merchant Steam Navigation Company, including the director of railroads, Chen Jingwen, and commissioner of mining and industry, Bao Geyong. Bao also became general manager of the "private" Taiwan Provincial Industrial and Mining Enterprises in January 1947. Bao was Yan Jiagan's brother-in-law. Yan later served as finance commissioner and chairman of the board of directors of the Bank of Taiwan from 1946 to 1949. In the latter post he controlled the supply of Taiwan currency. He eventually became minister of economic affairs from 1950 to 1954 and governor of Taiwan from 1954 to 1957, and later held important posts in the central government. See Memorandum from Blake to Stuart, Central Files, 894A.00/1-3147; Stuart to the secretary of state, Aug. 9, 1945, 894A.00/9-1446; Stuart to the secretary of state, Aug. 9, 1946, 894A.00/9-1446; and Kerr, *Formosa Betrayed*, 54.

24. Wang Shiqing, "Chen Fengyuan xiansheng," 161.

25. Conditions in Formosa, Central Files, 894A.00/3-1546.

26. Ibid.

27. Memorandum from Blake to Stuart, Central Files, 894A.00/10-3146.

28. Criminal networks extended across all the countries in the region. For example, among the roughly 20,000 Taiwanese in Japan (mainly laborers who had been drafted during World War II) in early 1947, were black marketeers and organized criminals in competition or cooperation with Japanese and Korean gangs. "Problems Regarding the Treatment of Formosans in Japan Raised by the Shibuya Incident," Department of State, Office of Intelligence Research Report, Feb. 10, 1947, UPA microfilm 484, part 6; and Memorandum from Blake to Stuart, Central Files, 894A.00/8-1246.

29. See the press reports in Central Files, 894A.00/5-2146; and Memorandum from Blake to Stuart, Oct. 31, 1946, 894A.00/10-3146.

30. Li Xiaofeng, *Daoyu xin taiji*, 51–52. According to Yin Naiping, post-retrocession inflation had its roots in the last years of Japanese rule, when the colonial government had the Taiwan Bank issue a huge amount of scrip to meet their expenses. The Japanese printed 3.57 times more scrip in 1945 than they had in 1944. From 1944 to 1945, prices increased by 5.13 times. In 1946, they increased by 5.3 times and in 1947, by 7.79 times. From 1945 to mid-1946 they skyrocketed 20-fold. Inflation was spurred by chaos on the mainland, over-issuing Old Taibi (*Jiu Taibi*, lit. Old Taiwan Dollar; the official currency), and increasing demands for goods as the Nationalists began their retreat. In June 1949, the government replaced the Old Taibi with the New Taibi (*Xin Taibi*; New Taiwan Dollar) at an exchange rate of 40,000 to one. The government also moved to control the gold supply and issue bonds to soak up excess currency. Yin Naiping, "Taiwan guangfu yilai de wujia wending zhengce"; and Yan Zhenhui, "Taiwan guangfu chuqi de jingji chongjian chutan."

31. Memorandum from Blake to Stuart, Central Files, 894A.00/10-3146.

32. For example, by early 1947, a desperate Gaoxiong city government was blaming profiteers (*jianshang*) for hoarding grain. It also urged that the provincial government distribute rice immediately. "Yanzhong qudi tunji jianshang" (Severely Punish Hoarding Profiteers), *Guoshengbao* (Jan. 31, 1947): 4.

33. Conditions in Formosa, Central Files, 894A.00/3-1546; and "Benshi zou fangyi zong dongyuan" (Yesterday City Begins General Mobilization Against Epidemic), *Zhonghua ribao* (July 29, 1946): 3.

34. Kerr, *Formosa Betrayed*, 171. There is no information to verify whether this is true or whether the more important cause was the collapse of the Japanese administration and lack of enforcement of sanitation regulations.

35. Huang Yingzhe, "Lu Xun sixiang."

36. You Mijian, "Taiwan wenhua xiejinhui de mudi."

37. The New Culture Movement was an attack on traditional Chinese values, which were blamed for China's poverty, disunity, and weakness against imperialism. Beginning with Chen Duxiu's "Call to Youth" in 1915, colloquial literature designed to awaken Chinese to perceived political and cultural defects became a key tool of young intellectuals, many of whom had Western or Japanese education. The New Culture Movement was further invigorated by the May Fourth Movement, which began when the warlord government that controlled Beijing accepted the humiliating provisions of the Treaty of Versailles in 1919. Intellectuals, students, and others took to the streets to protest imperialism and warlord rule. Although quickly crushed by militarists, the movement was a key step in radicalizing youth, increasing resistance to imperialism, and spreading a broad social and cultural critique of traditional China.

38. During the 1920s some young Taiwanese became familiar with the authors of the May Fourth era including Lu Xun. Understanding and readership of Lu Xun was limited on Taiwan, however, and Chinese publications were forbidden by the Japanese after 1937.

39. Huang Yingzhe, "Lu Xun sixiang," 304–17. See also idem, "Xu Shoutang yu Taiwan."

40. Xu himself was criticized by other Guomindang members who tied him to Lu Xun's leftist thinking. After the February 28 Incident, there was little discussion, much less state promotion, of Lu Xun. His works were forbidden after 1950. Xu himself was relieved of his post after Chen Yi left Taiwan in 1947. He was murdered on the campus of Taiwan National University in early 1948 during a bungled robbery of his home. Huang Yingzhe, "Lu Xun sixiang," 317–18.

41. On the language policies of the Nationalist government on Taiwan during this period, see Xu Xueji, "Taiwan guangfu chuqi de yuwen wenti."

42. In discussing the connections between nationalism, colonialism, and language in Indonesia, Benedict Anderson points out that "the acquisition of the colonial language implied a change in modalities of consciousness. It was far more than just the discovery of a radically different set of phonetic equivalents for the inventory of one's own language." Unfortunately, there does not yet exist an in-depth analysis of how the "modalities of consciousness" of Taiwanese (*Minnanhua*, also known as *Taiyu*), Hakka (*Kejiahua*), Japanese, and Mandarin Chinese contended on Taiwan. Anderson, *Language and Power*, 125.

43. Xu Xueji, "Taiwan guangfu chuqi de yuwen wenti," 166–67.

44. Ibid., 168. The Nationalist government explicitly connected the use of Guoyu to cultural affinity with the mainland and the rejection of colonial rule. Wei Jiangong, "'Guoyu yundong zai Taiwan de yiyi' shenjie."

45. Xu Xueji, "Taiwan guangfu chuqi de yuwen wenti," 173. For example, editorials in pro-Nationalist newspapers claimed that certain "beautiful young gentlemen" who persisted in using Japanese had a problem with their mentality (*xinli*) — namely that Japanese education had reduced their nationalist spirit. This was deemed a great disgrace to the Taiwanese. "Dajia dou jiang Guoyu" (Everyone Speak Chinese), *Zhonghua ribao* (Oct. 2, 1946): 1.

46. "Zhuantouyu" (Editorial at the Beginning of This Volume), *Xinxin* 3 (Mar. 20, 1946): 1.

47. Xu Xueji, "Taiwan guangfu chuqi de yuwen wenti," 184.

48. Ibid., 166–67. See also Lian Zhengdong, "Taiwanren de zhengzhi lixiang."

49. Historian Lin Hengdao states in his oral history that "Upon his arrival on Taiwan, Chen Yi supported a certain level of freedom of expression and permitted newspapers to reflect some practical questions." Chen Sanjing and Xu Xueji, *Lin Hengdao xiansheng*, 75.

50. Headed by Li Wanju, the staff of *Taiwan xinshengbao* included members of the China Youth Party, of which Li was a member, and Japanese-trained Taiwanese reporters. The paper openly attacked corruption among officials. Wu Zhuoliu, *Taiwan lianqiao*, 154–56. Li was forced out of his post in 1947. He then began to publish *Gonglunbao*, one of the few newspapers on the island that took a relatively independent stance toward the government after the February 28 Incident. Li's career is discussed in depth in Chapter 6.

51. "Zhengfu ziyou hefa baozhang" (Government to Guarantee Freedom in Accordance with the Law), *Heping ribao* (Nov. 23, 1946): 3.

52. Memorandum from Blake to Stuart, Central Files, 894A.00/1-3147. Wang's difficulties were part of an attempt to crack down on *Renmin daobao*, one of the newspapers most openly critical of the provincial government. This newspaper was one of the most important voices for Taiwanese outside of the Nationalist ranks. It was published until government pressure and financial problems forced it to close in mid-1946. Shortly after the paper had ceased publishing, the highest court on Taiwan announced that the case against Wang was being dropped due to the lack of evidence. "Wang Tiandeng wenzi huo'an gao fayuan xuanpan wu zui" (High Court Determines that No Crime Was Committed in the Wang Tiandeng Case), *Guoshengbao* (Jan. 31, 1947): 3; "Wang Tiandeng an you zhuanji" (A Turning Point in the Wang Tiandeng Case), *Heping ribao* (Jan. 29, 1947): 3. Wang was not the only prominent Taiwanese harassed by the state. Jiang Weichuan, former president of the Taibei Chamber of Commerce, which had ties to the C-C Clique, was sued for libel by the provincial government. Jiang's ties to the mainland-based faction may have also been a factor in his being named as a conspirator in the wake of the February 28 Incident. Chen Mingtong, "Paixi zhengzhi," 255–56. Taiwanese frequently cited Wang's case when complaining about the lack of press freedom. Bai Long, "Yanlun yao juedui ziyou."

53. They were Taibei mayor You Mijian, Xinju magistrate Liu Qiguang, and Gaoxiong mayor Xie Dongmin. Song Feiru, a Half-Mountain person who disappeared during the February 28 Incident, held the second most important post in the provincial government's Education Office.

54. Chen Mingtong, "Paixi zhengzhi," 270.

55. Several daily gazettes of Nationalist government actions and lists of important bureaucrats provide information on the fate of employees who had worked under the Japanese. These publications include *Taiwansheng xingzheng zhangguan gongshu gongbao* (Gazette of the Taiwan Provincial Administration), published daily in Taibei between December 1, 1945, and May 15, 1947. See also the *Shizheng baogao* (Administrative Report) issued by the Taiwansheng xingzheng zhangguan gongshu [2] in 1946, then by the Taiwansheng mishuchu (Taiwan Provincial Secretariat) beginning in 1947 entitled *Taiwansheng zhengfu shizheng baogao* (Report of the Taiwan Provincial Government).

56. Lai, Myers, and Wei, *A Tragic Beginning*, 65.

57. The consultative assemblies at the provincial level and below were designed by the Nationalists to serve as the limits of local self-government during the period of Political Tutelage (*xunzhi*), the middle stage of China's political development as defined by Sun Zhongshan in his Three Principles of the People. Rules for the assemblies are found in Shi Yangcheng, *Zhongguo sheng xingzheng zhidu yice*; and Li Xuexun, *Xianxing difang minyi jiguo zhidu*.

58. Shi Yangcheng, *Zhongguo sheng xingzheng zhidu yice*, 1

59. On the implementation of assemblies immediately after the war, see *Jiangsusheng zhengfu sanshisi, sanshiwu nian zhengqing shuyao*; and *Minzheng baodao*.

60. The Japanese division of the island into five districts (*zhou*) and three offices (*ting*) was revised by the Nationalists in late 1945 to eight counties (*xian*) and nine cities (*shi*). These jurisdictions were used for both the provincial administration and assembly elections. Most xian and shi assemblies selected one member of the provincial body but, based on their higher population, six of the largest counties and cities had two or three members. In 1950, the boundaries were changed again prior to the reform of the system of local self-government to include sixteen counties, five cities, and one administrative bureau (Yangmingshan, north of Taibei).

61. Wu Naide and Chen Mingtong, "Zhengchuan zhuanyi," 318–23.

62. Kerr, *Formosa Betrayed*, 196.

63. Memorandum from Blake, to Stuart, May 12, 1946, Central Files, 894A.oo/12-446.

64. Accounts of the Provincial Consultative Assembly come from Zheng Muxin, *Taiwan yihui zhengzhi sishinian*; and Li Xiaofeng, *Taiwan zhanhou*.

65. Min-Tai tongxun shebian, *Taiwan zhengzhi xiankuang baogaoshu*, 27–32, in Office of Strategic Services, National Archives, entry 173, box 11.

66. *Taiwansheng canyihui diyijie diyici dahui teji.* Hereafter cited as *Canyihui diyijie* and session number. *Canyihui diyijie*, 2.

67. Li Xiaofeng, *Daoyu xin taiji*, 25–27.

68. See the files at the Academia Historica (Guoshiguan) pertaining to the Taiwanese provincial government, such as file number 474/1786, which contains accusations against officials in the Gaoxiong tax office of assisting with the Japanese program of cultural assimilation during the late 1930s and early 1940s.

69. *Er erba shijian wenxian jilu*, 13–14.

70. Memorandum from Blake, to Stuart, Central Files, 894A.oo/8-1246.

71. The complete text of the plan can be found in "Taiwansheng difang zizhi sannian jihua" (The Three-Year Plan for Taiwan Province's Local Self-Government),

Zhonghua ribao (Jan. 15, 1947): 2, and (Jan. 16, 1947): 3. Speeches about and plans for local self-government can be found in Taiwansheng xingzheng zhangguan gong-shu [4], no. 20, Jan. 26, 1947.

72. "Bensheng xianshizhang minxuan yi zhongyang faling banli" (Popular Elections for Mayors and District Heads Will Be Managed According to Central Government Laws and Orders), *Heping ribao* (Jan. 22, 1947): 3. See also "Chongshi difang zizhi'an quanwen" (Complete Text of the Case to Complete Local Self-Government), *Guoshengbao* (Jan. 13, 1947): 3.

73. A Taiwanese author states that Chen Yi did not feel Taiwan was ready for the constitution that came into effect for the rest of China on December 25, 1947. According to the source, Chen felt that because of its colonial legacy Taiwan lacked the proper political consciousness. The province would require two or three additional years of political tutelage before the Taiwanese could become complete citizens. Deng Kongshao, "Cong er erba shijian kan," 73.

74. "Xingxian zhunbei gongzuo" (Work to Implement the Constitution), *Heping ribao* (Jan. 22, 1947): 3; and "'Chongshi difang zizhi'an' pingjia" (An Evaluation of "The Case of Fully Implementing Local Self-Government"), *Xinshengbao* (Jan. 13, 1946): 2.

75. Zhu Benyuan, "Taiwansheng duiyu xingxian de shiyingxing."

76. "Memorandum on the Situation in Taiwan," submitted by Ambassador Stuart to President Chiang Kai-shek, Apr. 18, 1947, *United States Relations with China*, 925.

77. "Puxuan zizhi shishi tiaojian" (Conditions for the Implementation of General Elections for Self-Government), *Guoshengbao* (Feb. 6, 1947): 3.

78. "Xianfa bingwu guiding Taisheng liewai" (The Constitution Does Not Stipulate that Taiwan Province Is an Exception), *Guoshengbao* (Jan. 25, 1947): 3.

79. "Shengxian zizhifa zhiding hou" (After the Introduction of Provincial and County Self-Government Laws), *Xinshengbao* (Feb. 9, 1947): 2.

80. "Xiao gan kun" (Little Heaven and Earth), *Minbao* (Feb. 20, 1946): 2.

81. This poem can be found in many publications. It was sometimes called "Five Heavens and Five Earths" (*Wu tian wu di*). "Taiwan xiaoxi" (Taiwan News), *Xin Taiwan* 3 (Apr. 1, 1946): 8. *Xin Taiwan* was published by islanders living in Beijing. Taiwanese who had lived in Japanese-occupied areas of the mainland had firsthand knowledge of the Nationalists' defects and greater sympathy for the colonial admin-istration. As a result, they tended to criticize the reintegration earlier and more force-fully than did other Taiwanese. Fang Hao, "Hong Yanqiu xiansheng."

82. Su Xin, "Zhuyi, jigou, renwu."

83. Chen Sanjing and Xu Xueji, *Lin Hengdao xiansheng*, 79; and Report on Current Public Opinion in Formosa, Nov. 23, 1945, Central Files, 894A.00/1-2846.

84. Li Xiaofeng, *Daoyu xin taiji*, 94–105.

85. "Suqing dou'ou zhi feng" (Exterminate the Fad of Brawling), *Zhonghua ribao* (June 25, 1946): 1.

86. Wu Xinrong, *Wu Xinrong huiyilu*, 213.

87. Li Xiaofeng, *Daoyu xin taiji*, 69–73.

88. Han Shiquan, *Liushi huiyi*, 75.

89. China Handbook Editorial Board, *China Handbook, 1950*, 189.

90. The open market currency exchange rate soared to 17,500 Chinese National Currency (CNC) to one U.S. dollar. In Shanghai, the economic heart of China, inflation jumped 20 percent from December 1946 to January 1947, then another 55 percent in February. Central Intelligence Agency, National Archives, "China Research Report SR-8," Aug. 1948.

91. For example, a newspaper editorial listed the effects of the mainland's problems on Taiwanese merchants: high interest rates, dumped goods from the mainland, reduced buying power, increased tax burdens, blocked shipments of goods, increased costs of investment, and lack of equipment and technical personnel. "Zhongguo de jingji weiji yu Taiwan" (China's Economic Crisis and Taiwan), *Guoshengbao* (Jan. 10, 1947): 1.

92. "Tuixing chaoran zhuji zhidu: Bingyi xiabannian ge shixing" (Promoting an Unprejudiced and Accountable System: Military Conscription to Begin in the Latter Half of the Year), *Xinshengbao* (Jan. 23, 1947): 2. For the actual regulations, see the Taiwansheng xingzheng zhangguan gongshu [4], nos. 7–10, Jan. 11–15, 1947.

93. "Mishang bimen hangshi wenluan" (Rice Market Closes, Market in Disorder), *Heping ribao* (Feb. 14, 1947): 3. A Taiwanese author raised two possible reasons for rising rice prices in early 1947. First, large quantities sugar and coal, two key commodities for stabilizing the Taibi, were being shipped to the mainland, thus increasing overall inflation. Second, merchants on the island itself were hoarding daily commodities. Wu Zhuoliu, *Wuhuaguo*, 212.

94. Tobacco was one of the products taxed and controlled by a state monopoly. Wu Zhuoliu wrote that the crowd assumed that the confiscated cigarettes would be kept or resold by corrupt authorities. Wu Zhuoliu, *Wuhuaguo*, 215.

95. American observers described this demonstration as "orderly." "Memorandum on the Situation in Taiwan," *United States Relations with China*, 926–27.

96. Li Xiaofeng, *Daoyu xin taiji*, 113–20 has an excellent short description of the incident and its aftermath in various towns and cities on the island. See also Lai, Myers, and Wei, *A Tragic Beginning*, 99–139, for the most detailed English-language account. For an account by Nationalist officials that emphasizes the violence against mainlanders, see "Taiwansheng er erba baodong shijian baogao" (A Report on Taiwan Province's February 28 Insurrection Incident), published by the Taiwansheng xingzheng zhangguan gongshu in 1947, reprinted in Chen Fangmin, ed., *Taiwan zhanhoushi ziliaoxuan*.

97. Lai, Myers, and Wei stress that there were relatively few Nationalist troops on the island to contain the incident. *A Tragic Beginning*, 65. However, at least as important was the poor quality of these soldiers. Official materials from the provincial government reveal a constant stream of deserters, many of whom were draftees from Fujian who had only served two or three months. For example, see Taiwansheng xingzheng zhangguan gongshu [4], no. 15, Jan. 21, 1947.

98. Memorandum from Blake, to Stuart, Mar. 7, 1947, Central Files, 894A.00/3.

99. Between March 1 and 7, Nationalist forces concentrated on maintaining control of the road from Jilong Harbor to Taibei. This route would prove vital for transporting Nationalist reinforcements from the mainland. Ibid.

100. On the variety of reactions to the chaos of February 28, see the collection of documents and oral histories in *Er erba shijian wenxian jilu*. Many Taiwanese were as confused and frightened as mainlanders were.

101. Japanese military service created a group of relatively well-educated youth, united by their shared experiences. On their role in the February 28 Incident see, for example, Chen Sanjing and Xu Xueji, *Lin Hengdao xiansheng*, 83–84; and Peng Mingmin, *A Taste of Freedom*, 65. One source stated later that Taiwanese who had served in the Japanese military, especially the imperial navy, were the main participants in the February 28 Incident. *Er erba shijian wenxian jilu*, 9.

102. Xie E moved to the United States a year later. Chen Sanjing and Xu Xueji, *Lin Hengdao xiansheng*, 83–84. Some sources state she made several radio broadcasts and that she tended to blame the people of Taibei for precipitating the incident — something that did not endear her to islanders. See Jiang Weichuan, *2.28 shibian shiweiji*, 5–6; Chen Cuilian, *Paixi douzheng*, 321–22; Ke Yuanfen, "Taiwan er erba shibian zhi zhenxian," 16.

103. Yan later rewarded him by making him head of Zhanghua Bank.

104. Chen Sanjing and Xu Xueji, *Lin Hengdao xiansheng*, 84–85.

105. "Zhangguan wanquan caina minyi" (The Administrator Completely Adopts the People's Will), *Heping ribao* (Mar. 2, 1947): 3. On Chen Yi's role in the incident, see Li Ao, ed., *Er erba yanjiu*.

106. "Chuli weihui zou kaihui: Kuoda zuzhi guangna minyi" (Resolution Committee Held Meeting Yesterday: Expand Organization and Incorporate the Popular Will), *Xinshengbao* (March 3, 1947): 1.

107. "Chuweihui zhianzu zoukai" (The Resolution Committee's Public Order Group Formed Yesterday), *Xinshengbao* (Mar. 4, 1947): 1. See also Li Xiaofeng, *Daoyu xin taiji*, 123.

108. They also attracted the most attention in — and won the approval of — the United States. A United States observer was probably referring to these men when he noted that "Today this literate population is highly organized throughout and has developed a keen sense of island-wide solidarity on governmental issues." Memorandum from Blake to Stuart, Alternate Courses of Action Open to the Chinese Government on Formosa, Central Files, 894A.00/3-1447.

109. The policy of the Chinese Communist Party (CCP) policy toward Taiwan is a matter of intense controversy. Prior to 1943 the CCP was ambiguous about the future status of Taiwan. Propaganda often suggested that the Taiwanese faced the struggle of a "weak and small nationality" separate from the mainland conflict. However, the CCP's policy toward Taiwan echoed that of the Nationalists' after the United States turned the tide of the war against Japan. The Communists could not allow themselves to appear less nationalistic than the Guomindang. As the war drew to a close, one of the few issues on which the Nationalists and Communists agreed was that Taiwan, like Tibet, was part of the sovereign territory (*bentu*) of China. Hsiao and Sullivan, "The Chinese Communist Party and the Status of Taiwan," 446.

110. Deng Kongshao, "Cong er erba shijian kan," 70.

111. Wu Zhuoliu, *Wuhuaguo*, 218.

112. I have modified a framework provided originally by Chen Cuilian, *Paixi douzheng*, 322–26.

113. Wu Xinrong, *Wu Xinrong huiyilu*, 213–24.

114. Ibid. Chen Yi's role in the incident is very controversial. We will probably never be certain whether he was negotiating with the Taiwanese in good faith.

115. Li Xiaofeng, *Taiwan zhanhou*, 197.

116. Ibid., 201–2.

117. For a more detailed account of self-government and the February 28 Incident, see Deng Kongshao, "Cong er erba shijian kan"; and Chen Fangming, "Zhanhou chuqi Taiwan zizhi yundong," 141–66.

118. Chen Mingtong, "Paixi zhengzhi," 275–80.

119. The translation of *yaoqiu*, which can mean "demand" or "request," has been politically charged. "Demand" suggests the Taiwanese were hostile or aggressive. The first definition of yaoqiu in the *Guoyu huoyong cidian* is "to sincerely request." The second definition is "insist." On the other hand, the well-known Mathews dictionary defines yaoqiu as "a demand; claims; to demand; to be importunate." When scholars want to make the Taiwanese appear aggressive, they translate yaoqiu as "demand"; when they think of the Taiwanese as moderate reformers, they tend to translate yaoqiu as "request." In reality, the Taiwanese requests became demands as the incident progressed. The Nationalists, focusing on the armed takeover by islanders, saw all yaoqiu as demands.

120. Chen Fangming, "Zhanhou chuqi Taiwan zizhi yundong," 157–63.

121. "Taisheng shijian chuli weihui tichu sanshier xian tiaojian" (Taiwan Province's Incident Resolution Committee Raises Thirty-two Conditions), *Shenbao* (March 10, 1947): 3.

122. "Taiwan zhixu yiqu zhengchang: Zhengfu juexin gaishan zhengzhi" (Taiwan's Order Already Returning to Normal: Government Determined to Reform and Improve Politics), *Shenbao* (March 7, 1947): 2.

123. An English-language version of the ten additional demands is in Lai, Myers, and Wei, *A Tragic Beginning*, 197–200. See also "Chuweihui chanming shijian zhenxiang: Xiang zhongwai guangbo chuli dagang" (Resolution Committee Makes Clear the Real Face of the Incident: Broadcasts Resolution Outline to the Central Government and Outsiders), *Xinshengbao* (March 8, 1947): 2; and Li Xiaofeng, *Taiwan zhanhou*, 204–6.

124. Li Xiaofeng, *Daoyu xin taiji*, 150–51.

125. The resolution committees had been funded in part by donations from wealthy islanders. Taiwansheng xingzheng zhangguan gongshu [4], no. 52, Mar. 13, 1947.

126. Li Xiaofeng, *Daoyu xin taiji*, 180–85. Ambassador Stuart reported that bodies were still turning up in Jilong Harbor during April, evidence of continued violence. "Memorandum on the Situation in Taiwan," *United States Relations with China*, 937.

127. On the implementation of policies to restore Nationalist control in Gaoxiong, see Xu Xueji, "Er erba shijian shi Gaoxiongshi de tuoqing."

128. "Memorandum on the Situation in Taiwan," *United States Relations with China*, 932–33; Wu Zhuoliu, *Wuhuaguo*, 223.

129. Wu Zhuoliu, *Taiwan lianqiao*, 204–5.

130. Interview with Lin Xinzhen, in Zhang Yanxian et al., eds., *Taibei Nangang er erba*, 177.

131. Interview with Wang Zhengtong, in ibid., 280.

132. Wu Wenxing, "Er erba shijian." On Chen Yi's meetings with various Taiwanese and his role in the massacre of early March 1947, see Li Xiaofeng, *Daoyu xin taiji*, 129–37. Lai Tse-han and his coauthors contend that Jiang Jieshi had decided on March 5 to dispatch troops to the island. Lai, Myers, and Wei, *A Tragic Beginning*, 142–51.

133. Peng Mengji, "Taiwansheng er erba shijian huiyilu," 59.

134. See Wu Wenxing, "Er erba shijian." According to Lloyd Eastman, the weaker the Nationalist regime felt, the more authoritarian it attempted to become. Eastman, *Seeds of Destruction*, chap. 1.

135. Even today, one of the most prominent historians of the February 28 Incident, Lai Zehan (also known as Lai Tse-han and Lai Jeh-hang), acknowledges that determining how many were killed, much less finding their graves, may be impossible. See also Kyne, "The Missing Victims of 2-28."

136. Nationalist officials were reluctant even to tell each other about the number of dead. Even as he was leaving the island on the fifth of April, Supervisory Yuan representative Yang Lianggong sought information on the number of arrested and killed in the incident. Chen Yi was unable or unwilling to provide the information and suggested that he contact Ke Yuanfen, head of the Garrison Command. Ke was of little help. Jiang Yongjing, Li Yunhan, and Xu Shishen, *Yang Lianggong xiansheng nianpu*, 373. The Nationalists provided a variety of estimates during early 1947. In May of 1947, the Taiwan Garrison Command, understating the number of casualties, reported as follows: military officers: 16 dead, 135 wounded, 3 missing; soldiers: 74 dead, 262 wounded, 37 missing; public employees: 64 dead, 1,351 wounded, 8 missing; citizens: 244 dead, 383 wounded, 24 missing. Thirty people were being held as "the most important criminals" in the incident. Eventually, about 500 people were arrested and charged with some sort of crime in connection with the incident. "Er erba shibian" (The February 28 Incident), *Guoshengbao* (May 28, 1947): 3. Another contemporary source claimed that only 1,000 people were killed, two-thirds of whom were from the mainland. "Agitation Quelled as Troops Moved In To Keep Order," *New Taiwan Monthly* (Mar. 1947). See also B. Stanway Cheng, "Bloodshed in Taiwan and Aftermath," in the same issue. Even in 1989, General Ke Yuanfen, then retired to California, wrote that only 408 people were killed. Ke Yuanfen, "Taiwan er erba shibian zhi zhenxiang," 36. On the various estimates of dead, wounded, and arrested, see Lai, Myers, and Wei, *A Tragic Beginning*, 155–64.

137. The *New York Times* reported the 10,000 figure as early as March 1947. Durdin, "Formosa Killings Are Put at 10,000."

138. Lai, Myers, and Wou estimate that 4,000 of those killed were part of the elite. They reckon 5 percent of the island's population of 6.5 million as the elite. *A Tragic Beginning*, 160. A United States Department of State observer noted that "It is probable that no Chinese military government can succeed on Formosa, though it may be able to paralyze all normal activities and wipe out — as it now appears to be doing — the open, intelligent and vocal leadership which sprang from every economic level." Memorandum from Blake to Stuart, Alternate Courses of Action Open to the Chinese Government on Formosa, Mar. 10, 1947, Central Files, 894A.00/3-1447.

139. Wu Naide and Chen Mingtong, "Zhengquan zhuanyi," 323–25.

140. On the promotion of Mandarin Chinese in the wake of the incident, see Xu Xueji, "Taiwan guangfu chuqi de yuwen wenti."

141. "Taiwan minzuhua de qiantu" (The Future of Taiwan's Democratization), *Guoshengbao* (May 2, 1947): 1. Indictments of prominent Taiwanese for their involvement in the February 28 Incident continued through the summer of 1947. "Gaojianchu tiqi gongsu" (Prosecutor's Office Submits Indictments), *Quanmin ribao* (Sept. 15, 1947): 3.

142. Wu Naide and Chen Mingtong, "Zhengquan zhuanyi," 329–31.

143. After the incident, the press, now tightly controlled by the government, occasionally discussed the uprising as a manifestation of traditional regionalism, and called for the eradication of such backward ideas in order to build a new China. Editorial, "Chedi xiaochu diyu guannian" (Thoroughly Erase Regionalism), *Heping ribao* (Mar. 18, 1947): 1. The Communists actually reinforced the Nationalists' propaganda. Many mainland books have attempted to put the Communist Party in the center of conflict between the Taiwanese and Nationalists. For example, see Wu Yuan, ed., *Taiwan de guoqu he xianzai*; Li Zhifu, *Taiwan renmin geming douzheng qianshi*; and Su Xin, *Weigui de Tai gong douhun*.

144. Jiang Yongjing, Li Yunhan, and Xu Shishen, *Yang Lianggong xiansheng nianpu*, 363. A Nationalist publication charged that "The recent riots in Taiwan were instigated by Taiwanese Communist members who had during the war been drafted by the Japanese to fight in the South Seas." Taiwan News Service, *An Infamous Riot*, 13.

145. This long-term/short-term approach appeared in many of the Nationalist materials examining the incident. For example, see the accounts of Generals Peng Mengji and Ke Yuanfen, and the Taiwan Provincial Administrator's Office in *Er erba shijian ziliao xuanji*, vol. 1.

146. Other commonly identified causes or contributing factors included inflation and unemployment, improper government policies, corruption and incompetence among officials, public opinion misled by a press tainted by fifty years of Japanese control, manipulation by evil politicians, weakness of the local military, and failure to prevent rebels from gaining control of the Taibei radio station. Jiang Yongjing, Li Yunhan, and Xu Shishen, *Yang Lianggong xiansheng nianpu*, 393–99.

147. Ibid., 400–402.

148. Ibid., 392.

149. Bai served as minister of national defense from 1946 to 1948. In 1949, he moved to Taiwan, where he held a position on the Guomindang's Central Executive Committee.

150. Memorandum from Blake to Stuart, Apr. 15, 1947, Central Files, 894A.00/4-1547. "Inside Story of General Pai Chung-hsi's Pacification Mission to Taiwan," *Xin Zhonghua ribao* (New China Daily), Chongqing (Chungking), (Apr. 4, 1947). Translation in Central Files, 894A.00/4-1547.

151. "General Pai Broadcasts on Cause of Taiwan Riots," in Taiwan News Service, *An Infamous Riot*, 27.

152. Ke Yuanfen, "Taiwan er erba shibian zhi zhenxiang," 7–12.

153. Ibid., 16–17.

154. For a version of the events surrounding the February 28 Incident that focuses

on the role of mainland Communists, and a discussion of the difficulty of creating a history of revolutionary Taiwanese, see Su Xin, *Fennu de Taiwan*, 119–66.

155. See for example, "Taiwan yixiang shangxinshi: juefei paiwai xingdong" (Taiwan's Heart-Rending History: Absolutely Not Anti-Outsider Activity), *Shanghai wenhuibao*, (Mar. 13, 1947), reprinted in Chen Mingtong, ed., *Taiwan zhanhoushi ziliao xuan*, 257–86.

156. Memorandum from Blake to Stuart, Mar. 7, 1947, Central Files, 894A.00/3-1447.

157. Ibid., Feb. 14, 1947, 894A.00/3-1447. A *Time* magazine report claimed that errors by Chen Yi and "carpetbaggers" from the mainland were responsible for increasing support for the Communists. "China: Snow Red and Moon Angel."

158. Xie soon fled to Hong Kong, and then to the mainland. In the PRC she was involved in various groups connected to Taiwan, the China Youth League, and the Political Consultative Conference. Her loyalty to her native place, however, made her a problem for the Chinese Communists. She was "sent down" to the countryside in 1958 for the error of *difang zhuyi* (localism) and suffered during the Cultural Revolution. She died in 1970.

159. *The Twenty-sixth Anniversary of the "February 28" Uprising*, 22.

160. Ibid., 4.

161. Peng Mingmin, *A Taste of Freedom*, 67.

162. On these issues, see Chen Fangming's massive biography of Xie Xuehong. Chen Fangming, *Xie Xuehong pingzhuan*.

163. *Canyihui diyijie*, 4: 29.

164. Several scholars have pointed out that at least a few Chinese continued to discuss decentralization, local autonomy, and even federalism in the PRC. See Waldron, "Warlordism versus Federalism"; and Schram, "Decentralization in a Unitary State."

165. Cohen, "The Contested Past," 83. As Cohen explains in his book, events like the Boxer Uprising or the February 28 Incident are understood as event (by historians), experience (by participants), and myth (by political leaders). In reality, the situation was even more complicated on the island, as both Taiwanese and Nationalists often combined all three roles. Cohen, *History in Three Keys*.

166. For a "taxonomy" of political agendas and understandings of the history of the incident, see Hou Kunhong, "Er erba shijian youguan shiliao yu yanjiu zhi fenxi."

167. Cohen, "The Contested Past," 107.

168. The balance of power established in the late 1940s shifted increasingly in favor of the Taiwanese in the 1980s. This had repercussions on interpretations of the incident. After political reform began on the Taiwan in the mid-1980s, Taiwanese dissidents and independence activists were able to publicly state their own interpretations of February 28. As will be discussed in Chapter 7, the incident has become a key justification of criticism of Nationalist rule.

CHAPTER 5: NATIONALIST CONSOLIDATION AND LOCAL SELF-GOVERNMENT

1. Wu Zhuoliu, *Taiwan lianqiao*, 206–7.

2. In April, the central government was reorganized, although Jiang Jieshi remained in his posts.

3. For example, Bai Chongxi's report on the incident, discussed in Chapter 4, formed the base for criticism of Chen Yi. Chen Yi's administration responded by highlighting the previous year's accomplishments, including the implementation of local self-government measures on the island. Taiwansheng xingzheng zhangguan gongshu [5], 20–46.

4. After deciding not to invade Taiwan during the war against Japan, the United States paid relatively little attention to the island. Although officials in the Office of Strategic Services, the Department of Defense, and the Department of State came to the island in late 1945, it was only after the February 28 Incident that concerns over Nationalist misrule of the island received a serious hearing in Washington. It was the collapse of Jiang Jieshi's regime on the mainland, not the problems of the Taiwanese, that stimulated increased American interest in — and interference on — the island.

5. Xue Ping, "Wo wei Taiwan shuohua."

6. George Kerr, Memorandum on Problems Faced by Governor Wei Tao-ming, Taiwan, May 31, 1947, Central Files, 894A.001/5-3147.

7. "Wei Daoming tan shizheng fangzhen" (Wei Daoming Discusses Present Policies), Zhonghua ribao (May 13, 1947): 1. In late 1947, Governor Wei reported to the Provincial Consultative Assembly that Taiwan was well-ordered and stable, and that "After researching the actual situation of Taiwan province over the last few months, [I believe that] the heart of our present problems lies in economics, not politics." Wei Daoming, "Bensheng shizheng zongbaogao," 4.

8. "Taizheng yinian jiantao" (A Review of Taiwan's Administration over the Past Year), Gonglunbao (May 16, 1948): 2.

9. "Wei zhuxi xuanbu sixiang jueding" (Chairman Wei Announces Four Decisions), Zhonghua ribao (May 17, 1947): 1. On administrative and organizational changes during Wei's tenure, see Taiwansheng zhengfu, Taiwansheng xingzheng jiyao, 1–5.

10. Chaffee, Area Handbook for the Republic of China, 84–85.

11. "Baozhi huifu Riwenban wenti" (Problems of Restoring the Use of Japanese in Newspapers), Guoshengbao (May 21, 1947): 1. Officials at the local level, often mainlanders, frequently went beyond the regulations. For example, the schools in Pingdong County in southern Taiwan mandated a variety of increasing penalties for employees who used Japanese. Tests of Mandarin Chinese ability were given to staff. "Tuixing Guoyu, jinyong Riyu, xiaoyong fangyan" (Promote Chinese, Prohibit Japanese, Reduce Dialects), Guoshengbao (May 19, 1947): 3. In fact, the issue was more complex than a simple division between Chinese-speaking mainlanders and Japanese-speaking Taiwanese. A member of the Provincial Consultative Assembly complained in late 1947 that too many officials from the mainland had studied in Japan, and were not promoting the Guoyu movement sufficiently because they were comfortable speaking Japanese with islanders. Canyihui diyijie, 4: 155–56.

12. On the composition of the committee, see Memorandum from Kenneth Krentz, U.S. consul in Taibei, to the secretary of state, Jan. 2, 1949, Central Files, 894A.00/1-249.

13. Ibid., Oct. 22, 1948, 894A.00/10-2248.

14. Wei's grip on power was never firm. For example, a contemporary editorial referred to widespread rumors about Wei's uncertain future, his lack of control over parts of the provincial government, and his need to discuss personnel problems with

top leaders in Nanjing. "Wei Daoming feijing shida shiming" (The Ten Great Tasks for Wei Daoming as He Flies to the Capital), *Taiwan chunqiu* 1 (Sept. 1948): 5.

15. A Taiwanese wrote later that Chen Yi's appointment as governor of Zhejiang stunned islanders. Li Zhenzhou, *Huoshaodao diyiqi xinsheng*, 70. Huoshaodao (Baked Island) is a nickname for Ludao (Green Island), off the southeast coast of Taiwan, site of major prison for dissidents. Li Zhenzhou's memoir provides a good introduction to the prison system under the White Terror.

Chen Yi attempted to surrender to the Communists. He proved no more adept at this than he had been at managing Taiwan or Zhejiang. In 1949 he was arrested, brought to Taiwan, and publicly executed in June 1950, much to the delight of many Taiwanese.

16. In November 1947, the exchange rate between the *Taibi* and *fabi* (the currency issued by the Nationalists in the rest of China) was 1:79. It increased to 1:248 by late April 1948, and eventually to 1:1,635 in August. This was devastating to newly arrived mainlanders, but it also spurred inflation on the island.

17. On the efforts to restore Taiwan's industry, see the remarks of Yao Hengxiu, manager of the China Petroleum Company. Liu Fenghan et al., *Yao Hengxiu xiansheng*.

18. Wu Zhuoliu, *Taiwan lianqiao*, 210–11.

19. Kerr, *Formosa Betrayed*, 348.

20. For example, see Wu Xinrong, *Wu Xinrong huiyilu*, 229.

21. Kerr, *Formosa Betrayed*, 349.

22. Zheng Zi, *Zhanhou Taiwan yihui yundongshi*, 54. See also Li Xiaofeng, *Taiwan zhanhou*, 209–24. Zheng Zi's book contains the most comprehensive analysis of the Provincial Consultative Assembly and its meetings.

23. Han Shiquan, *Liushi huiyi*, 86–92.

24. Ibid., 89.

25. A magazine article noted that, when the Supervisory Yuan sent an inspection team to the island in 1948, "the Taiwanese were silent, and were unwilling to speak." Xue Ping, "Wo wei Taiwan shuohua."

26. "Sheng canyihui diwuci dahui de shiming" (The Mission of the Fifth Session of the Provincial Assembly), *Gonglunbao* (July 1, 1948): 2.

27. "Dibaci hui gongqi jinzhang" (Atmosphere of Eighth Meeting Tense), *Gonglunbao* (July 9, 1948): 4.

28. "Taiwan jingji de jiben wenti" (The Basic Problems of Taiwan's Economy), *Gonglunbao* (May 8, 1948): 2.

29. "Bu chedi de kaifang zhengce" (An Incomplete Open Policy), *Gonglunbao* (Dec. 24, 1947): 2.

30. "Xian gei sheng canyihui sici dahui" (For the Fourth Session of the Taiwan Provincial Assembly), *Gonglunbao* (Dec. 1): 1947, 2.

31. "Richan fangshe jidai chuzhi" (People Anxiously Awaiting Handling of Japanese Property), *Gonglunbao* (Aug. 3, 1948): 3.

32. For example, a magazine article in late 1948 discussed how some adept at the "art of gaining access to political power" (*tongtian you shu*) used their connections to lobby to keep their property. Song Yanwen, "Taiwan yiqian ge xinxing caifa."

33. Han Shiquan, *Liushi huiyi*, 103.

34. "Tingzhi chanyi qixian biangeng" (The Time Period for Ending Transfers is Changed), *Gonglunbao* (Dec. 14, 1948): 3.

35. On the People's Liberation Army offensive in late 1948, see ambassador in China (Stuart) to the secretary of state, Sept. 22, 1948, *Foreign Relations of the United States: 1948*, 467. Hereafter cited as *Foreign Relations of the United States*. See also Pepper, *Civil War in China*. The failure to stem inflation was perhaps the single most important cause of the Nationalists' final defeat. Runaway inflation drove bureaucrats, low-ranking military officers, and the middle class to abandon Jiang Jieshi's cause. The Central Bank of China replaced the existing notes (fabi) with the Gold Yuan (*jinyuan*) in August 1948 in a failed attempt to control inflation. At the same time commodity prices were frozen. Jiang dispatched his son Jiang Jingguo to Shanghai to stem the inflation, but neither he nor economic experts elsewhere were able to bring it under control. Although the government undertook currency reform again in July 1949, it was ineffective. Eastman, *Seeds of Destruction*, 172, 180–81

36. The Nationalists also suffered a financial and intellectual drain as many wealthy and educated Chinese and Taiwanese fled to the United States or Hong Kong. John Macdonald, U.S. consul in Taibei, to the secretary of state, Sept. 7, 1949, Central Files, 894A.00/9-749.

37. "Lun 'taowang'" (Discussing Fleeing Disaster), *Quanmin ribao* (Nov. 26, 1948): 2.

38. Wu Zhuoliu, *Taiwan lianqiao*, 241.

39. Wu Xinrong, *Wu Xinrong huiyilu*, 279.

40. "Zai tan dangqian de wujia" (Again Discussing Current Prices), *Gonglunbao* (June 30, 1948): 2.

41. "Benshi fasheng miliang konghuang" (City Suffers Grain Shortage), *Gonglunbao* (Oct. 6, 1948): 3.

42. *Canyihui diyijie*, 6: 16–17.

43. A mainlander relates that oil refineries on the island laid off staff in 1949 because there was no one to sell to. Liu Fenghan, *Yao Hengxiu xiansheng*, 74–75.

44. Wu Zhuoliu, *Taiwan lianqiao*, 237.

45. Ibid., 232–33.

46. "Dangju jiaqiang liangshi guanzhi" (Strengthen Grain Controls), *Gonglunbao* (July 14, 1948): 3.

47. Memorandum from Krentz to the secretary of state, Feb. 7, 1948, Central Files, 894A.00/2-748. Wei complained that the C-C Clique was also interfering with his administration.

48. Ibid., Oct. 29, 1948, 894A.00/10-2948. When the central government changed the fabi to the jinyuan, the exchange rate between the new currency and the Old Taibi was 1:1,835. It fell to 1:370 in November 1948, 1:80 by January 1949, then 1,000:1 in May.

49. Memorandum from Krentz to the secretary of state, Nov. 23, 1948, Central Files, 894.00/11-2348. Krentz thought Wei's proposal was worth consideration.

50. Memorandum of Conversation with General Douglas MacArthur [and Department of State officials] at Tokyo, Dec. 7, 1948, Central Files, 894A.00/12-748.

In public, Wei followed the Nationalist line, attacking those who spread rumors of United States support for any independence movement. Wei Daoming, "Bensheng shizheng zongbaogao."

51. For example, L. F. Craig, Taiwan Regional Office, Economic Cooperation Administration, to Chief of Mission, Jan. 13, 1949, Central Files, 894A.00/1-1349.

52. Xu Dong, "Taiwan dixia zuzhi bibai wuyi."

53. *United States Relations with China*, 309.

54. Secretary of State Dean Acheson instructed United States diplomats as follows: "When situation develops to point where we know government groups US will have deal with on Formosa, US should seek develop and support local non-Comm Chi regime which will provide at least modicum decent govt Formosa. We should also use influence wherever possible to discourage further influx mainlanders. US should also discreetly maintain contact with potential native Formosan leaders with view future date being able utilize Formosan autonomous movement if it appears in US natl interest." Dean Acheson, secretary of state, to Livingston Merchant, U.S. consul in Taibei, Mar. 2, 1949, Central Files, 894A.00/3-2249.

55. The Acting Secretary of State to the Consul General in Taipei (Krentz), Nov. 23, 1948, *Foreign Relations of the United States*, 604.

56. Wei Daoming's career with the Nationalists entered a nearly two-decade-long hiatus. Wei and his wife quickly went to Hong Kong, then California. He returned to the island in 1966 and served as foreign minister until 1971, when he resigned in part in response to recriminations over the U.S. rapprochement with the PRC.

57. For example, see Fei Disheng, "Chen Cheng jiangjun tiemian zuofeng."

58. For an English-language account of his accomplishments, see Chen Cheng, *Land Reform on Taiwan*. See also Qi Xin, "Wei Daoming, Chen Cheng yu Taiwan."

59. Before Chen Cheng was appointed governor of Taiwan, his experience was almost exclusively in the military. He served as commander-in-chief of Chinese forces in Burma (1943–44), minister of war (1944–46), and chief of staff (1946–48). He later became as vice president of the Republic of China and president of the Executive Yuan on Taiwan.

60. Wu Zhuoliu, *Taiwan lianqiao*, 241.

61. Report to the National Security Council by the Department of State on the Position of the United States with Respect to Formosa, NSC 37/1, Jan. 19, 1949, Department of Defense, G-3 Decimal Files, 1949–50, box 154.

62. Dean Acheson, secretary of state, to Donald Edgar, U.S. consul general in Taibei, Mar. 9, 1949, Central Files, 894A.00/3-949.

63. This approach was made as part of the policy approved on March 1, 1949 by the National Security Council as NSC 37/5, United States Policy toward Taiwan.

64. Secretary of State Acheson seemed to accept this by November 1949, writing "DEPT believes Gimo [Generalissimo Jiang] is ultimate real authority on Formosa and that accordingly approach should be made him." "Approach" refers to a series of suggestions for improving the administration of Taiwan. Acheson to John Macdonald, U.S. consul in Taibei, Nov. 11, 1949, Central Files, 894A.20/10-3149.

65. Acheson to Edgar, June 24, 1949, Central Files, 894A.00/6-2449. Acheson stated that "you [should] continue informally to stress to Governor's inner circle . . .

political, economic consequences and disaffection risk inherent in idle troops in excess of island's defense needs." Observers in Taibei complained that Chen Cheng "lacks qualities [to] provide liberal efficient administration needed. Moreover, as GIMO man he cannot be relied on to prevent or discourage continued influx." Edgar to Acheson, Mar. 6, 1949, 894A.00/3-649. See also, Edgar to Acheson, May 10, 1949, 894A.01/5-1049.

66. Chen Cheng remained in Taibei, where he oversaw the evacuation of military and government units from the mainland.

67. Wu became increasingly critical of the Nationalist regime and the interference of Jiang Jingguo in the island's administration. He resigned in 1953 and fled to the United States.

68. The minister-counselor of embassy in China (Clark) to the director of the Office of Far Eastern Affairs (Butterworth), June 30, 1948, *Foreign Relations of the United States*, 332.

69. Until the Korean War, Secretary of State Dean Acheson and others in the Truman administration held out the hope of building diplomatic relations with the Chinese Communists. For this reason, they were not eager to see Jiang reestablish his regime on the island, nor did they want to see an independent Taiwan. For example, on March 3, 1949, Acheson stated before the thirty-fifth meeting of the National Security Council that "We are most anxious to avoid raising the specter of an American-created irredentist issue just at the time we shall be seeking to exploit the genuinely Soviet-created irredentist issue in Manchuria and Sinkiang [Xinjiang]. We cannot afford to compromise an emerging new U.S. position in China by overtly showing a pronounced interest in Formosa." Thirty-fifth Meeting of the National Security Council, National Archives, Record Group 319, Department of Defense, G-3 Decimal Files, 1949–50, box 154. Until forced by events in Korea and domestic political pressure to support Jiang's regime, Acheson sought to quash rumors that the United States might intervene to prevent a Communist invasion of Taiwan. For example, see the message from the secretary of state to the U.S. embassy in Manila, Dec. 19, 1949, Central Files, 894A.20/12-1949.

70. Central Intelligence Agency, National Archives, "China Research Report SR-8," Aug. 1948.

71. On Acheson's willingness to consider forging a diplomatic relationship with the new Beijing regime, see Cohen, "Acheson, His Advisers, and China." For a more detailed analysis of American policy on China at that time, see Tucker, *Patterns in the Dust*. For Acheson's own account of events, see his *Present at Creation*.

72. Memorandum from Krentz to Stuart, Jan. 26, 1948, Central Files, 894A.00/1-2648.

73. Memorandum from William Sebald, U.S. consul in Tokyo, to John Allison, deputy director, Division of Far Eastern Affairs, Apr. 12, 1949, Central Files, 894A.01/4-1249.

74. In 1949 and 1950, Taiwan was rife with rumors of plots against Jiang. Nancy Bernkopf Tucker has suggested that American-trained General Sun Liren was preparing a coup with American acquiescence, if not support. Tucker, *Patterns in the Dust*, 181. Robert Accinelli notes that "the odds were long that the Nationalist army com-

mander could depose the cunning Chiang [Jiang], a master of the art of political survival and intrigue." Accinelli, *Crisis and Commitment*, 21.

75. One of the best examples of the experiences of arrest and execution in the
White Terror can be found in the semifictionalized account of the arrest and execution of Zhong Haodong. Zhong had worked in the anti-Japanese resistance in
Guangdong and then became a school principal in Taiwan in the town of Jilong. His
involvement with the Communist Party and his publications critical of the
Nationalists led to his death. See Lan Bozhou, *Huangmache zhi ge*. See also works
of fiction such as the short story, "Hong xiezi" (Red Shoes) by Ye Shitao. In this work,
the protagonist is arrested in the early 1950s for not reporting a conspiracy in 1946.
At the end of the war, the young man had sought out several publications about politics on the mainland, not knowing they were Communist materials. Ye Shitao, "Hong
xiezi," in Lin Shuangbu, ed., *Er erba Taiwan xiaoshuo xuan*.

76. A good overview is Lin Delong, "Guofu qian Tai qianhou shehui kongzhi zhi
licheng."

77. Lan Bozhou, *Baise kongbu*, 62. As early as January 1948, the government
required the registration of anyone leaving or entering the island. "Luke churu
Taiwanshengjing sanyue yiri shixing dengji" (Visitors Entering or Leaving Taiwan
Will Register Beginning March 1), *Xinshengbao* (Jan. 29, 1948): 5. On identity cards,
see "Quansheng shenfenzheng zongjiancha" (General Inspection of All Identity Cards
in Taiwan Province), *Xinshengbao* (Apr. 24, 1948): 2.

78. On student, aborigine, and labor movements under the White Terror, see Lan
Bozhou, *Xunfang bei yinmie de Taiwanshi*, 101.

79. Li Zhenzhou, *Huoshaodao diyiqi xinsheng*, 68.

80. Wu Zhuoliu, *Taiwan lianqiao*, 244.

81. Li Zhenzhou, *Huoshaodao diyiqi xinsheng*, 72.

82. Wu Zhuoliu, *Taiwan lianqiao*, 206.

83. "'Fandui zhengfu' yu 'piping zhengzhi' " (Opposing the Government and
Commenting on Politics), *Quanmin ribao* (Aug. 5, 1948): 1.

84. On "crimes" and the White Terror, see the collection of oral histories and pho-
tographs in He Jingtai, *Baise dang'an*. For the story of the loan, see the oral history
of Chen Qichang contained in that volume.

85. On the Yang Da case, see Lan Bozhou, *Baise kongbu*, 53.

86. The assemblies did gain two additional powers. First, in 1947, they were
allowed to investigate the provincial budgets. Second, in early 1949, they obtained
the right to question and present views to central, not just provincial, government
organs. Zheng Zi, *Zhanhou Taiwan yihui yundongshi*, 98–99.

87. Some Taiwanese accepted the addition of unelected members from other parties as a way to check the Nationalists. Others were suspicious of their ability to win
future elections on the island. Were they in office to serve the people or simply to provide some sort of organized competition for the Guomindang? "Ping canyiyuan lin-
xuan" (Criticizing the Selection of Provincial Consultative Assembly Members), *Zili
wanbao* (Nov. 10, 1947): 2.

88. On the changing membership of the Provincial Consultative Assembly, see
Zheng Zi, *Zhanhou Taiwan yihui yundongshi*, 54–65.

89. Fu Sinian became chancellor of National Taiwan University in 1948. Gu

Youxiu who had been vice minister of education, a member of the Legislative Yuan, and professor at National Peking University, was selected as chancellor of National Chengchi University in 1947. Chaffee, *Area Handbook for the Republic of China*, 746, 756.

90. On arrests in the late 1940s, see Lan Bozhou, *Xunfang bei yinmie de Taiwanshi*, 158–62. One of the last major student protests was the April 6 Student Movement of 1949. The arrest of student leaders on that day led to a short-lived standoff at Taiwan Normal College in Taibei. Over three hundred students were arrested, although many were quickly released. Chen Cheng replaced the president of the school after the incident.

91. New magazines included *Taiwan chunqiu* (Taiwan Spring and Autumn), *Jinbu luntan* (Progressive Tribune), and *Dengta* (Lighthouse). One important exception was *Gonglunbao*, a newspaper managed by the prominent non-Guomindang politician Li Wanju. Li's newspaper was the publication most critical of the Nationalists in the late 1940s. On the press under Nationalist rule, see Chen Guoxiang and Zhu Ping, *Taiwan baoye yanjin 40 nian*.

92. Today, this organization is the Historical Research Commission of Taiwan Province (Taiwansheng wenxian weiyuanhui).

93. "Chuangkanci" (Words for the Inaugural Issue), *Taiwansheng tongzhiguan guankan* 1 (Oct. 15, 1948): 1.

94. Zhang Qun, head of the Executive Yuan, came in October 1947, Sun Liren in November, and a delegation of naval officers also in November. In February 1948, vice chairman of the Nationalist government Sun Ke visited the island. Guomindang secretary Wu Tiecheng came in March. General He Yingqin visited in October 1948. Memorandum from Stuart to the secretary of state, Dec. 30, 1948, Central Files, 894A.00/12-3048. Secretary general of the president's office Wu Zhongxin came in January 1949, along with boxes of records from Nanjing party offices.

95. "Zhang Xueliang zhu Taiwan wenquan: Lianlei le Xinzhu xianzhang" (Zhang Xueliang Visits Taiwan's Hotsprings: Gets Xinzhu District Magistrate in Trouble), *Taiwan chunqiu* 3 (Dec. 1948): 18. The "trouble" referred to in the article's title was the cost of entertaining visiting mainland dignitaries.

96. For a detailed, day-by-day account of Jiang and his son during 1949 and 1950, see Chiang Ching-kuo, *Calm in the Eye of a Storm*, 134–203.

97. Jiang's travels within China must be seen in the context of the debate among top Nationalist leaders over where the final redoubt might be. On possible capitals, see "Zhengfu jiang qian du Taiwan ma?" (Will the Government Move the Capital to Taiwan?), *Taiwan chunqiu* 3 (Dec. 1948): 2.

98. Historian and commentator Dai Guohui stresses that by the beginning of the Korean War, Jiang Jingguo was well on his way toward dominating the Guomindang and the ROC. He built this position on Mao's maxim of power growing from the barrel of a gun. Dai Guohui, *Taiwan zongtixiang*, 140–41. At the provincial level, in December 1948 Jiang Jingguo became a member of the Guomindang Provincial Committee Headquarters for Taiwan even before moving to the island. See "Jiang Jingguo guoran lai Tai" (As Expected, Jiang Jingguo Comes to Taiwan), *Taiwan chunqiu* 4 (Jan. 1949): 4. His brother Jiang Weiguo came to the island in February.

99. For information on Jiang's move see Krentz to Acheson, Jan. 2, 1949,

Central Files, 894A.01/1-249; and Stuart to Acheson, Jan. 1, 1949, 894A.01/1-149. Dai Guohui states that this occurred in August, as the Political Action Committee was formed. Dai Guohui, *Taiwan zongtixiang*, 125.

100. In 1954, the committee was renamed the High Commission for National Defense, and later the National Security Council. Several mainland political groups were conspicuous for their absence during the retreat to Taiwan. For example, the powerful C-C Clique, which had dominated the widely feared Guomindang Bureau of Investigation and Statistics, weakened dramatically as its two leaders dropped out of politics: Chen Lifu moved to the United States in early 1949 and Chen Guofu died in 1951.

101. On Jiang's consolidation of power, see Graphic Summary of the Formosa Situation, Office of Intelligence Research, report no. 5320, Aug. 21, 1950, Department of State, Division of Research for Far East, Office of Intelligence Research, in Office of Strategic Services/State Department Intelligence and Research Reports.

102. Other than a few small islands off the mainland coast (Jinmen [Quemoy], Mazu [Matsu], the Dachens), Taiwan province *was* the Republic of China.

103. For example, see "Shi difang zizhi zhenti" (Explaining the Real Meaning of Local Self-Government), *Heping ribao* (Apr. 25, 1948): 3.

104. A slightly different list can be found in Zhou Jixiang, "Xingxian yilai de Taiwan," 73.

105. On the laws for local self-government, see "Difang zizhi de zhibiao" (The Goals for Local Self-Government), *Gonglunbao* (Dec. 15, 1947): 2. See also Zheng Yanfen, "Guanyu shengxian zizhi tongze."

106. "Gaishan minsheng shi shouyao zhengwu" (Improving the People's Livelihood is the First Task of the Administration), *Gonglunbao* (Dec. 31, 1948): 3.

107. Zhang Lisheng was minister of the interior from 1944 to 1948, when be became vice president of the Executive Yuan. From 1954 to 1958 he served as secretary-general of the Central Executive Committee of the Guomindang, and from 1959 to 1963 he was ambassador to Japan.

108. On the organizations involved in implementing local self-government, see *Taiwansheng dizhi shinian jiyao*.

109. Li Zonghuang, *Li Zonghuang huiyilu*, 310.

110. Ibid., 306.

111. Li Zonghuang, *Taiwan difang zizhi xinlun*, 11.

112. "Shenghui dang zheng jun min ge jie zou shengda huanying Wu Tiecheng" (Provincial Meeting Yesterday of Political, Party, Military, and Representatives Gives Huge Welcome to Wu Tiecheng), *Xinshengbao* (Mar. 12, 1948): 2.

113. Li Zonghuang, *Taiwan difang zizhi xinlun*, 80–81.

114. Ibid., 1.

115. Ibid., 12–13.

116. Ibid., 11.

117. Ibid., 1.

118. Taiwansheng difang zizhi yanjiuhui, *Taiwansheng difang zhizhi yanjiuhui zhuankan*, intro.

119. "Weng Qian jiangyanci" (Speech of Weng Qian), *Xinshengbao* (Oct. 16, 1948): 5. Zhang Lisheng's list was nearly the same: widespread education, convenient transportation, developed agriculture and natural resources, and a household census. Taiwansheng difang zizhi yanjiuhui, *Taiwansheng difang zhizhi yanjiuhui zhuankan*, intro. Weng himself appears to have written relatively little. He was the publisher of a comprehensive work on local self-government, Wang Tingxi, Xiang Jike, and Xu Zhichen, *Taiwan difang zizhi*.

120. The requirements for local self-government were four, according to Sun's *Outline of National Reconstruction*: a census, a land survey, a high level of public order, and citizenship training for the people. Zhou Jixiang, "Xingxian yilai de Taiwan," 74.

121. Li Zonghuang, *Taiwan difang zizhi xinlun*, 37. Li wrote elsewhere: "What is 'self-government'? The self means oneself. Government means to manage (*guanli*). In other words, 'self-government' means to manage one's own affairs." Li Zonghuang, "Zizhi jingshen de fahui" (Bring into Play the Spirit of Self-Government), in *Li Zonghuang yanlun xuanji*, 310–11.

122. The specific activities of local self-government illustrated the important role on economic issues. What are the tasks of each locality? (1) Conducting censuses and household registrations, (2) setting land prices, (3) opening waste land, (4) overseeing construction, (5) arranging finances, (6) strengthening organizations, (7) training the masses, (8) developing transportation, (9) building schools, (10) promoting cooperation, (11) managing security, (12) promoting sanitation, (13) implementing welfare, and (14) encouraging the New Life Movement. Li Zonghuang, *Taiwan difang zizhi xinlun*, 37.

123. Wang Desheng, "Difang zizhi zhi lixiang yu shishi."

124. Zheng Yanfen, "Sheng zizhi de yiyi ye tezhi." See also Li Zonghuang, "Ping xianfazhong de difang zhidu."

125. "Zizhi juefei tuoyi" (Self-Government is Absolutely Not Severing), *Quanmin ribao* (Apr. 25, 1948): 3.

126. For an overview of Zhang's opinions, see Jin Tigan, ed., *Taiwan de difang zizhi*.

127. Li Zonghuang, *Zhongguo difang zizhi zonglun*, 17–18.

128. "Yanchang gongshan" (Extension Granted in Public Trial), *Guoshengbao* (June 27, 1947): 3; and "Taiji zhanzui qisushu quanwen" (Taiwan War Criminals: Complete Text of the Indictment), *Guoshengbao* (June 29, 1947): 3. On these charges, see Shen Zijia and Zhang Jueming, *Gu Zhenfu zhuan*, 13–16. All five of the activists — Xu Bing, Jian Langshan (both of whom had been named to the Japanese House of Peers for their loyalty), Gu Zhenfu, Lin Xiongxiang (named to the Japanese governor-general's Consultative Assembly), and Xu Kunquan (special agent for the Japanese) — had risen to prominence under Japanese rule.

129. Li Zonghuang, *Li Zonghuang huiyilu*, 246. Mainland intellectuals critical of the Nationalists frequently included expanded local self-government in their demands. Pepper, *Civil War in China*, 182–83.

130. Li Zonghuang, *Taiwan difang zizhi xinlun*, 11–13.

131. Ma Maoran, "Taiwan difang zizhi de jichu wenti."

132. Xie Bingkui, "Zizhi yu shishi xianzheng."

133. "Tizao shishi difang zizhi" (Implement Local Self-Government Soon), *Gonglunbao* (Mar. 19, 1948): 3.

134. "Bensheng gejie tongdian bianzheng" (All Walks of Life on Taiwan Argue Common Points), *Gonglunbao* (Apr. 24, 1948): 3. See also "Taiwan yaoqiu zizhi" (Taiwan Requests Self-Government), *Dagongbao* (Shanghai), (Apr. 12, 1948): 2.

135. Li Wanju, "Lishi zoudao fenquan de shihou."

136. Zheng Zi, "Zhongyan zhengfu," 10. For example, see "Suo wang yu Zhang yuanzhang zhe" (Hopes from Premier Zhang), *Gonglunbao* (Oct. 26, 1948): 2. This editorial, which was probably written by Li Wanju, argued that the Taiwanese were ready to elect county magistrates and mayors.

137. Han Shiquan, *Liushi huiyi*, 89.

138. Ibid., 89–92.

139. "Shengcan yihui xunwen minzheng" (Provincial Consultative Assembly Asks About Civil Affairs), *Gonglunbao* (Dec. 19, 1948): 3. Other assembly members repeated these complaints in 1949. See "Difang zizhi pan zao shixing" (Hopes for Implementing Local Self-Government Soon), *Gonglunbao* (June 17, 1949): 3. See also *Canyihui diyijie*, 6: 73.

140. "Duiyu bensheng difang zizhi de jidian yijian" (Some Opinions About This Province's Local Self-Government), *Gonglunbao* (July 20, 1949): 2.

141. "Difang zizhi xiehui chengli" (Association for Local Self-Government Established), *Gonglunbao* (July 9, 1948): 3; "Sheng difang zizhi xiehui" (The Provincial Self-Government Association), *Quanmin ribao* (July 25, 1948): 3; "Guanyu bensheng zizhi shifanchu" (Concerning the Province as a Model Self-Government Jurisdiction), *Heping ribao* (Apr. 27, 1948): 2.

142. Li Zonghuang, *Taiwan difang zizhi xinlun*, 97–98.

143. For example, see "Peizhi difang zizhi ganbu" (Cultivate Local Self-Government Cadres), *Gonglunbao* (July 28, 1948): 3.

144. "Xiezhu tuixing difang zizhi, shixian zhenzheng minzhu zhengzhi" (Help Promote Local Self-Government, Realize True Democratic Rule), *Gonglunbao* (July 14, 1949): 3.

145. "Peizhi difang zizhi ganbu" (Foster Local Self-Government Cadres), *Gonglunbao* (July 28, 1948): 3.

146. Zheng Zi, *Zhanhou Taiwan yihui yundongshi*, 106–7.

147. It was "provisional" because the Nationalists planned to return to the mainland, reunite China, then hold new elections. This body became the Taiwan Provincial Assembly (Taiwansheng yihui).

148. *Taiwan shengyihui sanshiwunian*, 3–5. On the background of members, see also chart in part 2, pp. 15–17.

149. Zheng Zi, "Zhongyan zhengfu," 32–33.

150. I use the term mass mobilization to mean the ability to involve the great bulk of the people in political activity. Political participation carries the connotation of better educated or wealthier citizens playing a role in government or political parties with the expectation of having direct influence over policies.

151. See Johnson, *Peasant Nationalism and Communist Power*; Selden, *The Yenan Way in Revolutionary China*; and Chen Yongfa, *Making Revolution*.

152. For example, Zheng Zi writes that local self-government represented an important facet of the Nationalists' reform after defeat on the mainland. Zheng Zi, "Zhongyan zhengfu," 4.

153. On the Blue Shirts, see Eastman, *The Abortive Revolution*. For the Youth Corps and the Renewal Movement, see Eastman, *Seeds of Destruction*, chaps. 4, 5. On the Nationalists drive to limit the activities of political parties, intellectuals, and students in 1945–49, see Pepper, *Civil War in China*. See also Sheridan, *China in Disintegration*, chap. 8. A particularly good example of the Nationalists' policy is the Three Principles of the People Youth Corps, created in 1938. The Nationalists seemed to spend half their time promoting the group, the other half reining in its members who were not following the Guomindang line. The corps was disbanded in the late 1940s. See Huang Jianli, *The Politics of Depoliticization*. On the Nationalists' enduring obsession with tightly controlling mass mobilization and molding good Nationalists on the mainland, see Dirlik, "Ideological Foundations of the New Life Movement; Pichon Loh, "The Politics of Chiang Kai-shek"; and Averill, "The New Life in Action." The great problem with using the historiography of Nationalist attempts to build support among the population is that mainland-based studies are always directed at how Jiang Jieshi attempted to counter the ideology and influence of the Communists — which simply was not a major problem on Taiwan.

154. Lloyd Eastman addressed Jiang Jieshi's own evaluation of the Nationalists' defeat on the mainland. Jiang frankly admitted that internal problems, including corruption and the lack of skilled personnel, plagued his regime. Thus he was unable to build the stable state he sought on the mainland. Jiang never repudiated, however, his drive to create a strong, highly centralized regime under his personal control. Eastman, *Seeds of Destruction*, chap. 9.

155. "Fadong minli jianshe xin Taiwan" (Spur the People's Power to Build a New Taiwan), *Zizhi tongxun* 3 (Nov. 3, 1946): 15.

156. Dai Guohui, *Taiwan zongtixiang*, 154–57. In 1951, American officers reported that "The basic tactical and strategical concept adopted by the Chinese Nationalist Military Establishment for ground troops is that of the Japanese or the World War II German concepts. Defense Commanders, Army and Division Commanders . . . attend an advanced school for four and one half months orientation and indoctrination. . . . The instructors are Japanese and Chinese, with German Military School background." Letter from the Office of the Chief, Army Section, Military Assistance and Advisory Group (MAAG), Formosa, Sept. 17, 1951, Department of Defense, G-3 Decimal Files, 1950–51, box 89.

157. Ambassador Rankin's Mutual Security Policy (MSP) Monthly General Report, Nov. 1951, Dec. 20, 1951, ibid.

158. Chargé d'Affaires Strong to Edmund O. Clubb, Sept. 6, 1950, Central Files, 794A.00/9-650.

CHAPTER 6: TAIWAN'S ELITE TRANSFORMED

1. The biographical information in this chapter comes from a variety of sources including the biographical dictionaries of Jin Shi, ed., *Taiwan shiren zhi*; idem, *Taiwan mingren zhuan*; *Taiwan mingren ji*; Bu Youtian, *Taiwan fengyun renwu*; and Zhang Yanxian et al., eds., *Taiwan jindai mingren zhi*.

2. I have modified slightly Wu's definitions. Wu Zhuoliu, *Taiwan lianqiao*, 208–9.

3. Cai Peihuo et al., *Taiwan minzu yundong shi*, 478–81.

4. There had been 1,183 candidates for the thirty posts in the provincial body. In fact, the total number of electors (city and county assembly members) was less than half the number of candidates in this election.

5. Wang served as a local leader of the corps in Taibei. Chen Mingtong, "Paixi zhengzhi," 353–55.

6. Li Xiaofeng, *Er erba xiaoshi de Taiwan jingying*, 57.

7. Wang Tiandeng, "Sheng canyihui de qianwan yan."

8. Taiwansheng xingzheng zhangguan gongshu [6], 15.

9. Ruan Meimei, *Yu'an jiaoluo de leisheng*, 57–62.

10. Ibid.

11. Ibid.

12. Interview with Wang Zhengtong, in Zhang Yanxian et al., eds., *Taibei Nangang er erba*, 274.

13. Ke Yuanfen, "Taiwan er erba shibian zhi zhenxian," 21.

14. The other three were Wu Sanlian, Guo Yuxin, and Li Yuanzhan.

15. He wrote a petition to then president Li Yuanhong requesting help in resisting the Japanese, but apparently received no reply. Zhang Yanxian et al., eds., *Taiwan jindai mingren zhi* 4: 174.

16. Zhou Shi, *Taiwan difang renwu pingzhuan*, 3.

17. Jin Shi, ed., *Taiwan mingren zhuan*, 139–40.

18. Taiwansheng xingzheng zhangguan gongshu [6], 18–19.

19. Zhou Shi, *Taiwan difang renwu pingzhuan*, 8–9.

20. Many Taiwanese sought to report to the police in the presence of many witnesses after receiving assurances of fair treatment. Zhou Shi, *Taiwan difang renwu pingzhuan*, 10–11.

21. "Canyiyuan Guo Guoji jinri panwuzui" (Today Assembly Member Guo Guoji Is Found Not Guilty), *Zili wanbao* (Feb. 13, 1948): 1.

22. Zhou Shi, *Taiwan difang renwu pingzhuan*, 10–11.

23. *Canyihui diyijie*, 4: 60–61.

24. Ibid., 5: 49.

25. Ibid., 113.

26. Ibid., 4: 83.

27. Ibid., 10:, 27.

28. Ibid., 9: 17.

29. Cai Xianchong, *Wang chunfeng*, 34.

30. *Canyihui diyijie*, 9: 60.

31. Ibid., 8: 4.

32. Ibid., 21.

33. "Juedui bu rongxu taren zhihui" (Absolutely Do Not Allow Others to Butt In), *Gonglunbao* (May 24, 1949): 2. In particular, he attacked a rumor that China would take Hong Kong in exchange for Anglo-American control over Taiwan.

34. *Canyihui diyijie*, 5: 51.

35. Ibid., 6:, 82, and 9: 35; and Taiwansheng xingzheng zhangguan gongshu [6],

14. Note: the last document is divided into unnumbered sections. This is p. 14 of the final section listing items raised by individual members of the assembly.

36. The land had been taken by the Japanese during the war and cleared as a firebreak to limit the damage from United States bombing.

37. *Canyihui diyijie*, 6: 119.

38. Zhou Shi, *Taiwan difang renwu pingzhuan*, 11–12, 20–21.

39. Cai Xianchong, *Wang chunfeng*, 32–33.

40. Tong Jianyan, ed., *Taiwan lishi zidian*, 240.

41. For a complimentary biography of Li Wanju, see Cai Xianchong, *Wang chunfeng*, 1–24.

42. Employees included Wu Zhuoliu, Wang Baiyuan, and other reporters-cum-political activists from the colonial era.

43. Wu Zhuoliu, *Taiwan lianqiao*, 154–56.

44. Taiwansheng xingzheng zhangguan gongshu [6], 17.

45. *Canyihui diyijie* 4: 156.

46. Ibid., and 9: 56.

47. Ibid., 10: 2–3.

48. The China Youth Party suffered from significant factional disputes in the early 1950s, when many members left.

49. Zhang Yanxian et al., eds., *Taiwan jindai mingren zhi* 1: 163–76.

50. *Dangwai* was the name given to legal opposition to the Nationalists before the legalization of new political parties (such as the Democratic Progressive Party) in the 1980s.

51. On Lin Xiantang's life, see Tong Jianyan, ed., *Taiwan lishi zidian*, 301.

52. United States government sources state Lin was one of the most popular and well-known figures among the Taiwanese. He was connected with "important industrialists, conservative politicians and social leaders and intellectuals, and landlords." Enclosure in report entitled "Formosan Independence Movements," Central Files, 894A.00/11-749.

53. Ye Rongzhong, *Taiwan renwu qunxiang*, 22.

54. Ye Rongzhong, "Mingzhi de lingdaozhe Lin Xiantang xiansheng" (Wise Leader Mr. Lin Xiantang), in Chen Yongxing and Li Xiaofeng, eds., *Taiwan jindai renwu ji*, 18.

55. Ibid., 26.

56. Lin Nanqing, "Sixiang he bu gui guli" (Thinking of Home But Not Returning), in Chen Yongxing and Li Xiaofeng, eds., *Taiwan jindai renwu ji*, 32–34.

57. On Lin's political activities after 1945, see Dai Baocun, "Shenshixing zhengzhi yundong lingdaozhe" (Gentry Political Movement Leader), in Zhang Yanxian et al., eds., *Taiwan jindai mingren zhi* 4: 66–71; and Zhou Wanyao, *Riju shidai de Taiwan*, 248–62.

58. Taiwansheng xingzheng zhangguan gongshu [6], 16.

59. Huang Chaoqin, *Wo de huiyi*, 170.

60. Lin Nanqing, "Sixiang he bu gui guli," 34–36.

61. In April 1949, the Taiwan Province Supervisory Committee for the Promotion of 37.5 percent Rent Reduction was established.

62. Wu Zhuoliu, *Taiwan lianqiao*, 234–35.

63. Land reform was one of the most successful and popular programs of the Nationalists. The land law of March 1, 1949, limited land rent to 37.5 percent of the total harvest. The Nationalists reported that in May and June of 1949 over 368,000 new leases — all, according to statute, to be for three to six years — were made. This gave farmers confidence in the new law. With American assistance, this program gradually purchased most large landholdings with government bonds.

64. On the impact of rent reduction and land reform on Taiwan's rural elite and farmers, see Hou Kunhong, "Guangfu chuqi Taiwan tudi gaige yundongzhong de zhengfu, dizhu, yu tiannong." Wu Zhuoliu noted that land reform was about controlling capital, not increasing farmers' incomes. Wu Zhuoliu, *Taiwan lianqiao*, 237.

65. Chen Sanjing and Xu Xueji, *Lin Hengdao xiansheng*, 99–101, 103–4.

66. Lin Nanqing, "Sixiang he bu gui guli," 39.

67. Lai Zehan et al., "Lin Zhong xiansheng." On at least two occasions, prominent Taiwanese were dispatched by the Nationalists to urge Lin to return to Taiwan, perhaps out of concern that he would become a rallying point for the independence movement. To date, there is no evidence that he supported the movement.

68. Ye Rongzhong, *Taiwan renwu qunxiang*, 22.

69. Other members included Yang Zhaojia, Wu Sanlian, Liu Mingchao, and Ye Rongzhong.

70. Han was active in the party's work in southern Taiwan.

71. Zhuang Yongming, *Han Shiquan zhuan*, 221.

72. Zhang Yanxian et al., eds., *Taiwan jindai mingren zhi* 1: 143. As a party official and Provincial Assembly member, he put forward four principles to the people: do not expand the violence, do not allow blood to flow, do not negate current administrative organs, and use political methods to solve political problems.

73. *Canyihui diyijie*, 4: 77–78.

74. Ibid., 3: 136–37.

75. Ibid., 5: 50.

76. Ibid., 6: 202.

77. Ibid., 8: 24.

78. Ironically, this dedicated doctor was not in attendance when Fu Sinian died during his interpellation in one of the last assembly meetings in December 1950.

79. Zhuang Yongming, *Han Shiquan zhuan*, 207–18.

80. Zhang Yanxian et al., eds., *Taiwan jindai mingren zhi* 1: 143–45.

81. *Taiwan mingrenji*, which was published in 1953.

82. Wu Zhuoliu, *Taiwan lianqiao*, 223.

83. Ibid., 221.

84. Wu Xinrong, *Wu Xinrong huiyilu*, 265–71.

85. See Zhang Yanxian et al., eds., *Taiwan jindai mingren zhi* 1: 169.

86. In the 1930s, Huang served as consul general in San Francisco and Calcutta. In 1942, he became a professor at the Central Political University and began to write official reports about Taiwan.

87. A recent and relatively favorable biography of Huang is Zhou Zongxian, *Huang Chaoqin zhuan*.

88. Huang Chaoqin, *Taiwan shouhuihou zhi sheji*, 1–2.

89. Huang Chaoqin, "Zai jianguo yundongzhong Taibei shimin duiyu ziyou ji shoufa yingyou zhi renshi."

90. Memorandum from Ralph Blake, U.S. consul in Taibei, to J. L. Stuart, ambassador to China, Central Files, 894A.00/12-446.

91. Huang Chaoqin, *Wo de huiyi*, 167–71.

92. There is no way to know what was actually said by the parties in the series of meetings held during Huang's short-lived resignation. The public statements of Huang and Lin toward each other were extremely polite and tell historians little.

93. Huang Chaoqin, *Wo de huiyi*, 169.

94. For example, see Huang Chaoqin, "Taiwansheng canyihui diyijie diyici dahui xianci, May 1, 1946" (Speech at the First Meeting of the First Session of the Taiwan Provincial Consultative Assembly), in *Huang Chaoqin xiansheng*, 250–51.

95. Wang Shaoqi, "Zhuihuai Huang Chaoqin xiansheng."

96. *Canyihui diyijie*, 4: 60.

97. Li Xinmin, *Huang Chaoqin zhuan*.

98. Huang Chaoqin, *Wo de huiyi*, 163–64.

99. *Canyihui diyijie*, 3: 22.

100. Ibid., 5: 26–27.

101. The essay was part of the Modern Citizen's Basic Knowledge series (*Xiandai guomin jiben zhishi congshu*), in Huang Chaoqin et al., *Guomin geming yundong yu Taiwan*.

102. Ibid., 1–13.

103. Huang Chaoqin, "Taiwan guangfu sizhounian xianci, October 1949" (Speech on the Fourth Anniversary of Taiwan's Retrocession), in *Huang Chaoqin xiansheng*, 3.

104. Lin Dingli, a native of Yunlin, was elected to the new assembly in 1951. To the surprise of many observers, he challenged Huang for the post of chairman. He narrowly lost the election, but became vice chairman of the Provincial Provisional Assembly.

105. Chen Sanjing and Xu Xueji, *Lin Hengdao xiansheng*, 95–96.

106. Zhang Yanxian et al., eds., *Taiwan jindai mingren zhi* 1: 179.

107. Tong Jianyan, ed., *Taiwan lishi zidian*, 422.

108. John Copper divides this problem into two parts in his *Taiwan: Nation-State or Province?*

109. Accepting that the relationship between the Taiwanese and the mainlander-dominated Nationalist government was colonial presupposes that the island is or should be an independent nation.

110. Michael Hechter, *Internal Colonialism*, 9.

111. Ibid., 33.

112. Ibid., 310.

113. There are, of course, many other possible case studies of Taiwanese who enjoyed political and material success under Nationalist rule. For example, Lian Zhendong went on to become chief of the Civil Administration Office in the 1950s; Ye Rongzhong, who became a banker in central Taiwan and later wrote histories of

political and cultural movements of the Japanese era; and You Mijian, who became mayor of Taibei in mid-1946.

114. Wu Zhuoliu, *Taiwan lianqiao*, 222.

CHAPTER 7: CONCLUSION AND EPILOGUE

1. Many scholars have commented on the militarized nature of Jiang Jieshi's government. Ch'i Hsi-sheng faults the Nationalists for pursuing manipulative, not integrative, state-building through military force. Jiang Jieshi subordinated the state and party to the military, this line of thinking goes, thus preventing the Nationalists from going about the vital business of state-building. Ch'i Hsi-sheng, *Nationalist China at War*. The late Lloyd Eastman argued that the strains of the War of Resistance exacerbated the structural flaws of this militarized regime. Eastman, *Seeds of Destruction*. See also idem, *The Abortive Revolution*.

2. Many scholars have examined the Nationalist effort to reinvigorate their state and party after the retreat from the mainland. See, for example, Dickson, "The Lessons of Defeat"; and Steven Tsang, "Revitalizing the Revolution." The Nationalists worked hard to promote this understanding of a "new" or "reborn" Guomindang. For example, see Chang Ch'i-yun, *The Rebirth of the Kuomintang*. Eastman argues that the Nationalists learned vital lessons in defeat that made them effective on the island. *Seeds of Destruction*, chap. 9.

3. The Republic of China was an innovator in developing export processing zones (the first around Gaoxiong in 1966) designed to promote exports and to attract investment and technology.

4. For example, Ralph Clough wrote that "Taiwan's economic development has been widely recognized as one of the outstanding success stories of the past thirty years. It grew out of an unusual combination of circumstances: the relatively developed infrastructure left by the Japanese; the influx of thousands of experienced and well-educated technicians, businessmen, and government administrators from China; large amounts of U.S. economic aid for the first fifteen years; political stability; and the willingness of top national leaders to accept the advice of technocrats." Clough gives the Taiwanese relatively little credit for the island's economic development and prosperity. Clough, "Taiwan under Nationalist Rule," 818. See also idem, *Island China*.

5. Lerman, *Taiwan's Politics*; and Jacobs, *Local Politics in a Rural Chinese Cultural Setting*.

6. While the debate rages on Taiwan over the adoption of an official romanization system, this work uses the hanyu pinyin romanization of Li Denghui for consistency.

7. Li was actually the second Taiwanese to be vice president under Jiang Jingguo. The first was Xie Dongmin (Hsieh Tung-min) who was elected in 1978.

8. On Li's visit to the United States, and his drive to reform the provincial government out of existence, see Tyler, "Tough Stance toward China Pays Off for Taiwan Leader"; and idem, "In Taiwan, A Mandate, But for What?" See also WuDunn, "Taiwan Plans to Drop a Fig Leaf."

9. The interview is in Shiba Ryōtarō *Taiwan jixing*, 319–39. For Li's explana-

tion of his views of Taiwan's relationship with the mainland, see his *Taiwan de zhuzhang*; and idem, *The Road to Democracy*.

10. Richburg, "Leader Asserts Taiwan is 'Independent, Sovereign.'"

11. *Guo* and *guojia* can be translated as nation, state, country, or nation-state. Li and ROC publications translate these terms as "state." For the text of the interview, see *Zhongyuan ribao* (Taibei), (July 10, 1999): 1.

12. Faison, "Taiwan President Implies His Island Is Sovereign State"; and Laris, "Taiwan Alters Old 'One China' Formula."

13. James Song (Song Chuyu) was a member of the Guomindang and the governor of Taiwan Province under Li Denghui. He quit the Nationalists to run for president in 2000 as an independent. Despite his loss, Song organized the People First Party. Song's party emphasizes that it is continuing the policies of the last mainland-born president of the Republic of China, Jiang Jingguo.

14. On this development, see Gold, *State and Society in the Taiwan Miracle*.

15. These demands were not always anti-Nationalist or necessarily part of the opposition, except insofar as they criticized those in power. On various interests groups that have sprung up in the last twenty years, see Hsin-Huang Michael Hsiao, "Emerging Social Movements and the Rise of a Demanding Civil Society on Taiwan."

16. Thomas Metzger and Ramon Myers write that the Nationalist state represented an "inhibited center" that was less democratic than the "subordinated center" of Western democracies and but much more tolerant of dissent than the "uninhibited center" of the mainland government. Metzger and Myers, "Introduction," in Myers, ed., *Two Societies in Opposition*, xvii–xviii.

17. The temporary provisions of the constitution that essentially made the document meaningless were repealed in 1990. A subsequent series of elections led to the replacement of legislators and National Assembly members (most of whom had been elected on the mainland in the late 1940s). In late 1994, elections were held for the provincial governor and mayors of the two largest cities (Taibei and Gaoxiong) and, in March 1996 for the presidency.

18. On the problems of democratization and Taiwanese identity, see Wachman, *Taiwan: National Identity and Democratization*.

19. See, for example, Zhang Yanxian's discussion of the connection between political developments and the growth of a "Taiwan-centered" history. Zhang Yanxian, "Taiwanshi yanjiu de xin jingshen." Many of the historiographical trends that began on Taiwan are starting to appear in American scholarship. See, for example, Rubinstein, ed., *Taiwan: A New History*.

20. For example, in the 1970s a pro-independence magazine devoted an entire issue to the February 28 Incident, which it described as "The February 28 Revolution: The Origins of the Establishment of the Taiwanese Nation." *Taidu* 59–60 (Feb. 28, 1977). Like many other pro-independence materials published before the 1980s, the authors are anonymous.

21. On various definitions of February 28, see the translator's introduction in Yang Yizhou, *Er erba minbian*, 13–16.

22. "Remembering '28 February 1947': A Memorial to Taiwan's Holocaust"; and "'Twenty-eight February 1947': Taiwan's Holocaust Remembered."

23. Peng Mingmin, *A Taste of Freedom*, 17.

24. Ibid., 92.

25. Had he won, this Taiwanese independence activist would have been, according to the official Guomindang line, head of state for all of China.

26. A typical discussion of Chen in the mainland press is "Yi ge Zhongguo yuanze jue bu chongxu huibi he hutu" (One China Absolutely Does Not Allow for Avoidance or Obfuscation), *Renmin ribao* (May 22, 2000): 4.

Glossary

Andō Rikichi	安藤利吉	
ba shiwu duli yundong	八十五獨立運動	August 15 Independence Movement
Bai Chongxi	白崇禧	
baise kongbu	白色恐怖	White Terror
banshanren	半山人	Half-Mountain people
baojia, hokō (J.)	保甲	local system of supervision
baoshou	保守	conservative
bendaoren, hontōjin (J.)	本島人	people of this island
bentu	本土	sovereign territory
buman fenzi	不滿分子	unsatisfied element
Cai Peihuo	蔡培火	
can'an	慘案	massacre
canmin zhuyi	慘民主義	"immiserate the people–ism"
canyihui	參議會	consultative assembly
chaoyuepai	超越派	transcendentals
Chen Cheng	陳誠	
Chen Fengyuan	陳逢源	
Chen Jiongming	陳炯明	
Chen Shuibian	陳水扁	

Chen Xin	陳欣	
Chen Yi	陳儀	
chuangzhiquan	創制權	legislative power
Chuli dagang	處理大綱	General Outline for Resolution
da chuantong	大傳統	Great Tradition
dangwai	黨外	outside the [Nationalist] party
Den Kenjirō	田健治郎	
difang zizhi, chihō jichi (J.)	地方自治	local self-government
difang zizhu	地方自主	local sovereignty
dikangpai	抵抗派	opposition clique
dizhu	地主	landlord
duli	獨立	independence
Er erba shijian	二二八事件	February 28 Incident
Er erba shijian chuli weiyuanhui	二二八事件處理委員會	February 28 Incident Resolution Committee
fabi	法幣	national currency
fei liuxingpai	非流行派	nonmainstream faction
fengjian	封建	feudal
fu	府	prefecture
Fu Sinian	傅斯年	
fujuequan	復決權	referendum
Ge Jing'en	葛敬恩	
genrō (J.)	元老	elder statesmen
Gotō Shimpei	後藤新平	
Gu Xianrong	辜顯榮	
Gu Zhenfu	辜振甫	
guan, jiao, yang, wei	管,教,養,衛	manage, teach, cultivate, protect

guangfu	光復	retrocession
guangfuqu	光復區	recovered area
Guo Guoji	郭國基	
Guo Yuxin	郭雨新	
Guomindang (Kuomintang)	國民黨	Nationalist Party
Guoyu	國語	"National Language" (Mandarin Chinese)
Han Shiquan	韓石泉	
Hanjian	漢奸	traitor (to China)
Hanzu	漢族	Han Chinese (ethnicity)
He Yingqin	何應欽	
hezuo	合作	cooperate
Hu Shi	胡適	
Huang Chaoqin	黃朝琴	
huawai	化外	"outside civilization"
Isayama Haruki	諫山春樹	
Itagaki Taisuke	板垣退助	
jiandu	監督	supervise
Jiang Jieshi (Chiang Kai-shek)	蔣介石	
Jiang Jingguo (Chiang Ching-kuo)	蔣經國	
Jiang Weichuan	蔣渭川	
Jiang Weishui	蔣渭水	
Jianguo dagang	建國大綱	General Outline for National Reconstruction
jianshang	奸商	profiteer
jieshou	接收	to receive
jiu Taibi	舊臺幣	old Taiwan dollar
junquan	均權	equal powers

kang E fan gong	抗俄反共	oppose Russia and resist Communism
kang Ri kao shan, kang luan kao hai	抗日靠山 抗亂靠海	To resist the Japanese, rely on the mountains; to resist chaos, rely on the sea
Ke Yuanfen	柯遠芬	
Kejiaren, also known as Hakka	客家人	"Guest People"
Kenpeitai (J.)	憲兵隊	police; military police
Kodama Gentarō	兒玉源太朗	
Kōmin hōkōkai (J.)	皇民奉公會	Imperial Subjects Service Society
kōminka (J.)	皇民化	becoming a subject of the Japanese emperor
laojia	老家	"old home"
Lei Zhen (Lei Chen)	雷震	
Li Denghui (Lee Teng-hui)	李登輝	
Li Wanju	李萬居	
Li Yizhong	李翼中	
Li Yuanzhan	李源棧	
Li Zhenzhou	李鎮洲	
Li Zonghuang	李宗黃	
Li Zongren (Li Tsung-jen)	李宗仁	
liansheng	聯省	federation of provinces
Lin Dingli	林頂立	
Lin Hengdao	林衡道	
Lin Lianzong	林連宗	
Lin Xiantang	林獻堂	
Lin Zhong	林忠	

Linshi quanguo daibiao dahui	臨時全國代表大會	Provisional National Assembly
lixiangpai	理想派	idealists
Long Yun	龍雲	
Lu Xun (Lu Hsun)	魯迅	
Mao Zedong	毛澤東	
Meiji (J.) (r. 1868–1912)	明治	emperor and era
minbian	民變	popular uprising
Mingchao	明朝	Ming dynasty (1368–1644)
minguo	民國	republic
Minnan	閩南	South of the Min River, an area in Fujian Province
Minnanhua	閩南話	spoken Taiwanese, also called Taiyu
Minzhengting	民政庭	Civil Administration Office
minzhi	民治	government by the people
Minzhongdang	民眾黨	Masses Party
Minzhu jinbudang	民主進步黨	Democratic Progressive Party
Minzhu shehuidang	民主社會黨	Democratic Socialist Party
minzu fuxing de jidi	民族復興的基地	base for the restoration of our race
naichi (J.), neidi	內地	interior or mainland (China); home islands (Japan)
naichi enchō neidi yanchang	內地延長	extension of the interior
Nakagawa Kenzō	中川健藏	

neidihua	內地化	assimilation (lit., becoming like the interior)
nuhua	奴化	enslavement
panluan or panbian	叛亂，叛變	rebellion
Peng Mengji	澎孟緝	
Peng Mingmin	澎明敏	
qianbei	前輩	elder generation
Qingchao	清朝	Qing dynasty (1644–1911)
qingxiang	清鄉	clearing the villages campaign
Qinmindang	親民黨	People First Party
Qisi xue'an diaocha weiyuanhui	緝私血案調查委員會	Committee to Investigate the Case of the Arrested Smuggler
Qiu Niantai	丘念台	
renmin zhi shang minsheng di yi	人民之上民生第一	the people are supreme, the people's livelihood comes first
renwen jiaoyu	人文教育	humanities education
Ribenhua	日本化	Japanization
san bu zhuyi	三不主義	three no-ism
san wei yi ti	三位一體	three positions in one body
sanmian quli	三面取利	grasping benefits from all sides
Sanmin zhuyi	三民主義	Three Principles of the People
sannian yi xiaoluan, wunian yi daluan	三年一小亂，五年一大亂	a small revolt every three years, and a large revolt every five years
Sanshi'er tiao yaoqiu	三十二條要求	Thirty-Two Demands

Sheng xian zizhi tongze	省縣自治通則	Principles for Provincial and County Self-Government
shi	市	city
shijian	事件	incident
shijun kikan (J.)	諮詢機關	advisory organ
shimon kikan (J.)	諮問機關	consultative organ
Shinnu (J.), Qingnu	清奴	Qing slaves
Shintō (J.)	神道	Way of the Gods
Shōwa (J.) (r. 1926–1989)	昭和	emperor and era
Song Feiru	宋斐如	
Song Meiling	宋美齡	
sōtoku (Chin. zongdu)	總督	governor-general
sujian	蕭奸	campaign to exterminate traitors
Sun Chuanfang	孫傳仿	
Sun Liren	孫立人	
Sun Zhongshan (Sun Yat-sen)	孫中山	
Tai ren zhi Tai	臺人治臺	Let Taiwanese Rule Taiwan
Taidu	臺獨	Taiwan independence
Taishō (J.) (r. 1912–1926)	大正	emperor and era
Taiwan	臺灣	
Taiwan chihō jichi renmei (J.)	臺灣地方自治聯盟	Taiwan League for Local Self-Government
Taiwan diaocha weiyuanhui	臺灣調查委員會	Taiwan Investigation Committee
Taiwan geming tongmenguhui	臺灣革命同盟會	Taiwanese Revolutionary Alliance

Taiwan minzhongdang	臺灣民眾黨	Taiwan Masses Party
Taiwan minzhu zizhi tongmeng	臺灣民主自治同盟	Taiwan Democratic Self-Government League
Taiwan sōtokufu (J.)	臺灣總督府	Taiwan Governor-General's Office
Taiwan sōtokufu hyōgikai (J.)	臺灣總督府評議會	Taiwan Governor General's Consultative Assembly
Taiwan tonghuahui, Taiwan dōkakai (J.)	臺灣同化會	Taiwan Assimilation Society
Taiwan wenhua xiehui	臺灣文化協會	Taiwan Cultural Association
Taiwan yishi	臺灣意識	Taiwan consciousness
Taiwan ziqiu yundong xuanyan	臺灣自求運動宣言	"A Declaration of Formosan Self-Salvation"
Taiwanhua	臺灣化	Taiwanization
Taiwansheng canyihui	臺灣省參議會	Taiwan Provincial Consultative Assembly
Taiwansheng difang zizhi xiehui	臺灣省地方自治協會	Taiwan Provincial Local Self-Government Association
Taiwansheng difang zizhi yanjiuhui	臺灣省地方自治研究會	Taiwan Provincial Local Self-Government Research Society
Taiwansheng jingbei zongsilingbu qianjin zhihuisuo	臺灣省警備總司令部前進指揮所	Taiwan Provincial Garrison Command Advance Office
Taiwansheng linshi yihui	臺灣省臨時議會	Taiwan Provincial Provisional Assembly
Taiwansheng tongzhiguan	臺灣省通誌管	Taiwan Provincial Gazetteer Office
Taiwansheng xingzheng zhangguan gongshu	臺灣省行政長官公署	Taiwan Provincial Administrative Executive Office

Taiwansheng xuanchuan weiyuanhui	臺灣省宣傳委員會	Taiwan Provincial Propaganda Committee
Taiwansheng zhengfu weiyuanhui	臺灣省政府委員會	Taiwan Provincial Government Committee
Tangshan	唐山	Tang Mountains (mainland China)
teshu	特殊	special characteristics
tianfu	天府	land of plenty
ting, chō (J.)	廳	administrative unit; government office
tonghua, dōka (J.)	同化	assimilation
tu huangdi	土皇帝	"local emperor"
tuoxiepai	妥協派	accommodationists
tuzhuhua	土著化	indigenization
Wang Baiyuan	王白淵	
Wang Jingwei	汪精衛	
Wang Tiandeng	王添燈	
Wei Daoming	魏道明	
wei hu zuo chang	為虎作倀	help an evildoer
Weng Qian	翁鈐	
wenhua chongjian	文化重建	cultural reconstruction
wu guo wu jia	無國無家	"no nation, no family"
Wu Guozhen	吳國楨	
wu hu jiang	五虎將	Five Tiger Generals
Wu Sanlian	吳三連	
Wu Xinrong	吳新榮	
Wu Zhuoliu	吳濁流	
wuzi dengke	五子登科	Five-Part Imperial Exam
xian	縣	county
xiaoji	消極	passive
Xie E	謝鵝	

Xie Nanguang	謝南光	
Xie Xuehong	謝雪紅	
xin Taibi	新臺幣	new Taiwan dollar
Xindang	新黨	New Party
Xing Zhong hui	興中會	Revive China Society
Xu Shouchang	許壽裳	
xuanchuan zuzhang	宣傳組長	propaganda chairman
Yamagata Aritomo	山縣有朋	
Yan Jiagan	嚴家淦	
Yang Lianggong	楊亮功	
Yang Zhaojia	楊肇嘉	
yangmin	養民	support the people
Yaxiya de gu'er	亞細亞的孤兒	Asia's Orphan
Ye Rongzhong	葉榮鍾	
yiban minzhong	一般民眾	average or common people
yiken shehui	移墾社會	frontier society
yimin shehui	移民社會	immigrant society
You Mijian	游彌堅	
Yuan Shikai	袁世凱	
yuanzhumin	原住民	aborigines "original people"
yuanzui	原罪	original sin
yuyong shenshi	御用紳士	collaborationist gentry
yuyongpin	御用品	items for the use of the emperor
zai andingzhong qiu fanrong	在安定中求繁榮	moving from stability to prosperity
zaibatsu (J.)	財閥	financial clique
Zhang Lisheng	張厲生	

Zhang Xueliang	張學良	
Zheng Chenggong also called Koxinga	鄭成功	
Zhengzhi xieshanghui	政治協商會	Political Consultative Conference
Zhengzhi xingdong weiyuanhui	政治行動委員會	Political Action Committee
zhidao	指導	to direct
Zhixian guomin dahui	制憲國民大會	National Assembly for Promulgating the Constitution
Zhongguo difang zizhi xuehui	中國地方自治學會	Chinese Local Self-Government Study Society
Zhongguo nongcun fuxing weiyuanhui	中國農村復興委員會	China Village Restoration Committee
Zhongguo qingniandang	中國青年黨	China Youth Party
Zhongguohua	中國化	Sinicization
Zhonghua minguo	中華民國	Republic of China
Zhongyang pingyi weiyuanhui	中央評議委員會	Central Advisory Committee
zhou, shū (J.)	州	administrative unit translated as province, prefecture or district
zhuquan duli de guojia	主權獨立的國家	sovereign, independent state
zifei	資匪	financing bandits
zigei zizu	自給自足	self-sufficient
ziqiang yundong	自強運動	Self-Strengthening Movement
zixin	自新	"turning over a new leaf"
zizhi	自治	self-government

Zizhi qingnian tongmeng	自治青年同盟	Self-Government Youth Alliance
zizhu	自主	autonomy
zongcai	總裁	Director General
zuguo	祖國	fatherland
zuguohua	祖國化	"fatherlandization"

Bibliography

CHINESE-LANGUAGE SOURCES

Official Documents and Publications, and Documentary Collections

Chen Wuzhong, and Chen Guangtang, eds. *Taiwan guangfu he guangfuhou wunian shengqing* (Taiwan's Retrocession and the Situation Five Years Thereafter). Nanjing: Nanjing chubanshe, 1989.

Chen Yunlong, ed. *Taiwansheng ge jiguan zhiyuan lu* (A Record of Professionals in Various Taiwan Provincial Organizations). *Jindai Zhongguo shiliao congkan xubian*, vol. 51. Taibei: Wenhai chubanshe, 1946.

Er erba shijian wenxian jilu (Historiographical Records of the February 28 Incident). Wei Yongzhu and Li Xuanfeng, eds. 3 vols. Taizhong: Taiwansheng wenxian weiyuanhui, 1992–94. Vol. 1 has no editor listed.

Fujiansheng zhengfu (Fujian Provincial Government). *Taiwan kaocha baogao* (A Report on the Investigation of Taiwan). 1937.

Guo Yimin. *Shoufu Taiwan yijianshu* (Views on the Return of Taiwan). N.p., 1944.

He Fengjiao, ed. *Zhengfu jieshou Taiwan shiliao huibian* (A Documentary Collection of Historical Materials on the Government's Recovery of Taiwan). Xindian: Guoshiguan, 1990.

He Taishan. *Taiwan zhanhou wenti* (Problems with Postwar Taiwan). N.p., 1943.

Hou Kunhong, ed. *Tudi gaige shiliao* (Historical Materials Related to Land Reform). Zhonghua minguo nongye shiliao (yi) (Historical Materials Related to Agriculture in Republican China, part 1). Taibei: Guoshiguan, 1988.

Jiangsusheng zhengfu sanshisi, sanshiwu nian zhengqing shuyao (An Overview of the Political Situation of 1945 and 1946 in the Jiangsu Provincial Government). N.p., n.d.

Junshi weiyuanhui (Military Affairs Committee). *Junshi weiyuanhui zhengzhibu Taiwan yiyongdui zhiduiyuan mingce* (Military Affairs Committee Political Bureau Roster of Members of the Taiwan Volunteer Corps). N.p., 1943.

Minzheng daobao (Fujian Political Report). Fujiansheng zhengfu mishuchu, 1945 and 1946.

Richan chuli weiyuanhui (Japanese Property Management Committee). *Taiwansheng Richan chuli faling* (Laws and Orders Concerning the Management of Japanese Property in Taiwan Province). 1946.

Taiwan geming tongmenghui zonghui ganbu mingce (Taiwan Revolutionary Alliance Cadre Name List). N.p., 1944.

Taiwan gongzuo gaijin yaogang (Requirements for Improving Taiwan Work). N.p., 1944.

Taiwansheng canyihui (Taiwan Provincial Consultative Assembly). *Diyijie di'erci dahui jueyi'an banli qingxing baogaoshu* (Report on the Situation of Handling Resolutions from the Second Meeting of the First Session). Taibei, 1946.

Taiwansheng canyihui diyijie diyici dahui teji (Special Record of the First Session of the First Taiwan Provincial Consultative Assembly). Taibei: Taiwansheng canyihui mishuchu (Taiwan Provincial Consultative Assembly Secretariat), 1946. This series continues for each session of the Consultative Assembly through 1950.

————. *Bannian lai gongzuo baogao* (Work Report on the Past Half Year). Taibei: Taiwansheng canyihui, 1947.

Taiwansheng difang zizhi yanjiuhui (Taiwan Provincial Local Self-Government Research Society). *Taiwansheng difang zizhi yanjiuhui zhuankan* (Special Publication of the Taiwan Provincial Local Self-Government Research Society). 1949.

Taiwansheng dizhi shinian jiyao (An Outline of Ten Years of Local Self-Government in Taiwan Province). Taibei: Minzhong ribao, 1961.

Taiwansheng gongye yanjiusuo jishushe (Taiwan Province Industry Research Institute Technology Office). *Taiwansheng jingji diaocha chugao* (Draft Report on the Investigation of the Economy of Taiwan Province). Taibei: Taiwansheng gongye yanjiusuo, 1946.

Taiwansheng Guoyu tuixing weiyuanhui (Taiwan Provincial Mandarin Promotion Committee). *Taiwansheng Guoyu jiaoyu shishi gaikuang* (The General Situation of Implementing Mandarin Education in Taiwan Province). Taibei: Taiwansheng guoyu tuixing weiyuanhui, 1946.

Taiwansheng mishuchu (Taiwan Provincial Secretariat). *Taiwansheng zhengfu shizheng baogao* (Report of the Taiwan Provincial Government). 1946.

Taiwansheng xingzheng zhangguan gongshu (Taiwan Provincial Administrative Executive Office).

[1]. Archival materials in the files of the Academia Historica (Guoshiguan), Xindian, Taiwan.

[2]. *Shizheng baogao* (Administrative Report). 1946.

[3]. *Taiwan minzheng* (Civil Administration on Taiwan). 1946.

[4]. *Taiwansheng xingzheng zhangguan gongshu gongbao* (Taiwan Province Administrative Executive Office Public Bulletin). 1945–47.

[5]. *Taiwansheng xingzheng zhangguan gongshu gongzuo baogao* (Taiwan Provincial Administrative Office Work Report). 1947. This report covers 1946.

[6]. *Taiwansheng xingzheng zhangguan gongshu tichu shengcanyihui diyijie diyici dahui shizheng baogao* (Taiwan Provincial Administrative Executive Office's Report on Administration to the First Session of the First Provincial Consultative Assembly). 1946.

Taiwansheng xingzheng zhangguan gongshu minzhengchu (Taiwan Provincial Administrative Executive Office, Civil Administration Bureau). *Taiwansheng minyi jiguan zhi jianli* (The Establishment of Organizations for Expressing Popular Will in Taiwan Province). Taibei, 1946.

Taiwansheng xuanchuan weiyuanhui (Taiwan Provincial Propaganda Committee).

Taiwan xiankuang cankao ziliao (Reference Material on Taiwan's Current Situation). Taibei: Taiwansheng xuanchuan weiyuanhui, 1946.

Taiwansheng xunliantuan (Taiwan Provincial Training Group). *Tuan zhuren jiangci* (Speeches of the Group Heads). Taibei: Taiwansheng xunliantuan, 1946.

Taiwansheng yihui (Taiwan Provincial Assembly). *Taiwansheng yihui sanshiwunian* (Thirty-five Years of the Taiwan Provincial Assembly). N.p., n.d. This overview of the Provincial Assembly, including name lists of past members, was probably published in the early 1970s.

Taiwansheng zhengfu (Taiwan Provincial Government). *Taiwansheng xingzheng jiyao* (Summary of the Administration of Taiwan Province). 1948.

Taiwansheng zhengfu minzhengting (Taiwan Provincial Government Civil Administration Department). *Taiwan minzheng* (The Civil Administration of Taiwan). Taibei: Dongnan yinshuguan, 1948.

Taiwansheng zhengfu xinwenchu (Taiwan Provincial Government Information Bureau). *Taiwan de jianshe* (The Rebuilding of Taiwan). Taibei: Taiwansheng zhengfu yinshuachang, 1962.

Xingzhengyuan xinwenju (Administrative Yuan, Information Bureau). *Er erba shijian zhuan'an baogao* (Special Case Report on the February 28 Incident). Taibei: Xingzhengyuan xinwenju, 1989.

Xue Yuexun, ed. *Ziyuan weiyuanhui dang'an shiliao huibian: Guangfu chuqi Taiwan jingji jianshe* (Documentary Collection of Historical Materials of the National Resources Commission: Taiwan's Economic Development, 1946–52). Taibei: Guoshiguan, 1993.

Zhang Ruicheng, ed. *Kangzhan shiqi shoufu Taiwan zhi zhongyao yanlun* (Selected Important Documents on Recovering Taiwan during the War of Resistance). Taibei: Guomindang dangshihui, 1990.

———, ed. *Shoufu Taiwan zhi chouhua yu shoujiang jieshou* (Plans for Recovering Taiwan, Receiving the Japanese Surrender, and Taking Over Taiwan). Taibei: Guomindang dangshihui, 1990.

———, ed. *Taiji zhishi zai zuguo de fuTai nuli* (Taiwanese Fighters' Endeavor on the Fatherland to Recover Taiwan). Taibei: Guomindang dangshihui, 1990.

Zhongyang shejiju (Central Planning Bureau). *Taiwan shouhui hou zhi sheji gangyao* (A General Outline of Plans for After the Return of Taiwan). N.p., 1944.

Zhongyang xunliantuan dangzheng xunlianban (Central Training Corps Political Training Class). *Difang zhengzhi* (Local Politics). N.p., 1944.

Zhongyang yanjiuyuan jindaishi yanjiusuo (Academia Sinica, Institute of Modern History). *Er erba shijian ziliao xuanji* (Documentary Collection Concerning the February 28 Incident). 3 vols. Taibei: Zhongyang yanjiuyuan, 1992–93. These materials were gathered by a committee of scholars organized by the Executive Yuan.

Periodicals and Newspapers

It is difficult to be certain of publication dates for the chaotic 1945–50 period. The dates listed below, and for the Japanese periodicals, are largely taken from Lang, "A History of Newspapers in Taiwan."

Damingbao (Clarity Daily). Taibei, 1946–47.

Difang zizhi (Local Self-Government). Various locations, 1934–50; Taibei, 1950–present.

Gonglunbao (Public Debate). Taibei, 1947–present.

Guoshengbao (Nation's Voice). Gaoxiong, 1946–47.

Heping ribao (Peace Daily). Taizhong, 1946–48.

Minbao (People's Daily). Taibei, 1946.

Quanmin ribao (All People's Daily). Taibei, 1947.

Renmin daobao (People's Report). Taibei, 1946–47.

Riyue tan (Discussing Life). Taibei, 1946.

Shenbao (Shanghai Journal). Shanghai, 1872–1949.

Taiwan pinglun (Taiwan Commentary). Taibei, 1946.

Taiwan qingnian (Taiwan Youth). Taibei, 1946.

Taiwan wenhua (Taiwan Culture). Taibei, 1946–50.

Taiwan wenxian (Reports on Historiographical Studies of Taiwan). Taizhong, 1955–present.

Taiwan xianfeng (Taiwan Vanguard). Fujian Province, 1941–42.

Taiwan xinshengbao (Taiwan New Life). Taibei, 1945–present.

Taiwan yuekan (Taiwan Monthly). Taibei, 1946–47.

Wenxian zhuankan (Historiographic Journal). Taizhong, 1948–55.

Xiandai zhoukan (Weekly Contemporary). Taibei, 1945–46.

Xin Taiwan (New Taiwan). Taibei, 1946.

Xinxin (New, New). Taibei, 1945–47.

Zhengjingbao (Political and Economic Report). Taibei, 1945–46.

Zhengzhibao (Political Record). Taibei? 1946.

Zhengzhi yuekan (Political Monthly). Taibei, 1947.

Zhonghua ribao (China Daily). Tainan, 1946–48.

Zhongyang ribao (China Central News). Various locations, 1929–49; Taibei, 1949–present.

Zhongyang zhoukan (Central Weekly). Shanghai, 1947.

Zili wanbao (Independence Evening News). Taibei, 1947–present.

Zizhi tongxun (Self-Government Report). Taibei, 1946.

Zuguo (Fatherland). Shanghai? 1945.

Books, Articles, Essays, and Dissertations

Bai Long (White Dragon) [pseud.]. "Yanlun yao juedui ziyou" (Speech Must Be Absolutely Free). *Xinxin* 2, 1 (Jan. 5, 1947): 25.

Bu Youtian. *Taiwan fengyun renwu* (Prominent Taiwanese). Hong Kong: Xinwen tiandishe, 1962.

Cai Peihuo, Wu Sanlian, Ye Rongzhong, Chen Fengyuan, and Lin Boshou. *Taiwan minzu yundong shi* (A History of the Taiwan People's Movement). Taibei: Zili wanbaoshe wenhua chubanshe, 1971.

Cai Qintang. "Huangminhua yundong qian Taiwan shehui jiaoyu yundong de fazhan" (The Development of the Social Education Movement Prior to the Kōminka Movement). Paper presented at the Taiwanshi guoji xueshu yanjiuhui, Tamkang University, May 1995.

Cai Xianchong. *Wang chunfeng: Taiwan minzhu yundong renwu fendou shi* (Await-ing the Spring Wind: A History of the Struggle of Taiwanese Democratic Move-ment Figures). Taibei: Cai Xianchong, 1981.

Chen Cuilian. *Paixi douzheng yu quanmou zhengzhi: Er erba beizhu de lingyi mian-xiang* (Factional Struggles and Power Politics: The Other Face of the February 28 Tragedy). Taibei: Shibao wenhua chubanshe, 1995.

Chen Fangming. *Xie Xuehong pingzhuan* (A Critical Biography of Xie Xuehong). Taibei: Qianwei chubanshe, 1991.

———. "Zhanhou chuqi Taiwan zizhi yundong yu er erba shijian" (The Self-Govern-ment Movement of the Immediate Postwar Era and the February 28 Incident). In *Er erba xueshu yantaohui lunwenji*. Taibei: Zili wanbao wenhua chubanshe, 1992.

———, ed. *Taiwan zhanhoushi ziliaoxuan: Er erba shijian zhuanji* (Postwar Taiwan Historical Materials Collection: Special February 28 Incident Collection). Taibei: Zili wanbao wenhua chubanshe, 1991.

Chen Guoxiang, and Zhu Ping. *Taiwan baoye yanjin 40 nian* (Forty Years of Evo-lution and Progress in Taiwan's Newspapers). Taibei: Zili wanbaoshe wenhua chubanbu, 1987.

Chen Hanguang. "Taiwan guangfu qianxi de shishi rizhi" (A Historical Journal of Taiwan on the Eve of the Retrocession). *Taiwan wenxian* (Reports on Historio-graphical Studies of Taiwan) 24, 2 (Mar. 1973): 56–70.

Chen Liyong, ed. *Jinji, yuanzui, beiju: Xinshengdai kan er erba shijian* (Taboo, Orig-inal Sin, Tragedy: A New Generation Looks at the February 28 Incident). Taibei: Daoxiang chubanshe, 1990.

Chen Mingtong. "Paixi zhengzhi yu Chen Yi zhi Tai lun" (A Discussion of Political Factions and Chen Yi's Rule of Taiwan). In Lai Zehan, ed., *Taiwan guangfu chuqi lishi*, 223–301.

———. "Weiquan zhengtixia Taiwan difang zhengzhi jingying de liudong (1945–1986): Shengcanyihuiyuan ji shengyihuiyuan liudong de fenxi" (Taiwanese Elite Fluidity under Authoritarian Rule, 1945–86: An Analysis of Fluidity in the Tai-wan Provincial Consultative Assembly and Taiwan Provincial Assembly). Ph.D. diss. National Taiwan University, 1990.

———, ed. *Taiwan zhanhoushi ziliao xuan* (A Collection of Historical Materials Concerning Postwar Taiwan). Taibei: Zili wanbao wenhua chubanshe, 1991.

Chen Qi'nan. *Taiwan de chuantong Zhongguo shehui* (Taiwan's Traditional Chinese Society). Taibei: Yunnong wenhua, 1987.

Chen Sanjing. *Zhongguo Guomindang yu Taiwan* (China's Nationalist Party and Taiwan). Taibei: Zhongyang wenwu gongyingshe, 1985.

Chen Sanjing, and Xu Xueji. *Lin Hengdao xiansheng fangwen jilu* (A Record of a Visit with Mr. Lin Hengdao). *Koushu lishi congshu* 42. Taibei: Zhongyang yan-jiuyuan jindaishi yanjiusuo, 1992.

Chen Yisong. *Chen Yisong huiyilu: Riju shidai bian* (The Memoirs of Chen Yisong: The Japanese Occupation Period). Taibei: Qianwei chubanshe, 1994.

———. "Muqian jinji de zhengzhi zhu wenti" (Some Questions About the Present Critical Political [Situation]). *Zhengjingbao* 1, 2 (Nov. 10, 1945): 3.

Chen Yongxing, and Li Xiaofeng, eds. *Taiwan jindai renwu ji* (A Record of Con-temporary Taiwanese). Taibei: Li Xiaofeng, 1983.

Cheng Qingyi, Wang Shiliu, and Gao Shufan, eds. *Taiwan shi* (A History of Taiwan). Taizhong: Taiwansheng zhengfu yinshuachang, 1977.

Dai Guohui. *Taiwan zongtixiang: Zhumin, lishi, xinxing* (The General Form of Taiwan: Inhabitants, History, and Attitudes). Trans. by Wei Dingchao. Taibei: Yuanliu chuban shiye gufen youxian gongsi, 1989.

Dai Guohui, and Ye Yunyun. *Aizeng er erba: Shenhua yu shishi, jiekai lishi zhi mi* (Love and Hate February 28: Myth and Historical Facts, Opening the Mystery of History). Taibei: Yuanliu chubanshe, 1992.

Deng Kongshao. "Cong er erba shijian kan minzhu yu difang zizhi de yaoqiu" (Looking at Democracy and Self-Government from the February 28 Incident). *Dangdai* 34 (Feb. 1, 1989): 66–79.

———, ed. *Er erba shijian ziliaoji* (Collection of Materials on the February 28 Incident). Taibei: Daoxiang chubanshe, 1991.

Fang Hao. "Hong Yanqiu xiansheng fangwenji" (A Record of an Interview with Mr. Yanqiu Hong). In Huang Fusan and Chen Lifu, eds., *Jinxiandai Taiwan koushu lishi*. Taibei: Lin Benyuan Zhonghua wenhua jiaoyu jijinhui, 1991.

Fei Disheng. "Chen Cheng jiangjun tiemian zuofeng" (The Inflexible Ways of General Chen Cheng). *Taiwan chunqiu* 3 (Dec. 1948): 15–16.

Ge Jing'en. "Lai Tai yinian de huigu" (Looking Back on Taiwan Over the Past Year). *Taiwan xinshengbao* (Oct. 5, 1946): 1.

Gu Ruiyun. *Taizhong de fenglei: Gen Xie Xuehong zai yiqi de rizili* (Taizhong's Wind and Thunder: My Days with Xie Xuehong). Taibei: Renjian chubanshe, 1990.

Guo Tingyi. *Jindai Zhongguo shigang* (An Outline of Modern Chinese History). Hong Kong: Zhongwen daxue chubanshe, 1979.

———. *Taiwan shishi gaishuo* (A General History of Taiwan). Taibei: Zhongzheng shuju, 1954.

Han Shiquan. *Liushi huiyi* (Memoirs of Sixty Years). Tainan: Han Shiquan xiansheng shishi sanzhounian jipianyin weiyuanhui, 1966.

Hao Yiwen, ed. *Guo-Gong neizhanzhong de Taiwanbing* (Taiwan's Soldiers in the Civil War). Taibei: Babilun chubanshe, 1991.

He Jingtai. *Baise dang'an* (White Archives). Taibei: Shibao wenhua chuban qiye youxian gongsi, 1991.

Hou Kunhong. "Er erba shijian youguan shiliao yu yanjiu zhi fenxi" (An Analysis of Historical Materials and Research Related to the February 28 Incident). *Zhongguo xiandaishi zhuanti yanjiu baogao* 16 (1994): 332–88.

———. "Guangfu chuqi Taiwan tudi gaige yundongzhong de zhengfu, dizhu, yu tiannong" (The State, Landlords, and Farmers in Taiwan's Post-Retrocession Land Reform). *Zhongguo xiandaishi zhuanti yanjiu baogao* 17 (1994): 273–329.

———. "You jisi dao baodong: Minguo sanshisannian Sichuan Jiangyouxian Zhongjuzhen 'sanerba' shijian" (From Investigating Smugglers to Uprising: The March 28 Incident of Zhongju Village, Jiangyou County, Sichuan, 1944). Draft, 1995.

Hu Chunhui. *Minchu de difang zhuyi yu liansheng zizhi* (Local Self-Government and Federal Self-Government during the Early Republican Era). Taibei: Zhengzhong shuju, 1984.

Huang Chaoqin. *Huang Chaoqin xiansheng lunyanji* (A Collection of Writings and Speeches of Mr. Huang Chaoqin). N.p., 1975.

———. *Taiwan shouhuihou zhi sheji* (Plans for Postrecovery Taiwan). N.p., 1944.

———. *Wo de huiyi* (My Memoirs). Taibei: Longwen, 1989.

———. "Zai jianguo yundongzhong Taibei shimin duiyu ziyou ji shoufa yingyou zhi renshi" (What Taibei Citizens Should Know About Freedom and Respect for the Law in the Movement for National Reconstruction). *Taiwan xinshengbao* (Nov. 28, 1945): 1.

Huang Chaoqin, et al. *Guomin geming yundong yu Taiwan* (The National Revolutionary Movement and Taiwan). Taibei: Zhonghua wenhua chuban shiye weiyuanhui, 1955.

Huang Defu. *Taiwan zhanji* (A Record of the War on Taiwan). Taibei: Taiwan shudian, 1946.

Huang Junjie, and Gu Weiying. "Xin'en yu jiuyi zhijian: Riju shiqi Li Chunsheng de guojia rentong zhi fenxi" (New Favors and Old Righteousness: An Analysis of Li Chunsheng's National Identity). In *Rentong yu guojia*, 275–300.

Huang Yingzhe. "Lu Xun sixiang zai Taiwan de chuanbo, 1945–49: Shelun zhanhou chuqi Taiwan de wenhua chongjian yu guojia rentong" (The Transmission of Lu Xun's Thought on Taiwan, 1945–49: A Discussion of Cultural Reconstruction and National Identification in Immediate Postwar Taiwan). In *Rentong yu guojia*, 301–22.

———. "Xu Shoutang yu Taiwan (1946–1948)" (Xu Shoutang and Taiwan, 1946–48). In *Er erba xueshu yanjiuhui lunwenji*, 115–39. Taibei: Er erba minjian yanjiu xiaozu, 1992.

Huang Zhaotang. *Taiwan zongdufu* (The Taiwan Governor-General's Office). Trans. from Japanese by Huang Yingzhe. Taibei: Qianwei chubanshe, 1994.

Ide Kiwata [Jingchu Jihetai]. *Riju xia zhi Taizheng* (Taiwan under Japanese Occupation). Trans. by Guo Hui. 3 vols. Taizhong: Taiwan wenxian weiyuanhui, 1977.

Jian Rongren. "Riben diguo de zhimin tongzhi yu Taiwan yishi de xingqi" (Imperial Japan's Colonial Rule and the Rise of Taiwan Consciousness). In *Lunwen jiyao*. Gaoxiong: Gaoxiong xian zhengfu, 1991.

Jiang Jieshi. *Taiwan zhi guangfu yu Zhongguo zhi qiantu* (The Restoration of Taiwan and China's Future). Taibei, 1946.

Jiang Weichuan. "Taiwansheng canyiyuan houxuan xuanyan (1)" (Statement of Provincial Consultative Assembly Candidate Jiang Weichuan, part 1). *Renmin daobao* (Apr. 7, 1946): 2.

———. *2.28 shibian shi weiji* (The Complete Story of the February 28 Popular Uprising). Xizhizhen: 1991.

Jiang Yongjing, Li Yunhan, and Xu Shishen. *Yang Lianggong xiansheng nianpu* (A Chronological Biography of Yang Lianggong). Taibei: Lianjing chuban shiye gongsi, 1988.

Jin Shi, ed. *Taiwan mingren zhuan* (Biographies of Famous Taiwanese). Taibei: Shangye xinwenshe, 1956.

———, ed. *Taiwan shiren zhi, di yi ji* (A Record of Current Taiwanese, Volume 1). Taibei: 1947.

Jin Tigan, ed. *Taiwan de difang zizhi* (Taiwan's Local Self-Government). Taibei: Zhengzhong shuju, 1950.

Ke Yuanfen. "Taiwan er erba shibian zhi zhenxian" (The Real Form of Taiwan's February 28 Incident). In *Er erba shijian ziliao xuanji*, vol. 1. Taibei: Zhongyang yanjiuyuan jindaishi yanjiusuo, 1992.

Lai Zehan, et al. "Lin Zhong xiansheng fangwen jilu" (A Record of a Visit with Mr. Lin Zhong). *Koushu lishi* 4 (Feb. 1993): 25–49.

———, ed. *Taiwan guangfu chuqi lishi* (The History of Immediate Postwar Taiwan). Nangang: Zhongyang yanjiuyuan Zhongshan renwen shehui kexue yanjiusuo, 1993.

Lan Bozhou. *Baise kongbu* (White Terror). Taibei: Yangzhi wenhua, 1993.

———. *Huangmache zhi ge* (Song of the Curtained Cart). Taibei: Shibao chuban gongsi, 1991.

———. *Xunfang bei yinmie de Taiwanshi yu Taiwanren* (Searching for Buried Taiwan History and People). Taibei: Shibao wenhua, 1994.

———, ed. *Chenshi liuwang er erba* (Hidden Corpses–Exiles–February 28). Taibei: Shibao wenhua chuban qiye youxian gongsi, 1991.

Lan Dingyuan. "Luzhou wenji" (A Collection of Essays on Luzhou). In Ding Rijian, comp., *ZhiTai migaolu*. Taibei: Taiwan yinhang jingji yanjiushe, 1959. First pub. in the 1860s.

Li Ao, ed. *Er erba yanjiu* (Research into February 28). 3 vols. Taibei: Li Ao chubanshe, 1989.

Li Chunqing. "Zhongguo zhengzhi yu Taiwan" (Chinese Politics and Taiwan). *Taiwan pinglun* 1, 1 (July 1, 1946): 4–5.

Li Denghui. *Taiwan de zhuzhang* (Taiwan's Point of View). Taibei: Yuanliu, 1999.

Li Guoqi. *Zhongguo xiandaihua de chuyu yanjiu: Min-Zhe-Tai dichu, 1860–1916* (Modernization in China, 1860–1916: A Regional Study of the Fujian, Zhejiang, and Taiwan Region). Taibei: Zhongyang yanjiuyuan jindaishi yanjiusuo, 1982.

Li Wanju. "Lishi zoudao fenquan de shihou" (History Has Come to the Time of Divided Powers). *Gonglunbao* (Dec. 10, 1948): 2.

———. "Taiwan minzhong bing meiyou Ribenhua" (The Taiwanese Masses Certainly Have Not Been Japanized). *Zhengjingbao* 2, 3 (Feb. 10, 1946): 4.

Li Xiaofeng. *Daoyu xin taiji: Cong zhongzhan dao er erba* (The Island's New Birthmark: From the End of the War to February 28). Taibei: Zili wanbao wenhua chubanshe, 1993.

———. *Taiwan minzhu yundong sishinian* (Forty Years of the Taiwanese Democracy Movement). Taibei: Zili wanbao, 1987.

———. *Taiwan zhanhou chuqi de minyi daibiao* (Representatives of the People's Will of the Immediate Postwar Era). Taibei: Zili wanbao, 1986. Revised in 1993.

———, ed. *Er erba xiaoshi de Taiwan jingying* (Lost Taiwanese Elite of February 28). Taibei: Zili wanbao, 1990.

Li Xinmin. *Huang Chaoqin zhuan: Aiguo, aixiang* (A Biography of Huang Chaoqin: Love of Country and Native Place). Taibei: Jindai Zhongguo chubanshe, 1984.

Li Xuexun. *Xianxing difang minyi jigou zhidu* (The Current System of Local Organizations for the Popular Will). Shanghai: Gebu Zhonghua shuju, 1946.

Li Yizhong. "Lingdao shehui yaoyi" (Key Points to Leading Society). *Haichao* 7 (Aug. 15, 1946): 3–4.

———. "Taibao dui xiankuang yingyou zhi taidu" (The Attitude Taiwan Compatriots Should Have toward the Current Situation). *Taiwan zhi sheng* (Voice of Taiwan) 1, 1 (1946): 2–3.

Li Zhenzhou. *Huoshaodao diyiqi xinsheng: Yi ge baise kongbu shounanzhe de huiyi* (The First Period of New Life on Baked Island: Memoirs of a Victim of the White Terror). Taibei: Shibao wenhua, 1993.

Li Zhifu. *Taiwan renmin geming douzheng jianshi* (A Brief History of the Taiwanese People's Revolutionary Struggle). Guangzhou: Hua'nan renmin chubanshe, 1955.

Li Zonghuang. *Li Zonghuang huiyilu: Bashisan nian fendou shi* (The Memoirs of Li Zonghuang: Eighty-three Years of Struggle). Taibei: Zhongguo difang zizhi xuehui, 1972.

———. *Li Zonghuang yanlun xuanji* (A Collection of Writings and Speeches by Li Zonghuang). Taibei: Zhongguo difang zizhi xuehui, 1969.

———. "Ping xianfazhong de difang zhidu" (Criticizing the Local System Contained in the Constitution). *Xinshengbao* (May 9, 1948): 2.

———. *Taiwan difang zizhi xinlun* (A New Discussion of Taiwan's Local Self-Government). Taibei: Zhongyang wenwu gongyingshe yinhang, 1951.

———. *Zhongguo difang zizhi zonglun* (A General Discussion of China's Local Self-Government). Taibei: Zhongguo difang zizhi xuehui, 1954.

Lian Wenliao. *Taiwan zhengzhi yundong shi* (A History of Taiwan's Political Movements), ed. Zhang Yanxian and Weng Jiayin. Taibei: Daoxiang chubanshe, 1988.

Lian Yatang [Lian Heng]. *Taiwan tongshi* (An Outline History of Taiwan). 2 vols. Taibei: Guoli bianyiguan Zhonghua congshu bianshen weiyuanhui, 1985 reprint.

Lian Zhengdong. "Taiwanren de zhengzhi lixiang he dui zuoguan de guannian" (Taiwanese Political Ideals and Views of Serving as an Official). *Zhengjingbao* 2, 2 (Jan. 25, 1946): 4–5.

Lin Delong. "Guofu qian Tai qianhou shehui kongzhi zhi licheng" (The Process of Social Control Around the Time of the Retreat of the Nationalist Government to Taiwan). *Taiwan shiliao yanjiu* 3 (Feb. 1994): 114–19.

Lin Hengdao, ed. *Taiwan kangRi zhonglielu* (A Record of Taiwanese Anti-Japanese Martyrs). Taizhong: Taiwan shengzhengfu yinshuachang, 1965.

Lin Hengdao, et al., eds. *Taiwanshi* (A History of Taiwan). Taibei: Zhongwen tushu, 1990.

Lin Manhong. *Sibainian lai de liang'an fenhe: Yige jingmaoshi de huigu* (Four Hundred Years of Unity and Division across the Straits: A Review of Economic and Trade History). Taibei: Zili wanbaoshe wenhua chubanshe, 1994.

Lin Muxun. *Taiwan eryue geming* (Taiwan's February Revolution). Taibei: Qianwei chubanshe, 1990.

Lin Shuangbu, ed. *Er erba Taiwan xiaoshuoxuan* (Selection of Taiwan Stories About February 28). Taibei: Zili wanbao, 1989.

Lin Tangchuan. "Xin Taiwan sanzijing" (New Taiwanese Three Character Classic). *Xin Taiwan* 4 (May 1, 1946): 9.

Lin Weisheng. *Luohanjiao: Qingdai Taiwan shehui yu fenlei xiedou* (Drifters: Qing Dynasty Taiwanese Society and Ethnic Conflict). Taibei: Zili wanbaoshe wenhua chubanshe, 1993.

Lin Zhen. "Kangzhan shiqi Fujian de Taiwan jimin wenti" (Taiwanese in Fujian during the War of Resistance). *Taiwan yanjiu congkan* 2 (1994): 71–78.

Lin Zhong. "Dui shichu fabiao zhengjian" (Expressing Political Views on the Current Situation). *Taiwan pinglun* 1, 3 (Sept. 1, 1946): 6–9.

Liu Fenghan, et al. *Yao Hengxiu xiansheng fangwenlu* (A Record of a Visit with Mr. Yao Hengxiu). *Guoshiguan koushu lishi congshu* 2. Xindian: Guoshiguan, 1993.

Liu Langbi. *Chongxiu Taiwan fuzhi* (Revised Taiwan Prefecture Gazetteer). Taizhong: Taiwan wenxian weiyuanhui yinhang, n.d. Written in 1742.

Liu Shiyong. "Chen Yi de jingji sixiang ji qi zhengce" (Chen Yi's Economic Thought and Policies). *Taiwan fengwu* 40, 2 (1990): 55–88.

Liu Zhuanlai. "Guangfu hou de huigu yu xinnian de xiwang" (A Look Back at Post-Retrocession and Hopes for the New Year). *Haichao* 12 (Jan. 1947): 12.

Lu Shaoli. "Shuiluo xiangqi: Rizhi shiqi Taiwan shehui de shenghuo zuoxi" (The Sound of the Conch: Life Activities of Taiwanese Society during the Period of Japanese Rule). Ph.D. diss., National Taiwan Chengchi University, 1995.

Lu Xiuyi. *Riju shidai Taiwan gongchandang shi* (A History of the Communist Party during the Era of Japanese Occupation). Taibei: Qianwei chubanshe, 1989.

Ma Maoran. "Taiwan difang zizhi de jichu wenti" (The Basic Problem of Taiwan's Local Self-Government). *Jinbu luntan* 1, 4 (Nov. 15, 1949): 10–11.

Min-Tai tongxun shebian. *Taiwan zhengzhi xiankuang baogaoshu* (A Report on the Present Status of Taiwanese Politics). N.p., 1946.

Peng Mengji. "Taiwansheng er erba shijian huiyilu" (A Record of Taiwan Province's February 28 Incident). In *Er erba shijian ziliao xuanji*, vol. 1. Nangang: Zhongyang yanjiuyuan jindaishi yanjiusuo, 1992.

Qi Jialin. *Taiwanshi* (A History of Taiwan). 2 vols. Taibei: Zili wanbao, 1993.

Qi Xin [pseud.]. "Wei Daoming, Chen Cheng yu Taiwan" (Wei Daoming, Chen Cheng, and Taiwan). *Taiwan chunqiu* 4 (Jan. 1949): 3–4.

Qiu Niantai. "Renshi Taiwan fayang Taiwan" (Understanding and Enhancing Taiwan). *Taiwan xinshengbao* (Mar. 6, 1946): 2.

———. "Zhanming Tairen wu Hanjian" (Clarifying That Taiwanese Are Not Traitors). *Renmin daobao* (Mar. 9, 1946): 2.

Rentong yu guojia: Jindai Zhong-Xi lishi de bijiao (Identity and Nation: A Comparison of Modern Chinese and Western History). Nangang: Zhongyang yanjiuyuan jindaishi yanjiusuo, 1994.

Ruan Meimei. *Yu'an jiaoluo de leisheng: Xunfang er erba sanlou de yizi* (The Sound of Tears in a Dark Corner: Locating the Scattered Survivors of February 28). Taibei: Qianwei chubanshe, 1992.

Shen Zijia, and Zhang Jueming. *Gu Zhenfu zhuan* (A Biography of Gu Zhenfu). Taibei: Shuhua chuban shiye youxian gongsi, 1993.

Shi Ming. *Taiwanren sibainian shi* (Four Hundred Years of History of the Taiwanese People). Taibei: n.p., 1979 reprint.

Shi Yangcheng. *Zhongguo sheng xingzheng zhidu yice* (A Volume on China's Provincial Administration). Chongqing: Shangwu yinshuguan, 1946.

Shiba Ryōtarō [Sima Liaotailang]. Trans. by Li Jinsong. *Taiwan jixing* (Travels in Taiwan). Taibei: Taiwan dongfan gufen youxian songsi, 1995.

Sima Xiaoqing. *Taiwan wu da jiazu* (Five Great Families of Taiwan). 2 vols. Taibei: Zili wanbao wenhua chubanbu, 1987.

Song Feiru. "Minzu zhuyi zai Taiwan" (Nationalism on Taiwan). *Zhengjingbao* 1, 4 (Dec. 10, 1945): 3–4.

Song Guangyu. "Lishi wenhua lun de tichu" (Raising Theories of History and Culture). In Song Guangyu, ed., *Taiwan jingyan: Lishi jingji bian* (The Taiwan Experience: A Volume on History and Economics). Taibei: Donghai daxue, 1993.

Song Yanwen. "Taiwan yiqian ge xinxing caifa" (Taiwan's One Thousand New Tycoons). *Taiwan chunqiu* 1 (Sept. 1948): 6–7.

Su Nanzhou, ed. *Jidujiao yu er erba* (Christianity and the February 28 Incident). Taibei: Yage chubanshe, 1991.

Su Shen [pseud.]. "'Neidi' yu 'neidiren'" (The "Interior" and "People of the Interior"). *Xinxin* 2, 1 (Jan. 5, 1947): 25.

Su Xin. *Fennu de Taiwan* (Outraged Taiwan). Taibei: Shibao wenhua, 1993.

———. *Weigui de Taigong douhun: Su Xin zizhuan yu wenji* (The Taiwanese Communist Spirit Who Will Not Return: The Autobiography and Writings of Su Xin). Taibei: Shibao wenhua, 1993.

———. "Zhuyi, jigou, renwu" (Isms, Structures, and People). *Zhengjingbao* 2, 3 (Feb. 10, 1946): 6.

Su Yunfeng. "Liansheng zizhi shengzhong de 'eren zhi e yundong': Jianlun shengji yishi zhi xingcheng ji qi zouyong" ("Let Hubei People Rule Hubei Movement" Amidst Calls for a Confederation of Provinces Self-Rule: A Discussion of Provincial Consciousness and Its Uses, 1920–26). In *Rentong yu guojia*, 215–48.

Taiwan chongjian xiehui (Taiwan Reconstruction Society). "Wei Taiwan tongbao jiang ji ju hua" (Speaking a Few Words on Behalf of Taiwanese Compatriots). *Xin Taiwan* 2 (Feb. 28, 1946): 10–11.

Taiwan mingren ji (Collection of Famous Taiwanese). Taibei: Xin Taiwan chubanshe, 1953.

Tang Zibing, ed. *Taiwan shigang* (Outline History of Taiwan). Taibei: Taiwan yinshua zhiye gongsi, 1946.

Ting Wenzhi. "Chen zhangguan lun 'guanliao ziben'" (Administrator Chen Discusses "Bureaucratic Capital"). *Heping ribao* (Aug. 1 and 2, 1946).

Tong Jianyan, ed. *Taiwan lishi cidian* (A Historical Dictionary of Taiwan). Beijing: Qunzhong chubanshe, 1990.

Wang Baiyuan. "Gao waishengren zhugong" (To All Mainland Gentlemen). *Zhengjingbao* 2, 2 (Jan. 25, 1946): 1–2.

———. "Zai Taiwan lishi zhi xiangke" (In the Imprint of Taiwan's History). *Zhengjingbao* 2, 3 (Feb. 10, 1946): 5.

Wang Desheng. "Difang zizhi zhi lixiang yu shishi" (The Ideals and Implementation of Local Self-Government). *Jinbu luntan* 1, 4 (Nov. 15, 1949): 6–7.

Wang Jiansheng, Chen Wanzhen, and Chen Yongquan. *1947: Taiwan er erba geming* (1947: Taiwan's February 28 Revolution). Taibei: Qianshu chubanshe, 1990.

Wang Junjie, and Gu Weiying. "Xin'en yu jiuyi zhijian: Li Qunsheng de guojia rentong zhi fenxi" (New Favors and Old Righteousness: An Analysis of Li Qunsheng's National Identity). In *Rentong yu guojia*, 275–300.

Wang Mingke. "Guoqu, jiti jiyi yu ziqun rentong: Taiwan de ziqun jingyan" (The Past, Collective Memory, and Ethnic Identity: Taiwan's Ethnic Experience). In *Rentong yu guojia*, 249–74.

Wang Shaoqi. "Zhuihuai Huang Chaoqin xiansheng" (Commemorating Mr. Huang Chaoqin). *Zhuanji wenxue* 14, 2 (Aug. 1986): 72–74.

Wang Shiqing. "Chen Fengyuan xiansheng fangwen jilu" (A Record of an Interview with Chen Fengyuan). In Huang Fusan and Chen Lifu, eds., *Jinxiandai Taiwan koushu lishi*. Taibei: Lin Benyuan Zhonghua wenhua jiaoyu jijinhui, 1991.

Wang Tiandeng. "Niantou zhi ci" (Words at the Beginning of the Year). *Xinxin* 2, 1 (Jan. 5, 1947): 2.

———. "Sheng canyihui de qianwan yan" (Some Words About the Provincial Consultative Assembly). *Xinxin* 6 (1946): 4.

Wang Tingxi, Xiang Jike, and Xu Zhichen. *Taiwan difang zizhi* (Taiwan's Local Self-Government). Taibei: Taiwan difang zizhishe, 1950.

Wang Xiaobo. *Taiwanshi yu Taiwanren* (Taiwan's History and People). Taibei: Dongta tushu gongsi, 1988.

———. *Zouchu Taiwan lishi de yinying* (Leaving the Shadow of Taiwan's History). Taibei: Bami'er shudian, 1986.

Wei Daoming. "Bensheng shizheng zongbaogao" (Overall Report on Taiwan's Provincial Administration). *Taiwan xunlian* 5, 6 (Dec. 16, 1947): 2–5.

Wei Jiangong. "'Guoyu yundong zai Taiwan de yiyi' shenjie" (An Explanation of "The Meaning of the Guoyu Movement on Taiwan"). *Xiandai zhoukan* 1, 9 (Feb. 28, 1946): 8–12.

Wo Ai Di [pseud.]. "Yu 'difang zizhi' tan dao xiubian Taiwan wenhuashi de biyaoxing" (From "Local Self-Government" to Discussing the Need for the Creation of A Cultural History of Taiwan). *Xin Taiwan* 4 (May 1, 1946): 3.

Wu Duanwen, ed. *Baise dang'an* (White Archives). Taibei: Shibao wenhua chuban qiye youxian gongsi, 1991.

Wu Naide, and Chen Mingtong. "Zhengchuan zhuanyi he jingying liudong: Taiwan difang zhengzhi jingying de lishi xingzheng" (The Transfer of Political Power and Elite Fluidity: The Historical Form of the Taiwanese Local Political Elite). In Lai Zehan, ed., *Taiwan guangfu chuqi lishi*, 303–34.

Wu Sanlian. *Wu Sanlian huiyilu* (The Memoirs of Wu Sanlian). Taibei: Zili wanbaoshe wenhua chubanshe, 1991.

Wu Wenxing. "Er erba shijian qijian guomin zhengfu de yinying yu juece zhi tantao" (An Investigation of the Nationalist Government Reaction and Policies during the February 28 Incident). In Lai Zehan, ed., *Taiwan guangfu chuqi lishi*, 107–26.

———. "Riju shiqi Taiwan shehui lingdao jiceng zhi yanjiu" (Research into Taiwan's Ruling Strata of the Japanese Era). Ph.D. diss., National Taiwan University, 1986.

————. *Riju shiqi Taiwan shehui lingdao jieji zhi yanjiu* (Research into Taiwan's Ruling Class of the Japanese Era). Taibei: Zheng Zhong shuju, 1992.

Wu Xinrong. *Wu Xinrong huiyilu* (Memoirs of Wu Xinrong). Taibei: Qianwei chubanshe, 1989

————. *Wu Xinrong riji: Zhanhou* (The Diaries of Wu Xinrong: Postwar). Taibei: Yuanjing chuban shiye gongsi, 1981.

Wu Yuan, ed. *Taiwan de guoqu he xianzai* (Taiwan's Past and Present). Beijing: Dongyou tuwu chubanshe, 1954.

Wu Zhuoliu. *Taiwan lianqiao: Taiwan de lishi jianzheng* (Taiwan Forsythia: Witness to Taiwan's History) Taibei: Qianwei chubanshe, 1994.

————. *Wuhuaguo: Taiwan qishinian de huixiang* (The Fig Tree: Looking Back at Taiwan over Seventy Years). Taibei: Qianfeng chubanshe, 1993.

————. *Yaxiya de gu'er* (Asia's Orphan). Taibei: Caogen chuban shiye youxian gongsi, 1995.

Xiang Ting [pseud.]. "Lun difang zizhi" (Discussing Local Self-Government). *Taiwan pinglun* 1, 2 (Aug. 1, 1946): 10–11.

Xie Bingkui. "Zizhi yu shishi xianzheng" (Self-Government and Implementing Constitutional Government). *Taiwan xunlian* 4, 9 (Aug. 1, 1947): 733.

Xie Nanguang. "Guangming puzhao xia de Taiwan" (A Taiwan with a Promising Future Shining upon It). *Zhengjingbao* 1, 4 (Nov. 25, 1945): 6–7.

Xu Dong. "Taiwan dixia zuzhi bibai wuyi" (Taiwan's Underground Organizations Must Be Defeated Without a Doubt). *Taiwan chunqiu* 2 (Nov. 1948): 4.

Xu Langxuan. *Zhongguo xiandaishi* (A History of Modern China). Taibei: Zhengzhong shuju, 1974.

Xu Xueji. "Er erba shijian shi Gaoxiongshi de tuoqing" (The Pacification of Gaoxiong during the February 28 Incident). In Huang Junjie, ed., *Gaoxiong lishi yu wenhua lunji*, 176–82. Gaoxiong: Weng Sishan jijinhui, 1994.

————. "Taiwan guangfu chuqi de yuwen wenti" (The Language Problem in Immediate Post-Retrocession Taiwan). *Si yu yan* 29, 4 (Dec. 1991): 155–84.

Xue Ping. "Wo wei Taiwan shuohua" (Speaking for Taiwan). *Taiwan chunqiu* 2 (Oct. 1948): 1.

Yan Zhenhui. "Taiwan guangfu chuqi de jingji chongjian chutan" (A Preliminary Investigation of Economic Reconstruction Immediately after Taiwan's Retrocession). *Zhongguo xiandai zhuanti yanjiu baogao* 17 (1995): 377–429.

Yang Shumei. "Guangfu chuqi Taiwan de shehui jingying (1945–1949)" (Taiwan's Social Elite Immediately After Retrocession, 1945–49). Master's thesis, National Taiwan Normal University, 1995.

Yang Yizhou. *Er erba minbian: Taiwan yu Jiang Jieshi* (The February 28 Popular Uprising: Taiwan and Jiang Jieshi). Trans. from Japanese by Zhang Liangze. Taibei: Qianwei chubanshe, 1991.

Yang Zhaojia. "Chuangli hou de zizhi lianmeng" (The Self-Government League since Its Creation). *Taiwan xinminbao* (Sept. 27, 1930): 4.

————. "Guanyu Taiwan difang zizhi lianmeng" (Concerning the Taiwan League for Local Self-Government). *Taiwan xinminbao* (July 6, 1930): 4.

————. "Taiwan difang zizhi zhudi" (Taiwan's System of Local Self-Government). In Chinese. In *Taiwan difang zizhi wenti*. Tokyo: Shinminsha, 1928.

Ye Rongzhong. "Taiwan guangfu qianhou de huiyi" (Memories of Taiwan's Retro-cession). In Li Nanheng and Ye Yunyun, eds., *Taiwan renwu chunxiang*, 400–35. Taibei: Shibao wenhua chuban qiye youxian gongsi, 1995.

———. *Taiwan renwu qunxiang* (A Portrait of Taiwanese). Li Nanheng and Ye Yun-yun, eds. Taibei: Shibao wenhua, 1995.

Ye Yunyun, ed. *Zhengyan 2-28* (Verifying February 28). Taibei: Renjian chubanshe, 1990.

Yin Naiping. "Taiwan guangfu yilai de wujia wending zhengce" (Policies for Price Stabilization since Taiwan's Retrocession). *Zhongguo xiandai zhuanti yanjiu bao-gao* 17 (1995): 330–76.

Yin Zhangyi. *Chou nong yan, he lie jiu, dasheng kangyi: Taiwan lishi yu Taiwan qiantu* (Smoke Strong Cigarettes, Drink Strong Wine, Loudly Resist: Taiwan's History and Future). Taibei: Taiwanshi yanjiuhui, 1988.

———. "Taiwan yishi de xingcheng yu fazhan: Lishi de guandian" (The Form and Development of Taiwan Consciousness: A Historical Perspective). In *Rentong yu guojia*, 363–88.

You Mijian. "Taiwan wenhua xiejinhui de mudi" (The Goals of the Association for Improving Taiwan Culture). *Xiandai zhoukan* 1, 1 (Dec. 10, 1945): 8.

———. "Wenxie de shiming" (The Mission of the Cultural Association). *Taiwan wenhua* 1, 1 (Sept. 15, 1946): 1.

Zhang Fumei. "Chen Yi yu Fujian shengzheng (1934–1941)" (Chen Yi and the Administration of Fujian Province, 1934–41). In *Er erba xueshu yantaohui lun-wenji*, 9–26. Taibei: Zili wanbao wenhua chubanbu, 1992.

Zhang Yanxian. "Taiwanshi yanjiu de xin jingshen" (The New Spirit of Taiwan His-torical Research). *Taiwan shiliao yanjiu* 1 (Feb. 1993): 76–86.

Zhang Yanxian, and Li Xiaofeng, eds. *Er erba shijian huiyiji* (Collection of Remembrances of the February 28 Incident). Taibei: Daoxiang chubanshe, 1989.

Zhang Yanxian, et al., eds. *Taiwan jindai mingren zhi* (A Record of Famous Tai-wanese of the Modern Era). 5 vols. Taibei: Zili wanbaoshe wenhua chubanshe, 1987–90.

———, eds. *Taibei Nangang er erba* (February 28 in Taibei and Nangang). Taibei: Wu Sanlian jijinhui, 1995.

Zhang Yuying. *Taiwan fuzhi* (Taiwan Prefecture Gazetteer). Xiamen: Xiamen daxue chubanshe, 1985. Reprint of 1685 edition.

Zhang Zhengchang. *Lin Xiantang yu Taiwan minzu yundong* (Lin Xiantang and Tai-wan's Peoples' Movement). Taibei: Dongmei caise yinshua youxian gongsi, 1981.

Zhe Ye [pseud.]. "Taiwanren de huhuan" (A Taiwanese Call for Help). *Xin Taiwan* 1 (Feb. 15, 1946): 6.

Zheng Muxin [Zheng Zi]. *Taiwan yihui zhengzhi sishinian* (Forty Years of Taiwan Assembly Politics). Taibei: Zili wanbao wenhua chubanshe, 1987.

Zheng Yanfen. "Guanyu shengxian zizhi tongze" (Concerning Principles for Provin-cial and County Self-Government). *Gonglunbao* (July 4, 1948): 4.

———. "Sheng zizhi de yiyi ye tezhi" (The Special Qualities and Meaning of Provincial Self-Government). *Taiwan xinshengbao* (June 7, 1948): 2.

Zheng Zi. *Zhanhou Taiwan de jieshou yu chongjian: Taiwan xiandaishi yanjiu lunji*

(The Takeover and Reconstruction of Postwar Taiwan: A Collection of Essays on Modern Taiwanese History). Taibei: Xinhua tushu, 1994.

———. *Zhanhou Taiwan yihui yundongshi zhi yanjiu: Bentu jingying yu yihui zhengzhi (1946–1951)* (Research into the History of the Postwar Taiwan Assembly Movement: Native Elites and Representative Politics, 1946–51). Taizhong: Zheng Zi, 1993.

———. "Zhongyang zhengfu qian Tai chuqi shixing difang xizhi zhi lishi tanyuan (1949–1950)" (A Historical Investigation into the Roots of Attempts to Implement Local Self-Government Immediately After the Central Government Moved to Taiwan, 1949–50). Paper delivered at the Conference to Mark the Hundredth Anniversary of the Founding of the Nationalist Party, Taibei, Dec. 1994.

Zhou Jixiang. "Xingxian yilai de Taiwan difang zizhi: Huigu yu zhanwang" (Taiwan's Local Self-Government since the Promulgation of the Constitution: Recollections and Prospects). *Jindai Zhongguo* 80 (Dec. 1990): 72–84.

Zhou Shi. *Taiwan difang renwu pingzhuan: Gaoxiong renwu* (Critical Biographies of Taiwan Local Notables: Gaoxiong). Gaoxiong: Shengfu shuju, 1975.

Zhou Wanyao. *Riju shidai de Taiwan yihui shezhi qingyuan yundong* (The Taiwan Assembly Petition Movement under Japanese Rule). Taibei: Zili wanbao wenhua chubanshe 1989.

Zhou Xianwen. "Ruhe kan Taiwan?" (How Should Taiwan Be Seen?). *Taiwan xinshengbao* (June 9, 1946): 1.

Zhou Zongxian. *Huang Chaoqin zhuan* (A Biography of Huang Chaoqin). Taizhong: Taiwansheng wenxian weiyuanhui, 1994.

Zhu Benyuan. "Taiwansheng duiyu xingxian de shiyingxing" (The Appropriateness of Implementing the Constitution on Taiwan). *Taiwan xinshengbao* (Dec. 29, 1946): 2.

Zhuang Yongming. *Han Shiquan zhuan* (Biography of Han Shiquan). Nantou: Taiwansheng wenxian weiyuanhui, 1993.

JAPANESE-LANGUAGE SOURCES

Newspapers and Periodicals

Taiwan. Tokyo, 1922–24.

Taiwan minpō (Taiwan minbao) (Taiwanese Daily). Tokyo, 1923–27; Taibei, 1927–32.

Taiwan shinminpō (Taiwan xinminbao) (New Taiwanese Daily). Taibei, 1930–41.

Books and Essays

Hara Kansyū. *Shin Taiwan no jinbutsu* (New Men of Taiwan). Taibei: n.p., 1937.

Taiwan tōki gaiyō (An Outline of Taiwan's Governance). Taibei: Taiwan sōtokufu, 1945.

Kitayama Fukujirō. "Taiwan o kyūshin toseru watashi ga nanhō seisaku no kaiko to kentō" (What To Do about Taiwan as the Center: My Review and Examination of the Southern Policy). In *Kinen kōinshū* 5. Taibei: Taihoku teikoku daigaku, 1937, 249–74.

ENGLISH-LANGUAGE SOURCES

Official Publications and Documents

Central Intelligence Agency. National Archives. Record Group 226. These records are also available at the Library of Congress, microfilm no. 86/212.

China Handbook Editorial Board. *China Handbook, 1950*. New York: Rockport Press, 1950.

Chinese Ministry of Information, ed. *China Handbook*. New York: Macmillan. Published annually, 1937–45.

Department of Defense, United States. G-3 Decimal Files, 091–Formosa. National Archives. Record Group 319.

Department of State, United States. Central Files. General Records of the Department of State. National Archives. Record Group 59. Also known as the "decimal files."

——. Office of Intelligence Research, Intelligence Report no. 7203. "Taiwanese Independence Movements, 1683–1956." Aug. 8, 1956. National Archives. Record Group 59.

——. Office of Public Affairs, comp. *United States Relations with China: With Special Reference to the Period 1944–1949*. Department of State Publication 3573. Washington, DC: Government Printing Office, 1949.

——. Records of the Office of Chinese Affairs, 1944–50. National Archives. Record Group 59. Lot 56 D 151.

——. United States State Department Confidential Files: Formosa (1945–49). University Publications of America microfilm.

——. United States State Department Confidential Files: Formosa (1949–54). University Publications of America microfilm.

Foreign Relations of the United States: 1948. Volume 7, The Far East. Washington, DC: Government Printing Office, 1974.

Government of Formosa. *Report on the Control of Aborigines in Formosa*. Taibei, 1911.

Important Documents Concerning the Question of Taiwan. Beijing: Foreign Language Press, 1955.

Office of Strategic Services, United States. National Archives, Record Group 226.

Office of Strategic Services/State Department Intelligence and Research Reports, 1941–1949. University Press of America microfilm collection. 6 reels.

Taiwan News Service. *An Infamous Riot: Story of Recent Mob Violence in Taiwan*. Taibei: Taiwan News Service, 1947.

United States Military Intelligence on Japan (1918–41). University Publications of America microfilm.

United States Military Translations of Japanese Broadcasts and Documents. CIS microfilm, at the Library of Congress.

BOOKS, ARTICLES, ESSAYS, AND DISSERTATIONS

Accinelli, Robert. *Crisis and Commitment: United States Policy toward Taiwan, 1950–1955*. Chapel Hill: University of North Carolina Press, 1996.

Acheson, Dean. *Present at Creation: My Years in the State Department.* New York: W. W. Norton, 1969.

Ahern, Emily M., and Hill Gates, eds. *The Anthropology of Taiwanese Society.* Stanford, CA: Stanford University Press, 1981.

Anderson, Benedict. *Imagined Communities: Reflections on the Origin and Spread of Nationalism.* Revised ed. New York: Verso, 1991.

———. *Language and Power: Exploring Political Cultures in Indonesia.* Ithaca, NY: Cornell University Press, 1990.

Arnold, Julean H. *Education in Formosa.* Washington, DC: United States Bureau of Education, 1908.

Aron, Raymond. *Politics and History.* Trans. and ed. by Miriam Bernheim Conant. New Brunswick, NJ: Transaction Books, 1978.

Asami, Noburo. *Japanese Colonial Government.* New York: n.p., 1924.

Averill, Stephen C. "The New Life in Action: The Nationalist Government in South Jianxi, 1934–1937." *China Quarterly* 88 (Dec. 1981): 594–628.

Ballantine, Joseph W. *Formosa: A Problem for U.S. Foreign Policy.* Washington, DC: Brookings Institution, 1952.

Barclay, George H. *Colonial Development and Population in Taiwan.* Princeton, NJ: Princeton University Press, 1954.

Bate, H. Maclear. *Report from Formosa.* London: Eyre and Scottiswoode, 1952.

Beasley, W. G. "Meiji Political Institutions." In Marius B. Jansen, ed., *The Cambridge History of China, Volume 5, The Nineteenth Century.* New York: Cambridge University Press, 1989.

Bello, Walden, and Stephanie Rosenfeld. *Dragons in Distress: Asia's Miracle Economies in Crisis.* San Francisco: Institute for Food and Development Policy, 1990.

Bigelow, Poultney. *Japan and Her Colonies.* London: Edward Arnold, 1923.

Boyle, John Hunter. *China and Japan at War, 1937–1945: The Politics of Collaboration.* Stanford, CA: Stanford University Press, 1972.

Cage, Eugenia. "Industrial Development in Formosa." *Economic Geography* 26, 3 (July 1950): 214–22.

Chaffee, Frederick H. *Area Handbook for the Republic of China.* Washington, DC: Government Printing Office, 1969.

Chai Chen-kang. *Taiwan Aborigines: A Genetic Study of Tribal Variations.* Cambridge, MA: Harvard University Press, 1967.

Chang, Carsun. *The Third Force in China.* New York: Bookman Associates, 1952.

Chang Ch'i-yun. *The Rebirth of the Kuomintang (The Seventh National Congress).* Trans. by Nee Yuan-ch'ing. Taibei: China Cultural Service, ca. 1953.

Chang Chung-li. *The Chinese Gentry.* Seattle: University of Washington Press, 1955.

Chang, Kwang-chih. *The Archaeology of Ancient China,* 2nd ed. New Haven, CT: Yale University Press, 1977.

———. "Chinese Archaeology since 1949." *Journal of Asian Studies* 36, 4 (Aug. 1977): 623–46.

———. *Fengpitou, Tapenkeng, and the Prehistory of Taiwan.* New Haven, CT: Yale University, Department of Archaeology, 1969.

Chen Cheng. *Land Reform in Taiwan*. Taibei: China Publishing Company, 1961.

Chen, Ching-chih. "Impact of Japanese Colonial Rule on the Taiwanese Elite." *Journal of Asian History* 22, 1 (1988): 25–51

———. "Japanese Socio-Political Control in Taiwan, 1895–1945." Ph.D. diss., Harvard University, 1973.

———. "The Police and the Hoko System in Taiwan under Japanese Administration (1895–1945)." In Albert Craig, ed., *Papers on Japan*. Cambridge, MA: Harvard East Asian Research Center, 1967.

Chen, Edward I-te. "The Attempt to Integrate the Empire: Legal Perspectives." In Myers and Peattie, eds., *The Japanese Colonial Empire*, 240–74.

———. "Formosan Political Movements under Japanese Colonial Rule, 1914–1937." *Journal of Asian Studies* 31, 3 (May 1972): 477–97.

———. "Japanese Colonialism in Korea and Formosa: A Comparison of Its Effects upon the Development of Nationalism." Ph.D. diss., University of Pennsylvania, 1968.

———. "Japanese Colonization in Korea and Formosa: A Comparison of the System of Political Control." *Harvard Journal of Asiatic Studies* 30 (1970): 126–58.

———. "Japan's Decision to Annex Taiwan: A Study of Ito-Mutsu Diplomacy, 1894–95." *Journal of Asian Studies* 37, 1 (Nov. 1977): 61–72.

Chen, Leslie H. "Chen Jiongming (1878–1933) and the Chinese Federalist Movement." *Republican China* 17 (Nov. 1991): 21–37.

Chen Yongfa. *Making Revolution: The Communist Movement in Eastern and Central China, 1937–1945*. Berkeley: University of California Press, 1986.

Cheng, Tun-jen, and Stephen Haggard, eds. *Political Change in Taiwan*. Boulder, CO: Lynne Rienner, 1992.

Chesneaux, Jean. "The Federalist Movement in China, 1920–1923." In Jack Gray, ed., *Modern China's Search for a Political Form*. New York: Oxford University Press, 1969.

Ch'i Hsi-sheng. *Nationalist China at War: Military Defeats and Political Collapse, 1937–1945*. Ann Arbor: University of Michigan Press, 1982.

Chiang Ching-kuo. *Chiang Ching-kuo: Calm in the Eye of a Storm*. Taibei: Li Ming Cultural Enterprise Company, 1978.

"China: Snow Red and Moon Angel." *Time* (Apr. 7, 1947): 35–36.

Chiu, Hung-dah, ed. *China and the Question of Taiwan: Documents and Analysis*. New York: Praeger, 1973.

Chu, Samuel C. "Liu Ming-ch'uan." *Journal of Asian Studies* 23, 1 (Nov. 1964): 37–53.

Clark, Cal. "The Taiwan Exception: Implications for Contending Political Economy Paradigms." *International Studies Quarterly* 31 (1987): 327–56.

Clough, Ralph. *Island China*. Cambridge, MA: Harvard University Press, 1978.

———. "Taiwan under Nationalist Rule, 1949–1985." In Denis Twitchett and John K. Fairbank, eds., *The Cambridge History of China, Volume 15, The People's Republic, Part 2: Revolutions within the Chinese Revolution, 1966–1982*, 815–74. Cambridge, Eng.: Cambridge University Press, 1991.

Coble, Parks M., Jr. *The Shanghai Capitalists and the Nationalist Government,*

1927–1937. Cambridge, MA: Council on East Asian Studies, Harvard University, 1980.

Cohen, Paul A. "The Contested Past: The Boxers as History and Myth." *Journal of Asian Studies* 51, 1 (Feb. 1992): 82–114

———. *History in Three Keys: The Boxers as Event, Experience, and Myth*. New York: Columbia University Press, 1997.

Cohen, Warren I. "Acheson, His Advisers, and China, 1949–1950." In Dorothy Borg and Waldo Heinrichs, eds., *Uncertain Years: Chinese-American Relations, 1947–1950*. New York: Columbia University Press, 1980.

Copper, John. *Taiwan: Nation-State or Province?* Boulder, CO: Westview Press, 1989.

Crozier, Ralph C. *Koxinga and Chinese Nationalism: History, Myth and the Hero*. Cambridge, MA: Harvard University Press, 1977.

Davidson, James W. *The Island of Formosa: Past and Present*. New York: Book World, 1903.

Deyo, Frederic C., ed. *The Political Economy of New Asian Industrialism*. Ithaca, NY: Cornell University Press, 1987.

Dickson, Bruce. "The Lessons of Defeat: The Reorganization of the Kuomintang on Taiwan: 1950–1952." *China Quarterly* 133 (Mar. 1993): 56–84.

Dikötter, Frank. *The Discourse of Race in Modern China*. Stanford, CA: Stanford University Press, 1992.

Dirlik, Arif. "Ideological Foundations of the New Life Movement: A Study in Counter-Revolution." *Journal of Asian Studies* 34, 4 (Aug. 1974): 945–80.

Duara, Prasenjit. *Rescuing History from the Nation: Questioning Narratives of Modern China*. Chicago: University of Chicago Press, 1996.

———. "Transnationalism and the Predicament of Sovereignty: China, 1900–1945." *American Historical Review* 102, 4 (Oct. 1997): 1030–51.

Durdin, Tillman. "Formosa Killings Are Put at 10,000." *New York Times* (Mar. 29, 1947): 6.

Eastman, Lloyd E. *The Abortive Revolution: China under Nationalist Rule, 1927–1937*. Cambridge, MA: Harvard University Press, 1990.

———. *Seeds of Destruction: Nationalist China in War and Revolution, 1937–1949*. Stanford, CA: Stanford University Press, 1984.

Eckert, Carter J. *Offspring of Empire: The Koch'ang Kims and the Colonial Origins of Korea Capitalism, 1876–1945*. Seattle: University of Washington Press, 1991.

Fairbank, John King. "Maritime and Continental in China's History." In John K. Fairbank, ed., *The Cambridge History of China, Vol. 12, Republican China, 1912–1949, Part 1*, 1–27. Cambridge, Eng.: Cambridge University Press, 1986.

———. *The United States and China*, 4th ed. Cambridge, MA: Harvard University Press, 1983.

Faison, Seth. "Taiwan President Implies His Island Is Sovereign State." *New York Times* (July 13, 1999): 1.

Ferro, Marc. *Colonization: A Global History*. New York: Routledge, 1997.

Fessler, Loren. *Taiwan Independence Advocate: Peng Ming-min*. American Universities Field Staff Reports, East Asia Series 19, 3. American Universities Field Staff, 1972.

Fincher, John. "Provincialism and National Revolution." In Mary Clabaugh Wright, ed., *China in Revolution: The First Phase, 1900–1913*, 185–226. New Haven, CT: Yale University Press, 1968.

Fitzgerald, John. *Awakening China: Politics, Culture, and Class in the Nationalist Revolution*. Stanford, CA: Stanford University Press, 1996.

Fix, Douglas Lane. "Taiwanese Nationalism and Its Late Colonial Context." Ph.D. diss., University of California, Berkeley, 1993.

Fogel, Joshua. *Politics and Sinology: The Case of Naito Konan (1866–1934)*. Cambridge, MA: Council on East Asian Studies, Harvard University, 1984.

Fu, Poshek. *Passivity, Resistance, and Collaboration: Intellectual Choices in Occupied Shanghai, 1937–1945*. Stanford, CA: Stanford University Press, 1993.

Furnivall, J. S. *Colonial Policy and Practice: A Comparative Study of Burma and Netherlands India*. New York: New York University Press, 1956.

Gellner, Ernest. *Nations and Nationalism*. Ithaca, NY: Cornell University Press, 1983.

Gluck, Carol. *Japan's Modern Myths: Ideology in the Late Meiji Period*. Princeton, NJ: Princeton University Press, 1985.

Goddard, William G. *Formosa: A Study in Chinese History*. East Lansing: Michigan State University Press, 1966.

Gold, Thomas. *State and Society in the Taiwan Miracle*. Armonk, NY: M. E. Sharpe, 1985.

Gordon, Leonard. "American Planning for Taiwan: 1942–1945." *Pacific History Review* 37, 2 (May 1968): 201–29.

———, ed. *Taiwan: Studies in Chinese Local History*. New York: Columbia University Press, 1970.

Grajdanzev, Andrew. "Cultural Policy in Taiwan and the Problem of Kominka." *Pacific Affairs* 14, 3 (1941): 338–60.

———. "Formosa (Taiwan) under Japanese Rule." *Pacific Affairs* 15, 3 (1942): 331–44.

———. *Formosa Today: An Analysis of Economic Development and Strategic Importance of Japan's Tropical Colony*. New York: Institute of Pacific Relations, 1942.

Gregor, James A. *Ideology and Development: Sun Yat-sen and the Economic History of Taiwan*. Berkeley: Institute for East Asian Studies, University of California Center for Chinese Studies, 1981.

Halbwachs, Maurice. *On Collective Memory*. Trans. and ed. by Lewis A. Coser. Chicago, IL: University of Chicago Press, 1992.

Hechter, Michael. *Internal Colonialism: The Celtic Fringe in British National Development*. New Brunswick, NJ: Transaction Publishers, 1999.

Hegel, Robert E. "The Search for Identity in Fiction from Taiwan." In Robert E. Hegel and Richard C. Hessney, eds., *Expressions of Self in Chinese Literature*. New York: Columbia University Press, 1985.

Himmelfarb, Gertrude. "Is National History Obsolete?" In *The New History and the Old: Critical Essays and Reappraisals*. Cambridge, MA: Belknap Press, 1981.

Ho, Samuel P. S. "Colonialism and Development: Korea, Taiwan, and Kwantung." In Myers and Peattie, eds., *The Japanese Colonial Empire*, 347–98.

———. *Economic Development of Taiwan, 1860–1970*. New Haven, CT: Yale University Press, 1978.

Hoston, Germaine A. *The State, Identity, and the National Question in China and Japan*. Princeton, NJ: Princeton University Press, 1994.

Hsiao, Frank S. T., and Mei-chu W. Hsiao. "Colonial Linkages in Early Postwar Taiwanese Economic Development." *Harvard Studies on Taiwan: Papers of the Taiwan Studies Workshop* 2 (1998): 91–117.

Hsiao, Frank T. S., and Lawrence R. Sullivan. "The Chinese Communist Party and the Status of Taiwan, 1928–1943." *Pacific Affairs* 52, 3 (1979): 446–67.

———. "A Political History of the Taiwanese Communist Party, 1928–1931." *Journal of Asian Studies* 42, 2 (1983): 269–89.

Hsiao, Hsin-Huang Michael. "Emerging Social Movements and the Rise of a Demanding Civil Society on Taiwan." *Australian Journal of Chinese Affairs* 24 (July 1990): 163–79.

Hsieh, Chiao-min. *Taiwan, Ilha Formosa: A Geography in Perspective*. Washington, DC: Butterworths, 1964.

Hsiung, James C., ed. *The Taiwan Experience, 1950–1980: Contemporary Republic of China*. New York: Praeger, 1981.

Hsiung, James C., and Steven I. Levine, eds. *China's Bitter Victory: The War with Japan, 1937–1945*. Armonk, NY: M. E. Sharpe, 1992.

Huang Fusan. "The Japanese Legacy and Nationalist Chinese Response in Postwar Taiwan: Some Observations." Conference on the Legacy of Japan in Postwar Taiwan, East Asian Studies, Washington University, St. Louis, Nov. 14–16, 1996.

Huang Jianli. *The Politics of Depoliticization in Republican China: Guomindang Policy toward Student Political Activism, 1927–1949*. New York: Peter Lang, 1996.

Hutton, Patrick H. *History as an Art of Memory*. Hanover, NH: University Press of New England, 1993.

Jacobs, Bruce. *Local Politics in a Rural Chinese Cultural Setting: A Field Study of Matsu Township, Taiwan*. Canberra: Contemporary China Centre, Research School of Pacific Studies, Australian National University, 1980.

———. "Taiwanese and the Chinese Nationalists, 1937–1945: The Origins of Taiwan's Half-Mountain People." *Modern China* 16, 1 (Jan. 1990): 84–119.

Jansen, Marius B. *The Japanese and Sun Yat-sen*. Cambridge, MA: Harvard University Press, 1954.

Johnson, Chalmers. "Introduction: The Taiwan Model." In James C. Hsiung, ed., *The Taiwan Experience, 1950–1980: Contemporary Republic of China*. New York: Praeger, 1981.

———. *Peasant Nationalism and Communist Power: The Emergence of Revolutionary China, 1937–1945*. Stanford, CA: Stanford University Press, 1962.

Kheng, Cheah Boon. *Red Star over Malaya: Resistance and Social Conflict During and After the Japanese Occupation, 1941–1946*. Singapore: Singapore University Press, 1983.

Kerr, George H. *Formosa Betrayed*. Boston, MA: Houghton Mifflin, 1965.

————. "Formosa: Island Frontier." *Far Eastern Survey* 14, 7 (Apr. 11, 1945): 80–85.

————. *Formosa: Licensed Revolution and the Home Rule Movement, 1895–1945.* Honolulu: University Press of Hawaii, 1974.

————. "Kodama Report: Plan for Conquest." *Far Eastern Survey* 14, 14 (July 10, 1945): 185–90.

————. "Some Chinese Problems in Taiwan." *Far Eastern Survey* 14, 20 (Oct. 10 1945): 284–87.

Kirby, William C. "China Unincorporated: Company Law and Business Enterprise in Twentieth-Century China." *Journal of Asian Studies* 54, 1 (Feb. 1995): 43–63.

————. "Continuity and Change in Modern China: Economic Planning on the Mainland and on Taiwan, 1943–1958." *Australian Journal of Chinese Affairs* 24 (July 1990): 121–41.

————. "Planning Postwar Taiwan: Industrial Policy and the Nationalist Takeover, 1943–1947." *Harvard Studies on Taiwan: Papers of the Taiwan Studies Workshop*, Fairbank Center for East Asian Research 1 (1995): 286–301.

Knapp, Ronald G., ed. *China's Island Frontier: Studies in the Historical Geography of Taiwan.* Honolulu: University Press of Hawaii, 1980.

Kuang, Paul, and Tsien Sih. *Taiwan in Modern Times.* New York: St. Johns University Press, 1973.

Kuhn, Philip. "Local Self-Government under the Republic." In Frederic Wakeman, Jr. and Carolyn Grant, eds., *Conflict and Control in Late Imperial China.* Berkeley: University of California Press, 1975.

Kumar, Ravinder. "From Swaraj to Purna Swaraj: Nationalist Politics in the City of Bombay, 1920–1932." In D. A. Low, ed., *Congress and the Raj: Facets of the Indian Struggle, 1917–1947*, 77–108. London: Heinemann, 1977.

Kyne, Phelim. "The Missing Victims of 2-28: A Quest for Truth and Bones." *China News* (Taibei), Features Sunday supplement. (Jan. 4, 1994): 9.

Lai Tse-han, Ramon H. Myers, and Wei Wou. *A Tragic Beginning: The Taiwan Uprising of February 28, 1947.* Stanford, CA: Stanford University Press, 1991.

Lamley, Harry J. "The Taiwan Literati and Early Japanese Rule, 1895–1915: A Study of Reactions to the Japanese Occupation and Subsequent Responses to Colonial Rule and Modernization." Ph.D. diss., University of Washington, 1964.

————. "The 1895 Taiwan Republic." *Journal of Asian Studies* 27, 4 (Aug. 1968): 739–62.

Lang, John L. "A History of Newspapers in Taiwan." Ph.D. diss. Claremont Graduate School, 1967.

Laris, Michael. "Taiwan Alters Old 'One China' Formula." *Washington Post* (July 13, 1999): A-14.

Lary, Diana. *The Kwangsi Clique in Chinese Politics, 1925–1937.* Cambridge, Eng.: Cambridge University Press 1974.

Lee, Robert H. S. "Changes in Taiwan Attitudes." *New Taiwan Monthly* (Jan.-Feb. 1947): 1.

Lee Teng-hui. *The Road to Democracy: Taiwan's Pursuit of Identity.* Tokyo: PHP Institute, 1999.

Legge, J. D. *Sukarno: A Political Biography.* Boston: Allen & Unwin, 1972.

Lerman, Arthur J. *Taiwan's Politics: The Provincial Assemblyman's World.* Washington, DC: University Press of America, 1978.

Levich, Eugene William. *The Kwangsi Way in Kuomintang China, 1931–1939.* Armonk, NY: M. E. Sharpe, 1993.

Liao, Thomas. *Inside Formosa: Formosans vs. Chinese since 1945.* Tokyo: Formosan Press, ca. 1960.

Lieberman, Henry R. "Obstacles Delay Formosan Output." *New York Times* (Aug. 30, 1946): 6.

Lindebarger, Paul Myron Anthony. *The Political Doctrines of Sun Yat-sen: An Exposition of the San Min Chu I.* Baltimore: Johns Hopkins Press, 1937.

Liu, Paul K. C. "Economic Development and Population in Taiwan since 1894: An Overview." In *Essays on the Population of Taiwan.* Taibei: Academia Sinica Population Papers, 1973.

Loh, Pinchon. "The Politics of Chiang Kai-shek." *Journal of Asian Studies* 25, 3 (May 1966): 431–52.

Malloy, James M., ed. *Authoritarianism and Corporatism in Latin America.* Pittsburgh, PA: University of Pittsburgh Press, 1977.

Mancall, Mark. *Formosa Today.* New York: Praeger, 1964.

McGovern, Janet. *Among the Head-Hunters of Formosa.* London: T. Fisher Unwin, 1922.

Mendel, Douglas. *The Politics of Formosan Nationalism.* Berkeley: University of California Press, 1970.

Moody, Peter R. *Political Change on Taiwan: A Study of Ruling Party Adaptability.* New York: Praeger, 1992.

Myers, Ramon H., ed. *Two Societies in Opposition: The Republic of China and the People's Republic of China After Forty Years.* Stanford, CA: Hoover Institution Press, 1991.

Myers, Ramon H., and Mark R. Peattie, eds. *The Japanese Colonial Empire, 1895–1945.* Princeton, NJ: Princeton University Press, 1984.

Naito, Hideo, ed. *Taiwan: A Unique Colonial Record, 1937–1938.* Tokyo: Kokusai Nippon Kyokai, 1938.

Peattie, Mark R. "Japanese Attitude Toward Colonialism, 1895–1945." In Myers and Peattie, eds., *The Japanese Colonial Empire,* 80–127.

Peng, Mingmin. *A Taste of Freedom: Memoirs of a Formosan Independence Leader.* New York: Holt, Rinehart and Winston, 1972.

Pepper, Suzanne, *Civil War in China: The Political Struggle, 1945–1949.* Berkeley: University of California Press, 1978.

Quigley, Harold S. *Japanese Government and Politics: An Introductory Study.* New York: Century Company, 1932.

"Remembering '28 February 1947': A Memorial to Taiwan's Holocaust." *Taiwan Communiqué* 65 (Apr. 1995): 1–2.

Richburg, Keith R. "Leaders Asserts Taiwan is 'Independent, Sovereign.'" *Washington Post* (Nov. 8, 1997): A-1.

Riggs, Fred W. *Formosa under Chinese Nationalist Rule.* New York: Macmillan, 1952.

Rubenstein, Murray, ed. *Taiwan: A New History.* Armonk, NY: M. E. Sharpe, 1999.

Rutter, Owen. *Through Formosa: An Account of Japan's Island Colony*. New York: Institute of Pacific Relations, 1948.

Schoppa, R. Keith. *Chinese Elites and Political Change: Zhejiang Province in the Early Twentieth Century*. Cambridge, MA: Harvard University Press, 1982.

———. "Province and Nation: The Chekiang Provincial Autonomy Movement, 1917–1927." *Journal of Asian Studies* 36, 4 (Aug. 1977): 661–74.

Schram, Stuart R. "Decentralization in a Unitary State: Theory and Practice, 1940–1984." In Stuart R. Schram, ed., *The Scope of State Power in China*, 81–125. London: School of Oriental and African Studies, University of London, 1985.

Selden, Mark. *The Yenan Way in Revolutionary China*. Cambridge, MA: Harvard University Press, 1971.

Shepherd, John Robert. *Statecraft and Political Economy on the Taiwan Frontier, 1600–1800*. Stanford, CA: Stanford University Press, 1993.

Sheridan, James E. *China in Disintegration: The Republican Era in Chinese History, 1912–1949*. New York: The Free Press, 1975.

Sih, Paul K. T., ed. *Taiwan in Modern Times*. New York: St. Johns University Press, Center for Asian Studies, 1973.

Simon, Denis Fred, and Michael Y. M. Kau, eds. *Taiwan: Beyond the Economic Miracle*. Armonk, NY: M. E. Sharpe, 1992.

Skocpol, Theda. *States and Social Revolutions*. Cambridge, Eng.: Cambridge University Press, 1979.

Stanford, Michael. *The Nature of Historical Knowledge*. Cambridge, Eng.: Blackwell, 1986.

Sun Yat-sen. *San Min Chu I: The Three Principles of the People*. Trans. by Francis W. Price. Shanghai: Commercial Press, 1928.

Sutherland, Heather. *The Making of a Bureaucratic Elite: The Colonial Transformation of the Javanese Priyayi*. Kuala Lumpur: Heinemann Educational Books, 1979.

Takao, Yasuo. *National Integration and Local Power in Japan*. Aldershot, Eng.: Ashgate, 1999.

Takekoshi, Yosaburo. *Japanese Rule in Formosa*. London: Longmans, Green, and Company, 1907.

Thompson, Roger. *China's Local Councils in the Age of Constitutional Reform, 1898–1911*. Cambridge, MA: Council on East Asian Studies, Harvard University, 1995.

Tien Hung-mao. *The Great Transition: Political and Social Change in the Republic of China*. Stanford, CA: Hoover Institution Press, 1989.

Tsai, Hui-yu Caroline. "One Kind of Control: The Hoko System in Taiwan under Japanese Rule, 1895–1945." Ph.D. diss., Columbia University, 1990.

Tsang, Steven. "Revitalizing the Revolution: Chiang Kai-shek's Approach to Political Reform in the 1950s." Centennial Symposium on Sun Yat-sen's Founding of the Kuomintang Conference, Taibei, Nov. 19–23, 1994.

Tsurumi, Patricia E. "Colonial Education in Korea and Taiwan." In Myers and Peattie, eds., *The Japanese Colonial Empire*, 275–311.

———. *Japanese Colonial Education in Taiwan*. Cambridge, MA: Harvard University Press, 1977.

Tucker, Nancy Bernkopf. *Patterns in the Dust: Chinese-American Relations and the Recognition Controversy, 1949–1950.* New York: Columbia University Press, 1983.

"'Twenty-eight February 1947': Taiwan's Holocaust Remembered." *Taiwan Communiqué* 74 (Feb. 1997): 1–2.

The Twenty-sixth Anniversary of the "February 28" Uprising of the People of Taiwan Province. Beijing: Foreign Languages Press, 1973.

Tyler, Patrick E. "In Taiwan, A Mandate, But for What?" *New York Times* (Mar. 29, 1996): A-10.

———. "Tough Stance toward China Pays Off for Taiwan Leader." *New York Times* (Aug. 29, 1995): A-1.

Vuyslsteke, Richard R. "A Research Field Comes of Age." *Free China Review* 44, 2 (Feb. 1994): 4–10.

Wachman, Alan M. *Taiwan: National Identity and Democratization.* Armonk, NY: M. E. Sharpe, 1994.

Waldron, Arthur. "Warlordism versus Federalism: The Revival of a Debate?" *China Quarterly* 121 (Mar. 1990): 116–28.

Welsh, William A. *Leaders and Elites.* New York: Macmillan, 1977.

White, Lynn, and Li Cheng. "China Coast Identities: Regional, National, and Global." In Lowell Dittmer and Samuel S. Kim, eds., *China's Quest for National Identity.* Cornell, NY: Cornell University Press, 1993.

Winckler, Edwin A. "Roles Linking State and Society." In Emily Martin Ahern and Hill Gates, eds., *The Anthropology of Taiwanese Society.* Stanford, CA: Stanford University Press, 1981.

Wu, Emma. "Local Scholars Take a Closer Look at Home." *Free China Review* 42, 3 (Mar. 1992): 4–19.

Wu, Kuo-chen. Chinese Oral History Project, Columbia University, Butler Library, Rare Book and Manuscript Library. 1946–53.

WuDunn, Sheryl. "Taiwan Plans to Drop a Fig Leaf: China May Grumble." *New York Times* (July 4, 1997): A-7.

Wyndham, H. A. *Native Education: Ceylon, Java, Formosa, Philippines, French Indo-China, and British Malaya.* London: Royal Institute of International Affairs, 1933.

Index